NEWNES'
PICTORIAL KNOWLEDGE

VOLUME FIVE

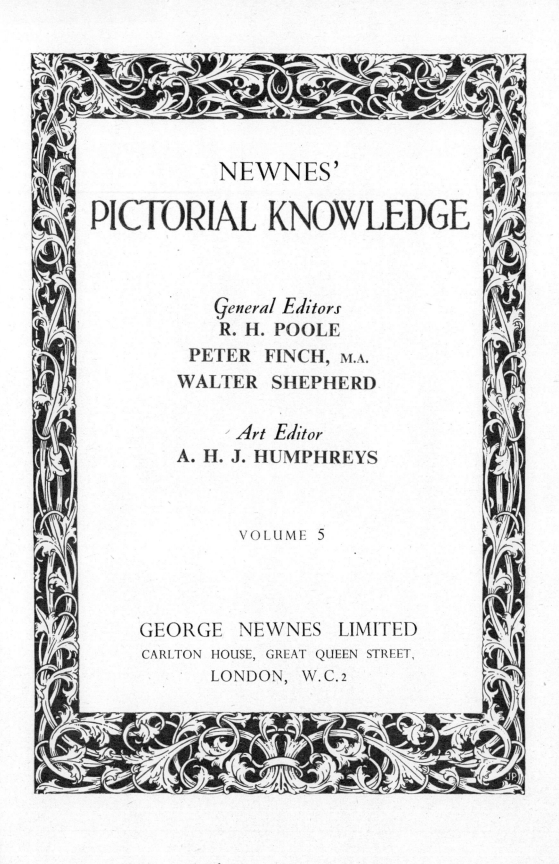

NEWNES'
PICTORIAL KNOWLEDGE

General Editors
R. H. POOLE
PETER FINCH, M.A.
WALTER SHEPHERD

Art Editor
A. H. J. HUMPHREYS

VOLUME 5

GEORGE NEWNES LIMITED
CARLTON HOUSE, GREAT QUEEN STREET,
LONDON, W.C.2

PRINTED IN GREAT BRITAIN
BY THE WHITEFRIARS PRESS LTD., LONDON AND TONBRIDGE, AND
BOUND BY HAZELL, WATSON & VINEY LTD. AYLESBURY AND LONDON
N.P.K. 7055.   W.P. 5316

CONTENTS OF VOLUME FIVE

FABLE, MYTH AND LEGEND

PAGE

Colour Plates

Special Colour Supplement

Photo=tone Supplements

Meteorology
and
What it Means

Sunshine and Storm
and how
They are Forecast

Wellcome Historical Medical Museum.

THE DISCOVERY OF THE BAROMETER

So long ago as the year 1640, an Italian named Torricelli filled a glass tube, open at one end, with mercury and then half-filled a bowl below with the same substance. In this manner he found out that a column of mercury can be upheld by the pressure of the air on other mercury in a bowl, and so discovered the principle of the mercurial barometer which we use to-day. Here you see Torricelli making experiments in the Alps with his tube of mercury.

THE WEATHER AND ITS WAYS

FROM earliest times men have watched the skies and the clouds and noted the way in which the wind has blown, and, as they have learned from experience, they have foretold coming changes in the weather. The fisherman and the farmer, the sailor and the shepherd, and all whose work is greatly influenced by weather conditions, generally learn to read the portents of the skies so far as their own areas are concerned.

"Red sky at night, shepherd's delight : red sky at morning, sailor's warning."

Some of the earlier observers kept records and even wrote on this subject. The famous sailor and navigator, William Dampier, compiled his "Discourse on Winds" in 1700 and described with great accuracy the main characteristics of the trade winds. The scientist, John Dalton, recorded over a

Fox Photos.

AT THE CLOSE OF A RAINY DAY

Here we have a photograph taken in the evening of London's skyline, dominated by St. Paul's Cathedral.   From the weather point of view the reading is that a cold front has passed and a narrow belt of rain was the result.   This has been followed by a rapid clearance of the sky and then the formation of cumulus clouds as seen in the picture.   The general outlook is now " bright periods with risk of occasional showers."

period of fifty-seven years from about 1780 onwards more than 200,000 observations on the weather. Many others also kept records and in some cases exchanged notes so that comparison could be made.

In 1867, Dr. Alexander Buchan, F.R.S., Secretary of the Scottish Meteorological Society, published a paper in which he gave six cold periods and three warm periods. The cold periods were February 9th–14th, April 11th–14th, May 9th–14th, June 29th–July 4th, August 6th–11th, November 6th–13th, and the warm periods July 12th–15th, August 12–15th, and December 3rd–14th, and were based on records taken in Scotland over a long period. Buchan only claimed that there was a

tendency for these short spells to occur at the times mentioned.

About the middle of the nineteenth century there grew up in most countries organisations for the collection and discussion of information about the weather. The science of meteorology had emerged from its early stages and was studied by men possessed of scientific knowledge. Meteorology is not an experimental science, but, like astronomy, an observational one. It can be defined as the science dealing with the processes going on in the earth's atmosphere which manifest themselves as weather and it seeks to give an explanation of these processes.

When the Nations Combine

During the past century meteorological stations have been established all over the world and international conferences have been held to ensure similarity in systems and reports in all countries. In recent years a knowledge of what the weather is likely to be in the next twenty-four hours and the outlook for a further period is of tremendous importance to a variety of people. In particular, the ever-growing volume of air traffic has made weather forecasts a vital need. To-day there are many hundreds of meteorological stations throughout the world where experts receive and send reports. Pilots in their planes in America or in Europe learn in advance the kind of weather they may expect whether their journey is North, South, East or West. By radio they can receive regular reports and forecasts of the changing conditions.

In the same way fishermen at sea may be warned of approaching gales many hours before there is any outward sign of them in their area. Farmers learn in advance the prospects regarding the weather for seed-time and harvest and can make arrangements accordingly.

It is on the observations of its own meteorologists, combined with information received from many other stations, that our Meteorological Office issues its regular forecasts which are nowadays a familiar feature of the B.B.C. services. "Here is the official weather forecast for the next twenty-four hours . . ." followed by a further outlook for the succeeding period.

Measuring the Air Pressure

What is weather, and how are the different changes brought about? Simple questions but not quite so

Planet.

WHEN THE FLOODS CAME

On the night of January 31, 1953, the eastern shores of Britain and the coast of the Netherlands suffered one of the most terrible storm and flood disasters in modern history. The worst-hit areas on the British coast were around the Thames Estuary where thousands of people were rendered homeless and many lives were lost. In this photograph Canvey Island is seen on the day after the storm.

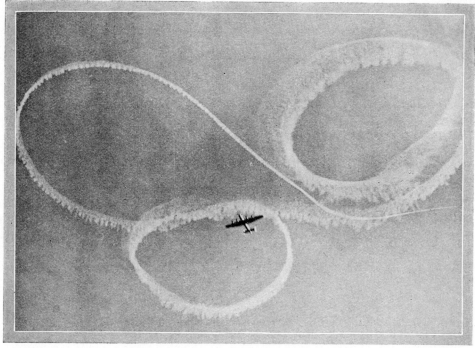

M. *Hubbard.*

TRAILING CLOUDS FOLLOW THE PLANE

The amount of water vapour the air can hold depends on the temperature ; the warmer the air the more water vapour it can contain. If heated, air can absorb extra water, but when cooled suffi- ciently this water vapour comes out in the air as mist, fog or cloud. An aeroplane flying at high altitudes discharges heated air carrying water vapour into the very cold atmosphere through which it is travelling and the water vapour condenses as trailing clouds in the wake of the plane.

simply answered. Our earth is a sphere surrounded by an envelope of gas, or rather a mixture of gases called air. This envelope is in two layers, the first consisting of the more dense air (which is called the *troposphere*) and extends to a height of about seven miles in our latitude. Beyond this is another layer of more rarefied air (the *stratosphere*). We are mainly con- cerned with the lower layer.

This envelope of air which surrounds the earth has a definite weight, roughly about 15 pounds to the square inch. Slight variations in the pressure which this column of air exerts have their effect on the weather. These variations can be measured by means of the baro- meter, familiar to most of us as a weather glass. There are three types of barometer in general use :—

The Mercury barometer is one in which the pressure is measured by reading the height of a column of mercury. The scale used to be marked in inches but is now generally marked in millibars (1,000 millibars equal approximately 29½ inches). Normal variations of pressure in this country range from 960 to 1,040 millibars.

The Aneroid barometer is one in which the pressure of the air causes contractions and expansions of an air- tight metal bellows which work a moving pointer. This is the type which is in popular use in our homes. The Barograph is also an aneroid barometer in which the pointer is re- placed by a pen that records the move- ment of the bellows on a rotating clockwork drum and so gives a con- tinuous record of the variations.

How the Wind Blows

The wind is caused primarily by pressure differences. There are, however, other forces, the chief of which is due to the rotation of the earth upon its axis. This is known as the Coriolis force and can be explained in this way : when the atmosphere is calm at the pole it is moving *through space* at the same speed as the earth beneath it. When it is calm at the equator the atmosphere is not only moving through space at the same speed as the earth, but also at about 1,000 geographical miles an hour from west to east owing to the rotation of the earth.

At the equator, therefore, the wind is blowing from the west at about 1,000 miles an hour compared with the calm at the pole. A person at the equator does not notice this because he is also moving from west to east at about 1,000 miles per hour. If a wind blows from the tropics towards the north, that is, a southerly wind, it moves over a surface that is not moving so fast as the place from which it comes. It tends to become a westerly wind and, in the same way, a wind blowing from the north tends to become an easterly wind. A third force which acts on the air is the centrifugal force, which becomes very important in tropical revolving storms such as typhoons, where the air moves along a very curved path.

Nearly a century ago a Dutchman, Christoph Buys-Ballot, discovered that the relative arrangement of high and low pressure areas determines the directions in which the wind blows. If you stand with your back to the wind you will have lower pressure on

H. J. Shepstone.

IN THE CANADIAN ROCKIES

You have all heard of the Canadian winters, with dry intense cold and deep crisp snow. Nothing could bring home to you the severity and yet the beauty of these winters more than the illustration above, which is reproduced from a photograph taken in the Rocky Mountains. During the winter in Canada the thermometer drops far below zero.

Government of New Zealand.

A CAVE FORMED IN THE ICE

It may seem strange to hear about intense cold in far-away New Zealand, yet in the neighbourhood of Milford Sound there are great glaciers within 600 feet of the sea. In these Southern Alps of New Zealand is the great Tasman glacier, as majestic as any in the world, and the above print shows us a cave within the glacier formed completely of ice.

your left-hand side and higher pressure on the right in the Northern hemisphere. In the Southern hemisphere it is the opposite.

Thus, if you are in London when a south-westerly wind is blowing and stand with your back to the wind with arms extended, your right arm will point towards Hastings where pressure will be high ; your left will be pointing towards Birmingham where pressure will be low. If the barometer at Hastings reads 10 millibars higher than it is in Birmingham then the wind will be blowing twice as hard as it would be if there were only 5 millibars difference between them.

The meteorologist requires to know the pressure as shown by the barometer from different quarters when he prepares his report. It is on record that shortly after the Allied landing in Normandy in June, 1944, there was a north-easterly gale in the English Channel which caused considerable damage to shipping and to the Mulberry harbours off the Normandy coast. Pressure in France had fallen rapidly while the barometers in southern England showed little change.

The Sun's Radiation

Any substance gives off heat at a rate dependent on its temperature and surface. If its temperature is low it gives off heat slowly, and if its temperature is high it gives off heat quickly. Thus the earth and its atmosphere are losing heat all the time, and to maintain their temperature they must receive heat. This heat they receive comes almost entirely from the sun. The solar radia-

tropics towards the poles. The necessity for this transport of heat is one of the basic causes of the winds and movement of water in the oceans. Solar radiation consists of energy mainly in the form of light and heat. Both travel in the form of waves of similar character, but the human eye can only perceive such radiation over a small range of wavelengths, in fact from that of blue light to that of red. The white light from the sun consists of all the wavelengths on this range, and can be broken up into the various colours by means of a prism.

When the sun's radiation reaches the earth's atmosphere

PICTURES IN THE ICE

In this illustration we see how moisture has condensed evenly on a pane of glass and the fern-like tracery of crystals brought about afterwards by Jack Frost.

tion the earth receives is almost constant from year to year, but varies at any one place during the year. The tropics receive much more of the sun's radiation than do the polar regions. Also the tropics receive considerably more radiation from the sun than they lose by radiation from the surface of land and sea and from the atmosphere, whereas the reverse is true in the polar regions. Thus as the temperature of the tropics and the polar regions remains almost constant for one time of the year over a great number of years there must be a net transport of heat from the

Photos : John J. Ward, F.E.S.

IN LITTLE RIVULETS

Here drops of water have been trickling down a pane of glass till arrested by sharp frost and turned into crystals of a different type.

TRUE CIRRUS CLOUDS
Cirrus clouds, here depicted, are high and light. They often show that the fine weather will not last long.

warmed up in consequence. The earth's surface is also giving out heat all through the day and night. During the hours of daylight in the forenoon the solar radiation reaching the earth's surface exceeds the heat leaving the surface and so normally its temperature rises till about 2 or 3 p.m. At about this time the radiation from the sun, which decreases after noon, becomes less than

some is reflected back from clouds. When there are no clouds the radiation reaches the earth's surface with only a very small fraction of it having been lost to the atmosphere. When this radiation reaches the ground part of it is reflected and part absorbed by the earth's surface, which is

Cloud photos : G. A. Clarke.

A BRINGER OF HAILSTONES
This is an example of cumulonimbus cloud. This great sullen mass in the sky is often a portent of squalls and a downpour of rain or hail.

A " MACKEREL SKY "
These are cirro-cumulus clouds, which produce a mackerel sky.

that leaving the earth's surface and hence the temperature begins to drop and normally continues to do so until about sunrise next day.

When the Temperature Rises

Temperature is the condition which determines the flow of heat from one substance to another. It can be measured by making use of the well-known fact that substances expand when heat flows into them and contract when it flows out. To measure the temperature a thermometer is used. This is simply a bulb containing mercury with an outlet in the fine tube of the glass stem to which it is attached. When heat flows into the bulb the mercury expands and

SEEN IN WAVES

These clouds are "alto-cumulus," made up in waves and presenting another type of mackerel sky.

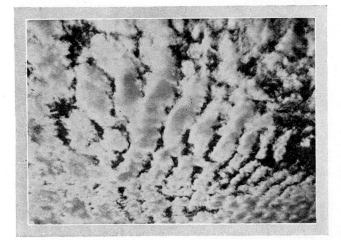

OF MEDIUM HEIGHT

A further example of "alto-cumulus" clouds, which are usually at medium height in the sky.

usually go higher than 120°. Boiling point of water under certain standard conditions is fixed at 212°.

Water requires two to three times the amount of heat, volume for volume, as does land to raise its temperature. Any large stretch of water is con-

the thread rises in the stem. By the side of the tube is a scale marked with different degrees. Most of the thermometers in this country are marked on the Fahrenheit scale in which the melting point of ice (or the point lower than which water will begin to freeze) is taken as 32°. Our thermometers do not

ON A SUMMER'S DAY

The cumulus cloud, soft and feathery, and lit by the sun.

THUNDER THREATENED

The cumulo-nimbus or thunder-cloud, dark and angry, and often building up vertically at great speed.

stantly stirred by the winds and the heat received or lost is therefore distributed down to considerable depths whereas it is only the top few inches of earth which are really affected by a warm day or a cold night. Because of this, land surfaces become hotter in summer and colder in winter compared with the wide expanse of the seas, and the further one goes from the sea the more pronounced does this become. That is why the British Isles, being sur-

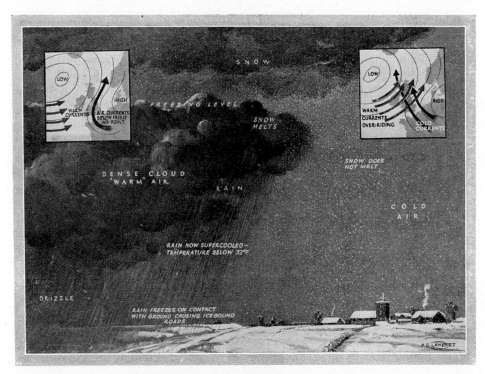

WHEN THE WARM AIR MEETS THE COLD

The picture above shows not only why our weather has earned the description " changeable " but also some of the difficulties facing the forecaster.   Cold air from the Continent has brought snow and ice to Britain.   From the Atlantic, however, warm air has advanced and this is expected to override the cold.   Snow formed at higher levels falls through warm air and then, as rain, falls into the freezing lower layers, eventually freezing when it reaches the cold ground.   This results in dangerous icy roads, impassable for motorists and cyclists and very difficult for pedestrians.

rounded by water, experience less extremes of heat and cold than inland places in the same latitude on the continent.

Over the oceans water is continually passing into the atmosphere as water vapour. The amount of water vapour the air can hold depends on the temperature. The warmer the air the more water it can contain. Air is often heated on its passage over the earth's surface. This causes it to expand, become lighter and rise. Where two sorts of air from different parts of the

MICRO-BAROGRAPH AND CASE

The instrument seen above is a Micro-barograph or precision-recording barometer. It shows the smallest fluctuations of pressure.

Negretti & Zambra.

THE STEVENSON SCREEN

To ensure correct conditions for the different thermometers this double-louvred screen has been designed by the British Meteorological Office. It houses the maximum, minimum, dry bulb and wet bulb thermometers.

world meet, boundary lines are formed where the colder, heavier air runs under the warmer and lighter air and compels it to rise. Or again air may come up against hills or mountains and be pushed up their sides. In each case the air cools as it rises and may drop its moisture in the form of droplets which float suspended in the atmosphere as clouds.

Different Kinds of Clouds

There are the high

clouds which float above 20,000 feet and are formed in a cold region where the temperature is well below freezing point. Among high clouds, known as *cirrus*, we find the stratus type as seen in the thin whitish veil which often gives the sun or moon a halo. *Cirrus* may also be seen as isolated tufts branching feather-like plumes across a blue sky.

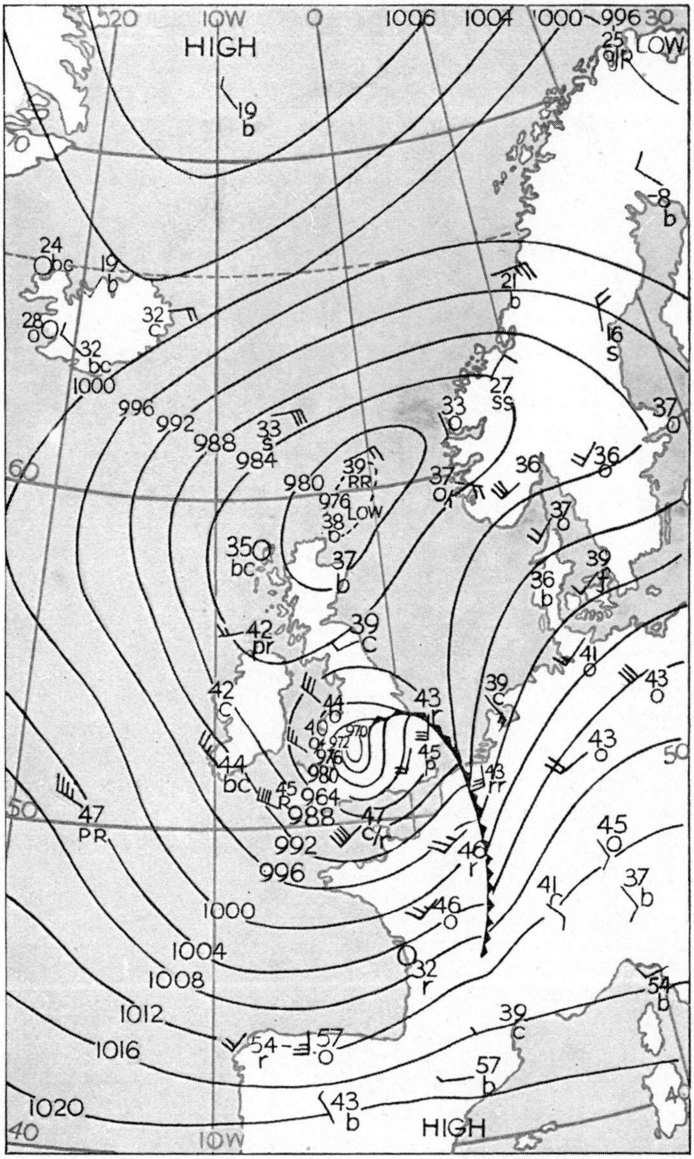

The medium clouds frequently float between 8,000 and 20,000 feet and often consist of ice crystals at the top and usually water droplets at the bottom. Among these are seen the stratus type known as *altostratus* and the cumulus type known as *altocumulus*, rounded masses arranged in rows, sometimes with blue lanes between them.

Low clouds float below 8,000 feet though they may on occasion build up with tops well above 20,000 feet. Among these the stratus type are well-known: grey woolly layers of cloud, perhaps in parallel folds, or the sheets of low grey clouds from which rain falls. There is also the cumulus type of low cloud, rounded islands of fair weather cloud sailing across a summer sky, or the towering domes and pinnacles that bring the showers.

When the Rain Comes

Clouds that form below 20,000 feet are most frequently

Crown Copyright.

THE METEOROLOGIST'S MAP

The weather forecaster plots on an outline map the reports received from many other stations, all of which are based on readings and records taken at the same hour. In the map, or synoptic chart, shown above, the progress of secondary depressions in relation to the British Isles, is indicated. This is an actual chart made in the course of the day's work and is published by permission of the Controller of H.M. Stationery Office.

" FOR SEA AREAS—GALE WARNING "

In the Shipping forecasts which are regularly broadcast by the B.B.C. different areas are named, just as in the case of forecasts for the country generally various districts are given, as, for instance, London and South-east England. The chart seen above, which is published by permission of the Controller of H.M. Stationery Office, shows how the seas around the British coasts are divided into areas, each of which has a distinctive name.

made up of tiny droplets so small that they float in the air. As cooling and condensation continues upon them the droplets grow larger until they reach a size when they cannot float but must fall slowly down to earth as fine rain or drizzle. If the upward currents of air are strong enough they will support the droplets until they have reached a size where they come to earth as rain-drops. When there are very strong up-draughts as in towering cumulus clouds, the tiny

drops will become very large before they fall and when at last the upward current can no longer support them they fall as heavy showers or pelting rain.

If the temperature in the cloud is below freezing point the droplets form as beautiful ice crystals and begin their journey earthwards as snow flakes. Snow rather than rain can be expected if the surface air temperature is less than 37° F. If, however, violent up-draughts keep carrying the ice crystals up and down

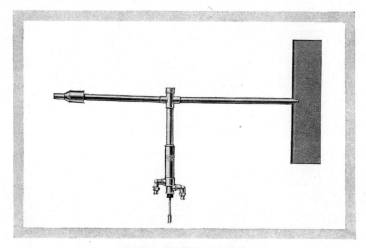

WIND VELOCITY HEAD

This instrument is part of the anemometer which records wind velocity. The open-ended tube is set into the wind by means of the vane, and a suction tube is exposed on all sides to the wind.

denses on the inside of windows when the air outside is cold.

At sea the commonest kinds of fog are formed when air which is warm and moist blows over fairly cold sea. The air in contact with the surface of the sea is cooled to a point where the moisture condenses and forms a cloud lying on the sea.

What the Winds Tell

The direction of the wind is that from which it blows. The wind is said to *back* if its direction changes against the hands of the clock, and to *veer* if the change is the other way. If a wind blowing from the south gradually changes until it is blowing from the west it is said to have veered. If it changes to the east it has backed.

South-west winds come from the warmer waters of the Atlantic farther south and are being cooled at the surface of the sea as they travel towards Britain. They bring warm moist air, therefore, and this drops its moisture as low cloud covering most of the sky. Grey, gloomy, cloudy weather is the result. In late spring and early summer when the sea is still comparatively cold, fog and mist may be expected.

North-west winds have just the opposite characteristics. They bring cold air from the polar regions or northerly latitudes which is warmed as it passes over the relatively warm sea around Britain. The air therefore has a tendency to rise and form high towering cumulus clouds. Showers fall from these, often as snow in winter, but are usually separated by intervals with blue sky predominating. If the wind is strong the uprushing air causes

they become balls of ice and may fall as hailstones.

Fog and Mist

Fog and mist are really clouds down to earth level. They are usually formed overland when air condenses its moisture through being cooled by contact with the earth's cold surface and not because air is cooled through rising. There is no difference between fog and mist except in degree. The meteorologist speaks of fog when visibility is under 1,100 yards.

On clear nights a sharp drop in temperature occurs about sunset when the earth loses heat into space and cools down the air in contact with it. If the sky is cloudy the heat cannot get away into space and little cooling takes place. If the sky is clear then sufficient cooling takes place to allow the air in contact with the earth to shed its moisture as mist or fog. A gentle breeze is necessary for this so-called radiation fog to form. If the wind is strong enough the air becomes stirred up too much for mist to form. If there is no wind at all the moisture is condensed as dew, or, on very cold nights, as hoar frost in the same way that water con-

gusts and squalls and "bumpiness" generally.

Our two most common winds are from the South-west and the West. Westerly winds bring a variety of weather, but often a westerly wind shifts to south-west or north-west. North-east winds usually come from Scandinavia and North Russia : the air is cold in winter

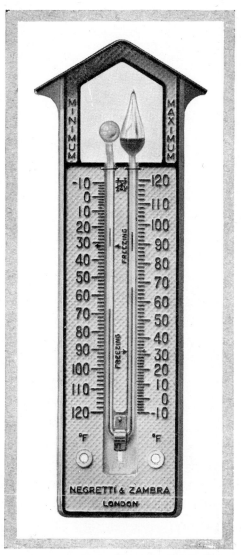

Photos : Negretti & Zambra.

ANOTHER TYPE OF THERMOMETER

This "Six's" Thermometer registers the maximum and minimum readings during a set period. The ordinary thermometer records only the temperature at the moment of reading.

BAROMETER AND THERMOMETER

In this illustration we see the barometer and thermometer in close company. The barometer carries a second and marking hand. If this hand is set overnight over the recording hand, we can see in the morning to what extent pressure has changed.

and cool in summer. Overcast skies and sometimes drizzle may accompany them, but occasionally in winter towering clouds build up from which showers fall, largely depending on whether the air is warmer or cooler than the surface waters of the North Sea across which it travels *en route*.

East and south-east winds come to us from Central Europe and are cold and dry in winter and warm and dry in summer. An easterly wind frequently brings grey overcast skies while a south-easter often has little cloud but picks up smoke from the industrial regions of Belgium and the Ruhr and brings in a smoke haze over south-east England. A backing wind, especially from north or west, is often a sign of unsettled weather.

Wind, Sky and Glass

The fishermen round our coasts and the farmers on the land have their own ways of reading the skies and understanding the warning of the winds. The city man has his glass, but generally speaking the indications given by the barometer, and the sky, too, for that matter, are short-range warnings. The barometer tells in broad terms if the weather is likely to change. It also usually gives short notice of approaching gales, but not always so. The case already quoted of the north-easterly gales at the time of the Allied landings in France is an example of the exception which may occasionally occur.

A steady glass often means that conditions will remain much as they are for probably another twelve hours. A rising glass means an eventual improvement, providing of course that the rise is maintained. A falling glass betokens increasing cloud, probably rain, possibly increasing wind and poor visibility. If the barometer falls steadily over a fairly long period it may mean the approach of a series of depressions, each with bad weather belts, bringing unsettled weather for some days. But a sudden fall usually denotes the approach of a short bad spell followed fairly soon by an improvement.

If the barometer falls steeply and the wind backs, a gale within a

News Chronicle.

ON THE AIR MINISTRY ROOF

Our weather forecasts are based on the reports from many stations throughout the world. Readings of the different instruments are made at regular intervals and from the knowledge thus gathered the forecaster plots his weather map. In the picture above a meteorological assistant is taking the readings shown by the instruments on the roof of the Air Ministry in Kingsway, London.

few hours is probable with heavy rain and poor visibility. There may then be a sharp veer of wind. If the backing is pronounced the gale will often be violent and the veer great. The gale will continue for some time from about north-west with the rising glass. Gales with a rising barometer are frequently squally.

Gales are more frequent in winter, especially early winter, than in the summer, and occur more often in the north than in the south of the North Atlantic ocean. In the winter there is a gale on the average on five to ten days a month in the western entrance to the Channel, but in the summer the average is only one or two days a month.

High Clouds and Low

The clouds, the colour of the sky, and the clarity or otherwise of the atmosphere are other indications of the weather to be expected. Generally, however, low clouds tell little about anything except the present weather since they are formed by air rising locally. High and medium clouds show what is going on in the upper layers and so help us to form some opinion of the weather ahead.

Fleecy, woolly low clouds floating separately against a pale clear blue background are fine weather clouds. If they collect together and rise upwards with dark centres there may be scattered showers, but the clouds will usually flatten out and dissolve in the evening over land. Very high towering clouds with silver linings and radiating shafts of light against a deep blue sky mean heavy showers. If they fan out into anvil-shaped heads having fibrous texture of threadlike appearance, differing from the dome-shaped, rounded clouds nearer the ground, very heavy showers can be

Crown Copyright.

A RECORDING RAIN GAUGE

A rain gauge is an instrument for recording the fall of rain. Our photograph shows the changing of the daily chart of a rain gauge at Kew Observatory. On this chart a pen automatically records the rainfall during a period of twenty-four hours.

A SUNSHINE RECORDER

In this instrument the sun's rays are focused by means of a glass sphere upon prepared and printed cardboard strips. The "Campbell-Stokes" Sunshine Recorder seen above is designed for use in latitudes 45° to 65°.

expected, probably of hail in winter, and possibly with thunder. This is the sky brought by the northerly or north-west winds from the polar regions behind a depression. These clouds often occur behind a bad weather belt.

Clouds that seem to writhe and twist as they tower upwards and send down pouch-like folds also indicate thundery conditions. A gloomy pall of grey roller-shaped clouds will often persist for some time.

Among the high and medium clouds, cirrus of the fibrous type, often in long bands, white and transparent, covering more and more of the sky until there is little blue left, denote the approach of a depression with rain, low cloud, and probably poor visibility within the next twenty-four hours.

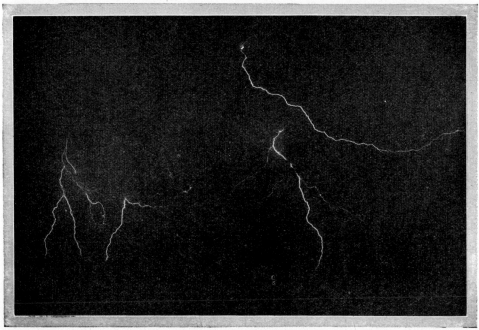

Fox Photos.

WHEN THE LIGHTNING FLASHES

To the naked eye lightning gives the appearance of a blinding streak of light. When photographed it appears a sinuous line, usually branched and often resembling a map of a large river and its tributaries. Our photograph shows the forked lightning normally seen; sheet lightning is caused by the glow from lightning below the horizon or a considerable distance away.

The next stage in the approach of bad weather is a thin whitish veil with a halo round the sun or moon. If the barometer is falling with a southerly wind, continuous rain may be expected to begin within the next twelve hours or so. The veil develops into a sky that looks like ground glass with a hazy sun or moon that gradually becomes completely obscured. This is the " wet sky " that tells of rain within four to eight hours.

A low sunset, with the sun setting on the horizon beneath a bank of cloud is a good sign of fair weather, but a high sunset, with the sun setting behind a bank of cloud, is usually a sign of rain during the night. A red sunrise, as the old lines already quoted indicate, generally means rain, but it is not altogether a good rule by itself. The type of cloud and shade of red have to be taken into consideration. If the redness at morning is caused by high and medium clouds spreading from the west it is fairly safe to assume that bad weather is in the offing. But light red low clouds, or pink and soft-looking clouds at sunrise, may not mean bad weather. A rosy sunset, however, probably means good weather all the next day.

With the Met. Men

These general indications are for the amateur. The Met. men of the Meteorological Office of the Air Ministry and those in the Naval service have their instruments, reports from other areas, and sound scientific knowledge on which to base their forecasts. During the 1914–18 war two Norwegian meteorologists, father and son named Bjerknes, made numerous observations and evolved the polar front theory of depressions and their formation. This theory has now been generally accepted and forms the basis of modern forecasting.

According to Bjerknes depressions are

LIKE A VACUUM-CLEANER IN THE SKY

This wonderful photograph gives you some idea of what a tornado is like. The snapshot was taken near Jasper, Minnesota, in the United States of America, and shows the tornado stretching across the heavens in the form of a gigantic tube. The " broom " at the earthward end was 300 feet across, and the destruction wrought can be well imagined.

WHAT IS A WATERSPOUT?

Photo : Acme-Sennecke.

One of the most amazing freaks of climate is a waterspout, normally observed at sea. The spout seen above was captured for this pictorial reproduction on the River Yangtse in China. Strictly speaking, it is not a column of water, but a portion of a cloud brought down to earth with a twirling motion as though it were one of Nature's spinning tops.

Topical Press.

READY FOR DUTY IN THE ATLANTIC

In agreement with several other nations who are anxious to have accurate meteorological forecasts, Great Britain now maintains four of the fleet of weather ships necessary to maintain the ten weather ship stations in the Atlantic. Our picture shows one of these ships, *Weather Observer*, all ready to sail from the docks for her turn of duty at sea. Other British weather ships are named appropriately *Weather Watcher*, *Weather Explorer* and *Weather Recorder*.

formed in a region where a cold polar current of air comes in contact with a humid warm equatorial current. Owing to the geostrophic force, of which we have read, the tendency of these currents of air is to flow in opposite directions : the cold air tends to flow west while the warm equatorial air inclines to the east. The boundary between these masses of warm and cold air is known as the polar front and is in the form of a slope upwards towards the cold air.

Owing to the difference in temperature and humidity between these two air masses, the boundary or polar front is a region of upward movement. Disturbances on this boundary cause the warm air current to form a wave over the polar front. It is from this wave of warm air encroaching further and further

into the cold air that a depression forms.

At the warm front the warm air blows against the side of the cold air and rises over it. As it rises it gets colder; the moisture condenses and heavy rain falls from nimbo-stratus and alto-stratus clouds.

At the cold front the cold, heavier air undercuts the warm air and causes it to rise. The warm humid air is forced up at a greater speed than at the warm front with the result that heavy rain is experienced, usually of shorter duration than the rain at a warm front, and is followed by clearing showers and broken cumulus clouds.

So long as there is a warm front and a cold front the depression increases in depth and severity. When the two fronts become close together and form a combined front it is known as an occlusion. The majority of depressions reaching the British Isles are occluded, and once a depression becomes occluded it gradually fills up and dies away.

On the Weather-Man's Chart

For the purpose of forecasting, synoptic charts or weather maps are prepared : a synoptic chart is an outline map of the area for which the forecast is required and on this are plotted the meteorological observations, all of which have been made at the same time. At the Air Ministry in Dunstable, now the

Central Forecast Office of the meteorological service in this country, observations are received at three-hourly intervals from land stations as well as from voluntary observing merchant ships and ocean weather ships at sea, and these are marked on the chart. They show, in symbols, the direction and force of the wind, the pressure, the temperature, and the amount of cloud and visibility at that particular place at that particular time.

When all these observations have been plotted, lines are drawn of varying shapes through places of equal pressure. These are called isobars and are usually drawn in for every two millibars. The direction of the wind is shown by small arrows variously feathered to indicate the force. Sometimes lines are drawn through places of equal temperature and these lines are known as isotherms.

The meteorologists have reduced the many possible arrangements of these isobars into six fundamental forms. The three we hear most often are the Depression or Cyclone; the Secondary Depression; and the Anti-cyclone or High. The depression is rarely stationary and in the North Atlantic usually follows a path from west to east. As the depression passes any given place the barometer continues to fall until the centre of low pressure has passed when it begins to rise again. Depressions may be of any size from local disturbances to wide-spread systems covering the Atlantic.

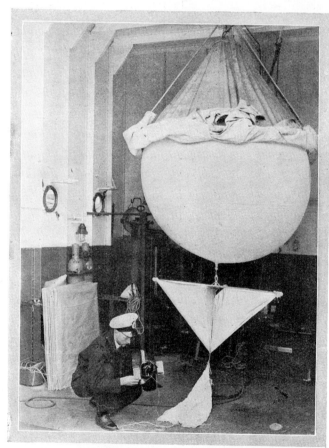

Topical Press.

FIXING THE RADIO TRANSMITTER

In this picture we see a member of the crew of the weather ship fixing a radio transmitter to an observation balloon. The course of the balloon is plotted by radio and radio-frequencies are sent out from the balloon in a known order, picked up by the ship and measured. Each balloon with its equipment costs £30 and two balloons are used every twenty-four hours

In the case of secondary disturbances these may form in any part of the main depression, but they usually reach their greatest development on the south side. They often bring more intense weather conditions with rain. Between the depression and the secondary disturbance there will probably be light variable winds.

The anti-cyclone is an area of high pressure and may remain stationary in one area for days. Generally the anti-cyclone brings fine, dry weather with light winds and blue skies in the summer, but in winter it will probably mean overcast skies.

This is merely a general idea of the lines on which the meteorological experts gather their information, and from the synoptic charts they compile work out the shape of things to come so far as the weather is concerned. The value of this work has become increasingly recognised, not only to the airman and the sailor, but to the fruit-grower, for instance, to whom an early warning of frost may result in the saving of valuable crops.

Topical Press.

CHECKING THE RADAR AERIAL

Many scientific devices which will enable the meteorologist to obtain the fullest information about the state of the atmosphere high above the earth have been fitted to the weather ships now manning the Atlantic. Our picture shows the Radar operator carrying out the necessary tests and checks on an important part of this equipment, the Radar aerial.

Warning of Gales

In addition to the gale warnings broadcast, visual gale warnings are shown by means of the North and South Cones. These cones are hoisted at certain points around the coast to indicate that a gale (wind with a mean speed of thirty-nine miles an hour or gusts of forty-seven miles per hour or more) is probable in the near future.

Aboard the Weather Ships

For about 100 years merchant ships of many nations have voluntarily made regular weather observations all over the oceans. Great Britain now has over 500 selected merchant ships reporting, and most other nations also arrange for a proportion of their ships to make meteorological observations. So important is weather forecasting now considered to be by the governments of Europe and America that eight nations agreed in 1946 to equip a fleet of weather ships for service in the Atlantic. Great Britain has four of these ships, two being on duty at the same time. They are fitted with the latest meteorological instruments and special radar equipment. The radar operators are able to give transatlantic air pilots their minute-to-minute bearings. Every twelve hours a balloon carrying a special transmitter is released from the weather ship. Trailing from these balloons are tinfoil kites so

prepared that the ship's radar can pick up the signals they send out. By these automatic sound signals details of the upper air temperature, humidity, pressure and wind are obtained. What happens high up will eventually affect the weather below.

Working in these weather ships is one of the toughest jobs in a meteorological service and only men who are physically fit and not seriously liable to sea sickness are able to undertake the work. Already an American weather ship has been responsible for thrilling rescue work from an aeroplane forced down to the sea. This is among the additional duties which the weather ships are fitted to undertake. Other scientific work is also carried on while the ships are at sea.

These vessels are at sea for twenty-seven days and the four British ships are named *Weather Observer*, *Weather Watcher*, *Weather Explorer* and *Weather Recorder*, all ex-corvettes and each carrying a total of fifty men on board. From these ships reports are transmitted to Dunstable and then sent to foreign stations in all parts of the world.

Many of us, of course, simply take the weather as it comes, although even the amateur gardener is grateful to the B.B.C. when it gives warning of a ground frost just when the early potatoes are promising well. Recently in America warning was given of the coming of a cyclonic storm several hours before it swept

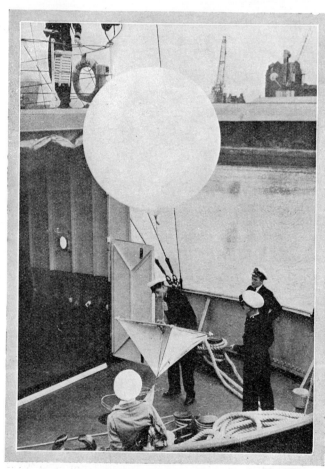

Central Press.

READY TO GO ALOFT

Every twelve hours a balloon fitted with special equipment is released from the weather ships now stationed in the Atlantic. These balloons rise to a height of between 50,000 and 60,000 feet when they burst. By means of these the experts aboard the weather ships learn the barometric pressure, the humidity, the temperature and wind in the atmosphere far above sea level.

Whites Aviation Ltd., N.Z.

A REMARKABLE CLOUD FORMATION IN NEW ZEALAND
Probably the finest and most unusual cloud photograph ever seen is the one shown here. It was taken by Mr. L. S. White, a well-known New Zealand aerial photographer, while flying near Middlemarch in South Island. In spite of the impression it gives of sweeping across the countryside, the cloud is stationary, though the meteorologists explain that the wind is actually blowing at high velocity through it.

across certain parts on the south-westerly coasts. The warning enabled urgent steps to be taken to minimise the terrible loss that might have ensued. Damage and loss did occur but it was little compared with what might have taken place but for the warning.

Tornadoes, Typhoons and Waterspouts

That particular storm was similar to the great circular storms which occur in the sub-tropical belt. They may be as much as 1,200 miles in diameter and within about 300 miles of the centre the wind may blow at 100 miles per hour. The rainfall is enormous and thunder and lightning add to the terror. In the centre is a small area of dead calm in which the sun shines brightly.

The typhoon of the China seas is an example of this type of storm. Then there is a smaller but even more terrible type of circular storm, the tornado or whirlwind, sometimes no more than a

hundred yards in diameter. It shows as a funnel-shaped cloud, purple-black in colour, with edges white as snow, and it leaps and dances across the country like a mad giant. Nothing can stand against its force. A waterspout is really a tornado at sea. It is a violent whirl-pool which produces a dark, funnel-shaped cloud tapering downwards towards the sea so that it resembles a spout or trunk joining the sea to the cloud.

On the whole Britain is comparatively free from these highly destructive types of storm, but there are several instances of them in this country. One of the worst was the tornado of May 21st, 1950. It moved from Wendover to Linslade and in its track trees were felled, roofs of old buildings were removed and vehicles in farmyards lifted; thunderstorms also occurred with heavy rain and large hailstones, the largest individual stone consisting of an irregular mass of ice with several centres and measuring

$6\frac{1}{2}$ inches round. The storm resembled a true American tornado.

There have been other fierce storms in Britain. The gale on January 15th, 1952 was very severe in the north of Scotland, reaching hurricane force in places and causing great damage in the Orkney Islands. Among the highest gusts recorded on this day were 108 miles per hour at Stornoway, 102 at Lerwick and 81 at Millport and Tiree.

About Electric Storms

Generally our weather can claim few records and the description usually applied—temperate—is a very fair summary of what we experience. Java is probably the most thundery region on earth but parts of Central America and certain places in Africa might possibly contest the claim. One of the worst British thunderstorms occurred in July, 1927. It covered some 10,000 square miles and it was calculated that at least £100,000,000 worth of electrical energy was released that night. Possibly one day some means will be found of harnessing the mighty electric power in a thunderstorm and making good use of it.

Yet even in Britain there is an average of one thunderstorm every two days. Over the whole surface of the earth there are at any given moment about 1,800 thunderstorms occurring while lightning flashes are appearing at the rate of 100 every second. And each flash of lightning releases sufficient electrical energy to supply all London with the power it requires for eight minutes.

Lightning appears in three separate forms : forked or zig-zag, sheet lightning, and the mysterious ball lightning. It is produced by the discharge of electricity between two clouds, or between the cloud and the earth. Forked lightning gives the appearance to the naked eye of a blinding streak of light; photographically it appears as a sinuous line, usually branched and often resembling a map of a large river and its tributaries. Sheet light-

ning is caused by the glow from lightning below the horizon or at a considerable distance away. Ball lightning, which is only rarely seen, appears as a luminous ball moving slowly in the air and breaking up explosively on contact with some object.

Cherrapunji in Assam is probably the wettest place in the world; yearly averages of between 424 and 499 inches have been recorded. In Britain annual totals of 240 inches have been recorded twice at The Stye, Borrowdale, and once at both Ben Nevis Observatory and at Llyn Llydaw, Snowdon, this century. Margate recorded the smallest annual rainfall, 9.29 inches, in 1921. The highest rainfall in a single day was recorded at Bruton, Somerset; 9.56 inches, on June 28th, 1917.

The scientist has made great progress in his efforts to control the forces of Nature; but few attempts have ever been made to control the forces which make our weather. Our real progress in fairly recent times has been not in the direction of control but in accurate anticipation by scientific means of what the weather will be in any given area.

Two examples of how man has endeavoured to change the weather on a small scale are the dispersal of fog at certain airfields by the use of flame burners at the sides of a runway and the production of rain from clouds which might not otherwise have given it. The artificial production of rain has been carried out in Australia and America by the " seeding " of clouds, often by ice or silver iodide particles. The experimental results, however, show that the occasions on which the " seeding " of clouds will produce rain which otherwise would not have fallen are strictly limited.

The meteorologist is a scientist and a prophet, telling us from his observations just what Nature intends to give us on the morrow. We can guard against the frost by night or prepare in advance for the storms of the day because we have been warned.

THE MYSTERY OF THE TIDES

A ROUGH SEA OFF THE ENGLISH COAST

The power and the grandeur of the sea has inspired writers and artists through the centuries.
In this photograph is seen a typical example of stormy seas breaking against the rocky fringe of
the English Coast. In the chapter below, the phenomenon of the tides is explained.

EVERY visitor to the seaside is almost bound to notice that about twice in every 24 hours the tides rise and fall: that the water advances up the shore and is deeper at high tide: and that at low tide the water has receded, sometimes far out on low flat shores, and is shallower. Wise holiday-makers will even consult the local tide-tables—will there be swimming and boating to-day? Yes, if the tide is " in." Will the family be able to play on the beach, to hunt for treasures there safely? Yes, if the tide is " out " most of the day. Does the flood tide " come in " gradually? Or does it advance rapidly so as to cut off unwary little paddlers before they can retreat to safety? These, and many other questions affecting the success of a seaside holiday, can be answered by the local tide-table.

Dwellers by the sea can tell us more about the tides. They have noticed, especially at certain points on some coasts, that the tides create definite currents in the sea—anchored vessels point one way when the tide is rising and the opposite way when the tide is falling. In the Thames Estuary, for example, anchored ships point up towards London at *ebb*-tide, when the tide is falling ; but at *flood*-tide, when the tide is rising, they point east towards the North Sea. Seaside dwellers, too, have noticed that the tides are about 51 minutes later each day, and that the moon rises about 51 minutes later each night—which at once suggests an important connection between the tides and the moon. In very early times the ancients observed this phenomenon and recorded the coincidence of tidal changes with certain changes in the moon.

When the Moon Wanes

Another important fact well-known to seaside dwellers is that just as the moon waxes gradually to full moon, and then slowly decreases, so the flood tides become higher as the moon increases to full, or at new moon, and then become lower at half-moon. The highest tides are known as *Spring tides*, when the flood tide is deepest and strongest and the ebb-tide is lowest. The lowest tides are the *Neap* (*nipped*) *tides* at half-moon when the flood is shallowest and weakest and the ebb-tide is not so low as it is at Spring tide. In other words, the tidal " range "

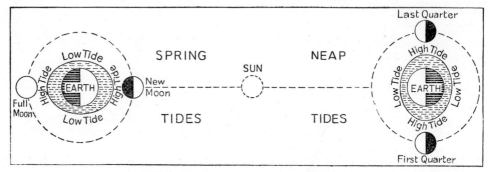

SPRING AND NEAP TIDES IN THE OCEAN

At the time of the Full Moon, the Earth is between the Sun and the Moon ; at the time of the New Moon, the Moon and the Sun are pulling together. At both these times the tidal bulge is greatest and we have Spring tides. When, however, the Moon is in its first quarter or in its third quarter (half moon at both times), the tidal bulge beneath the Moon is less owing to the modifying pull of the Sun. At these times we get Neap tides, whose range is considerably less than that of Spring tides.

(difference between high tide and low tide) is greatest during Spring tides and least during Neap tides.

Normally, the flood tide reaches full height in about 6 hours and then ebbs to low water in another 6 hours. But coastal features, capes and bays, estuaries and sandbanks, for example, may alter this considerably. The flood tide may sweep up an estuary like the Severn or a great long inlet like the Bay of Fundy in Canada in a swift " bore " or " tidal wave " in a very short time; but the ebb may be many hours beyond the normal six. At Stonebench, below Gloucester, people often gather to watch the " bore " coming up the river. A low roar is heard, like the sound of a distant water-fall, then a wall of water, crested with foam, comes rushing along, travelling as fast as a man can run. Venturesome boys think it great sport to go out in their boats and meet " Flood's Head " as they call it, which carries them flying up-stream. The Bay of Fundy, sepa-rated by a neck of land from the Gulf of the St. Lawrence, is 145 miles long, and the sight as the tide pours into it is a very wonderful one. The sea races across the broad mudflats and sand as fast as horse can gallop, and anyone caught there by the tide has small hope of surviving.

The Secret of the Tides

The tides are primarily due to Gravi-tation, " the force that rules the Universe ": the force that keeps the Sun and its attendant planets in place and establishes the rotation of the Sun's family of planets and satellites in their regular orbits: the force whose " pull " acting from the centre of each heavenly body affects all others and keeps us and other " movables " in our places on the earth's surface, even at the Equator which is rotating at least at a thousand miles an hour.

Since by gravitation all bodies attract each other according to their masses and their distances apart, the Earth is influenced by the gravitational " pull " of both Sun and Moon. Vastly the greater mass—2,700,000 times that of the Moon—the Sun is much farther away from the Earth than the Moon, which therefore exercises greater " pull " on the earth than the Sun, despite its very much smaller mass. The Sun's " pulling power " is less than half of that of the Moon.

The Earth has a great thick covering of water over three-quarters of its sur-face, and water responds more readily to the gravitational attraction of Sun and Moon than does the solid land. It is the differential attraction of Sun and Moon upon the great waters of the Earth

A "BORE" AND A HIGH TIDE

James's Press Agency.

In some parts of the world, strong Spring tides run up a fast-narrowing river in the form of a bore, which advances with a low roar like a distant waterfall.   Here we are shown the Haining bore which flows up the River Tseintang in China every twenty-four hours, being especially strong when the Moon is full.

G. Brocklehurst.

Sweeping forward, these surging waves beat against the shores in high tide.   We get the highest tides when the Moon is full and when it is new because at these times the Sun and Moon are pulling together.   The time of harvest moon in September appears to bring particularly high tides.   The roar of the flood shown here could be heard distinctly a mile away.

that causes the Tides. At certain times in the month, Sun and Moon are (1) pulling together in conjunction, (2) pulling in opposition to each other, or (3) pulling against one another in quadrature. These three relative positions govern the Tides of the Earth's waters.

Effect of Land Masses

To understand how this works let us suppose the globe—our Earth—is covered entirely with water. *If* the Earth stood still, gravitational pull of Sun and Moon (but chiefly that of the Moon) would cause the water to rise in a broad shallow bulge opposite the Moon. But the Earth rotates continuously and each part in turn would come opposite the Moon whose influence would apparently cause a tidal bulge that would seem to travel round the world—although actually the Earth would be rotating under the bulge.

But the Earth is *not* an all-water sphere. The land masses, great and small, break up the tidal bulge, causing many changes in the timing and the character of the Tides, deflecting the passage of the " tidal wave " and producing freak conditions in certain places. Generally speaking, however, the Moon is the chief tide-producer, although the Sun plays a part. The diagram on page 28 explains Spring and Neap Tides in the ocean.

Let us imagine the tidal wave in the wide Pacific travelling westwards (the Earth rotates from west to east). It is very broad and not very high in the open ocean. In about 12 hours it

Fox Photos.

THE POWER OF THE TIDES

High tides combined with violent winds on the last night of January, 1953 caused one of the worst disasters for many years along the coasts of Britain and Holland. This photograph shows the end of the jetty at Margate, with a portion of the wrecked lighthouse after the fury of the tide and the storm had died down. Damage amounting to millions of pounds, as well as a tragic loss of life, was the result of one night of storm and high tides.

THE SEVERN BORE

The flood tide sweeps up the Severn in a swift " bore " or " tidal wave," as you can see from this picture. A low roar is heard like the sound of a distant waterfall, then a foam-crested wall of water comes rushing along, travelling as fast as a man can run. Stonebench, below Gloucester, is a favourite spot for watching the Severn bore.

reaches New Zealand and Australia; both land masses impede its progress and break it up, but it sweeps on to the west and in 30 hours has reached Africa, passing the Cape of Good Hope to join the Atlantic tide, and passing north-west at great speed to reach New York in 40 hours from the Pacific and then eastward to reach London in 66 hours or so. All the while the land masses and coastlines, as well as contrary winds, have impeded it.

When the tidal wave reaches the continental platform of Western Europe, from which rise the British Isles, it is further impeded by rapidly shallowing water. This causes the tide to set up definite " tidal streams " or currents, one passing up the English Channel, another up St. George's Channel, and a third along the western shores of Ireland and Scotland which passes north, through the Pentland Firth and into the North Sea, turning south and eventually meeting off the Thames Estuary an English Channel tide twelve hours older than itself, and creating in the Thames Estuary a double tidal effect that is of vast importance to the Port of London. The Port of Liverpool has similar advantages, for a branch of the northerly tide, to the west of Scotland and the north, reaches the Irish Sea via the North Channel to meet the tide that has come direct by way of St. George's Channel.

Tidal Conditions at Southampton

Tidal conditions at Southampton are peculiar, largely as a result of the narrowing of the English Channel eastwards. The English Channel is rightly called by the French *La Manche*, " The Sleeve," with its cuff or wristband at the Straits of Dover. Southampton has double tides—a second highwater

THE INCOMING TIDE   . *L.E.A.*

In wind-swept fury, the surging breakers rush towards the shore. In some parts of the world, the tide comes in at such speed that anyone caught by it has little hope of surviving. On our seaside holidays, it is always safest to find out the habits and times of the tides before venturing very far out from the shore at low tide.

occurs two hours after its predecessor. Between them the ebb is only slight and the general effect of this phenomenon is to prolong high-water conditions for some three hours. The advantage to shipping is obvious, especially to the large vessels using Southampton; in addition to deep, quiet, sheltered water the high tide is prolonged, enabling the slow and cautious manœuvring of big ships into the docks to be carried on unhindered.

The causes of Southampton's double tides are still a matter for debate. Some authorities say that one tide enters the Solent past the Needles and the second enters Spithead two hours later as a throw-back of the main Channel tide owing to the sudden and sharp northerly trend of the French coast between Le Havre and Boulogne. Others, however, point out that this double tidal effect is experienced as far west as Weymouth and even across the Channel at the mouth of the Seine, and that it is definitely the effect of the sharp constriction of the Channel eastwards and northwards.

Whatever may be the causes of these favourable tidal conditions in Southampton water, their effect has been to make Southampton the premier British port for large vessels, especially as there are first-class railway and road transport systems from the docks inland.

The Work of the Tides

Every reader of the terrifying tales of Edgar Allan Poe will remember the fearsome Maelstrom which he described. This is formed by a tidal race among the Lofoten Islands off the Norwegian coast. Although there is no such

A RAINBOW IN THE SKY

The beautiful colours of the rainbow are produced by the reflection of the sun's rays caused by the spherical globules of raindrops, and the size and shape of the arc are determined by the position of the sun: the higher the sun the lower the rainbow. "My heart leaps up when I behold a rainbow in the sky," Wordsworth sang, and this wonderful phenomenon showing all the colours of the spectrum in their right order has excited admiration through the ages since the first rainbow appeared in the heavens.

" THE BRIDGE " IS SYDNEY'S MOST PRIZED POSSESSION

Sydney is justly proud of the magnificent bridge which spans the harbour and connects the city with its northern suburbs. The bridge, which is the most spectacular engineering achievement in Australia and one of the engineering wonders of the world, was officially opened in 1932, six years after construction work had started. It contains some 52,300 tons of steel and is the widest bridge in the world. The cost of construction itself was more than £A7 millions, and other expenses brought the total cost to nearly £A9¾ millions. The highest point of the great arch is 445 ft. above water level and there is a clearance of 170 ft. for shipping.

ON THE EVENING TIDE

G. Brocklehurst.

Here we see the evening tide at Gainsborough in Lincolnshire, which has produced that phenomenon known as the bore or ægir when the incoming tidal waves meet the fresh water pouring down stream. In Norse fairy lore, Ægir was the giant of the seashore, and from him this famous bore takes its name.

frightening whirlpool as Poe described, the eddies formed among the rocks are deep and dangerous.

There are other places where dangerous conditions are created by a great volume of tidal water being forced through a narrow channel. " The Great Gulf," which runs between the Scottish mainland and the islands of Jura and Scarba, is a tidal " race " which at times has a current of eleven miles an hour, and it would take a fairly powerful steamer to force its way against it.   Another ugly place for sailors is the Blanchart Race, between the Channel Islands and the French coast, where the current runs at a speed of ten miles an hour.

But the Tides, especially along the shorelands and in shallow water, are prodigious workers.   Tidal currents scour coastlines, removing vast quantities of material and depositing them in other places.   Tides keep the navigation channels of important estuaries clear, especially at ebb tide when vast quantities of silt and rubbish are swept out to sea.   They bear upon their bosoms ships of all kinds, helping them up to the docks and back again to sea.   Often,

as in the case of the familiar Thames lighters, the Tides are the transport-power, not the bargees at the long sweeps which only guide the lumbering craft along.

The   Tides   are   excavators   and builders, carriers and scavengers, transporters and destroyers.   When a strong north-east gale pushes a high Spring tide into the Thames Estuary, the normal outflow of the river is arrested and the Thames " floods "—still a great   anxiety   to   the   responsible authorities—are the result.   Tidal currents can form bars across estuaries and inlets, blocking them completely unless the waterway is kept open by constant dredging.   Coastal regions open to sea erosion (e.g., on the east coast of England) are often protected from further damage by a system of groynes.   Each groyne thrust out over the badly scoured shallow serves to hold back some of the shingle, sand and other debris carried along by tidal currents ; in time, the deposits on both sides of the groyne often grow so considerable that nowadays parts of shorelands formerly swept by flood tidal currents are firm land.

G. Brocklehurst.

LIKE A CORRUGATED SHEET

This second view of the ægir or bore at Gainsborough was taken early in the month of May and in particularly favourable weather conditions. On this account the formation of the incoming waves is particularly smooth and even.

Our
Engineers
and
Their Work

Roads, Bridges,
Canals,
Water Power
and Irrigation

E.N.A.

ALONG THE APPIAN WAY

The Appian Way, as it appears to-day, is illustrated above, and we see the ruins of the Tempio di Ercoli. This most historic highway dates back to the time of Ancient Rome, having been commenced by Appius Claudius in 312 B.C. The Romans were great builders of roads, and this highway ran from Rome to the East. The ruins along its course are deeply interesting.

THE WONDERS OF MODERN ROAD MAKING

THE roads of the ancients were mere rough paths for foot passengers and beasts of burden. We read in Isaiah: " Make straight in the desert a highway for our God. Every valley shall be exalted, and every mountain and hill shall be made low; and the crooked shall be made straight, and the rough places plain." Here we have a picture of what was done when a king announced a royal progress through his dominions: a hurried making of embankments and cuttings, which were allowed to fall into disrepair as soon as the progress was over.

Linking up the Country

The Romans were the first people to realise the great value of wide, durable roads as a means of binding their country together, and enabling their armies to move quickly to and fro between the capital and conquered provinces. Their roads ran the whole length of Italy, and crossed the Alps into France and Spain. When they invaded Britain their legions, aided by native labour, built a splendid road system spreading north, east, west and south from London, and linking up all their great military centres. Their

3—2

best roads were works of art, solid structures, 2 or 3 feet thick, of stones cemented together and covered with closely-fitted slabs. So thoroughly was the work done that some of them are in use to-day.

The strata, or layers, of stone used for the making of Roman roads have given us our word " street," and they survive in the names of Stratford, Streatham, Chester-le-Street, and some other old towns built along the military routes. Not till Napoleon the First's time were such fine roads seen again. That great soldier, for the same reasons as the Romans, constructed wide roads through France and over the Alps to Italy, through the Mont Cenis and Simplon passes.

After the departure of the Romans from Britain, and throughout Europe after the decline of Roman power, the great roads were neglected, and their condition became worse and worse. When Prince George of Denmark visited Petworth in 1708 to meet Charles VI. of Spain, it took his coach over six hours to travel the last nine miles. A courtier who accompanied him complained that he had been able to stretch his legs only when the coach overturned or stuck fast in the mud!

The " Flying Coach "

In those days it took a week to reach York from London, and two days to travel from the capital to Tunbridge Wells. Exeter was five days away, and even in the second half of the eighteenth century getting from Edinburgh to London by a so-called " flying coach " was a matter of a fortnight's bumping over ruts and holes in badly paved tracks. During the winter the coach services on many roads were suspended altogether, as floods, unbridged rivers, and deep mud made travel on wheels quite impossible.

Dozens of laws were passed to bring about a better state of things. Toll-gates were set up, at which every vehicle had to pay a small sum towards the upkeep of the roads. They were greatly resented, and caused many riots, often accompanied by bloodshed, though the principle was just.

What in the end gave us good roads was the return to Roman methods of roadmaking.

A Wonderful Blind Boy

About 200 years ago there was born, at the small Yorkshire town of Knaresborough, a boy named John Metcalfe. When but six years old he fell ill of smallpox and lost his sight. His parents were humble working folk, able to do little to lighten the boy's affliction, and he was left to amuse himself as best he could. " Blind Jack of Knaresborough," as he was called far and wide, had good stuff in him. He set himself to sharpening his remaining senses, and taught himself to swim, climb trees, wrestle, box, and play bowls and the violin. He walked unaided from Yorkshire to London and back twice; he was present at the battle of Culloden; and he engaged in many other adventures which there is no space to relate. When at last he " settled down," he took to road making.

A Sightless Surveyor

By means of an uncanny sixth sense he was able to survey country and lay out routes in a manner which would have done credit to any engineer blessed with eyesight. In the course of thirty years' work Metcalfe constructed 200 miles of highways such as Britain had not known since Roman days, and to him we owe the beginnings of our magnificent system of roads, as well as a splendid example of what a brave spirit can accomplish in the face of difficulty.

Macadam and Telford

After Metcalfe came two even more famous road makers, Loudon Macadam and James Telford. Macadam's name is still used whenever we speak of a macadam road. His principle was to

SOME ROADS IN SECTION

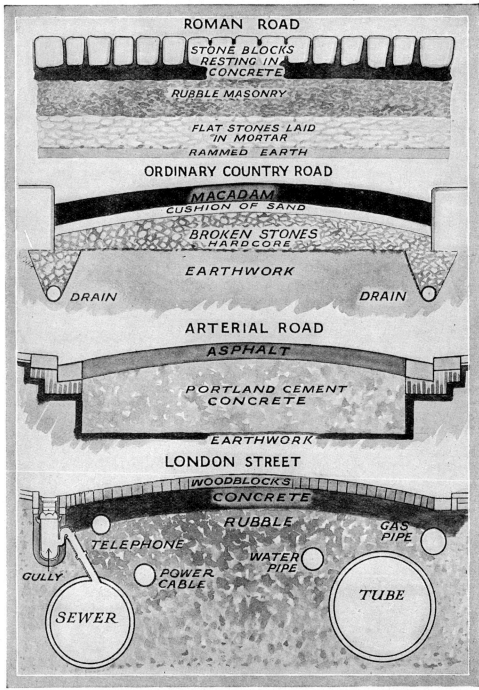

ROMAN ROAD

STONE BLOCKS RESTING IN CONCRETE

RUBBLE MASONRY

FLAT STONES LAID IN MORTAR

RAMMED EARTH

ORDINARY COUNTRY ROAD

MACADAM

CUSHION OF SAND

BROKEN STONES HARDCORE

EARTHWORK

DRAIN   DRAIN

ARTERIAL ROAD

ASPHALT

PORTLAND CEMENT CONCRETE

EARTHWORK

LONDON STREET

WOODBLOCKS

CONCRETE

RUBBLE

GAS PIPE

TELEPHONE

WATER PIPE

GULLY   POWER CABLE

SEWER   TUBE

Specially drawn for this work.

If you could cut through roads as though they were plum-cakes, the above sections show what you would most likely find. The Roman invaders faced their highways with substantial stone blocks, and to-day we use wooden blocks in some of our city streets. The Romans did not arch or " camber " their road surfaces so that the water could run off on either side, as we do.

MAKING TWENTIETH=CENTURY ROADS

Central Press.

With many of the newest arterial and by-pass roads, gas pipes, water mains, electric light mains and similar services are accommodated in special reinforced tunnels, often topped with steel girders. Here, for example, is such a tunnel on the Great West Road in England. Such tunnels make it possible for repairs to be carried out without interfering with the roadway.

Topical Press.

Modern roads usually have a thick bed made of broken bricks, pieces of masonry and other "hard core." This is rolled well and then faced with heavy-gauge wire-netting upon which concrete is laid, to be afterwards coated with asphalt, tarred stones or some other composition. Here we see workmen laying the netting on one of the main Highways of Northern Ireland.

cover the roadway with evenly-spread layers of hard stone broken small, which the weight of the traffic would jam together till they gave a hard, smooth surface. Telford employed a foundation of large stones, covered with smaller broken stone, and a facing of fine gravel.

One of Telford's greatest works was the Shrewsbury-Holyhead road, 105 miles long, running through the mountainous district of North Wales. It was splendidly laid out, and, with modern improvements, is still the main route between the towns named.

The Era of Stage-coaches

With improved roads to run on, the stage-coaches flourished. In the early part of last century there were in Great Britain thousands of miles of highways, including many fine roads, kept in excellent condition. Among the most famous of them were the Great Bath Road, the Brighton Road, the Holyhead Road, the Dover Road and the Great North Road. Along these the coaches averaged ten miles an hour.

Here is a list of the vehicles which passed through Colnbrook, on the Bath Road, during one day in 1834 : 77 coaches, 105 post-chaises and private carriages, 95 phaetons and gigs, 52 spring carts, 29 stage carts, 80 waggons. This makes 438 in all, so the road must have been pretty busy.

Then came the railway and the rapid decay of the roads. Famous inns fell into disrepair, and stables which once had held hundreds of horses stood empty. This state of things lasted for many years. Even in the 'nineties of last century some of our chief roads were so deeply rutted or so thickly covered with mud or dust as to be dangerous to cyclists.

Topical Press.

ALONG ONE OF ENGLAND'S MODERN ROADS
Here is an excellent example of modern road-making in this country. The photograph shows the Mickleham by-pass road, taken from Box Hill, a well-known Surrey beauty spot. There are separate tracks for motorists, cyclists and pedestrians.

Motor Cars Appear

The present century brought with it the motor car; and the motor car brought with it whirling clouds of dust and the rapid destruction of road surfaces. The " dust nuisance " began to abate in 1907, when the practice of spraying roads with tar was adopted. The next step was to give the broken stone used for surfacing roads a coat of tar or bitumen, which stuck the stones together and prevented water getting through and breaking up the road in wet or frosty weather.

But when heavy commercial motor-vehicles, such as omnibuses and lorries, became numerous, more than a good surface was needed. Under it must be placed a thoroughly sound foundation, such as roads in towns already enjoyed where they were paved with wood or granite blocks.

The last forty years have therefore seen great improvements in road engineering, which is now, at any rate as far as new roads are concerned, on much the same footing as railway engineering. The words of Isaiah might well be applied to some of the broad arterial roads made since the War of 1914–18, to cope with the ever-increasing stream of motor traffic. As we traverse some of these roads we pass over great embankments and bridges, and through deep cuttings or broad ledges made in hill sides, such as in the past were associated only with the " iron horse."

Our Modern Highways

The Roman sojourners did not hesitate to go straight over any hill that lay on the course of a road. The modern road engineer does all that is possible to avoid a steep gradient, even if doing so means spending a great deal of money; for every penny so spent means the saving of many pence in wear and fuel to the vehicles which will use the road.

The modern road may be said to begin in the quarry, where huge masses of granite or other hard rock are blasted down, broken into lumps with hammers, and passed through the jaws of ponderous machines. In a twinkling lumps weighing half a hundredweight or more are split and crushed into fragments as easily as you crush a nut with a pair of crackers. The broken stone is then sent through screens, which sort it out into several different sizes, and return any overlarge pieces to the crushing machine.

Besides stone, the slag from

New South Wales Government.

THROUGH THE RAIN FOREST

Road-making in Australia was a tough problem in the early days of the country's history. Machinery has eliminated some of the difficulties in more recent times. Here we see the early stages of road-making in the rain forest district at Doyle's River in New South Wales.

BUILDING AUSTRALIAN COUNTRY ROADS

Gangs of men building and maintaining Australia's roads beyond the towns and cities live in camps that can be struck and moved along at short notice. In this photograph a high-powered road grader, built in Australia with a British engine, works ahead of multi-tyred rollers in preparing a new road over the mountains in Victoria for tarring and bitumening.

Photos: Victorian Country Roads Board.

In sparsely-settled regions the Australian road-builders spend much of the year away from home and fix their camps on the job. In this photograph a bridge required to carry the road across a stream is being pre-fabricated by the road-builders in their camp at Kiewa in Victoria. Pre-fabricating bridges in road-making is a technique recently introduced in Australia.

steelworks, once considered perfectly useless and a nuisance, is treated in the same way, and provides the road maker with very useful material.

The stone or slag is now carefully dried and heated in large ovens and coated with tar or bitumen. It is then ready for being spread and rolled flat by our old friend the steam-roller, which first came on the roads in 1865. The modern roller is fitted with stout steel spikes that can be lowered to tear up an old surface in need of repair. One also sees nowadays on the road strange machines which spread tar and grit and roll at one operation; and even machines which spread stone right across a road and give it the proper camber, or sideways curve from the centre to the edges.

But we find road making in its most advanced form where a new main road for very heavy traffic is in course of construction. The fences on each side of the road may be as much as 120 feet apart, to give ample room for a roadway 50 or 60 feet wide, and to allow for possible future widening. Between roadway and fences are footwalks and grass verges, under which any pipes that have to follow the road are laid. There is to be no tearing up of these new roads when water or gas companies want to make repairs and alterations.

Some of these new highways have separate tracks for the two streams of traffic, divided by a long, narrow island, and others possess special tracks at the side for cyclists or, in some cases, for trolley buses. The Great West Road is one such highway, a by-pass constructed to relieve congestion in the main streets of towns. Another example is the Mickleham By-pass Road in Surrey.

In the next few years many new roads will be constructed in Britain to deal with the steady increase in motor transport. In May, 1946, the Minister of Transport announced a programme of road building which was planned to take place as soon as circumstances permitted. Among other proposals which have been made is a scheme for roads which will be restricted entirely to motor traffic. This plan has already been adopted with success in certain other countries.

Copyright.

FOR QUICK ROAD-MAKING IN UNDEVELOPED REGIONS

This remarkable road-making machine, known as the Single Pass Stabilizer, digs out the soil, adds the necessary proportion of cement or other stabilizing agent, mixes them, and then lays the mixture on the road at the required thickness. The particular mixture varies according to the nature of the soil. Over this a wearing coat, possibly tar spraying, is applied.

SOME TRIUMPHS OF THE BRIDGE BUILDER

The High Commissioner of Canada.

ACROSS THE ST. LAWRENCE

At the time when it was built, Quebec Bridge, across the mighty St. Lawrence River, was the longest clear-span bridge in the world. From end to end this bridge is upwards of 3,000 feet, and the bottom of the central span 150 feet above water level. Quebec Bridge is built on the canti-lever principle, as is the Forth Bridge, near Edinburgh, and the new Howrah Bridge at Calcutta.

THE cave man was much troubled by a swift, narrow river running between his cave and the good hunting ground on the farther side. It was difficult and dangerous work cross-ing from boulder to boulder when the water was low enough to expose them. In times of flood, crossing was alto-gether impossible. Yet a distance of only 20 or 30 feet separated the banks.

Then one day the cave man had a brilliant idea. He remembered having once crossed a stream on a fallen tree. Looking about, he noticed a tall pine leaning slightly towards the river. From his skin belt he took his stone axe, and with it began to hack away at the butt of the tree. After a week of hard work with his primitive tool, the tree cracked, snapped, and fell forward over the stream. Man had *made* a bridge for the first time: the simplest form of bridge, in which a single beam is supported at each end.

Bridges of Cane

Probably the earliest type of bridge requiring skill in the making was the suspension bridge, which the Chinese were using thousands of years ago. It consisted of ropes or chains hung side by side, and connected by crossbars on which to walk.

The natives of the hills north of Assam in India, though savages in many ways, are wonderfully clever at making suspension bridges from rattan, a kind of cane. One of these spans a river chasm 200 yards wide, and is about 800 feet long. The centre part is like a great tube, woven of cane, through which passengers may walk safely when the bridge sways in a strong wind. It is a really marvellous piece of engineering for such a people. One would like to know how they got it into place.

This simple form of suspension bridge is not suitable for road traffic, owing to the sag in the middle and the steep slopes at the ends. The modern sus-pension bridge uses steel chains or cables running over high towers and anchored firmly to the ground. From these a

THE PAINTERS' NEVER=ENDING TASK

Topical Press.

It is absolutely necessary to keep the ironwork of great bridges protected by paint from the ravages of the weather. The artisans who apply the paint have many perils to face, as this photograph shows. The scene, taken from the top of the pier on the Anglesey side of the Menai Suspension Bridge, gives us a splendid idea of painters actually at work upon the cables.

Central Press.

In this picture we see painters walking along the stays of the Forth Bridge, many hundreds of feet above the water level. This bridge over the Firth of Forth carries the main railway line from England to the North of Scotland. The bridge is one and a half miles in length.

BRIDGES OF VARIOUS TYPES

ARCH

SUSPENSION

GIRDER

CANTILEVER

Specially drawn for this work.

Bridges are of many types, but the four examples illustrated above are of special interest. The first is built of arched masonry, the piers designed to withstand heavy flood waters. The second is a suspension bridge, the carriage-way supported by overhead cables. Our railway engineers favour the steel girder bridge for its strength and simplicity. Cantilever bridges, shown in the fourth picture, are found in several parts of the world.

platform is hung at the same level as the road at each end. This arrangement makes a convenient use of the ability of steel to stand great stretching strains.

A Plucky Cobbler

Probably the first metal suspension bridge of great length was that built by Thomas Telford across the Menai Strait, to carry the Holyhead road from Wales into Anglesey. It was opened in 1825, and is still the only road connection between the mainland and the island. The main span of the bridge is 550 feet long, and is approached by great masonry viaducts carrying the roadway about 100 feet above high water level. At each end of the central span is a high tower, with cast-iron saddles on the top to bear the sixteen chains, each a third of a mile long, and 24 tons in weight, from which the roadway platform is hung.

The great bridge-builder, Thomas Telford, had not the experiences of earlier engineers to guide him in designing and constructing this bridge, and until the chains had been lifted safely into position he suffered terribly from anxiety. We are told that when the first chain had been hoisted, a local cobbler crawled out to the centre of it and calmly stitched a pair of shoes—to the great admiration, one need hardly say, of many of the onlookers.

For the biggest things in the way of suspension bridges we must go to New York. That capital is of necessity a city of great bridges, because Manhattan Island, in which all the great business offices are, is separated by rivers from the suburbs where most of the workers live. To the south and east of it is the East River; on the west side is the much wider Hudson River; and in the north is the narrow Harlem River, joining the other two.

Paul Popper.

THE BIRCHENOUGH BRIDGE IN SOUTHERN RHODESIA

Forming part of the scheme of trunk roads in Rhodesia, the Birchenough Bridge is the third largest single-span bridge in the world and is of similar construction to Sydney Harbour Bridge, being built by the same British engineering company. Birchenough Bridge spans the Sabi River and links Fort Victoria to Umtali and the Eastern Districts of Southern Rhodesia.

Fox Photos.

A NEW RAILWAY BRIDGE ACROSS THE TIGRIS AT BAGHDAD

The first railway bridge ever to span the River Tigris is here seen in course of construction at Baghdad, Iraq, in 1949. British contractors, using Iraqi labour, have carried out the work to link the railway systems of the West bank, carrying traffic to Mosul, Basra and Turkey, with the East bank (Persia and the Kirkuk oilfields). The photograph shows the approach viaducts on steel trestles leading up to the main steel girder span.

Since 1883 the lower end of Manhattan has been given access to Brooklyn, on the other side of the East River, by three great suspension bridges, the Brooklyn, Williamsburgh, and Manhattan bridges. They were opened in this order. The first two have a main span of about 1,600 feet; that of the last is 1,470 feet, but it carries a much heavier load. All have tracks for railways, trams, road vehicles and foot passengers.

Cables of Wires

The enormous weight of the great girders forming the roadway of one of these bridges is carried by a large number of upright bars connected at the top ends with four great cables. Each cable is composed of a vast number of wires about $\frac{1}{5}$ inch thick, running side by side. Steel wire is steel in its strongest form. About fifty

years ago a Mr. John A. Roebling, of New York, devised a method of " spinning " cables with a steel wire carried to and fro from anchorage to anchorage over the towers of the bridge. Every turn of the wire was adjusted exactly to the curves it must have, to take its proper place in a cable, and then all the turns were bound together by being clamped and wrapped. Each wire then bore an equal share of the load, which is not the case when wires are *twisted* together, as in a wire rope. The cables of the Manhattan Bridge contain 9,472 wires each; and enough wire almost to girdle the earth at the Equator went into their making. Between them these wires can stand a strain of nearly 100,000 tons.

The World's Largest Bridge

But all these bridges are now dwarfed by one which has been made across the Hudson River at a point where it is well over a mile wide. As it was neither possible nor allowable to build a pier in mid-channel, the two towers for carrying the cables are built in the shallow water near the banks. They are 3,500 feet apart, and to allow for the necessary sag of the cables and a headway for ships of about 150 feet at high tide, they rise over 600 feet high—great steel structures encased in concrete and granite to protect them from the weather. One can speak of the cables with the greatest

respect, for each is a yard thick and has nearly 27,000 wires in it, and the wire needed for them would suffice to encircle our globe five times. They will support in mid-air a structure weighing 90,000 tons. Enormous blocks of masonry have been formed on shore to which to anchor the cables, containing about half a million tons of material.

We now pass to another type of bridge, in which the load is carried by metal girders resting on piers, and the thrust is straight downwards on to the ground under the piers. If conditions allow it, a long bridge of this kind will be divided up into short spans, and be supported by a large number of piers. A good example is the bridge across the River Tay in Scotland, just over two miles long, with seventy-four spans, resting on piers sunk in the river bed.

Across Menai Strait

Large gaps have to be spanned by special forms of girders. In building the famous Britannia railway bridge across the Menai Strait, Robert Stephenson made use of great square iron tubes, inside which the trains would run. Four of these were 460 feet long, and they weighed about 1,400 tons each. They were built on shore, floated out on huge rafts, and lifted by hydraulic rams into position 100 feet above the water. If you travel by train to Holyhead you have to pass through them. They are now more than ninety years old, and apparently as good as ever.

The late Sir Benjamin Baker, when set the task of designing a railway bridge to cross the Forth near Edinburgh, had to provide for jumping two stretches of water, each a third

General Photographic Agency.

THE HUDSON RIVER BRIDGE

Here we see the concrete base and two of the towers for the Hudson River Bridge, connecting Washington Heights with Fort Lee, near New York, U.S.A. This is one of the finest examples in the world of a monster suspension bridge.

LOWER MANHATTAN, BROOKLYN BRIDGE AND THE EAST RIVER

The skyscrapers of Lower Manhattan form an impressive skyline when viewed from Manhattan Bridge. Nearer to us, spanning the East River, is Brooklyn Bridge, one of many that link Manhattan with other parts of the great city of New York. Henry Hudson came this way in 1609, searching for the north-west passage and in 1626 Manhattan was bought from the Red Indians for a few dollars. To-day, this narrow tongue of land is the heart of the largest city in the United States and the home of nearly two million of its people. The East River, with its busy wharves and docks, is sometimes called " New York's watery main street."

Specially painted for this work.

THE DIVER USES HIS BLOW PIPE

Divers examine sunken ships and test the piers of bridges. In some instances, as at Winchester Cathedral, they inspect submerged foundations of buildings. Their dress for work at moderate depths is entirely watertight, air being pumped into the helmet through a tube from the surface. As will be seen above, spent air is released through a valve at the side of the helmet whilst a lifeline is the man's method of communication. In this picture the diver is opening the strong room of a foundered liner by means of an oxy-hydrogen blow pipe which cuts rapidly into the steel.

General Photographic Agency.

STEEL CABLES IN POSITION

This view shows the Hudson River Suspension Bridge at a later stage in its growth. By this time the steel cables have been carried from anchorage to anchorage over the two towers. The need for strong anchorage is obvious when one considers the immensity of the structure.

of a mile across, separated by a rock in mid-channel. He solved the problem by raising three huge towers of steel tubes, nearly 400 feet high, on the rock and on the banks of the river. Great triangular girders, called cantilevers, were built out on opposite sides of a tower, in the line of the bridge, and at the same speed, so that each balanced the other.

In this way they were able to form six girders, the two end ones of which extended to the shore, while the other four were joined together in mid-air, forming two spans of 1,710 feet. This great structure, containing 50,000 tons of steelwork, was opened in 1890, and is still one of the engineering wonders of the world. Since its construction other great cantilever bridges have been thrown across the St. Lawrence at Quebec, the East River at New York and the Hooghli at Calcutta.

At the Shore Ends

The principle of building outwards from supports has been used in the making of some of the greatest arch bridges in places where it was impossible to support the arch from below during construction. Crossing the gorge of the Niagara River below the Falls is the Clifton Bridge, a single huge arch 840 feet long. The two halves were begun at the shore ends, and as they were lengthened the girders were at intervals connected by tie-bars to anchorages on the cliffs. When the two halves met the bars were removed.

The 500-foot arch carrying the railway across the Zambezi just below the Victoria Falls was made in much the same way. Before it could be begun, a ropeway had to be strung over the gorge to transport the materials for the northern half. A rocket was fired across, with a cord attached. The cord

THE LONGEST-ARCHED BRIDGE

In this illustration we see men at work with a pneumatic hammer, putting rivets into the bridge which now spans Sydney Harbour, in New South Wales. This bridge possesses the longest arch in the world. It stands 170 feet over water level at the centre, and its cost was nearly six million pounds. The actual span of the arch is 1,650 feet.

The ends of the arch of Sydney Harbour Bridge press against abutment towers, the southern one of which is here illustrated. It is estimated that the two points of this tower against which the arch is fixed have each to take a thrust equal to about 20,000 tons.

HOW WILL THE ENDS MEET?

The building of the gigantic Sydney Bridge began simultaneously at each side of the harbour, the arms of the arch growing upwards and outwards. So thoroughly was the work of the engineers carried out that when the time came the two sections met one another exactly.

This is another type of single-arch bridge under construction, the one that was opened in 1928, over the River Tyne at Newcastle. There is so much traffic on this river that considerable head-room had to be allowed for steamers. Note how the two parts of the arch are temporarily supported by cables from the shore.

hauled a wire over, and the wire a steel rope, on which an engineer crossed to superintend the dragging over of a heavy cable. The last was supported on towers, and along it ran an electric trolley with loads up to 10 tons. As there was a 400-foot drop into the boiling torrent below, a great net was slung under the line of the bridge to give the workmen confidence. It had just the opposite effect, for the sight of it made them nervous, and eventually it was taken away!

Sydney Harbour Bridge

By far the largest of such bridges is that between Dawes Point and Milson's Point in Sydney Harbour. This has a central arch with a span of 1,650 feet. The top of the arch is 440 feet above the water; and the deck of the bridge, which carries four lines of electric railway, as well as a wide roadway and two footways, gives a clear headroom of 170 feet for shipping. The bridge contains 51,000 tons of steel, all of which was made in England and shipped to Australia.

This great bridge, like so many others which have been erected in various parts of the world in the past forty years, was built by the well-known Dorman Long Company of Middlesbrough, Yorkshire. In bridge-building British engineers have led the way.

In some cases a bridge has to cross a busy river at such a level that it would block shipping if it were made solid. Such bridges have to contain parts which swing round horizontally or lift vertically, leaving a gap for ships to pass through. The lifting bridge is now more widely used. The finest example in England is the Tower Bridge, with its two great balanced leaves, each 100 feet long and weighing 1,200 tons, which swing upright on mighty pins 21 inches thick, to give ships a way through the bridge. The Americans have invented another kind of lifting bridge, which has one end rounded and heavily weighted. When the bridge is opened the round end rolls back on steel tracks till the girder is almost upright. The rolling leaf of a certain one of these bridges is over 230 feet long, and when raised would easily overtop the Nelson Column in Trafalgar Square.

Copyright.

A FAMOUS BRIDGE IN INDIA

The Howrah Bridge, seen in the photograph above, connects Calcutta with its populous suburb, Howrah, on the other side of the Hooghli river. The bridge is of the cantilever type, having a main span of 1,500 feet. Like so many other great bridges it is a fine example of British engineering skill and was opened for public service in 1943.

THE STORIES OF SUEZ AND PANAMA

E.N.A.

LINKING THE NORTH SEA WITH THE BALTIC

The tall, slender structure in the background is the Rendsburg Bridge over the Kiel Canal. This canal, nearly sixty-one miles in length, was commenced in the year 1887, and forms a waterway connecting the North Sea with the Baltic. At the opening ceremonies in 1895, a string of warships belonging to many nations steamed through the Canal. Air attacks on and around this Canal frequently figured in the news during the Second World War 1939–45.

IF anyone had been shown a map of the world eighty years ago, and been asked to lay his finger on the places where a big canal, cut through a few dozen miles of land, would most benefit navigation, he would without doubt have pointed at the Isthmus of Suez and the Isthmus of Panama.

The first of these isthmuses compelled ships sailing between Europe and India to voyage round the Cape of Good Hope. The second, from the sailor's point of view, pushed the Atlantic and Pacific oceans thousands of miles further apart than they are at the narrow neck joining the two Americas, and drove ships southwards round Cape Horn.

Shortening the Voyage

So in this section you will read the story of how canals capable of passing great liners were cut through these natural barriers. There are other great ship canals: that joining Manchester with the sea; that through the isthmus of Corinth; the Kiel Canal, linking the North Sea with the Baltic; the Bruges Canal; and so on. But the Suez Canal and the Panama Canal are by far the most important of their kind. The first

shortened the voyage to India and the East by over 4,000 miles, the second has lessened distances between points on American coasts by a great deal more.

There are two interesting facts to note about the canals chosen for description. The Suez Canal passes through a flat desert, and is open from end to end. It was the first of the great ship canals. The Panama Canal had to cross high ground by means of locks, and is the most recently opened, as well as the largest, in width and depth of channel, of ship canals.

The Suez Canal

This canal will always be associated with the name of the famous Frenchman, Ferdinand de Lesseps, whose statue overlooks Port Said harbour. It was he who thought out and carried through the gigantic scheme of making a path for ships from Port Said, on the Mediterranean, to Suez on the Red Sea, about eighty miles away. On the route selected were some small lakes, and large depressions below sea level which, when the sea was given access to them, would become lakes and so reduce the amount of digging needed.

There is a saying that there is nothing new. In fairness to the ancients, one should mention that, long before the Christian Era, Rameses II. of Egypt made a canal for small boats through the isthmus; that Darius I. of Persia found this filled up, and re-opened it; and that for a third time the Arab conquerors of Egypt, many hundreds of years later, brought it into use again. But the desert sands overwhelmed it once more. Since it was a mere ditch compared with the present canal, it would in any case have been useless for modern purposes.

Ships of the Desert

When trade with India became great an "overland route" was organised across the isthmus. Ships landed cargoes at Cairo, and the goods were thence transported on "ships of the desert" to Suez, where they were again put aboard ship. But as thousands of camels were needed to deal with a single cargo, this method proved very expensive. In 1857 a railway between Cairo and Suez improved matters considerably, and was much used by passengers and mails, but it was at best a makeshift.

Meanwhile de Lesseps had been surveying the desert and satisfying himself that the levels of the Red Sea and Mediterranean were the same. He decided that there were no unconquerable difficulties in the way. His plans were put on paper and submitted to the Khedive of Egypt, who refused his consent. Poor de Lesseps, bitterly disappointed, retired to his farm in France.

The Desert Encampment

For some years the matter remained in abeyance. Then one day de Lesseps happened to see the death of the Khedive announced in a newspaper. Without losing a moment he took ship

E.N.A.

ON THE GRAND CANAL OF CHINA

We read of canals in the history of ancient Greece, but to China probably belongs the credit of first making these waterways. In the photograph above, picturesque native boats are seen sailing placidly along the Grand Canal, passing the famous Three Pagodas at Kashing. The Grand Canal is of great length, and links the basins of several important rivers.

TAKING A SHIP DOWN STAIRS

Michigan is the second largest of the Great Lakes of North America, and the State of Michigan has many lakes and rivers, as well as a magnificent ship canal capable of accommodating large vessels. Here we see the steamship *James A. Farrell* being lowered in the water of Satin Lock. Locks in a canal system serve the purpose of steps or stairs.

The Corinth Canal, depicted above, gives to coasting steamers a much shorter journey from the Ionian Sea to the Port of Athens. It is a particularly wonderful ship canal, because it was cut almost entirely through solid rock. Though the Canal is only about four miles in length, it saves ships a voyage of more than 200 miles. The Canal was opened in 1893.

for Egypt to approach the new ruler. He found him encamped in the middle of the desert. Being asked to put his scheme into writing, de Lesseps galloped back to his own tent, and soon returned with a brief, but clear, statement of his plans, written on a small foolscap sheet. The Khedive read it, was convinced, and gave his permission for the work to begin.

We need not go into de Lesseps' troubles in raising the necessary money, nor dwell on the refusal of British capitalists to interest themselves in the Canal, while French peasants emptied their stocking-foot savings-banks to aid their countryman. Let it suffice to say that on April 25th, 1859, M. de Lesseps turned the first spadeful of sand at Port Said.

At first work went ahead very slowly despite the army of 30,000 conscripted labourers that the Khedive had supplied. There were 80,000,000 cubic yards of sand, earth and rock still to be moved when the Khedive suddenly withdrew the men. The engineers, faced with a crisis that threatened ruin to the scheme, hired what men they could and replaced human muscles with huge steam dredgers, which cut a channel for themselves and constantly lengthened it, sending the sand clear of the course through long chutes.

From Sea to Sea

The last barrier between sea and sea was broken away on August 15th, 1869. Ten years of hard and anxious work had produced a canal 150 to 300 feet wide at the top, and 26 feet deep, at a cost of over £16,000,000.

Since the opening in 1869, the depth of the Canal has been increased to $34\frac{1}{2}$ feet, and its width almost doubled. Traffic is worked much as on a single-line railway, by a system of block signals, being divided up into sections and provided with " gares," or sidings, in which a ship ties up to allow another to pass. All the signal stations are connected by telegraph with a head office at Ismailia, half-way along the Canal, where there is a model of the Canal with dummy ships which are moved as the vessels represented by them advance. A ship is taken through the Canal by a special pilot, and at

E.N.A.

BETWEEN MEDITERRANEAN AND RED SEA

If you could stand on the sandy desert at the edge of the Suez Canal, you would observe ships coming through one after another, as is illustrated. Even in the days of Rameses II. of Egypt there was a small canal across the desert, but it was left to Ferdinand de Lesseps, a brilliant French engineer, to cut the 103 miles of waterway (of which twenty-one miles are in lakes) connecting the Mediterranean and Red Sea.

" SHIPS THAT PASS "—ON THE SUEZ CANAL

The Suez was the first of the world's great ship canals. It was constructed with less difficulty than the Panama Canal, for it threads its course through flat desert, whilst the waterway of the New World has to flow over very high ground. Here we see two large steamers passing one another in the Suez Canal, one homeward bound to England, and the other maybe making a trip to New Zealand.

night while under way she carries a strong searchlight in her bows to illuminate her course.

The Panama Canal

Having won a great triumph in the Egyptian desert, de Lesseps turned his attention to the Isthmus of Panama. This was already crossed by a railway, opened in 1853, to carry the crowds hurrying to the newly-discovered gold-fields of California. The railway reaped a huge fortune for its promoters, and its success started people hunting up and down the isthmus for a suitable route for a canal which would make the journey by sea continuous from the east coast to the west coast of America.

Among the latter was de Lesseps, who, after much consideration, chose the line that the Canal now takes. The work before him was a vastly greater one than that at Suez. Instead of a flat desert he had to cross land along which ran a backbone of hills over 300 feet high. The Chagres and other rivers, which at times become raging floods, traversed the course, and must be dealt with. A third difficulty, the greatest of all, was the pestilential climate of the isthmus, which wrought havoc with the health of people who had to live there.

Nothing daunted, however, de

Lesseps persuaded thousands of his countrymen to invest their savings in a scheme for piercing the isthmus. He had succeeded once brilliantly, and they showed their faith in him by subscribing many tens of millions of francs. The most elaborate machinery was sent in shiploads to the isthmus and set to work on digging a canal at sea level.

The Engineer's Disaster

Much of the money was wasted, and de Lesseps came to see that it would be impossible to carry through his original scheme. He decided to make a canal with locks, and so reduce the excavation work. But in 1889 the crash came. Five years later a new company was formed, and this struggled on till 1902, when the Government of the United States bought from it, for £8,000,000, what had cost French pockets over £60,000,000

For this huge expenditure there was to show a partly-finished trench, from which over 80,000,000 cubic yards of material had been taken, and a vast array of machines more or less buried in the mud. The failure was a terrible disaster to many humble homes in France, and it broke de Lesseps' heart.

To ensure that the Canal, if finished, should be entirely their own, the United States bought from the Republic of Colombia a strip of land running on each side of the centre line of the Canal from ocean to ocean.

By American Energy

The Americans then turned their energies to completing what the French had begun. One of the first things to be done was to protect the army of white and coloured workers that would be needed from the ravages of malaria and yellow fever, now known to be spread not, as formerly supposed, by mists from swamps, but by the bites of mosquitoes. It is one of the romances of medical science how Colonel Gorgas organised his "mosquito brigade," filled in swamps and stagnant waters, or flooded them with petroleum, and took other measures which killed off the mosquitoes and made the canal belt one of the most healthy places in the tropics.

After their custom, the Americans left as little as possible to chance. They decided to make the River Chagres an ally instead of a foe, by building a dam across it and collecting its waters into a huge lake, 170 square miles in extent, with its surface 89 feet above sea level. Ships would be lifted into the lake by a group of three locks at its Atlantic end, and a single lock and two locks, in different places, on the Pacific side.

This brilliant way out of a difficulty reduced enormously the amount of excavation that had to be done, though even so it totalled over 200,000,000 cubic yards.

Broken by Dynamite

The greatest collection of excavating and other engineering machinery that has ever been brought together in one place presently appeared on the isthmus: huge steam navvies, machines that would lift many yards of railway track and heave it sideways into a fresh position; ploughs which in a few minutes cleared a whole train of flat dirt cars of their loads; shovels which pushed the dumped material well away from the rails. Machinery in its most perfected form was matched against the earth and rock over which, 400 years earlier, Balboa had passed to his discovery of the Pacific.

For years the isthmus resounded with the explosions of dynamite charges, the clang of the steam navvy, and the panting of locomotives. Eventually a huge cleft, nearly 300 feet deep and over half a mile wide, traversed the high ground near the Pacific coast. The Chagres, pent up by the largest earth dam in the world, spread out into a lake, and this lake was joined to both oceans by channels deep enough to float the largest ships likely to be built, and

AT THE GATUN LOCKS

E.N.A.

The system of locks and lock-gates here illustrated is to be seen on the Panama Canal. Taken from the top of the operating tower, this is the view that would confront us if we were looking towards the Atlantic Ocean. At this stage ships are raised to the level of Lake Gatun. Four electric locomotives in front tow each large vessel through the locks, whilst two astern keep the craft on a straight course. The lock-gates are 60 feet wide and 80 feet high.

wide enough to allow two vessels to pass one another.

In all, over 280,000,000 cubic yards of earth and rock had been moved, including the work of the French excavators, and £160,000,000 spent before the way was clear from ocean to ocean. The minimum width of the Canal at the bottom is 300 ft. and the minimum depth is 41 ft. On either side of the Canal is a strip of land, 5 miles wide, which is known as the Canal Zone.

On August 15th, 1914, the Panama Canal, the most wonderful of all engineering feats, was opened by the steamer *Ancon*, flying the flags of all nations. An event which should have stirred the whole world passed almost unnoticed, for the outbreak of the War of 1914–1918 a few days earlier had centred men's thoughts on things of much less peaceful import.

A Trip through the Panama

We are on a ship bound from England for New Zealand by the Panama route. Our vessel enters an artificial channel 500 feet wide at Colon, named after Columbus, and follows it southwards—the Canal runs roughly north and south—for about eight miles. We then find ourselves at the foot of a huge staircase with three steps in it, each step a pair of locks side by side, one for the "up" and the other for the "down" traffic. The locks are the largest in the world, being 1,000 feet long and 110 feet wide.

As we approach the first lock a great guard chain is seen to stretch across the channel. If the ship has not come to a dead standstill before reaching it, the chain, which is attached to powerful hydraulic buffers, will bring the vessel quickly to rest.

The Biggest of Gates

Two enormous steel gates, about 60 feet wide and 80 feet high—surely the biggest of all gates!—now swing open, and fold back into recesses in the lock walls, the chain sinks out of sight, and the way is clear into the first lock, the water in which is at sea level. But the ship is not allowed to enter under her own power.

Four great electric locomotives, running along tracks on the lock walls, take her in tow, and two more hang on to her stern to keep her straight. As soon as she is inside, the gates behind are closed, and water is let into the lock chamber through large openings in its walls. The ship rises slowly till she has been raised some 30 feet. Then the entrance

Will. F. Taylor.

MAKING THE PANAMA CANAL

The Panama Canal is considered to be one of the most wonderful of the engineering feats of man, for it forms a water link between two oceans. Machinery of the most advanced types was matched against the rock and earth, as seen above; but whereas soil in some parts had to be excavated, in others building-up was rendered necessary.

LINKING PACIFIC AND ATLANTIC

The famous engineer, Ferdinand de Lesseps, who constructed the Suez Canal, designed the Panama Canal, but was broken in health before the work was properly undertaken. Eventually the U.S.A. took the task in hand in 1905 and the Canal was completed in August, 1914. This photograph shows the Pacific entrance to the Canal, with the coaling plant and docks.

Planet News.

During their voyage to Australia and New Zealand, H.M. Queen Elizabeth II and the Duke of Edinburgh went ashore at Cristobal and visited the Miraflores Locks on the Panama Canal. They are seen here with the Governor-General of the Canal Zone crossing one of the lock gates.

gates to the next lock swing open;
the locomotives haul again; the gates
are shut; water is let in; and we rise
another 30 feet. The same series of
operations follows once more at the
third lock, which raises us to the level
of Lake Gatun.

The electricity driving the locomotives
and all the other machinery of the Canal
comes from a station in the Gatun dam,
where some of the overflow water from
the lake is sent through turbines.

Through the Great Cut

We are soon on the lake, a vast sheet
of water through which we steam briskly
for thirty miles. Then we enter the
defile of the Culebra Cut (now Gaillard
Cut), the great gash through the hills
already mentioned. Here our ship is
dwarfed by the man-formed cliffs, which
represent the biggest excavation ever made.

Presently we arrive at a single lock,
and drop down through it to a small
artificial lake, the crossing of which
brings us to two locks. These let us
into the channel which leads to Panama
and so to the Pacific Ocean.

The passage through the Canal from
sea to sea takes seven to eight hours, four
of which represent the time taken for the
passage through the twelve locks.

Under the arrangements made when
the Canal was planned, a strip of land,
ten miles in width, was granted to the
United States Government, which has
sovereign rights over this Canal Zone.
The Canal itself is built through the
centre of this territory, and a Governor
of the Panama Canal is appointed by
the U.S.A. to carry out the administra-
tion of the Zone.

E.N.A.

LAKE GATUN, PANAMA CANAL

No photograph could better illustrate how ocean-going steamers are made to move up or down
" stairs " by means of locks. These are the three famous Gatun Locks on the Panama Canal,
with the Lake beyond. The electric locomotives make light work of the gradients as the
lock-gates are approached.

ELECTRIC POWER FROM WATER

" THUNDER OF THE WATERS "

Government of Ontario.

The tremendous force behind the rushing waters of the famous Falls at Niagara was first harnessed to produce electric power in 1881. In this photograph the power house of the Lower Niagara is seen. Although it is not now quite the largest in the world the Niagara Falls power station to-day distributes over a million horse-power of electric current over an area some tens of thousands of square miles in extent.

IN Great Britain most of the power stations, with their tall chimneys, employ steam-driven turbines to provide the electricity we use in our homes and factories. In some countries, however, there are no steam-power stations at all; and in the world as a whole just over half of the requirements for electric power are supplied by harnessing the reserve of energy that lies in running water.

Water-power is really power derived from the sun. The sun shines on the sea and on the lakes, and evaporates the water which then forms clouds, and these in turn break up into rain which descends on high ground. This water has to flow back again to the sea, and in doing so man can make use of its energy for his own purposes.

The history of the development of water-power extends back to 2,000 years B.C., when to irrigate their rice fields the Chinese used primitive water-wheels which elevated water into ditches, running through the drier parts, thus making the crops grow. For nearly 3,000 years, however, water-power was only used to drive corn mills or other simple mechanical devices, because man had not yet found a way of transmitting the energy from the running wheel for any distance, and, moreover, the slow, ponderous water-wheel did not provide energy in a suitable form for the majority of his requirements in the new industrial age.

Steam *versus* Electricity

It was the development of the steam engine which hindered the development of water-power during the nineteenth century. With coal readily available there was no need to depend on water-power to turn the mills or drive the machines in the way they had done to a limited extent. The steam engine was much more convenient than any older form of power.

Then came electricity as a competitor of steam power. With the development of the dynamo water-power began to return to its old position. Many new manufacturing processes required large amounts of cheap energy, and water turbines, erected at some convenient site, opened up new possibilities.

To-day, the need for electric power obtained from water without the use of costly fuels such as oil and coal, has led to the building of hydro-electric stations in many countries throughout the world. In Canada, 90 per cent. of electrical energy is generated from water-power, while in Switzerland, Norway, Sweden, Spain, Tasmania, New Zealand and several other countries, almost the whole of the power arises from the harnessing of the natural water resources. By its aid, some countries, such as Switzerland, have achieved a very high standard of living, since electricity is cheaply and abundantly available everywhere not only in the homes of the people, but to drive trains on the electrified railways, to heat buildings, and to give ample light wherever it is needed.

Fuel Supplies Limited

The Fourth World Power Conference, held in London in 1950, showed that in many areas of the world the resources of solid or oil fuels are definitely limited. The demand for electric power continues to increase, and, for example, in Great Britain itself it was shown that at the present rate of mining coal there is only enough for about the next 200 years. The rate of mining, to satisfy the power demand should, theoretically, increase, and if this happens, through increased mechanisation in the pits, possibly a very much shorter period might see us at the end of our reserves of solid fuel.

Careful surveying in recent years has shown that comparatively few areas of the world's surface have very large deposits of solid or oil fuel of a size which indicates that they will be available for an unlimited period in the future.

In view of the continued spread of industry in countries which have hitherto been mainly agricultural, and of the fact that man is constantly inventing new ways in which to utilise electrical energy, it is thus imperative that all possible sources of water-power should be harnessed and developed. An estimate made in 1950 shows that in the whole world there is likely to be no less than 7,520,000,000 horse-power which can ultimately be made available from hydro-electric sources.

English Electric Co. Ltd.

A MODERN WATER WHEEL

Water wheels are the oldest means of utilising water power, but the old wooden wheels of the flour mills have been considerably improved upon in modern times. This photograph shows the bucket or " Pelton " type of runner used when the height of the fall is very high.

BRIDGES BIG AND LITTLE

Venice, a city and seaport of Italy, stands at the head of the Adriatic and is built mainly on piles in the Venetian Lagoon. Most of its streets are waterways with many bridges. Of these the most famous is the Bridge of Sighs seen in this picture. It owes its name to the fact that it joins the Hall of Judgment in the Doge's Palace with the prison, and hundreds of prisoners in the years gone by have been marched across the covered way from prison to judgment hall and then back to await their fate.

BUILT OF GRANITE IN THE MIDDLE AGES

Fox Photos

The English tinners of the Middle Ages who worked on the lonely wastes of Dartmoor carried all their stores on horseback and took the tin away in the same manner. To cross the rivers they built what are called Clapper Bridges made from slabs of granite as shown in the photograph above.

E.N.A.

The Menai Strait separates the Isle of Anglesey from the mainland of Carnarvonshire, Wales, and is crossed by two bridges. Stephenson's Britannia tubular bridge carries the railway while the highway crosses the famous Menai Suspension Bridge, seen in the photograph above. It was constructed by Thomas Telford and was completed in 1825. Telford was one of the great road-makers of Britain and was the first President of the Institute of Civil Engineers.

ACROSS CALIFORNIA'S GOLDEN GATE AND GREAT VALLEY

Mondiale

At the entrance to San Francisco Harbour is the Golden Gate Bridge spanning the Golden Gate Strait. An Indian legend says that a range of mountains once separated the lake from the sea but the Sun God divided the mountains and formed the strait. The central suspension span of the bridge is 4,200 ft. long.

H. Armstrong Roberts

California, sometimes known as the Golden State of the U.S.A., has a coast-line of about a thousand miles, while the interior consists of the Great Valley enclosed by mountain masses which are world-famed for their grandly picturesque scenery. It is a land where the skill of the road-maker, the railway engineer and bridge-builder is heavily taxed, and our photograph shows the work of all three at North Fork, Feather River, near Oroville.

Department of Railways, N.S.W.

Typical examples of the outstanding achievements of Australian engineers are the two fine bridges for road and railway traffic over the Hawkesbury River, some thirty miles from Sydney. This photograph shows the Hawkesbury Railway Bridge, opened July 1, 1946. It replaced an earlier one, the first big bridge in Australia, originally built in 1889.

E.N.A.

One of the most famous mountain passes in the world is that over the St. Gotthard mountains in Switzerland. Here we have a view of the Pass showing two of the bridges across the River Reuss.

Dorien Leigh

Burma is a land of mountains and jungle and the crossing of its ravines and gorges calls for much ingenuity. Our picture shows a suspension bridge made of loosely woven cane, in Upper Burma.

ACROSS BRITAIN'S TYNE AND THAMES

E.N.A.

Among the many fine bridges in Britain is the one which spans the River Tyne at Newcastle. The tremendous arch of steel has an air of strength and carries the broad roadway at a height which does not interfere with the shipping below. The main span of the bridge is 531 ft. in length and 4,000 tons of steel were used in making this span alone.

Fox Photos

Work on the building of the new Waterloo Bridge, seen in the photograph above, was begun towards the end of 1937. The roadway was first opened in August 1942, and the whole bridge in November 1944, though the formal opening was not until December 1945. It is built of reinforced concrete with a facing of Portland stone and has five spans, each about 240 ft. wide.

TWO MARVELS OF ENGINEERING

Canadian National Film Board

The Quebec Bridge which spans the St. Lawrence River in Canada is one of the largest cantilever bridges in the world. Its enormous central span has a clear height above water level of 150 ft., thus allowing ocean steamers to pass unhindered beneath. It carries two railway tracks and a footwalk and was first opened to traffic in 1917.

General Steam Navigation Co., Ltd.

One of London's most famous bridges is Tower Bridge near the Tower of London. It is the last bridge towards the mouth of the Thames. Begun in April 1886, it was opened in June 1894, and its total cost was over £1,000,000. It carries a roadway 49 ft. wide, and, to allow ocean-going steamers to pass, the central bascules are raised by hydraulic machinery to a vertical position against the towers.

CANTILEVER AND SUSPENSION DESIGNS

L.N.A.

From the engineer's point of view the Forth Bridge, begun in 1882, and opened in 1890, marked an epoch in bridge-building. Its enormous clear spans of 1,710 ft. were rendered possible by the use of steel and by the cantilever design of the superstructure. Across it runs the railway from Edinburgh, capital of Scotland, and vessels of any size can pass below it.

Fox Photos

At Clifton, a suburb of the historic port of Bristol, the River Avon passes through a gorge. Its magnificent suspension bridge across this gorge was built by the famous engineer, Brunel, and was constructed partly of material taken from the old Hungerford Bridge at Charing Cross, London. It has a length of 702 ft. and is 275 ft. above low water. The bridge was opened in 1864.

BRIDGES ENDURE THOUGH TIMES CHANGE

Right in the centre of the broad village street of Crowland in the English Fens stands this old triangular bridge, known as the three-way Trinity Bridge. It was built over the River Welland in the fourteenth century, but the river has disappeared. This photograph shows the crowned figure of the Saviour on the south side.

Photos: E.N.A.

Peking first became the capital of China in 1264, but lost the title 1368-1403, and again from 1928-1949. Though the Emperors have ceased to rule, something of their former greatness still remains in the imperial palaces and pleasure grounds. In this picture is seen the Marble Bridge on the Lotus Lake of the summer palace of Peking.

In a number of countries, all the most convenient water-power sites near to centres of industry have already either been developed or are at present being surveyed for development in the immediate future. New problems, therefore, arise — how the energy from distant waterfalls, such as those in the north of Sweden, for example, can be harnessed and the power brought economically to the centres of industry many hundreds of miles away. Electrical engineers have developed methods of transmitting more and more power at high voltages, such as 400,000 volts, and there are schemes for using high voltage direct current (as opposed to the normal alternating current) to assist in solving the problem of transmitting bulk power over great distances.

English Electric Co. Ltd.

THE KAPLAN TYPE RUNNER

This is the Kaplan type of turbine propeller runner, showing the feathering blades in the open position. These blades are adjustable and because their pitch can be regulated this type is particularly suitable where the head of water varies widely from time to time.

One of the problems that all engineers concerned with electricity supply have to solve is that of meeting the peak demand. During any one twenty-four hours the demand for electrical energy varies very widely. Enough generating plant has to be available to meet the peaks which occur at 8 o'clock in the morning, when all the factories are starting, and in the evening when the lights come on at a time which overlaps the factory working hours. Certain water-power schemes are particularly useful here, since the stored water in the reservoir or lake can be released when the load reaches peak proportions. The modern method of utilising water-power is to endeavour to create as great a storage area as possible. In France, Switzerland, and Italy particularly, where already many of the water-power resources are completely harnessed, engineers are constructing still higher dams to trap more water for use not only at the peak periods, but during dry seasons. In a few cases, part of the energy available when the demand from the consumers is low is used to pump water back from the lower levels into the reservoir, so that it can once more fall back through the turbines and again release useful energy.

Types of Turbine

There are three main types of water-power plant. The first, known as the Pelton wheel or impulse turbine, is used where the " head " (that is, the height of the fall) is very high, say, 1,000 feet or more. In this case water is led through steel pipes into the jets of the turbine where a steel wheel with specially shaped buckets attached to the frame is situated. The jets of water play on the buckets and drive the wheel round, and in so doing drive the electrical generator attached to the shaft. As many as six jets may be used on a single wheel.

This type of installation is generally used where relatively small quantities of water at high pressure have to be dealt with. In other cases where the head is lower, the reaction turbine is employed. In this case water from the pipes is carried to a spiral casing, which is like a giant snail. It flows inwards through guide vanes which can be moved to regulate the flow, on to the water-wheel, and from thence down through another tube, known as the draft tube, to the tailrace, and so away into the river. This type of machine is capable of handling vast quantities of water, and by its use power can be derived from very low heads even down to 20 or 30 feet. In cases where a relatively slow flowing river is dammed, turbines of this kind can be used very successfully.

The third type of water turbine is a modification of the reaction wheel, and employs the same kind of spiral casing, but this time the runner is shaped like a ship's propeller. The blades of the

English Steel Corporation Ltd.

LIKE A GIANT SNAIL

The size of this piece of mechanism can be realised by looking at the two men who are seen in this photograph. The enormous " snail " is an important part of certain types of water-power plants where the head is low. The actual inlet is 15 feet 6 inches in diameter. The circular casing is built up of steel plates held together by countless rivets and bolts.

SUPPLYING POWER FOR THE GRID

Wm. McCallum.

The Galloway water-power scheme has been planned in such a way as to preserve the natural beauties of the locality. Our picture shows how the impressive arches of the Loch Doon Dam have been blended into the surrounding landscape.

British Electricity Authority.

Before the North of Scotland Hydro-Electric Board was formed in 1943 there were already thirteen stations, among them the five plants known as the Galloway scheme for supplying current to the electricity grid in Britain. At the Tongland power station 40,000 horse-power is developed, and our photograph shows the tailrace of this station, where the water emerges after passing through the turbines.

propeller are movable as to their pitch, like the blades of a modern aeroplane propeller. By regulating the pitch of the blades not only can the turbine be governed, but also the maximum power can be derived from a head of water which varies widely from time to time. The other two types of turbine do not operate efficiently at a head which is greatly different from that for which they were designed.

There have been, for many years, schemes for utilising the energy of the tides, by trapping the high tide water in a basin, and letting it run back through water turbines. The Severn Barrage is one of such schemes, but neither this one nor any of the others has yet been started. The Kaplan turbine, with its power of accepting a variable head, would be extremely valuable for tidal power projects.

Harnessing a Million Horse-Power

As an indication of the size of some of the world's great water-power schemes, it may be mentioned that the Grand Coulee project, on the Columbia River in America, uses nine Francis turbines, each having the enormous output of 165,000 horse-power each. Thus one station has an output of nearly 1½ million horse-power, and, at the same project, there is a second power house, on the other bank, with 1,350,000 horse-power, also in nine units. Pelton wheels are made up to 75,000 horse-power.

Although not quite the largest, the Niagara Falls Power Station is one of the most interesting hydro-electric projects in the world, mainly because of the spectacular nature of the wonderful Niagara Falls with which it is associated.

At Niagara, water from a chain of lakes totalling 900,000 square miles in area, slips over the edge of a precipice and falls with terrific roar into a foamy cauldron 170 feet below. The natural flow over the falls would fill a tank a mile square and 40 feet deep in one hour. The energy of the water is equal to that which could be derived by burning 150,000 tons of coal every twenty-four hours.

It was in 1881 that Niagara was first harnessed for generating water-power, and to-day a visitor will see, on the shores of the river both above and below the Falls, several large and handsome buildings from which over a million horse-power is sent in all directions and distributed over an area some tens of thousands of square miles in extent.

In one of the stations, above the Falls, the water is taken from the river into deep pits in which are situated the turbines. A tunnel connects the bottom of the pits with the foot of the Falls.

Perhaps you would like a peep into the pit of one of the above-Falls stations. It is 150 feet deep, 416 feet long, and 22 feet wide; and dark, but for electric light, as the floor of the power house covers in the top. Down one side run eleven huge steel tubes, 10½ feet in diameter. These are the penstocks leading water to as many turbines on a platform at the bottom. At three different levels the pit is spanned by arches in which are the bearings in which the turbine shafts turn. Descending the staircase, we at last reach the turbines, each spinning with the force of 15,000 horses. We are therefore in the presence of over 160,000 horse-power.

A short journey through an opening gives us a view of foaming water, dashing away from the turbines in a huge tunnel, 33 feet across and nearly 2,000 feet long. Hung from the roof of it is a footway along which we tramp until daylight appears, and we see in front of us, through a cloud of spray, a curtain of water, while our ears are filled with a deafening roar. We are looking at Niagara Falls from the *back !*

There are now a number of power stations associated with the Niagara

IN RHODESIA AND BRITISH COLUMBIA

Water from the Zambezi River in Southern Rhodesia is conveyed through a pipe-line, which can be seen in the picture above, to the hydro-electric power station which is situated in the gorge at the foot of the Victoria Falls. Automatic gear controls the turbines, and, apart from the daily inspection, no attendants are needed to control the speed of the turbine and to shut off the power in case of any mishap occurring.

Photos : English Electric Co. Ltd.

This fine hydro-electric station is built on the shores of Stave Lake, British Columbia. The overflow from Lake Alouette passes through the tunnel and enters Stave Lake after passing through the turbines in the power house shown above. In so doing it generates nearly 14,000 horse-power to drive the electrical generators supplying current to the surrounding districts. This station also operates on the automatic system and can be closed down or switched on from a distance, according to the demand for current.

Topical Press.

THE DAM OF THE LOCH SLOY HYDRO-ELECTRIC POWER STATION
The culmination of five years' work in some of Scotland's wildest country was reached in October, 1950, when Queen Elizabeth (the Queen Mother) inaugurated the Loch Sloy hydro-electric power scheme. This was the first of the major North of Scotland projects which will " see new strength surging into the very arteries of Scotland's being." Above is seen the dam at Loch Sloy.

Falls and others are being planned, although care is taken not to divert too much water so that the wonderful scenic beauty of the Falls will be preserved.

The Victoria Falls on the Zambezi River in Africa are equally famous for their scenic grandeur and these falls have been utilised as a source of electric power. Under the supervision of the engineers of the English Electric Company an automatic hydro-electric station has been erected.

Water is conveyed to the settling tanks and reservoir direct from the Zambezi River just above the Falls. From the reservoir a pipe-line takes water down to the generating station, which is in the gorge, at a spot known as the " Silent Pool."

One interesting feature of this hydro-electric scheme is that the station runs automatically and no attendants are required to control the speed of the turbine and to shut off the power in case of any mishap. It is only neces-sary for the station to be inspected each day.

Another automatic station of this kind has been built within recent years near Lake Alouette in British Columbia.

In Australia big irrigation schemes are being developed and some of the stored water will be used for producing electric power. Tasmania is the State which possesses the greatest potential water-power resources, and it is esti-mated that $1\frac{3}{4}$ million horse-power will eventually be available.

British Water-Power

In Great Britain, water-power is never likely to be a major source of electrical energy, as it lacks great rivers, flowing down from extensive mountain ranges with enormous rainfall catchment areas. It is estimated that when all hydro-electric schemes are fully de-veloped, about one-sixth of British power requirements will be supplied from water.

There are a group of hydro-electric

WATER POWER IN TASMANIA

Australian News and Information Bureau.

Tasmania, the smallest State in the Commonwealth of Australia, is potentially the most important water-power State. In this island the lakes and rivers are harnessed by such power stations as the one at Tarraleah shown here. With four turbines working, 485 million gallons of water pass through the station each day. Notice the great penstocks, or pipes, which convey the water to drive the turbines producing electric power.

stations in North Wales, yielding together about 50,000 kW, and a few small isolated plants in Yorkshire, Cornwall, and the Lake District.

In Scotland, before the development of hydro-electric power was tackled in a full-scale manner, there existed, up to 1943, thirteen stations, developing 320,000 kW. Included in these were the five plants known as the Galloway scheme.

In 1943, the North of Scotland Hydro-Electric Board was formed, and since that date a very great deal of survey work has been carried out in all parts of Scotland. As a result 46 hydro-electric stations have been planned, with a total capacity of almost 1,000,000 kW.

Among those already completed is Loch Sloy, which is likely to remain as the largest hydro-electric station in Great Britain.

The station was opened by Queen Elizabeth (the Queen Mother) in 1950. It is situated on the banks of Loch Lomond, while the loch itself, 910 feet above, lies in a wild valley overshadowed by the glowering peaks of Ben Vane and Ben Vorlich. Here a giant concrete dam, 1,160 feet long and 160 feet high, has been built. The level of the loch itself has been raised by 155 feet, and the water stored is equivalent to 20 million units of electricity. From the dam, a horseshoe-shaped tunnel, two miles long, carries the water through Ben Vorlich to a point directly above the power station. From there four steel pipe-lines carry the water to the four turbines. Each of these pipe-lines is 1,500 feet long and 7 feet in diameter.

Inside the elegant power house there are four vertical Francis-type turbines, each developing 46,000 horse-power.

The power is carried away, by means of lines of steel pylons with conductors operating at 132,000 volts, to the Grid system.

In the dim ages of Scottish history, the country around Loch Sloy was the scene of some of the fiercest clan warfare; midnight forays resulted in the moon being known as "MacFarlane's Lantern." Now, millions of modern lanterns are supplied with power from the same wild countryside, by the quietly-humming turbines which, between them, translate the rainfall on the glens and bens into a force of 184,000 horse-power.

English Electric Co. Ltd.

INSIDE THE LOCH SLOY POWER HOUSE

The power house itself is situated on the banks of Loch Lomond, famed in song and story. The four 46,000 horse-power Francis-type water turbines operate under 910 feet head of water. At full load 220,000 tons of water pass through the pipe-lines to the power house every hour.

TURNING DESERTS INTO GARDENS

H. J. Shepstone.

GIVING A DRINK TO THIRSTY LAND

By means of irrigation, thousands of acres of ground that would otherwise be barren are brought under fruitful cultivation, and this illustration shows how water is made to flow along the furrows of land to give sustaining moisture to thirsty crops. In some parts of the world there is practically no rainfall, but this deficiency can profitably be made good by artificial methods.

CENTURIES before the birth of Christ the plains near and between the great Rivers Tigris and Euphrates were fed with water from those rivers by means of a wonderful system of canals. So fertile were the plains that each nation which rose to power in Western Asia coveted them and fought for their possession. Assyrians, Babylonians, Medes and Persians, and Arabs all held them in turn, and left behind them the ruins of the once mighty cities of Nineveh, Babylon, Ctesiphon, and Seleucia.

Presently, through invasion by Tartar races, the inhabitants of this fruitful region were swept away. The canals silted up, water no longer reached the plains, and they became a desert, since the rainfall was too small to support vegetation. A desert they remained for hundreds of years, though their natural fertility remained. Engineers are now at work on restoring the water supply, so that, once more, " if tickled with a hoe, they shall laugh with a harvest."

For the Thirsty Land

In many other parts of the world there are wide stretches of naturally fertile soil, with little or no rainfall, and great rivers running through and near them. One of the most important branches of modern engineering is concerned with diverting the water of such rivers on to the thirsty lands.

The general principle of an irrigation scheme, as a plan for watering land artificially is called, is to build a dam across a river to raise its level. From points above the dam large canals are dug on a slope less than that of the river, and running more or less parallel to it downstream, a considerable distance away. These main canals throw out branches to right and left, and the branches feed a number of still smaller channels, until at last we come to the irrigation ditches in the fields which the water is to feed. At places the water may have to be lifted by pumps, but as far as possible matters are so arranged that it will flow naturally wherever it is needed.

Irrigation Wonders in India

There are probably few of us who realise the wonderful work British irrigation engineers have done for India, especially in the north and north-west, where rain is scanty and so uncertain that not so long ago large tracts were quite uninhabited.

Some of the greatest schemes have been carried out in the Punjab, the " Land of the Five Rivers "—Beas, Chenab, Jhelum, Ravi and Sutlej, all tributaries of the Indus. Let us glance at one of them, the Chenab scheme, watering three million acres between that river and the Ravi.

By Canals and Ditches

Most of the country was absolutely barren, a prey to drought and shimmering heat, which caused mirages that sometimes deceived the engineers sent to survey it. Through this arid waste a huge canal was dug, 250 feet wide at the bottom, carrying as much water as the Thames does in times when it is out in flood. This water is delivered to a network of canals and ditches, which divide the whole district up into squares of about 25 acres.

Topical Press.

DELTA BARRAGE ON THE NILE

By means of this wonderful dam at the delta (*i.e.*, near the mouth) of the River Nile, the upper level of the stream is so raised that there is sufficient water available to refresh vast tracts of fertile country, and help enormously in the production of great crops of cotton. Now that the Nile is dammed, there is little likelihood of a recurrence of the " seven lean years " of Pharaoh's dream. Our photo was taken from an aeroplane.

ROUGH WATER AT THE SENNAR DAM

H. J. Shepstone.

The Sennar Dam, seen above, is on the Blue Nile, 170 miles south of Khartoum. It was built in 1914–25 at a cost of £11,000,000. There is a railway running along the top of the wall, here 23 feet wide, though the width at the bottom is 90 feet. The water which is making such a troubled cascade below the dam, comes through no fewer than eighty sluice gates.

IN INDIA AND AFRICA

One of the greatest irrigation schemes in the world was carried out with the building of the giant dam at Sukkur, on the River Indus in Pakistan. The photograph shows the famous Lloyd Barrage which forms part of these irrigation works, completed in 1933. Some five million acres of waterless desert in Sind were turned into a vast fertile area, producing wheat, rice and cotton.

Egypt and Britain have joined in the plans for building a dam at Owen Falls, below Jinja, where Lake Victoria joins the White Nile in Uganda. This vast scheme will make better use of the Nile waters both for irrigation and, in due course, for the supply of electric power to the British protectorate of Uganda and probably later to Ethiopia as well.

LOOKING DOWN ON THE BOULDER DAM

Dorien Leigh.

The Colorado is the fifth longest river in the United States of America and has an estimated length of over 2,000 miles. It is remarkable for the number of gorges or canyons through which it flows. American engineers have controlled its turbulent waters by a series of dams which supply electric power and serve to irrigate valleys that have now become rich farming areas. Our photograph shows the famous Boulder Dam and power plant, seen from the highest mountains below the dam.

As soon as the water was available people were brought in by hundreds of thousands and settled in villages. A once unpopulated waste now has well over a million inhabitants, busy tilling millions of acres of land.

What irrigation means to the peasants of India can be gathered from an engineer's own description. At one time he was responsible for a district on both sides of a large river. The land on one side was irrigated, that on the other side was not. A drought came and the crops on the unwatered land failed. Here and there a scanty ear of rice might be seen, hardly worth the gathering. The famine-stricken people crowded to relief works set up by the Government to earn enough food to keep themselves alive.

This food was bought from farmers on the farther side of the river, where irrigation had produced a bumper crop, sold at very high prices to meet the demand from the famine district.

A Gigantic Scheme

Far more important even than the Chenab scheme is one which taps the main stream of the Indus near Sukkur. A low dam, called a barrage, has been built across the river. It contains sixty-six huge iron gates, each weighing 50 tons, which can be raised to let the water pass freely in times of flood. By itself the dam is a great work, but the system of canals into which it turns the water is a greater work still. The task before the engineers who had to make the canals—of which there are some 1,450 miles—was to move 370,000,000 cubic yards of earth. This is a far larger quantity than had to be shifted even in the making of the Panama Canal.

As it was totally impossible to house and feed, in the middle of a desert, the army of about 60,000 labourers who would have been needed to carry out the work by hand, huge digging-machines and trenching-machines were brought into service. These ate their way through the desert soil, leaving behind them cleanly cut channels that were to be part of a scheme watering an area of land a quarter the size of England and Wales.

In the Land of the Pharaohs

Ever since the dawn of history the River Nile has supported millions of people living on narrow strips of land on each bank and in the Delta at its mouth. It has been well said that Egypt is the Nile, and the Nile Egypt. For the Egyptians depend entirely for their crops on the waters of the great river.

At certain seasons it overflows its banks and soaks the ground in the valley to east and west of it. When it returns to its bed, it leaves behind a deposit of fertile mud, in which the crops are sown. You can understand, then, why the Egyptians have always watched anxiously for the rising of the waters; and why in many places on its banks there are gauges, called Nilometers, to show what level it reaches. Some of these are thousands of years old.

The Seven Lean Years

Again and again Egypt has been overtaken by famine, due to the Nile not rising sufficiently to flood the land. You will remember the " seven lean kine " of Pharaoh's dream, which Joseph interpreted as seven years of famine. During those seven years the Egyptians suffered from a " low " Nile and crop failure.

Until the middle of last century the Nile was left to its own devices, and Egypt was entirely at its mercy.

In 1856 a beginning was made on work to control the water, with dams near Cairo, but they were constructed so badly that they could not be used till repaired in 1890.

But the country above the dams was no better off than before, so a scheme was prepared for taking away much more of the Nile's liberty. It was, briefly, to break the Nile up into great steps by low dams in two or three places,

U.S.A. Bureau of Reclamation.

AN AERIAL VIEW OF THE SHASTA DAM IN CALIFORNIA

The magic of irrigation and drainage has turned a desolation of swamp and desert in the Central Valley of California into an area of rich farms and pleasant cities. Bigger schemes to utilise the water of smaller streams were inaugurated by President Truman in 1951. The key structure of the Central Valley Project is the giant Shasta Dam which spans the Sacramento River at the Valley's northern tip and has created a lake of 47 square miles.

each turning water into large canals, and to barricade the stream still higher up with a very lofty dam at Assouan, where the Nile tumbled over a rocky slope called the First Cataract. All the dams were to have gates, which would be opened during the flood season but closed as the river subsided. The Assouan Dam would be high enough to bank up 1,000 million tons of water which would be let out during the dry season and maintain a better *average* flow throughout the year.

In the Dry Season

The building of this great dam was a formidable task, as 1,000,000 tons of masonry had to be placed across channels through which the water rushed at a speed of sixteen miles an hour. It was, of course, impossible to carry on when the river was in flood, and the engineers had to work at high pressure during a dry season and then wait for the next. Yet the dam was built in four years. Five years after it had been put into use it was found to be much too low. It has since been raised 23 feet by adding another 400,000 tons of masonry, and to-day holds up to two and a half times as much water as it did at first. When the reservoir behind the dam is full, it forms a lake 150 miles long.

The great dam and the barrages cost several millions of pounds between them, but the money was well spent, for it has brought prosperity to millions of people. The nightmare of " lean kine " no longer afflicts the Egyptians.

A Magic Change in the Sudan

A thousand miles above the Assouan Dam the two great feeders of the Nile, the Blue Nile and the White Nile, come together at Khartoum. The country between the rivers is named Gezira, which means " The Island." Till recently it was a dry, dusty country, very subject to famine. But after the War of 1914–18 engineers came in by way of the Red Sea and built a great dam, nearly two miles long, across the Blue Nile.

This dam was opened in 1925. Its effect has been magical. To-day a traveller finds in Gezira hundreds of thousands of acres of flourishing cotton fields, producing some of the finest cotton in the world.

Much work has still to be done: on the main Nile in the Sudan, on the Blue Nile in Ethiopia, and on the White Nile in Uganda. The new dam and hydro-electric works at Owen Falls, Jinja, on Lake Victoria, opened in 1954, will presently provide power for Kenya as well as Uganda, which it now serves. This is part of a series of schemes to harness the Nile completely, not only for irrigation, but for electric power. Huge storage lakes, the reclamation of the Sudd swamps, and the extension of the Gezira cotton-growing area have been planned, and it is estimated that this great work will take at least 25 years.

Water for American Deserts

Moving on to the United States we find a great country whose rainfall is divided into three main belts running north and south. Nearly all its eastern

U.S.A. Bureau of Reclamation.
TWO MILLION GALLONS A MINUTE
This huge concrete pipe is part of the Central Valley irrigation scheme in California. Every minute two million gallons of water flow through the pipe and its size can be judged from the man walking along it. Water which would flow uselessly into the sea is carried to the Delta-Mendota Canal for irrigating dry lands.

Australian National Publicity Association.

ON AUSTRALIA'S GREATEST RIVER

With its tributaries, the Murray drains a watershed of 414,000 square miles. From its source in the Australian Alps to Lake Alexandrina in South Australia where it enters the sea, it has a length of 1,520 miles. The most important irrigation scheme in Australia has been the control of the Murray River, and the biggest of several dams is the Hume Dam near Albury, seen in this photograph.

half has a good rainfall; most of its western half has a poor rainfall; and between them is a narrow belt of uncertain rainfall.

Since the beginning of this century many great projects have been carried through, or set on foot, in the arid western states, over large stretches of which agriculture is impossible without irrigation. Many streams which feed the Rivers Missouri, Colorado, Columbia and Sacramento have been barred by dams, and their waters diverted to the farmer. Wheat, maize, lucerne, apples, dates, plums, and other fruits now grow on millions of acres on which even sagebrush and cactus could hardly keep alive.

Work of the Ancients

While certain works were being carried out in Arizona and New Mexico, traces were found of the irrigation systems of some prehistoric race. These were on such a scale as to suggest that, perhaps 3,000 years ago, a large population lived there. The land had gone back to desert long before the Spaniards discovered it in the sixteenth century. How that ancient people hewed its canals in many places through solid rock is a mystery.

River Barriers

American engineers have thrown great dams across narrow valleys, controlling the rivers and creating huge lakes of storage water that can be released when required. The lovely orange-groves around Phoenix,

Arizona, flourish on what was once desert, thanks to the Salt River Irrigation which—through its Theodore Roosevelt dam—waters 750,000 acres.

The famous Tennessee Valley Authority, by chaining the waters of the Tennessee, has saved millions of acres of fertile soil from being swept away in terrible floods and produced fruitful terraced fields where once farmers were abandoning their land because of erosion.

Then there is the Shoshone Dam, in Northern Wyoming, the highest masonry dam in the world. It resembles a great wedge, 328 feet high, driven into the narrow chasm through which the river flows. This wedge means water for over 150,000 acres of desert.

A Daring Piece of Work

In South-Western Colorado the River Uncompahgre runs through an open valley, and parallel to it, on the other side of a high ridge, the Gunnison flows through a gorge half a mile deep. The water of the Gunnison was needed badly for irrigation on the Uncompahgre scheme, and the engineers decided to drive a tunnel through the intervening ridge to get it. The Gunnison gorge was first explored by two daring men, A. L. Fellows and W. W. Torrence, who floated down the foaming torrent on an inflated rubber mattress. They escaped with their lives and brought back invaluable notes and photographs.

A third engineer was lowered on ropes into the gorge to do further surveying. This dangerous work lasted for weeks, but it resulted in the tunnel being driven and the Gunnison being turned aside through the mountain.

The Colorado, the fifth longest river in the United States, has had its wild flood controlled by such famous engineering feats as Boulder Dam, Parker Dam, and Imperial Dam. From the last-named, irrigation channels carry water to the Imperial and Yuma-Gila valleys, which are now among America's richest farming areas. But for the waters of the Colorado, the lush green crops here would die in ninety days.

Paul Popper.

WELL SINKING IN AUSTRALIA

In the hot dry summers many sheep stations are dependent on their artesian wells for watering sheep and cattle. These wells draw from vast underground lakes, and our photograph shows the sinking of an artesian well in Southern Australia.

FROM RIVER TO FARMLANDS

This shows one of the several weirs on the Murray River in Australia which convey water into the irrigation channels and then on to the farms. By this means pastures and fodder crops are watered and dairy farmers are able to keep their flocks and herds in areas which would normally be parched and arid for many months in the year.

Photos : Paul Popper.

Here we see one of the irrigation channels conveying water from the Murray River to farms over hundreds of square miles in northern Victoria. All the water is conveyed by gravity. On either side of the channel can be seen the water wheels which measure the amount of water consumed in the area.

Water for Australian Farms

During the past fifty years thousands of acres of arid land in the great Commonwealth of Australia have been transformed into fruitful farms and orchards by irrigation. The first scheme of this kind was at Mildura where, late in the last century, the Chaffey brothers built pumping machinery to lift water from the great Murray River to the dry lands.

Since then, far greater projects have been carried out. In the mountains of New South Wales, the Murrumbidgee river is barred by the Burrinjuck Dam. The Murray River now feeds the Curlwaa, Renmark, Mildura, and other irrigation areas. Hume Dam, on the Murray, near Albury, pens the water in Hume reservoir, the largest of its kind in the Southern Hemisphere.

In January, 1949, further irrigation and power schemes for this part of the Commonwealth were announced. At a cost of over 170 million pounds, the headwaters of the Snowy river are being diverted as part of a gigantic project that will take many years to complete. There will be many power stations and seven main dams in this project; nearly 100 miles of tunnels will have to be driven through the Australian Alps, and 500 miles of race lines constructed. When the scheme is complete there will be an enormous increase in the amount of electric current available as well as in the water available for irrigation in the Murrumbidgee valley.

Australia is the driest continent and in wellnigh every State of the Commonwealth schemes are in hand to develop and harness water supplies. Every Australian knows that drought is a real danger, even for those who live in the cities. Not so many years ago, the great city of Sydney was on the brink of a water famine ; in fact, if the drought had persisted, it would have been necessary to evacuate part of the population. That is why a big new dam, capable of holding back 445,000 million gallons of water, is being built across the Warragamba River to the west of Sydney.

Victoria has already done much to turn the mallee scrub country of the northeast into fertile wheatlands. Her new Rocklands Dam on the Glenelg River will help to provide water supplies for this part of the State and will include a tunnel through the Dividing Range to carry precious water to the Wimmera district. Another important project in Victoria is the Cairn Curran Reservoir, on the Loddon River. The Eildon Dam on the Goulburn River may also be extended.

In some parts of the Commonwealth water is piped many miles to feed towns and industrial centres. In Western Australia, water is piped 346 miles from Mundaring Weir to Kalgoorlie and the Eastern Goldfields. In South Australia, a pipe line 223 miles long carries water from Morgan, on the Murray River, to the important ore-smelting and shipbuilding centre of Whyalla.

The Radio Physics Division of the Australian Scientific and Industrial Research Organisation has recently developed ways of *making* rain, although at present they are too expensive for general use.

Speaking in Melbourne in September, 1953, Dr. E. G. Bowen, Director of the Division, said that economical methods might be found within the next five years. Rainfall could be increased by as much as 50 per cent. in many areas, especially in the inland marginal rainfall areas. Lands now used only for grazing might become suitable for cultivation, rainfall in some areas might be made more regular, and certain kinds of drought prevented.

But Australia's greatest problem, which has still to be solved, is how to provide water for the dry interior of the island continent. Many suggestions have been made, the best known being the scheme put forward by the late Dr. Bradfield, an engineer who had much to do with the building of the Sydney Harbour Bridge, but a way has still to be found which holds certain promise of success.

The Story that
Scientists
can tell us

About Heat,
Light
and Sound

Specially drawn for this work.

HOW PRIMITIVE MAN MADE FIRE

It is difficult for us to realise a world without such simple things as matches, or everyday existence
that had no ready means of making fire. In ancient days men and women worshipped fire, and
this illustration shows us a primitive savage, whose only method of producing first sparks, then
glowing heat, and finally flame, was to rub one stick against another.

WHAT IS FIRE ?

ACCORDING to a legend of Greek mythology, one of the Titans, Prometheus by name, stole fire from heaven to give to men. Zeus, king of heaven, angered to think that men should receive a gift that would raise them nearer to the gods, had Prometheus chained to a rock, and sent an eagle to gnaw his liver, which grew afresh every night. So Prometheus suffered terribly for his rashness until Hercules came and released him, after slaying the eagle.

The Titan could hardly have selected a finer gift. Human civilisation is based on fire, which gave man heat to cook his food and warm his body, light to drive away the darkness, and the possibility of working metal into the tools and other devices used in agriculture and all the arts. We can hardly wonder that the ancients worshipped fire, and that fire-worship still survives in some parts of the world.

Good Servant, Bad Master

And what is this wonderful thing which the savage coaxes into being by rubbing one stick against another, and the civilised man conjures up in a moment by striking a match? It is nothing more than the combining of some other element with the oxygen of the air. In the fuels which we use—

wood, coal, peat, oil—the other element is carbon. As soon as this is heated up to a certain extent, its atoms spring to meet those of oxygen and combine with them to form carbonic acid gas, giving out great heat in the process. It is of no use to apply a match to a lump of coal. You must first warm up paper till it bursts into flame, then with the paper heat sticks till they too take fire, and depend on the sticks to heat the coal. The spreading of a fire through a building, town, prairie, or forest is but a succession of warmings-up of cold carbon into hot and combustible carbon. When conditions are favourable, this spread is so rapid that it justifies the old proverb about fire being a good servant but a bad master.

One does not get flames unless gas be present. Gas is merely a substance with its atoms very widely spread by heat. And in this condition they unite fiercely with oxygen. The flame of a candle is the burning gas from the carbon of the grease. The as yet unburned particles of carbon are made white-hot by the burning particles and give out light. On the surface of the sun, vast quantities of hydrogen gas burn daily, as flames which stretch outwards into space to distances reckoned in hundreds of thousands of miles.

The Giant Heat

When one stands in front of a blazing fire it feels hot to us. A snowball feels cold. In the first case heat enters the

Specially drawn for this work.

SOME SECRETS OF THE GREENHOUSE

Why is the air inside a greenhouse always hotter than that outside? To answer this question we must remember that heat waves are both long and short. Thus, the shorter heat waves get through the glass of the conservatory, fall upon things inside, are converted into longer waves, and cannot get back through the glass. So, put very simply, the greenhouse acts like a trap to Giant Heat.

HOW WORK CHANGES INTO HEAT

Photo : *By permission of the Science Museum, London.*

Once upon a time people thought that all artificial heat must come from the burning of certain substances. James Prescott Joule, an eminent physicist, made the above machine or calorimeter, however, and was able to prove that work can produce heat. Thus, by turning the handle vigorously and setting in motion the stirring paddles beneath, he actually caused water in the tank to become heated. Indeed, the faster he stirred the hotter the water became,

body; in the second, some is taken from it. So far as our bodies are concerned, heat and cold are mere sensations, as light is a sensation.

But what is it that *causes* this feeling called heat?

The answer is, heat is a form of *motion*. This may appear an unsatis-

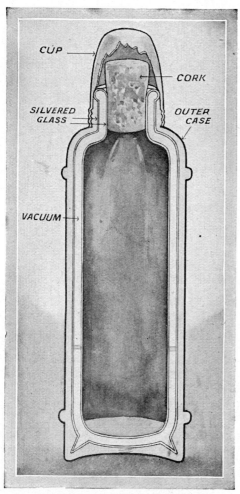

Specially drawn for this work.

GIANT HEAT IN A PRISON

Our illustration shows a vacuum or thermos flask cut down the middle so that you can see it in section. You will thus notice that there are two glass walls, as it were, the space between containing no air. As heat cannot pass through two thicknesses of glass and the vacuum space, a hot liquid placed in the container keeps its heat. In the reverse way, a cold liquid remains cool because heat cannot enter.

factory answer. But let us examine it a little. Take sun heat. The atoms of the sun are in violent motion among themselves. They stir up the ether and agitate it into light waves, heat waves, and other waves. The ether transmits these waves to the earth. The heat waves, acting on the particles of matter of which the earth and everything on it, including ourselves, are made, produce in them that form of motion called heat. The ether itself is not heated. It is merely a *transmitter* of heat energy, just as a telephone wire is a transmitter of sound in a form which is not itself sound.

About Heat Waves

We may assume that heat waves, like light waves, are of different lengths, occupying, as it were, an octave or more on the scale of ether vibrations. For this will explain the action of a greenhouse. We may picture to ourselves some of the sun waves—the longer—being stopped by the glass, as a blue glass will stop the longer red light rays, the shorter getting through. These strike the things inside the greenhouse, and are converted by them into longer waves, which cannot get back through the glass. So the greenhouse acts as a heat-trap.

It is the same with a glass fire-screen, which allows the short light waves to come through, but stops most of the heat waves, which are probably much longer than those from the vastly hotter sun. But the screen itself gets hot. The heat waves affect the ether in the glass itself, and set the atoms surrounded by it in more vigorous motion.

The spreading of heat through a body is called *conduction*. If you stick a poker into a roaring fire, you may protect your hand from the radiant heat by interposing a piece of cardboard as a kind of shield on the poker, for ray heat travels only in straight lines. But the heat passed along by the atoms of the poker will presently reach your hand whether the poker be straight or much bent, for the matter of the poker " conducts " the heat. Yet only part of the heat reaches you, since the ether all round the poker is being agitated, and heat is being radiated from the poker in all directions. You can prove this by drawing the poker out of the fire and holding your hand some distance from it.

KEEPING THE HANDLE COOL

Metals are good conductors of heat, and to prevent the handle of a teapot from getting too hot to hold, the handle is either made of wood, which is a bad conductor of heat, or an insulating material such as plastic or bone is used between the handle and the teapot.

Fur and Feathers

While metals are good conductors of heat, other substances, such as rock and earth, are bad conductors. Their atoms object to being roused up by the heat waves. It is lucky for us that this is so. For what otherwise would become of us, living as we do on a great wall which is terrifically hot inside, as witness the molten lava flung out by volcanoes ? The outer crust, having lost its original heat, fortunately refuses to pass on the heat of the uncooled mass which it covers.

Air also, like other gases, is a bad conductor of heat. What we call warm clothes are not warm in themselves, but being of thick, loose materials they imprison tiny pockets of air which obstruct the escape of heat from our bodies. It is the same with felt and other substances used for covering boilers, the feathers of birds, and the fur of animals.

Heat Insulation

When we dress in the morning one of the main objects is to insulate our bodies against the varying temperature of the air. Our object is to keep the natural warmth of the body from travelling. This word *insulate* comes from the Latin *insula* meaning island, and an island is insulated from the mainland by the sea. In the case of a metal teapot, for example, the heat from the hot water would travel to the handle and make it too hot to hold unless the handle is made of some material which is a poor heat conductor, or some

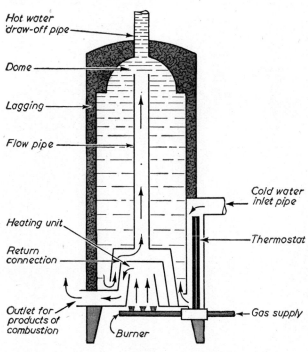

A GAS-HEATED GEYSER

Cold water flows into the geyser and passes through a narrow pipe which is heated by gas burner. This burner heats the water almost instantaneously and so gives an unlimited supply of hot water.

Specially drawn for this work.

IRON IS A GOOD CONDUCTOR

The man sheltering from the sun beneath this canopy of corrugated galvanised iron feels the power of the rays terribly. This shows us that the metal is a good conductor of heat.

Just as materials differ in their readiness to conduct heat so do different kinds of surfaces vary greatly in their readiness to receive and absorb heat. Generally speaking, dark and rough surfaces absorb heat much better than white or bright and shiny surfaces which turn the heat rays back and reflect them. On a hot day, when the warmth of the sun would raise the natural heat of our bodies, light-coloured clothes are the coolest. In the tropics most people wear white clothes as these reflect the heat rays from the sun and turn them back before they reach the body.

How Giant Heat is Humoured

Nearly all solids and liquids, and all gases, expand with heat and contract

Specially drawn for this work.

IN A GRATEFUL SHADE

It is useful to us to understand which substances possess the property of conducting heat. Earth and rock, for example, are bad conductors, and the man in this sketch, sheltering beneath a covering of turf and soil, is protected from the sun's rays.

insulating material such as bone or ebony is placed between the actual teapot and the handle.

Hot-water tanks are often clothed with a layer of asbestos, and the top may be covered with cork. Both these are bad conductors of heat and so the heat which might be radiated from the metal of the tank is prevented from travelling and the water in the tank is prevented from cooling down after the heat which supplied the hot water has been cut off.

Why are wooden spoons used for cooking? Simply because wood is a poor conductor of heat and the cook can hold a wooden spoon for stirring a boiling liquid, but would find that a metal spoon would become too hot to hold as metal is a good conductor of heat.

with cold. If boiling water be poured into a cold tumbler of thick glass it will probably crack it. The inside expands suddenly before the outside, and this is more than the glass can stand. Steam should not be raised too quickly in a cold boiler, lest one part should expand before the other and cracks, or leaky joints result.

You have probably noticed— you certainly have felt—the small gaps between the ends of rails in a railway track. These have to be left to allow for expansion during hot weather. Tramway rails are without joints, as the concrete in which they are laid overcomes the expansive force of heat.

Balancing the Movements

The rods working points require what are called compensating joints, which keep the total length of the rods the same in cold and heat. The towers of a suspension bridge have saddles at the top to carry the wire cables. These saddles run on rollers and allow movement to and fro as the cables lengthen or shorten. Long steam pipes and hot-water pipes are provided with sliding

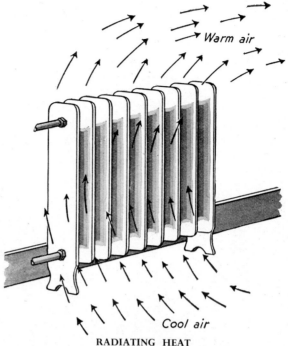

RADIATING HEAT

Rooms and passages are often heated by radiators. Air which is near the radiator rises as it is warmed and cool air takes its place and also rises as it becomes heated. In this way a constant current of hot air is circulated through the room.

joints, usually like those of a telescope. The power of expansion is very great, and if heat be not humoured there will be trouble with great continuous lengths of metal.

The rate at which a clock's pendulum swings, or a watch's balance-wheel vibrates, varies with changes in temperature, unless means are taken to overcome this. The pendulum "bob" of an expensive clock is often a tube of mercury, fastened above a crossbar on the end of the rod. As the rod lengthens downwards with heat, the mercury lengthens upwards in the tube, and the two movements balance.

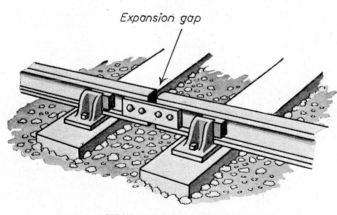

HEAT EXPANDS METAL

Heat causes many metals to expand. To allow for the expansion which inevitably occurs on hot days a gap is left between each length of rail when making the track on which trains run.

But expansion is useful in some ways. It gives us the thermometer. It enables us to shrink tyres on to wheels ; and to draw bulging walls together with steel bars, by heating the bars, tightening up the nuts on their ends, and allowing them to cool. And devices for keeping water at a steady heat generally depend on the expansion of a metal bar connected to a valve.

How Giant Heat is Harnessed

Imagine a solid block of coal, one mile high, one mile long and one mile broad. The sun's heat is equal to that which would be obtained by burning 700,000 million blocks of this kind every hour. Though but a tiny fraction of this enormous heat falls on the earth, that fraction grows our crops and maintains animal life, and in past ages it created our coal deposits.

An enormous amount of the sun's heat that reaches us is, however, wasted, and radiated back into space. Except on a very small scale, we cannot turn sun heat directly to account for purposes which demand intense heat. For the present we have to harness the heat energy of the sun by indirect means.

In the first place, we burn coal, wood and petroleum—for all of which we must thank the sun — in countless boilers, stoves and fireplaces. The heat passes into water and raises steam, which is applied to many purposes, but specially to driving engines. Or the heat may be radiated to warm our houses directly or with the aid of hot-water pipes.

The heat energy of petroleum, and of the very inflammable petrol or gasolene got from petroleum, can be used in the cylinders of what are called internal-combustion engines, such as the engines of motor cars. The liquid is heated till it changes into gas, or squirted through a nozzle as a fine spray and mixed with air. The mixture is then drawn into the cylinders, squeezed by the pistons, and set alight. The explosion causes great heat and a swelling of the charge, and the pressure on the pistons provides the thrust.

Where intense heat is needed, as for smelting metals, the rate at which coal or coke burns is hastened by driving a blast of air through the fuel, so that the

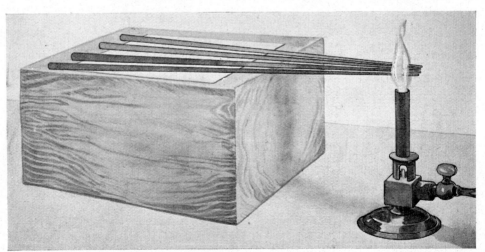

Specially drawn for this work.

AN EXPERIMENT IN HEAT CONDUCTING

Some substances can lead heat along far better than others, and even different metals vary considerably in the speed with which they act as conductors. In the experiment here illustrated bars of lead, copper, iron and brass respectively are laid upon a sheet of waxed paper resting on a block of wood. When the bunsen gas burner is lit it will be seen that the wax under the rods is not all melted by heat at the same time. Thus one metal is a better conductor than another.

FALLING WATER TURNED TO HEAT

ELECTRIC
FURNACE

GENERATORS

PIPE
CONVEYING
WATER TO
TURBINE

REVOLVING
SHAFT →

ROWELL

Specially drawn for this work.

It seems wonderful that man can harness a waterfall and convert its energy into heat for his own
use. This diagram explains in detail how this great engineering feat is accomplished, and we
see that a portion of the water is diverted into a monstrous pipe. This captive water, before it
is allowed to run to waste, sends turbine machinery spinning round, so that a shaft is caused to
revolve. The shaft conveys power to the generators, and these create electrical energy.

supply of oxygen shall be increased. We use the same principle when we " blow up " the fire with bellows.

Heating a Furnace by Water

But great heat may be obtained in another way altogether by using the power of falling water. A waterfall can be made to turn a water turbine driving a dynamo. The electricity is led away to an electric furnace, and treated in a manner which changes it into heat.

This form of furnace is used in making some of the world's finest steel; carbide of calcium, from which acetylene gas is produced ; carborundum, for grinding-wheels ; and aluminium, now a very important metal. We practically owe these last three materials to the electric furnace, and through it to the sun, since it was the sun that sucked up water as vapour from the oceans,

to fall again on to high land and run back to sea level.

Other applications of Giant Heat include the blowpipe, burning a mixture of oxygen and acetylene gas, the flame of which will cut through steel plates several inches thick quite easily. Then we have the whirling disc of iron, like a toothless circular saw, able to cut steel bars by melting a path through the metal with the heat of friction.

Heat energy is measured in Thermal Units, often referred to as B.T.U. (British Thermal Units). A British Thermal Unit of heat is needed to raise the temperature of one pound of water by 1° Fahrenheit. Gas is measured by the therm and there are 100,000 British Thermal Units in one therm. Electricity is measured by the unit, and one electrical unit equals 3,412 British Thermal Units of heat.

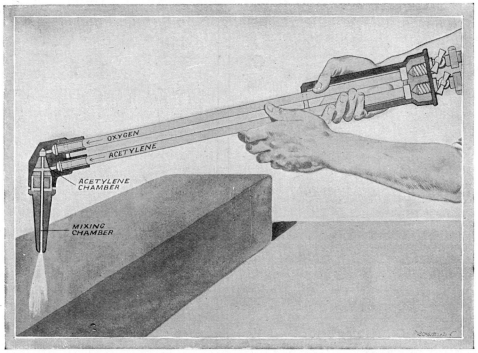

Specially drawn for this work.

FOR CUTTING THROUGH SOLID STEEL

You will have seen bellows employed for blowing up the sitting-room fire or larger ones in use at a blacksmith's forge. Much the same principle is employed with the oxygen-acetylene blow-pipe, whose flame will cut through steel plates several inches in thickness. In this sectional diagram we see oxygen and the gas from acetylene being forced into a mixing chamber, from which they emerge with an intense energy.

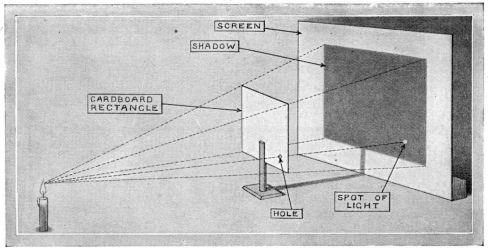

Specially drawn for this work.

HOW LIGHT TRAVELS IN STRAIGHT LINES

It is a very simple matter to prove that light travels in straight lines. Try the experiment explained in the diagram above. The piece of cardboard between the candle and large sheet of paper causes a deep shadow to be thrown, but the rays of light from the candle flame to the corners and then to the paper are perfectly straight, as you can prove with a piece of taut string. The pencil of light which gets through the hole in the cardboard is equally straight.

HAVE you ever heard of ether? We do not mean the strong-smelling liquid, the fumes from which are used to render a person unconscious before an operation. What we are referring to is a something—it cannot be called a substance—which, so scientists tell us, fills all space not occupied by matter. It is found even between the atoms of a grain of sand; and the vast expanses of the heavens, though containing no atmosphere such as surrounds our globe, are not truly empty, for they are full of ether.

Ether's Scale of Waves

We can't see, or taste, or weigh ether. If we pump all the air out of a vessel, we still leave the ether behind. We assume its existence, because only by assuming it can we explain light, radiant heat, wireless waves, X-rays, certain other rays, and their actions.

If a rope is lying on the ground, and you take one end and give it a jerk, a ripple of movement will run right along the rope, though the rope itself won't move endways. We must imagine ether to behave somewhat like the rope. If it be repeatedly jerked in one place it will pass along the jerks; or, if you like it better, send waves, in all directions.

Now, of course, you can imagine a succession of quick or slow jerks, each sending out a wave. And you know that a piano has a scale of sounds or notes getting higher and higher towards the top. In the same way the ether has a scale of waves. The bottom octave—slow waves—are wireless waves; above them come in turn heat waves, light waves, and X-rays, the last corresponding to the piano's "treble" notes. We will just add that waves of the first three kinds at any rate appear to travel at about the same speed through the ether. Quite a super-express speed, too, for light has been definitely "timed" at about 186,000 miles a second! Which means that light leaving the sun on the stroke of noon, reaches us at between eight and nine minutes past twelve, having done a "hop" of about 93 million miles in the interval!

J. F. Corrigan.

A PHOTOGRAPH IN NEGATIVE FORM

This picture shows us a photographic film or plate, and we observe that it is exactly the reverse from what our eyes would see if gazing upon the old cottage. In other words, the picture is a negative or opposite, with left-hand to right, darkness where there should be light and deep tones where we know clear ones to exist.

lengths, each giving rise to a different *colour*. The longest of them, the red waves, run 35,000 to the inch — the width of a half-penny—and the shortest, the violet waves, 67,000 to the inch. Waves of the other colours in between them, orange, yellow, green, blue, and indigo —in this order from red upwards—are of intermediate lengths. Ordinary sunlight contains them all in a certain proportion, and they blend into the colour called white.

It is extraordinary that the eye should be able to respond to these tiny waves. Even red, the "slowest" colour, demands that something should happen in the eye 400,000,000 million times a second, for that number of waves strikes it in a second. And when we look at a white object the eye has to respond to seven different sets of waves at once. Wonderful, is it not?

But the ether thinks nothing of such trifling distances as this. There is a star named Betelgeuse, in the constellation of Orion. Light travelling from it to us is 186 *years* on the journey. And Betelgeuse is quite a close neighbour as compared with some other visible stars!

Our Magical Eyes

So much for the speed of light. But how do light waves differ from other ether waves? In this way : they alone have the power of affecting our eyes, and becoming what we call visible. As the aerial of a wireless set is a receiver of wireless waves, so our eyes are two receivers given us to catch light waves sent off from any glowing body, or reflected from any object, so that we may *see* it. Cut off all light, and we are completely blind for the time; our eyes have lost their job.

Now light waves are not all of the same length from crest to crest. They can be shown to be of several different

What Causes Light ?

The mystery of light was one of the first natural phenomena to interest the earliest scientists. The famous Greek philosopher and mathematician, Pythagoras, was one of the first to set forth a theory which is now known as the corpuscular theory. Vision, he said, was caused by material particles projected from the surfaces of objects into the pupil of the eye.

Another famous Greek, Aristotle, took the view that light was an action of a medium which he called the *pellucid,* and later scientists carried his ideas still farther. Very slowly information was gathered about the conduct of light when it passed from one transparent medium to another. The reflection of light and the manner in which it was affected by lenses and prisms, were all carefully studied. With the invention of the telescope and microscope other ideas were advanced.

Isaac Newton was among the scientists of his day who studied the mystery of light, and since his time it has never ceased to be of interest. It is a remarkable fact, however, that, although many theories have been put forward since Newton's day, the latest theories of modern scientists resemble very closely the ideas put forward by Newton. True, the modern scientist speaks of electrons and attendant wave-train while Newton wrote of corpuscles and waves, but the theory is much the same.

We need not concern ourselves too much about these various theories since we already have a considerable amount of knowledge which the scientists through the ages have learned. Let us go back to the beginning of things and talk a little about the *cause* of light. We stick a poker into the fire. Presently its dark surface turns a dull red, then a bright red. If it be now taken into a dark place it will be seen to glow with a very visible light.

What has happened to it? Why, the heat of the fire has set the atoms of the poker jumping about so vigorously that they jerk the ether, sending out both heat waves and light waves. Further heating in a fierce fire would rouse the poker to emit other colour waves, until it became white hot, and very bright. As it cools it becomes first red and then black. Light waves are sent out no more, though heat waves are still given out.

The sun is our great source of light. And well it may be, for that huge globe, 866,400 miles across, is a mass of unbelievably hot matter. Even its surface, which is far cooler than its interior, is five times hotter than molten steel! No wonder, then, that it keeps the ether in violent motion, flooding with both heat and light that side of our earth which is turned towards it.

Making Light Work for us

Light works for us in many ways

J. F. Corrigan.

THE POSITIVE PHOTOGRAPHIC PRINT

Here we have ordered light to pass through the negative plate or film on to a sheet of sensitised printing paper. Thus the objects appear in positive form, precisely as we see them, light tones and dark ones in their proper place. In this manner light becomes our servant and we make it do our bidding.

Specially drawn for this work.

LIGHTS WITHOUT REFLECTORS

The motor car here depicted has its normal electrical bulbs switched on, with the same volume of current as customarily passes from the storage battery. The lights, though, seem strangely feeble and totally ineffective for the simple reason that their rays are spread about and sent scattering to waste in all directions.

a chemical solution called a developer, the effect becomes visible. Wherever the light has struck it, the silver bromide darkens. The tint it assumes at any point is in proportion to the strength of the light that fell on that point. Wherever no light reached the plate the film remains white, and when the unchanged silver bromide is dissolved away by another chemical we have an image in which the tones are the reverse of those of the object. But matters are put right when light is allowed to pass through this " negative " image on to another film. For the parts under the clear glass are most affected and turn black, while those under the black get no light at all and remain white. The negative, moreover, like type set up for printing, is able to be used for making any number of copies.

Collecting and Directing Light

The bulb of a motor car's headlight gives a very feeble light when burning

without any effort on our part, but we have had to find out for ourselves ways of making it meet our special needs.

Take photography, for example. A glass plate, covered on one side with a coating of gelatine and silver bromide, is exposed to light which can reach it only through a lens. The rays reflected from an object or view are focused on to the plate, and wherever they strike the silver compound they change it mysteriously in a manner invisible to the eye.

Yet when the plate is flooded with

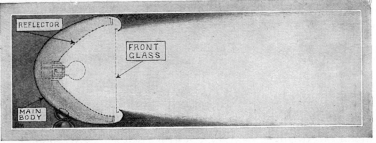

Specially drawn for this work.

A LIGHT IN HARNESS

In this diagram one of the electric bulbs of the car has been enclosed in its proper bowl-shaped reflector. We have harnessed the rays now so that the reflector seizes them, concentrates them together and sends them as a dazzling beam a hundred yards down the dark road.

THE SEARCHLIGHT'S GLARE

Imperial War Museum.

Here is a Royal Air Force searchlight at a Northern Bomber station. In time of war it may be used for detecting enemy aircraft, and we employ it in peace like a sky lighthouse to guide our own aeroplanes. The principle of the searchlight is that a powerful electric arc-light shines like thousands of candles, its rays gathered in a blinding sheaf.

7—2

in the open and sending its rays in all directions. The same bulb, placed in the focus of a bowl-shaped reflector, sends a dazzling beam of light 100 yards or more down the road. The reflector has caught most of its rays and bent them all in one direction, thus concentrating them enormously.

The searchlight used in warfare for spotting aircraft, and in peace for guiding them, works on just the same principle. But the place of a small incandescent bulb is taken by a powerful electric arc light. Light equal to that from hundreds, or even thousands or millions, of candles is gathered into a blinding sheaf, which, as it sweeps the heavens, may be seen by the airman when he is 100 miles or more away.

The lighthouse for aircraft has its counterpart in the lighthouse for ships, without which navigation round our coasts would be dangerous indeed. At the top of a massive granite tower stands a light surrounded by clusters of lenses and prisms. These gather up the light and send it out in horizontal bands. The framework carrying them floats on a trough of mercury, and is revolved with remarkable ease by clockwork, so that at regular intervals the mariner sees a bright flash of light. In a few cases powerful searchlights are used in place of lights with lenses.

Signalling Across 100 Miles

Of the kinds of apparatus used for merely reflecting light we will mention just two.

One is the heliograph, a mirror mounted on a tripod, and able to be tilted by pressing a key. With it sunlight can be flashed by reflection in any direction. Heliograph signs have been read at distances of over 100 miles.

Then there is the reflecting galvanometer used in receiving very weak telegraphic signals. A tiny mirror mounted on a bar magnet—the two together weigh hardly one grain—reflects a beam of light from a lamp on to a fixed scale. The slightest current makes the needle waggle and a dot of light move from the centre of the scale towards one or other end. So sensitive is this instrument that it has received signals sent by cable across the Atlantic and back with a battery consisting of— what do you think? A silver thimble, a fragment of zinc, and a few drops of acid and water!

Through the Looking-Glass

During the first voyage made right round the world, in 1519–1522, by a small fleet under the command of Ferdinand Magellan, the members of the expedition passed a winter in port off the shores of Patagonia. One day a huge native appeared dressed in skins and with his face brightly painted. When brought aboard one of the ships he displayed no alarm until someone suddenly held up a mirror in front of him. On seeing his reflection, the giant sprang backwards in astonishment, laying four of the Spaniards flat on the deck.

In Nature's Mirror

The native no doubt thought the mirror to be a magic device, and what he saw in it to be another man staring at him. He did not at the moment realise that the image was as unreal as the things which Alice met with during her famous adventures on the farther side of the looking-glass. But if he had had time to think matters out he would probably have fathomed the mystery; for he must have seen the reflections of the sun, moon and cliffs in Nature's mirror—a sheet of smooth water.

The water mirror appears in several stories. In that, for instance, of the dog which, while crossing a stream, dropped his own bone to seize the image of it. And, again, in the legend of the beautiful Greek youth, Narcissus, who fell in love with his own reflection, died of grief because he could not get at it, and was changed into the flower which still bears his name.

TO GUIDE THE MARINER'S PATH

Specially drawn for this work.

All round our coasts are tall towers, usually built of granite, from which a bright light flashes through the hours of darkness, not merely to warn the sailor of danger but also to guide him along a safe course. In the light-room clusters of lenses and prisms gather the rays together and send them flashing through space in horizontal bands. The framework which causes the light to flash at regular intervals is revolved by clockwork.

The ancients used mirrors of polished metal, which at best were probably very imperfect. St. Paul, in one of his epistles, has the words, " Now we see through a glass, darkly," that is, indistinctly. What is meant here by the word "glass" is no doubt the metal mirror of his times.

By the fourteenth century the Venetians were making looking-glasses like those of to-day, consisting of a perfectly flat sheet of polished glass, coated on the back with a film of metal. Being protected from the air by the glass, the metal keeps very bright.

Building an Image

Why is it that, if we look at a table or door, we see the table or door; whereas, if we peep into a mirror, we do not see the mirror itself, but only the objects reflected in it? The better a mirror is, the less visible it becomes. Most of us have, at one time or another, almost charged into a mirror reaching to the ground, or stopped short at the sight of another person coming unexpectedly towards one.

To get back to the question. A door has a comparatively rough surface, which scatters light in all directions, so that some light will reach the eye from every point on it, and we see it directly. But a mirror, that is, the film on the back of it, being perfectly flat, makes light rays bounce off it at the same angle as they strike it at, but in the opposite direction. So of all the rays coming from, say, the top right-hand corner of the door, the eye receives from the mirror only those which strike it *at a particular point*, and it seems to see the corner of the door through that point. The same thing is happening with rays from all parts of the door, bouncing off at different points, and among them they build up an image or reflection, apparently as far behind the mirror as the door is away from it in front.

Tricks that Light Plays us

You have no doubt made the acquaintance of the toy called a kaleidoscope. It is a metal tube with an eye-hole at one end and a circle of ground-glass at the other. Three long narrow mirrors are fixed in the tube, at an angle of 60 degrees to each other. A number of small pieces of coloured glass between the ground glass and a disc of clear glass tumble over when the tube is rolled round.

The mirrors reflect images from one to the other, so that one sees five of them as well as the object itself. There is thus a constant change of regular patterns, grouped round the points where two mirrors meet, and the eye is completely tricked. If you buy a couple of cheap, square-cornered mirrors and stick them together along one edge with a strip of strong paper acting as a hinge, you can have a lot of fun in watching the designs they weave when drawn upright over a paper with coloured patches painted on it. Changing the angle between the mirrors alters the nature of the patterns.

A Desert Mirage

Many other tricks can be played by mirrors. Years ago an illusion called " Pepper's Ghost " was a popular spectacle. The figure of a person under the stage was reflected upwards through a hole on to a sheet of plate glass leaning over towards the audience. A dim image—the " ghost "—coming from the front surface of the glass could be seen, but the glass did not screen actual people on the stage behind it. Another mirror trick makes use of a three-legged table, with mirrors running from leg to leg, and set with one leg turned towards the footlights. The audience sees only the reflections of black cloths at the sides of the stage, and this makes the space under the table seem empty. A person sitting under the table, with his head projecting through it, therefore appears to be a head lacking a body!

Perhaps the strangest of all tricks— and sometimes a very tantalising one—

THE HELIOGRAPH: A LOOKING-GLASS WHICH TURNS SUN-RAYS INTO MESSAGES

Sometimes on a bright day your eye catches a bright gleam where a sun-ray has lighted upon a piece of glass or shimmering tin. These flashes of light have been put to use in a simple apparatus known as the heliograph, which is illustrated above. This device consists of a mirror (A) mounted on a tripod so that it faces the sun. The different parts of the instrument are (B) Tangent box and screw; (C) Lever arm; (D) Beat regulating screw; (E) Key; (F) Screw in Socket; (G) Jointed arm; (H) Clamping screw for arm; (I) Jointed sighting rod; (K) Sighting vane. By pressing the key the operator catches sun-rays and throws them by reflection to form short and long flashes, equivalent to the dots and dashes of other signalling systems. Even in these days of radio, the heliograph is still a useful military signalling appliance. Cases are on record where messages have been sent direct over a distance of 100 miles.

is the mirage of the desert. It is due to there being layers of air of different heat over the sand, the lowest the hottest. Now, when light passes from colder to hotter, or from hotter to colder air, it is bent out of its course a bit. The rays from the top of, say, a palm tree travelling downwards are turned more and more horizontally by each layer till at last they bounce off a layer and begin to move upward. They are now turned more and more vertically, and if they strike a person's eye he appears to see the top of the palm below ground, with the trunk above it. The air has acted as a mirror. Sometimes clouds are treated in this way, giving the thirsty traveller promise of water which he never tastes, for the mocking " lakes " recede as he advances.

And, again, mirages are sometimes seen at sea, ships appearing upside down in the sky. In such a case the coolest layers are near the water and the hottest far above. The eye then catches rays which have been turned first upward and then downward.

Splitting up Sunlight

You must often have noticed the beautiful colours which seem to be imprisoned in a pendant of a chandelier, the cut-glass stopper of a decanter or a bevelled edge of a mirror.

The colours are those of sunlight, separated by the action of the glass.

The ordinary way of splitting-up sunlight is as follows : A beam of sunlight is allowed to enter a darkened room through a vertical slit in a blind or shutter. It falls on a horizontal triangular bar—a prism—of glass, arranged with its top lying level. The

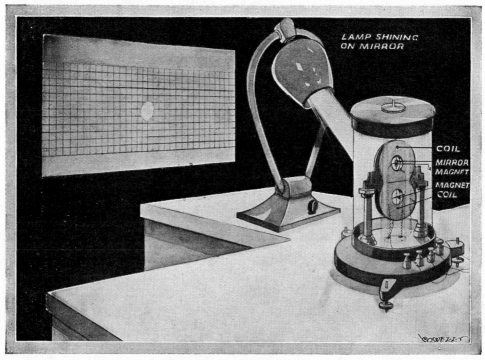

Specially drawn for this work.

A SENSITIVE SIGNALLING DEVICE

The appliance here depicted is a reflecting galvanometer which can receive telegraphic signals. It consists of a tiny mirror mounted on a bar magnet and reflects a beam of light from a lamp on to a fixed scale. So sensitive is this instrument that it has recorded cable signals sent across the Atlantic Ocean and back again to our shores with the current from a battery which consisted of a silver thimble, a fragment of zinc, and a few drops of acid and water.

From " Scientific Ideas of To-day," by courtesy of Messrs. Seeley, Service, Ltd.

WHEN BEAMS OF LIGHT ARE TWISTED

You may often have noticed how strange beams of light appear when passing through say a gold-fish bowl. This diagram explains the reason, for you can follow the strong ray from the lantern to the reflecting mirror and then through a tank of water to the clear air above. In this case the beam of light has had its direction changed completely by passing through water.

light strikes the sloping side nearer it, is bent towards the top side while passing through the bar, and as it leaves the glass on the farther side again bends in the same direction. But the rays of different colours are taken out of their original paths in different degrees. The result is that the white screen on to which the rays are cast reveals an upright strip of bands of colour. Violet, which has been bent most, stands at the top, and then, in order downwards, come indigo, blue, green, yellow, orange and red. This strip of colours is named the *solar spectrum*.

The bands of colour in it are not sharply separated like those on a striped ribbon, but blend gradually into each other. The spectrum thus includes very many hues, the strongest and purest of which are selected for naming.

About the Rainbow

The order of the colours never varies. Whenever Nature shows us the spectrum in the form of the rainbow, we see the order maintained, from violet on the inside of the bow to red on the outside. If there be a second bow outside the first, as sometimes happens, the same order persists, but the other way round—red inside, violet outside.

Why does a rainbow appear? Why is it curved?

One always sees a rainbow in the quarter of the sky away from the sun. That is, one must have one's back to the sun in order to behold it. The reason for this is that the rainbow is the product of millions of *reflections* from millions of raindrops, each acting as a tiny prism. Take any one raindrop for consideration. Sun-rays enter it at a point, say, near the top, are bent downwards, reflected from the inside of the curved back surface of the drop, and come forward again, passing out near the bottom. Rays of different colours will take different paths, as we have already noticed.

From Drops of Rain

This process is happening all over the sky, but we get reflections only from those drops in the right positions to reflect light to us. The drops which send us red must therefore be in a line different from that of the violet-reflecting drops. The red from the last miss us, so to speak, and the same is the case with the violet from the " red " drops. And so we get the various bands of colour.

Next, what about the curve of the rainbow? To make the reason for this clear, imagine a string to run from the eye to, say, a " green " drop, and from it to the sun. Imagine, too, an airman holding the string at the point where it bends and flying through space, keeping the string tight the while. He will describe part of a circle. It is evident that all the drops through or near which the bend passes, and they only, are correctly placed to reflect green. And this is why the rainbow is curved.

What is Colour ?

From near sea-level the bow is semi-circular. But as we go higher up more of the circle becomes visible. From a balloon or very high mountain a complete circle of colours—one cannot in this instance speak of a bow—is seen.

It is hardly necessary to ask you whether you have ever blown a soap-bubble, for, of course, you have done so, probably many times. You took a colourless film of soap on a pipe and made it swell out into a globe, rendered

very beautiful by the different colours it displayed.

A drop of colourless oil falling on to a wet pavement spreads out into rings of different colours, like those of the soap bubble.

In both cases a substance which is neither blue, red, nor green, has been able to take on all these, and other colours. Nothing has been done to it except to make it spread itself out very thinly. Nothing has been added; nothing taken away.

Red and Green Reflections

Keeping this in mind, it will be easier to accept the statement that the colour of an object is not something put into it, like currants into a bun, but merely a certain arrangement of its atoms, which enables it to reflect or pass through it light-waves of a certain colour. If the state of the surface changes, the colour will change too. Cheap green paint tends to turn blue if exposed to weather and a strong light. A gate painted a pleasing red to start with may presently be clad in an unpleasant pink. And all of us know how dyed curtains are apt to " fade " in the sun.

Here is a geranium with green leaves and red flowers. The flowers take in all the colours of the sunlight except red, with which they will have nothing to do. So they reflect it, and we get the benefit. Similarly, the leaves take in all colours but green, and reflect that colour.

A white flower is unfriendly to light-waves of all colours, and reflects them all equally; while a black object is hungry for colours of all kinds, and gives back none at all to the eye.

Deceptive Colours

There is another interesting fact about colour, which is, that a thing will be dressed in its true day-light colour only when the light falling on it contains that colour. You must have noticed how red the clouds look at sun-

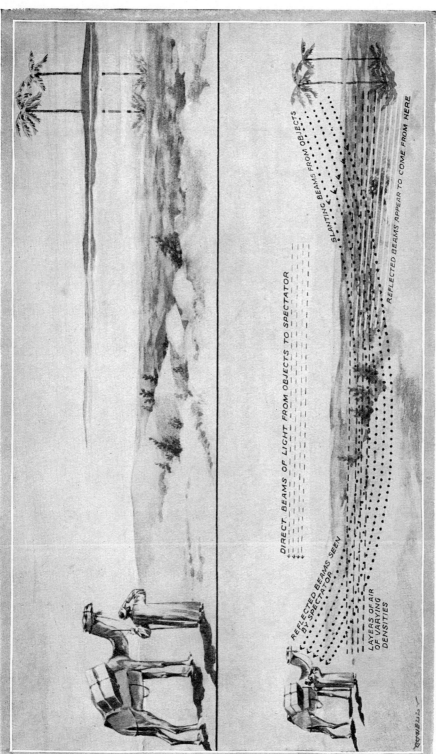

Specially drawn for this work.

DIRECT BEAMS OF LIGHT FROM OBJECTS TO SPECTATOR

SLANTING BEAMS FROM OBJECTS

REFLECTED BEAMS APPEAR TO COME FROM HERE

REFLECTED BEAMS SEEN BY SPECTATOR

LAYERS OF AIR OF VARYING DENSITIES

WHY THE BEDOUIN OF THE DESERT SEES A MIRAGE

Almost certainly you will have heard of desert mirages when an observer can see in the sky a landscape which he knows is really not there at all. This strange trick on the part of Nature is the outcome of rays of light being bent out of their course and is explained in the above pictorial diagram. In the desert the air is in layers both hot and cold, and one stratum of this air in reality acts during a mirage as a mirror to the human eye. In a mirage at sea the objects noted in the sky are invariably upside down, so that one might watch a ship apparently clinging funnel downwards to the clouds.

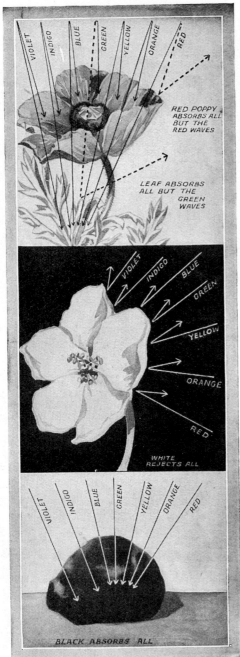

VIOLET INDIGO BLUE GREEN YELLOW ORANGE RED

RED POPPY ABSORBS ALL BUT THE RED WAVES

LEAF ABSORBS ALL BUT THE GREEN WAVES

VIOLET INDIGO BLUE GREEN YELLOW ORANGE RED

WHITE REJECTS ALL

VIOLET INDIGO BLUE GREEN YELLOW ORANGE RED

BLACK ABSORBS ALL

Specially drawn for this work.

HOW COLOUR AFFECTS FLOWERS

In the rainbow, in a drop of rain, in a soap bubble or in a splash of colourless oil on the pavement the order of the colours seen never varies. With our flowers, red blooms will take in all the hues of sunlight excepting red. Only a black object (third in the diagram) is hungry for all the colours.

set. They haven't themselves changed in any way to lose their mid-day fleecy whiteness, but the colour of the sunlight has. It has lost most of its violet and blue, and the red gets the upper hand.

Concerning Paints and Dyes

So far we have talked only of reflected colours. A word should be added about the colours of transparent objects, such as the red and green glasses of a railway signal. In this case the colour which the substance dislikes—if we may put it so—is allowed admittance, but is at once shown out through the back door! All other colours are captured and held prisoner.

Then what about paints and dyes? The first are merely substances for giving surfaces the power of reflecting this colour or that. Dyes bite deeper. A grain of indigo will stain a ton of water blue.

Cold Light

Glow-worms, fireflies, and some other beetles have the power of emitting light from parts of their bodies. Certain tiny living creatures, called bacteria, which swarm in decaying fish and rotting wood, possess the same property. And all of us are acquainted with that queer substance, phosphorus, used for making the hands of watches and other objects visible in the hours of darkness.

How these things produce their light is not known. It may be that they are able to change invisible ether waves into visible ones. Phosphorus undoubtedly can store up sunlight and give its energy out again.

By Living Lamplight

The strange thing is, that the light is not accompanied, like sunlight and artificial light, by heat, or at any rate, by measurable heat. The glow-worm possesses some secret which would win a fortune for any one who could discover it.

MARVELS OF SOUND

ONE OF MOTHER NATURE'S SOUNDING BOARDS

A very simple experiment in the movement of sound can be made when next you happen to see a length of solid tree trunk. If you listen carefully at one end by pressing your ear against the log you will hear clearly when your companion scratches the other end with a pin. Nor need he scratch heavily for the experiment to be successful.

HOW would you like to spend a holiday on the Moon? The idea may sound rather attractive. But there are some serious difficulties in the way, apart from that of getting to the " parish lantern." The moon is terribly cold, and you would be frozen to death in a few minutes, if you had not already died from lack of air. For there is no atmosphere on the moon.

Even if we could do altogether without heat and air, we should find the moon a very unsociable place, since it would be impossible there to talk with one another. Most sounds reach our ears through the air, and it therefore follows that, if we take air away, we become practically deaf.

Why the Tick is Loud

It would, however, not be quite correct to say that sound is a succession of *air* waves. To get things quite right, we should rather put it this way: that sound is waves in matter. Air is matter spread out very thinly, and for this reason is a poor conductor of sound as compared with liquids and solid bodies, in which the particles of matter are packed much more closely together. Haven't we all been annoyed sometimes by the loud ticking of a watch placed under the pillow, and removed the watch to a table or chair? The air between us and it being much less solid than the pillow, the watch now ceases to worry us.

Even thin string is a fine carrier of sound. Try this simple experiment: Tie a long, heavy poker to the middle of a piece of string, and press the ends of the string against the ears. If the poker be kept clear of the ground and struck, it will give out a deep booming note worthy of " Big Ben " himself.

Wood behaves even better than string. If you press your ear against one end of a big log, and someone scratches the other end lightly with a

Specially drawn for this work.

HOW STRING CARRIES SOUND

Tie a heavy poker to the middle of a length
of string and press the ends of the string
against your ears. When the poker strikes
gently against the table leg it will give forth
a deep booming note.

pin, you will hear the sounds easily.
Sir Charles Wheatstone, the inventor of
the first practical telegraph, used to
mystify people with what he called his
" Enchanted Lyre." It was nothing
more than a lyre-shaped sounding-
board, connected by a wooden rod with
a piano in another room. When the
piano was played, the sounds ran up
the rod and seemed to come from the
board.

Sounds under Water

The fisherman knows that the slightest splash will scare fish away, and he
is careful to drop his fly or float as
quietly as possible into the water. For
water, like other liquids, conducts sound
readily. This quality is of use to
mariners, as it enables sound-signals
to be sent farther and with greater
certainty than through air. In many
places, near a dangerous rock or shore,
a buoy of a special kind is moored to
the sea-bottom. As it bobs up and
down on the waves internal mechanism
keeps striking a bell inside it, surrounded by the water. The sounds of
the bell travel through the water in all
directions, and may be picked up by a
ship several miles away by means of a
pair of microphones below water and
connected with ear-pieces in the chart
room.

One microphone is on each side
of the ship, and only one of them is
used at a time. By using them alter-
nately the listener can easily tell
whether the buoy is to port or starboard of the ship, as he will hear the
sounds more clearly through the microphone on that side. Perhaps both may
give equally strong sounds, and then
he knows that the ship is heading
straight for the buoy.

Enough has now been said to show
that sound travels through matter, and
through matter only. It is therefore
quite different from the waves in the
ether—light waves, wireless waves, and
so on — to which matter is only a
hindrance.

Specially drawn for this work.

THE BELL BUOY WARNING TO SHIPS

Over dangerous reefs and in shallow channels bell buoys are placed to warn sailors. The bell is sounded automatically as the waves send the buoy dancing up and down, and the notes travel far afield in all directions. Sound moves well through water, and many ships carry microphones so that they can the more readily pick up the sonorous boom of the floating watchman. In addition to bells, these captive buoys often carry lights.

Sound under Discipline

If you drop a heavy book on to the floor you get one kind of sound. If you strike a bell you get sound of another sort. What is the difference between them?

The first is simply a jumble of air waves, producing what we call a mere noise. The second is a series of waves reaching the ear at regular intervals and giving rise to a musical note. One may compare the first to a galloping mob of horses, and the second to the measured tread of a body of soldiers marching in step.

A Curious Instrument

Almost any solid body will give out a note of its own if the conditions for doing so are right. There is a story

of a great musician who was staying with a friend in town. One day, on returning from a walk, he found that he had forgotten the number of the house, which formed part of a very long row. He got over the difficulty by going from house to house and drawing his foot gently over the door scrapers till he found one that sounded " A sharp." Then he knew where he was, for he *could* remember the note of his friend's door scraper.

The writer once heard an entertainer play tunes on things which he had picked off a rubbish heap. They included bones, bits of jampots, and glass bottles. Each had been selected for its natural note, and hung up in its proper place on a string, so that it could vibrate freely when struck.

Of course, an instrument—if such it may be called—of this kind is quite unsuitable for serious musical use. But its principles are found in the xylophone, which is merely a series of bars of wood fixed in a frame, and struck with little wooden hammers; and in the piano with a number of strings, each tightened till it emits a certain note if made to vibrate; and in the organ with every pipe of a certain length, so that the column of air inside it shall respond only to one note.

Notes and their Secrets

From the earliest times most musical instruments have fallen into one or other of two classes, the stringed instruments and the wind instruments. The piano is the most complicated member of the first class, as the organ is of the second class. In the violin, four strings are made to do the work of a much greater number on the piano. The performer, by pressing his finger down on a string here or there, can make it give out any one of a number of notes. Similarly, the cornet is able to replace many organ pipes, as by means of keys the player can give its tube any one of four lengths, and with each of these lengths he can produce any one of several different notes.

Has it ever struck you as at all curious that different kinds of instruments give out sounds of different qualities? One cannot possibly mistake a flute for a cornet or a violin. The reason for the difference is that any note contains smaller notes, called its harmonics, but how many of them are present depends on the instrument. A certain kind of apparatus changes musical notes into wavy lines drawn on paper. A note —say, middle C— would produce waves of one fixed *length*, whatever the instrument might be, but the *shapes* of the waves would differ with the instrument.

The Speed of Sound

One dark night, rather more than 100 years ago, a small group of men, holding very accurate watches in their hands, stood on a hill near Paris, looking for the flashes of a gun which was being fired, at intervals of ten

Specially drawn for this work.

WAVES OF SOUND WHEN A BELL RINGS

You will all know that when you toss a pebble into a pond circular ripples form which grow bigger and bigger until they reach the water's edge. Much the same thing occurs when you ring a bell, for the waves of sound increase in size as they travel farther away. A large circle of sound, however, decreases the volume, which is why at twice the distance from the bell you hear the clang only a quarter as loudly.

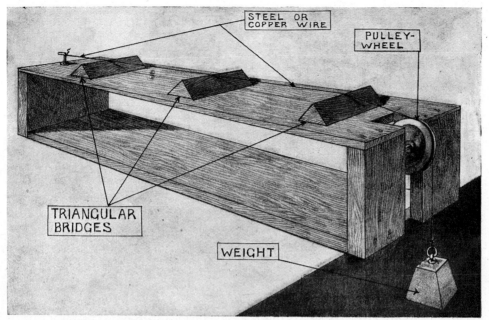

Specially drawn for this work.

THE PRINCIPLE OF THE FIDDLE STRING

Often you may have wondered just why you can obtain such a variety of notes from a one-stringed fiddle. The principle is explained in this diagram, which shows that the greater the stretching force on the wire the higher becomes the note produced. On the other hand, a short length of wire between two points gives a still higher note, and you may make interesting experiments by moving the triangular bridges in such a framework as is here illustrated.

minutes, on another hill about eleven miles away.

These men were making a careful experiment to find out the speed at which sound travels through air. As the distance had been measured exactly beforehand, and the speed of light is so great that the flash was seen at the moment when it left the gun, they had merely to divide the distance by the number of seconds elapsing between seeing the flash and hearing the report to get the answer. They took the average of twenty-four tests, and found the speed of sound through air to be · 1,120 feet a second.

Through Water and Steel

This speed is decidedly lower than that of a bullet fired from any army rifle. The bullet would reach a man a mile away two seconds before the report. In water, which is 800 times denser than air, the speed is nearly a mile a second;

and through steel sound travels four times faster than through water.

Many scientific facts which may seem of little importance in themselves have very useful applications. Here is a ship lying fog-bound off a dangerous coast. A station on shore is sending signals to her by strokes on a bell hanging in the water and, at the same moment, wireless signals. On the ship someone is picking up the sound signals through a microphone in the ship's side and the wireless signals with a wireless receiver. The wireless signals arrive instantaneously; the sound signals lag behind them. The delay in seconds, multiplied by the known speed of sound in water, tells the listener how far he is from the land station.

Echo and Its Uses

Among the many stories in old Greek mythology is one about a daughter of Air and Earth, named Echo. This young goddess offended Juno, the queen of heaven, and as a punishment she was struck dumb, except for the power of repeating any question put to her.

And this is why the reflection of a sound from a surface is called its echo. There are many places in the world where sounds are thrown to and fro between hillsides with wonderful clearness, and shouted words may be repeated twenty or thirty times.

Making Echoes Useful

Echo can be useful as well as amusing. If one measures the time that passes between the moment of making a sound and the arrival of its echo, one can calculate easily the distance away of the surface which throws back the sound.

It sometimes happens that an important drain or sewer gets blocked somewhere, perhaps by the sides collapsing. Should other methods of finding the exact position of the obstruction fail, echo is resorted to. A pistol is discharged in a manhole and the echo is timed. If the echo arrives, say, a second after the report, the block must be 560 feet away, that is, *half* the distance that sound travels through air in a second. For the report has had to reach the block and come back again.

A new kind of apparatus for taking soundings at sea works on the same principle. A sound signal is made under water and the time of its echo from the sea bottom is measured. The apparatus is so accurate that it may be relied on when there are only a few fathoms of water under the ship's keel, and it has the great advantage over other depth-finders of giving continuous soundings while the ship is moving fast.

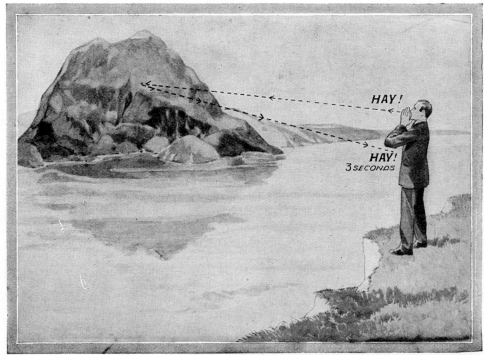

Specially drawn for this work.

MEASURING DISTANCE BY ECHO

An echo is like a reflection of sound, for it is sound thrown back to its source by some substance with which it meets, such as a hillside. It is possible to calculate distances by noting the period of time occupied by sound in reaching the surface which throws it back and returning to you in the form of an echo.

How
Steam and
Petrol
Work for Man

The Story
of our
British
Railways

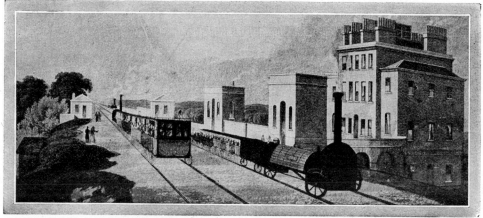

Rischgitz.

MORE THAN ONE HUNDRED YEARS AGO

The above reproduction, after a picture by Calvert painted at the time, shows trains running on the Liverpool and Manchester Railway. Though the Stockton and Darlington line is actually our oldest iron road, it was the system here illustrated that really set the steam locomotive on its path to triumph. This line was opened in 1830.

THE EARLY DAYS OF STEAM

ABOUT 4,000 years ago, Cheops, King of Egypt, decided to build for himself a tomb that should be the greatest tomb of all time. An army of workmen, including practically all his male subjects, and no doubt a large number of prisoners of war, were put on to the work. They hewed huge stones weighing up to 60 tons apiece, in the quarries near Assuan, in Upper Egypt, dragged them to the banks of the Nile, loaded them on boats, floated them hundreds of miles down-stream, unloaded them again, and hauled them to the site of the Great Pyramid.

How this vast mass of stone, weighing nearly seven million tons, was put together we do not know for certain. But we may be sure that most of the hard work was done by human muscles, and that thousands of men must have died from hardship and exhaustion before the great burial place was completed.

Brains and Labour

To-day, if we can imagine anyone foolish enough to copy Pharaoh, steam would be used to quarry and carry the stones, and lift them into position. A man with his hand on a lever would take the place of a gang of perhaps hundreds of hard-driven slaves, hauling on ropes under the burning Egyptian sun. A small fraction of the men impressed by Cheops would, aided by Giant Steam, do the work in much less time. Brains would direct, and steam would labour.

Though steam now has powerful rivals in electricity generated by water power and the internal combustion engine burning fuel in its own cylinders, it still does most of the hard work of the world. It moves ourselves and the things we need from place to place by land and sea; it drives the machinery of millions of factories, either directly

Rischgitz.

A MODEL OF NEWCOMEN'S ENGINE

The model illustrated, to be seen in the Museum of King's College, London, is one of a pumping engine brought out by Thomas Newcomen, who was born at Dartmouth in 1663. A great see-saw beam, one end of which was connected to a pump and the other to a piston, was the chief feature of this engine.

or with electricity generated by it; it raises minerals from the bowels of the earth; it digs our canals; it pumps our water; and does a thousand other things which help to make life less laborious and more pleasant.

There is a story told of George Stephenson that is worth relating. He and a friend were one day watching a locomotive haul a train. "What moves the train?" asked Stephenson. "The engine," was the reply. "And what moves the engine?" "Why, the steam, to be sure." "And what produces the steam?" "Coal." "Yes! But what produced the coal?"

Stephenson himself had to answer his last question: "The sun, my friend!"

Bottled-up Energy

Stephenson was right. The sun heat of far distant ages gave life to the vegetation which afterwards became coal, bottling up, as it were, the energy of the sun. In the boiler furnace this energy is released and imparted to water, changing it into steam, the pressure of which gives motion to engines of many kinds.

The power of steam was realised many centuries ago. The earliest apparatus which used it in any way was probably invented by Hero, of Alexandria, about 120 B.C. Hero made a hollow metal sphere, and mounted it on two supports with curved ends which entered holes bored at two opposite points in its "equator." One of the supports was hollow, and led steam into the sphere from a boiler beneath. The steam spurted out through two short bent tubes at the "poles," and the push-off it gave the air made the sphere spin rapidly.

It is curious that many centuries had to pass after the invention of this toy—it was nothing more—before steam was put to any practical use. We have to stride almost to the end of the seventeenth century to take up the tale.

At that time the mining of coal and other minerals was being carried out on a considerable scale in many parts of Britain. But it was sadly hampered by the difficulty of keeping the mines free of water. We are told that at one Cornish mine over 500 horses were employed in turning machines which lifted water in great buckets up the shafts. The deeper a mine, the greater was the expense of unwatering it, and the depth to which mine owners found it profitable to go was, therefore, very limited.

Pumping by Steam

About this time—in 1698—a Mr. Thomas Savery invented a steam pumping engine. It consisted of a metal vessel placed near the water to be raised. Steam was blown into it and then condensed by flooding the vessel with cold water outside. A vacuum being thus formed inside, the pressure of the air forced water up into the vessel. Then steam was turned in again to drive the water out through the delivery pipe. These two operations were repeated over and over again.

A few years later one Thomas Newcomen brought out another, and much more successful, pumping engine. He mounted a great see-saw beam at the top of the shaft. A heavy rod, running down to a pump at the bottom of the mine, was hung from one end, while the other was connected to a piston working in an upright, open-ended steam cylinder. The weight of the rod pulled the piston upwards, and the pressure of the air forced it downwards when steam under it was condensed at the end of the upstroke. Though it used a great deal of steam, and therefore was costly to run, the Newcomen engine opened up a new era in mining. There is a case of one of these old engines remaining at work for 150 years!

Watt and the Kettle

A far greater man than Newcomen now appears on the scene—James Watt. We all know the story about Watt and the tea kettle—how the jumping of the lid drew his attention to the power of steam. Unfortunately the same story is told of other inventors, so there may be nothing in it. But Watt undoubtedly was a very observant person. He thirsted for exact

By permission of the Science Museum, London.

PUMPING BY HIGH PRESSURE

Richard Trevithick, a Cornish mining engineer, was the first man to invent a high-pressure steam pump. An engine of this type is here depicted, and similar ones were in use for generations in the mining districts of Cornwall and South Wales.

knowledge about the properties of steam, and set out to make the steam engine useful to man in many ways. He succeeded so well in doing this that he is with good reason called the "Father of the steam engine." He found it a crude machine, able merely to move a beam up and down: he left it a well-thought-out device, able to revolve shafts and drive machinery, fitted with a governor for controlling its speed, and using steam much more economically than Newcomen's pumping engine.

Poor Watt was at times almost driven to distraction by the difficulty of making his cylinders circular. In the later half of the eighteenth century there were no lathes for turning and boring large metal parts, and Watt had to rely on the skill of his workmen in beating a cylinder by hand out of sheet iron, or casting it of true shape. In writing to a friend he says with some satisfaction that a cylinder 18 inches in diameter was only $\frac{3}{8}$ inch bigger one way than the other! To-day, a much larger cylinder would be rejected if its bore were $\frac{1}{100}$ inch out of truth anywhere; and, when we come to motor car cylinders, the allowance is far smaller still. Watt and his predecessors were in much the same position as you would be if you were asked to carve a wooden panel nicely with an axe. All the more credit to them for their success!

The invention of what are called machine tools, early in the nineteenth century, was an enormous help to engineers, especially to those building steam engines. Metal could then be turned, bored, and planed with accuracy, and we hear no more of such things as pistons being packed with pieces of old hat to keep them steam-tight, or of the tops of cylinders being made of wood.

To Replace the Horse

While Watt was busy on the stationary engine—one which is fixed to the ground—other people had an eye on Giant Steam as a substitute for wind power on the sea and horse power on land.

About the year 1776 there was launched on a river in France the first *steamboat*. It was about 150 feet long,

Rischgitz.

LEARNED FROM A KETTLE LID

James Watt, who was born at Greenock in Scotland in 1736, first had his attention drawn to the power of steam by watching the jumping lid of a tea kettle. As a boy he was very delicate, and so spent most of his time at home. He is shown above making his first experiment with a kettle, aided by his mother. The picture is after a painting by G. W. Buss.

BY BEAM AND WHEEL IN 1788

Pioneers of steam motive power were mainly in search of a powerful appliance for pumping water. At this period, at one Cornish mine, no fewer than 500 horses were employed in turning machines for lifting water in buckets. The appliance shown here was fashioned by Matthew Boulton, a Birmingham man who became the partner of James Watt, and was known as Boulton and Watt's Rotative Beam Engine, because it caused a wheel to be turned in conjunction with the beam—a vital step towards the building of a locomotive.

weighed as many tons, and had a big paddle wheel on either side. But as the village blacksmith of the place had constructed the engines with his rude tools, the ship was not a success. Several American and British inventors afterwards built small steamboats which, at any rate, managed to move themselves through the water; and in 1807 Robert Fulton, an American, put his *Clermont*, the first steamboat to carry passengers, into service on the East River, New York.

Marching on the Tides

The early steamboats burned wood as fuel, and flames often rose from their funnels. We have a rather amusing account of the effect that this "new-fangled steam-kettle," the *Clermont*, had on spectators. "Notwithstanding the wind and tide were averse to its approach," we read, "they saw with astonishment that it was rapidly coming towards them; and when it came so near that the noise of the machinery and paddles was heard, the crews in some instances shrank beneath their decks from the terrific sight, and left their vessels to go on shore; while others prostrated themselves, and besought Providence to protect them from the approach of the horrible monster which was marching on the tides, and lighting its path by the fires which it vomited."

Henry Bell's *Comet*, which began to

BRITAIN'S FIRST PASSENGER STEAMSHIP

Rischgitz.

In this picture we see the original engine of the first British passenger-carrying steamer, *Comet*, built by Henry Bell, who ran her on the River Clyde and then took her round Gt. Britain and Ireland. The ship was 40 feet in length, and the engine, which operated paddle-wheels, was of about 3 horse power. The portrait is that of John Robinson, the engineer.

RAILWAY ENGINES—Plate 1—EARLIEST TYPES

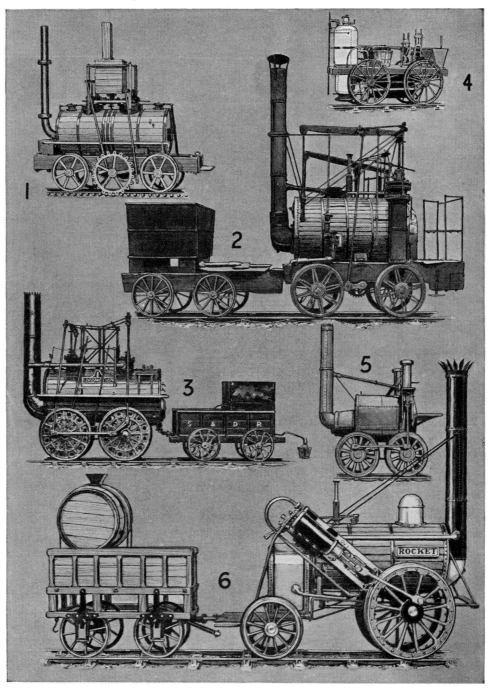

In the Science Museum at Kensington some of the earliest locomotives ever built are still preserved: 1. Blenkinsop's engine built in 1812 had a geared tooth wheel which engaged in notches on one of the rails. 2. "Puffing Billy," designed by William Hedley in 1813. 3. George Stephenson's "Locomotion," the first to run on the Stockton & Darlington Railway, 1825. 4. The "Novelty," designed by John Braithwaite and John Ericsson in 1829. 5. "Sans Pareil," built by Timothy Hackworth, 1829. 6. Most famous of all, Stephenson's "Rocket," winner of the Rainhill competition in 1829.

RAILWAY ENGINES—Plate 2—BRITISH

Though the old names of the different companies have gone and "British Railways" appears instead, the same types of locomotive are still in regular use. Here, with their old identities we see, at the top, a locomotive of the "King Class," which hauls the well-known Cornish Riviera and other expresses. Just below is one of the 3-cylinder A/2/1 expresses employed in taking heavy passenger trains over such steep gradients as those between Edinburgh and Aberdeen. The third is the "City of Leicester" belonging to the "Princess Coronation" class. The locomotive at the bottom is one of the "West Country" class, Southern Region.

Although the locomotives employed in long runs across whole continents differ in certain particulars from those used on the comparatively short runs on British railways, their general form and design is much the same. The main difference is in weight, since trains up to 3,000 tons have to be taken up long, steep gradients and heavier engines up to 400 tons are required. Our picture shows at the top a South Australian locomotive; immediately below is a Selkirk class engine of the Canadian-Pacific Railway. The third is employed on the Pennsylvania Railway, U.S.A., while the fourth is a freight locomotive of the Texas and Pacific Railway, U.S.A.

Some unusual types of locomotives have been designed to meet special demands in certain parts of the world. The "Garratt" engine at the top has extended girder frames; it is used on the Kenya-Uganda Railway. The one below, a 4-cylinder engine, has the tender fitted with a booster, and is in use on the Delaware-Hudson Railway. The third picture is a "Fairlie" type "two engines in one" employed on the Festiniog Railway, N. Wales, on a 1 foot 11½ inch gauge. The bottom illustration shows a "Shay" 12-wheeled locomotive, driven by gearing by three vertical cylinders, used on the Peru Railways.

OUR EARLIEST ROAD ENGINE

It is difficult now to realise what our roads would be like without vehicles propelled by motive power contained within themselves. To appreciate the above print, however, we must imagine indifferent highways used only by horses and cumbersome coaches or wagons. To such roads Richard Trevithick brought a carriage moved along by this curious steam engine.

ply on the River Clyde in 1812, was the first European passenger steamboat. By 1820 over thirty British steam vessels were in use, and the American steamer *Savannah*—she also carried sails—had crossed and re-crossed the Atlantic. Since that year steam has been steadily ousting sail, and a sailing ship of any great size is now almost a rare sight.

The Railway Locomotive

Many men share the glory of developing the railway locomotive, but to a Cornishman, Richard Trevithick, belongs the credit of building the first. This was put into use on a mine tramway near Merthyr Tydvil, South Wales, on February 15th, 1804. Despite its queer appearance, it contained all the chief arrangements of a modern locomotive, and hauled a train of 10 tons of iron and seventy persons nine miles.

But its weight broke the iron rails,

and the Welshmen would have no more of it. So for the second stage of the locomotive's history we have to go to the North of England, where Blenkinsop, Hedley, and George Stephenson in succession improved it for hauling coal wagons. In 1825 it appeared on the first public steam railway—that between Stockton and Darlington; and when the Liverpool and Manchester Railway, the first passenger steam railroad, was completed in 1830, it finally established itself as a rival to the stage horse.

Having brought the history of steam so far, we must leave it, for its later chapters belong to the stories of the railway and the steamship, given elsewhere in this work. In conclusion, the reader is reminded that if he visits the Science Museum, South Kensington, London, he can see there some of the actual engines of which we have written, as well as working models of them.

By permission of the Science Museum, London.

FOR EXPRESS PASSENGER TRAINS

In this picture we see a model of an express passenger engine as used on the London and South-Western Railway about the beginning of the century. These locomotives, with their bell-shaped smoke-stacks and extended bogie platforms, had a great turn of speed, but loads were much lighter in their time. The weight of these engines was not much more than half that of the modern mainline locomotives, many types of which are shown in the following pages.

AS USED ON EARLY RAILWAYS

George Stephenson built his first locomotive in 1814 and it was his " Locomotion " engine which was the first to run on the Stockton and Darlington railway in 1825. Succeeding locomotives were steadily improved and in this picture we see a model of one with a long boiler, built by Stephenson in 1845.

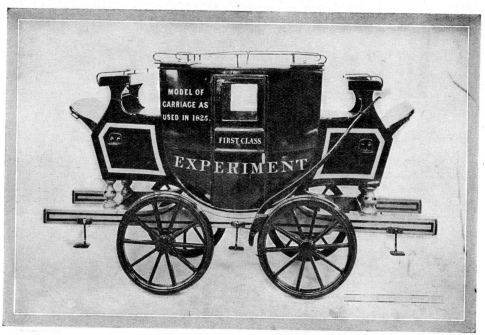

Photos by permission of the Science Museum, London.

Our early railways were very much influenced by the stage coach, and the pioneers of the iron road were inclined at first to adopt the old coach design for the new rail travel. Here we have the model of a first-class carriage, as run on the Stockton and Darlington Railway.

THE ROMANCE OF THE IRON ROAD

CELEBRATING A RAILWAY CENTENARY

The Times.

To celebrate the centenaries of the opening of King's Cross Station, London, and of the " Towns Line," the Centenaries Express was arranged by the Eastern Region of British Railways and a group of railway enthusiasts in October, 1952. The train was hauled by the class A4 streamlined locomotive " Sir Nigel Gresley " and is seen here speeding through Hadley Wood on its way to York.

IF when you are cycling you happen to pass over a stretch of soft ground, you find yourself compelled to pedal hard. The wheels must compress the ground in front of them until it will bear them, and this has much the same effect as riding uphill. Directly you get on to hard ground again, the work that your legs have to do becomes much lighter, since no effort is now wasted on packing down the surface.

As with bicycles, so with vehicles of all kinds, and hence the introduction of roads. But keeping a road hard and level is an expensive matter, as the whole width of it must be in equally good condition since wheels may pass over any part of it.

How Rails Came

Many years ago it occurred to some-one to use two hard *strips* of stone or wood for coal wagons **to** run over between a colliery and the wharf at which the coal was shot into ships. A foot or so for each line of wheels was all that was needed, and these narrow strips could be kept in repair fairly cheaply.

The next stage was to use cast-iron plates with turned-up rims, called flanges, along their edges. The rims prevented the wagons going astray and saved a lot of time.

A little later it was decided to put the flanges on the wheels instead of on the plates, and to use narrow, deep rails instead of wide plates. Here was another saving, as the actual wheel-track was reduced to a few inches of width, less metal was needed, and there were fewer breakages.

In a Hundred Years

And so we got the railway, which is kept in order by men still called *plate-layers*, because the first of their kind laid flat plates for wheels to run on.

Out of the small colliery railway

worked by horses has developed the railway as we know it. What would a man living in 1825, when passenger trains were still a dream of the future, have thought if he had been told that, when a hundred years had passed, there would be over 750,000 miles of track with continuous parallel steel bars laid on it, each yard of bar weighing 70 to 100 pounds ? That these tracks would run from the Atlantic coast of Europe to the Pacific coast of Asia. That they would traverse the American Continent in many places. That they would form a network in every civilised and thickly-populated country; climb over lofty mountain ranges, cross rivers, lakes, swamps and even the open sea. That along them huge steam engines, weighing up to 450 tons apiece, would haul passengers at a speed of a mile a minute or more amid luxurious surroundings, and at a price much lower than that charged for a seat on a stage coach. That a man might take his evening meal in New York and his breakfast next morning at Chicago, 900 miles away, after a night spent comfortably in bed.

It would have strained his powers of belief, we fancy.

But one must not forget the hundred years. Not till 1844 was the third-class passenger legally entitled to have a roof over his head, and a seat to sit on, while travelling on the railway, and even then the sides of a carriage were without windows. The railway companies seem to have treated him as an interloper, too mean to take a first-class or second-class ticket. It is said that one company went so far as to hire sweeps to enter third-class carriages, and drovers to drive pigs into them, to make things even more uncomfortable than they were without such invasions!

Copyright.

A MODERN LOCOMOTIVE AND ITS ANCESTOR

No picture could show more clearly the advance made in engine construction over a period of more than a century than this photograph of two British locomotives. On the left is " City of Birmingham," one of the " Coronation " class streamline locomotives. On the right is the historic engine " Rocket."

INSIDE THE DRIVER'S CAB

Left-hand drive for all locomotives has become standardised on British Railways. Previously it had varied on different lines. In this photograph the standard driving cab is seen from the inside. The figures marked on the illustration show : 1. The regulator, controlling the admission of steam to the cylinders ; it has the same effect as a car's accelerator. 2. The vacuum brake lever applies the brakes right down the train ; the guard also has a lever, and a passenger can apply the brakes by pulling the " communication cord." 3. The steam brake lever applies the brakes on the engine only. 4. The whistle ; there is another lever on the right of the cab, so that the fireman can also operate it. 5. Reversing gear. This wheel alters the " cut off " (period of steam admission). At high speeds an engine works on " early cut off " ; at low speeds on " late cut off." If moved far enough the motion is reversed. 6. Sand ; with this lever the driver blows steam down the sand-pipe, forcing a spray of sand under the driving wheels, giving them a grip when starting up on a wet rail. There are two sets of sand-pipes, one for forward and one for reverse running.

SCHOOLS FOR RAILWAY SIGNALMEN

There are many important and responsible tasks to be done by the men who keep our railways working efficiently. Few posts demand more care than that of a signalman in a main line box. In recent years new technical schools have been opened in different railway centres in Britain where future signalmen receive training on a full size track.

Photos : Topical Press.

In the top photograph on this page a pupil at the Bristol school for training signalmen is receiving instruction on the working of a signal lever. The lower picture shows a class being instructed in the working of hand generating joining points. A class takes a three months' intensive course on all aspects of signal working.

Corridor Trains

The corridor train did not come to England till about 1892, bringing with it the dining-car and the sleeping-car. Any long-distance traveller now enjoys a well-padded seat, electric lighting, steam heating, good ventilation and a restaurant car. On some of the " super " trains of the world luxury runs to drawing-room cars, library cars, barbers' shops and bathrooms. In fact, it would be rather difficult to think out any way of making railway travelling more comfortable than it is already.

Railway Engineering

Many of the world's greatest engineering feats have been connected with the building of railways. There are bridges such as those over the Forth, the St. Lawrence, the Zambezi at Victoria Falls, the Mississippi at St. Louis, the Menai Strait and Niagara Falls. Then we have viaducts such as that across the Sioule River in France, 435 feet high; the 27½-mile Lucin Cut-off crossing Salt Lake, Utah; and the Key West Extension of the Florida East Coast Railway which runs 114 miles out into the Bay of Florida.

All of the world's longest tunnels were drilled through mountain ranges to serve the railway. In the Alps we have the Simplon (12½ miles), St. Gothard (9¼ miles), Loetschberg (9 miles), Mont Cenis (8½ miles), and Arlberg (6⅓ miles). In New Zealand is the Otira or Arthur's Pass Tunnel, 5¼ miles long. Nor must we forget the Severn Tunnel, driven not through rock, but through gravel and clay, right under the River Severn. It may be described as 4½ miles of almost superhuman difficulties overcome.

The Romance of the Rail

There is hardly a great railway in the world the making of which does not

Central Press.

A STANDARD TYPE FOR BRITISH RAILWAYS

In use on British Railways are some 400 different types of locomotives. Gradually some of these will disappear and, instead, standard types of locomotives will be used on all British Railways. The first of the twelve standard types, the " Britannia," a new express locomotive, made its first run early in 1951, and is seen above. It embodies the best features of many other designs.

CROSSING THE FORTH BRIDGE

Fox Photos.

Across the Firth of Forth on the east side of Scotland is one of the longest bridges in the world. It was constructed in 1882–90 to make direct connection between Edinburgh and the north side of the Forth and to avoid the long detour which had previously to be made to continue northwards. In this photograph we see the famous " Cock o' the North " locomotive taking the passenger train from London across the Forth Bridge.

TRAINS FOR HOLIDAY-MAKERS

The " Devon Belle " is one of the best-known of Britain's special holiday trains and is composed of all Pullman coaches, with every seat a restaurant seat.   The train is drawn by a locomotive carrying a distinctive headboard, with red wings on each side of the boiler casing, bearing the name.

Fox Photos.

As part of its holiday attractions the " Devon Belle " has an observation car at the rear of the train. This has been specially designed to give passengers a better view of the lovely Devon scenery through which they travel.   The train runs from Waterloo Station to Devonshire resorts.

"SILVER JUBILEE" AND "GOLDEN ARROW"

Central Press.

Despite the tendency on the railways, as elsewhere, towards standardisation, many different types of locomotives are still required according to the work for which they are designed. The "Silver Jubilee" locomotive, seen above, is among the leading express engines in Britain.

Fox Photos.

Another famous name in railway history is the "Golden Arrow," the Continental express train which takes business men and holiday-makers on the first stage of the journey from London to France and other countries of Europe. The photograph above was taken at Victoria Station, London.

afford a romantic story. In practically every case great physical obstacles had to be surmounted. The very spying-out of the land by the surveyors entrusted with selecting the best route has often needed feats of mountaineering and exploration which have gone unnoticed merely because they were parts of the surveyor's job. When the Canadian Pacific Railway was being built, men spent ten years or so finding a way through the Rocky Mountains and parallel ranges. Hundreds of times they had to take their lives in their hands, crawling along narrow ledges, hanging over dizzy precipices, and crossing dangerous ice-fields. Several lives were lost before the survey ended. The difficulty of the work is shown by the fact that the surveyors were the first men, white or brown, to find a way through some of the country afterwards crossed by the railway.

The hardships of railway surveying are by no means confined to mountains. The laying out of a line through waterless deserts, unhealthy swamps and dense forests brings with it much suffering from thirst, hunger, and disease. Plotting a route for the Grand Trunk Pacific Railway in Canada entailed fighting a way for hundreds of miles through a tangle of standing and fallen trees. One must not forget that the engineer responsible for this work has all the time to be taking measurements, recording levels, and gathering information which, if incorrectly given, may mean the wasting of large sums of money later on.

Laying the Sleepers

So whenever we travel over a railway taken across country that we should not like to go through on foot because of its dangerous or inhospitable character, we should spare a thought for the brave and patient men who spent

Topical Press.

A MAIN LINE DIESEL-ELECTRIC LOCOMOTIVE

It is only in very recent years that diesel-electric engines have been brought into service on British Railways. The first of these was the " L.M.S. 10,000," and the photograph above shows the locomotive just before beginning its run from Euston Station.

WHEN ROYALTY TRAVELS

Queen Victoria made her first railway journey in June, 1842 and soon afterwards special carriages were designed for Royal journeys. The Great Western Jubilee Train of 1897 was the first to have a corridor throughout. In the photograph above is seen the day compartment of Queen Alexandra's saloon, built in 1903 and used by Royal travellers for some 40 years.

Photos : British Railways.

The changes in furnishing and decorating styles which have come about in the intervening years can be seen in the comparison between two Queen's saloons seen on this page. In the lower picture is the lounge of the present Queen's saloon now in use for Royal journeys on British Railways. The vehicle itself was constructed by the L.M.S.R. in 1941.

months, and perhaps years, preparing the plans on which the actual work of construction was based.

And we should think, too, of the army of men who followed them, blasting away rock, cutting great trenches through rising ground and along hillsides, collecting earth into embankments, building bridges over rivers and chasms, and driving piles into swamps to support a track; and of the gangs who formed the bed, and on it laid sleepers, and to the sleepers fixed the rails and so made the path ready for the " iron horse."

In the main, rail-making in the wilderness is peaceful, if trying, work. But it is not always so. When the Union Pacific Railway, the first railway to cross the American continent, was being built during the sixties of last century, the Indians gave a great deal of trouble. It has been said that they shot an arrow for every spike that was driven into a sleeper. Perhaps this is merely a picturesque way of describing their many attacks on the white workers, who had to be as handy with the rifle as with the pick and shovel. Many a desperate fight took place between " paleface " and " redskin," and victory did not always lie with the first, as many a lonely grave beside the track witnessed.

The Klondike Line

Jumping thirty years and some thousands of miles we find ourselves in Alaska, where, in 1898 and 1899, a railway rather more than 100 miles long was built from Skaguay, on the seashore, over the terrible White Pass. Many men, and thousands of wretched horses, had died in the mad rush of gold seekers to the newly found goldfields of the Klondike while climbing over this snow-clad and precipitous slope.

Then the railwaymen took things in hand. They blasted a way up the hills, sometimes roped together and standing

British Railways.

POWER SIGNALLING AT EUSTON STATION

Euston was the first main-line terminus in London and was opened on July 20th, 1837. Many changes have been made since then and here we see the interior of the signal-box which came into use in 1953. The photograph shows the 227-lever frame, illuminated diagrams, train describers, block bells, telephones and other apparatus.

ON THE TRANS=AUSTRALIAN RUN

The Trans-Australian Railway runs for 1,051 miles between Port Augusta and Kalgoorlie and helps to link up Perth, capital of Western Australia, with Adelaide, capital of South Australia. Across the great Nullarbor Plain the heat may be intense, but in the lounge of the express it is cool and comfortable, with afternoon tea making a pleasant diversion.

Photos : Camera Press.

Here is another diversion on the long journey across the Plain as the passengers gather in the lounge for community singing in the evening. Spacious sleeping cabins with hot and cold showers are among the amenities provided for the comfort of passengers. The Trans-Australian Railway was opened in 1917, a mule-drawn mail coach being one of the principal means of transport until then.

E.N.A.

AN EARLY AMERICAN PASSENGER TRAIN

After the opening of the first passenger railway in Britain other countries were not slow to adopt the new system of transport. In the U.S.A. the first regular steam railway was opened in 1831. Their locomotives developed special features of their own, as seen in this photograph of the first passenger train to be operated on the Rock Island Railway in 1852. Wood was burnt as fuel.

on logs chained to the rock, sometimes on platforms hung from ropes. During the winter they had to work in icy winds, when the thermometer showed 50 to 70 degrees of frost, so numbed with cold that they could hardly hold their tools. In places snow 30 feet deep had to be cleared away, and everything needed for the work was carried up steep zig-zag paths on men's backs.

Afloat in a Tank

Another picture. We are now in the early years of this century, and have been transported to a chain of coral islands forming stepping-stones from the southern tip of Florida to Key West, a hundred miles away in the waters of the Bay of Florida. Thousands of men are engaged in making a railway across these islands, and joining the gaps by great viaducts built in the shallow water between them. Many of the men live on large two-storey houseboats.

A hurricane sweeps across the Bay. Several houseboats are carried away. One runs aground and most of the men aboard are drowned.

Two more go out to sea. Of the forty-nine men on them one man

British Railways.

THE PRINCESS ANNE LOCOMOTIVE

Named after the Queen's daughter, the " Princess Anne " is a four-cylinder reciprocating locomotive of the " Princess " class and is numbered 46,202.

escapes alive. A cement barge is torn from her moorings and blown out into the Atlantic. The solitary man in charge loosens the water-tank on the deck and gets into it. The barge sinks under him, but the tank keeps afloat, and several days later he reaches land in the Bahamas, after surely as strange a voyage as ever man made in the open sea.

Yes! There is plenty of romance and not a little danger about the building of railways.

Railways with Teeth

Some railways are so steep that ordinary locomotives could not take trains over them. To get the necessary grip, toothed racks are laid between the wheel rails, and cogwheels on the engine claw their way along them.

These rack railways, as they are called, scale several well-known mountains—such as Snowdon in Wales, Pilatus in Switzerland and Pike's Peak in the United States. The last is the highest and longest of its kind, climbing about 7,005 feet in nine miles to a height of over 14,000 feet above the sea.

Next to it comes the electric line that burrows its way up the great mountain mass crowned by the Jungfrau. We say " burrows," because the uppermost six and a quarter miles of it are in a tunnel, driven not far from the surface of the rock. Thus protected, avalanches cannot injure it.

Here and there, at the stations, openings are made to give passengers a view of the glorious scenery.

Travel on these railways is very slow, as the rails rise 1 foot in every 4, or even 3 feet. So the locomotive has to work very hard going up; and coming down it must move with extreme caution to check the carriages, which are always on the uphill side of it.

Australian News and Information Bureau.

AN AUSTRALIAN INTER-STATE EXPRESS

The C.38 passenger engines of the New South Wales Government weigh 200 tons, carry 14 tons of coal, 8,100 gallons of water, and maintain a speed of 70 miles an hour on straight runs. Our photograph shows the Melbourne-bound inter-state express. Crews for these trains are specially selected and receive higher rates of pay.

But the rack railways are not the highest climbers among railways. For these we must go to South America, where three railways without racks beat the Pike's Peak track. First among them is the Antofagasta and Bolivia Railway, which conquers the Andes at a point 15,817 feet above the sea—a few feet higher than the summit of Europe's loftiest mountain, Mt. Blanc.

Over the Mountains

Some hundreds of miles north the Oroya-Lima line surmounts the same range through a tunnel driven at an elevation of 15,665 feet, which makes it the world's highest tunnel. This line was a marvellous feat of engineering. It runs continuously up hill from the port of Callao, in Peru, to the Galera tunnel mentioned, and then descends gently a couple of thousand feet to its terminus at Oroya. A car can travel 100 miles from the tunnel to the sea by gravity only—the longest " coast " in the world. One who made the journey on a light truck said of it: " You start under the eye of the eternal snows, and you finish among humming birds and palms."

The railway was begun in 1870 by an American contractor, Henry Meiggs. As far as the tunnel it follows the gorge of the River Rimac, running on ledges cut in the cliffs, leaping the chasm here and there by bridges built at dizzy heights by sailors. One of these bridges connects two tunnels on opposite sides of the ravine. It is indeed a very wonderful line.

Central Press.

MAKING A NEW UNDERGROUND RAILWAY STATION

Work on the extension of the Central London Underground line from Liverpool Street had begun when war broke out. Completed sections of the tunnel were then used as an aircraft factory, and in this photograph workmen are seen drilling the old railway line then used, while the new Underground rails can be seen below. The section shown here is now Gant's Hill Station, finally completed and opened to the public in 1948.

Central Press.

ONE OF LONDON'S UNDERGROUND STATIONS

Engineers and architects from all parts of the world have visited the great Underground " Con-
course " at Gant's Hill Station on the Central Line extension from London. The lofty domed
hall, seen in this photograph, is 40 feet below ground level, and is 150 feet long and 20 feet high. The
white ceiling, illumined by strip lighting, is supported by sixteen pillars.

Mole Railways

From these lofty railways we plunge
well below-sea-level into the wonderful
" tube " railways of London. These
underground railways are called
" tubes " because they run through
circular tunnels lined with iron from
end to end, there being a separate
tunnel for each track. The first of
them, the City and South London Railway, was opened in 1890. Since then
they have been added to and extended
by stages, until at the present time they
include 72 miles or so of tunnel.

They burrow through clay and gravel
under London at a depth averaging
about 100 feet below the streets, which
they follow in most places. The engineers who made them used a kind of
mechanical mole, the Greathead shield,
so named after its inventor. It may be
described as a short cylinder, rather
larger across than the tunnel, with a
sharp cutting edge in front.

Through the " Air-Locks "

The men inside dig away the ground
ahead of it, and the lining is put in
behind it, the tail end always overlapping a ring or two of the finished
lining. When the shield has to be advanced it is forced forward by hydraulic
rams, pushing backwards against the
lining. Some of the shields had revolving cutters to slice away the ground.
Where water proved troublesome, the
tunnel was walled across and filled with
air at a pressure sufficient to keep the
water out. Men and materials passed in
or out through chambers with a door
at each end, called air-locks.

Most of the " tubes " were driven
from several places at once to save time.
Though the tunnels twisted both side-

ways and up and down, the shields were steered so cleverly that they came together with wonderful accuracy.

In the days when the Metropolitan and District Railways in London were steam railways, the tunnels were at times filled with stifling fumes, especially in hot weather.

The "tube" railways, much deeper down and much more difficult to ventilate, could not have been worked by steam. It was the electric haulage of trains that made them possible, for electricity may be generated in one place and used in another place, provided that a conductor joins the two places. Whereas a steam locomotive must itself create the power it uses, an electric locomotive has a partner, the power station, to feed it, and all the dirt and smoke connected with the burning of coal is kept far from the train.

Our State-owned "British Railways"

At various stages in the history of Britain's railways the smaller companies have been absorbed or amalgamated with the larger ones. After the war of 1914–18 they were formed into four main-line companies: London, Midland and Scottish; London and North Eastern; Great Western; and Southern. Then during the last war the government inevitably controlled all railways, until, on January 1st, 1948, they passed finally under the ownership of the State.

All our railways, with a very few exceptions, now belong to British Railways, though they still remain in similar groups as under the former companies: the London Midland Region; Western Region; Southern Region; the North Eastern Region; the Eastern Region; and the Scottish Region.

The exceptions mentioned are chiefly light railways of short mileage, and having a narrower gauge than the standard 4 feet $8\frac{1}{2}$ inches. There is, for instance, the Romney, Hythe and Dymchurch Light Railway, which has

EIGHTY FEET ON MOVING STAIRS   *London Transport.*

This escalator is at Leicester Square Station, London, beneath which two electric tube lines run. It is the longest railway station escalator in the world and from the bottom to the top it raises passengers upwards of 80 feet.

THROUGH COMMONWEALTH COUNTRIES

This illustration shows a Beyer-Garratt articulated locomotive used on the Rhodesian Railways. One of the first of this type was used on the Royal Tour through Rhodesia, and sixty more are being employed on Rhodesia's 3 foot 6 inch gauge railways.

Above is seen the ten-car Royal train that carried Princess Elizabeth (now Queen Elizabeth II) and the Duke of Edinburgh across Canada during their tour of the Dominion in Oct.–Nov., 1951.

On the right is seen the locomotive used during the Royal Tour of South Africa in 1947. On the left is the Pilot Train just about to leave Harrismith station. From this point electric locomotives hauled the Royal train, as the line from Harrismith to Durban is electrified.

A GAS=TURBINE LOCOMOTIVE

Topical.

The first gas-turbine locomotive to be used on British Railways is this 2,500 horse-power model which was made in Switzerland. It came into service in 1950, hauling heavy express trains from London to Plymouth. The locomotive is seen here as it passed through Maidenhead on the way to London. It has reached a speed of over 80 miles an hour.

Copyright.

Here we see one of the latest locomotives used for the Southern Pacific (U.S.A.) stream-lined train "The Daylight" between Los Angeles and San Francisco. For comparison, the same company's first locomotive "C. P. Huntingdon" is seen on the right-hand side of the photograph.

ON THE RAILWAYS OF THE U.S.A.

Chesapeake and Ohio Railway.

This Chesapeake and Ohio Railway's " 500 " is the first coal-burning, steam turbine-electric loco-motive ever built and the largest single-unit passenger locomotive in the world. Measuring 154 feet from its nose to the end of its 25,000 gallon water tender, the " 500 " weighs 411½ tons and has a top speed of 100 miles per hour.

Santa Fé Railway.

In this photograph is seen a 6,000 horse-power " Alco " diesel-electric engine which is in regular use on the Santa Fé Railway in California. The picture was taken in the Cajou Pass and shows the heavily-powered engine drawing ten light-weight cars through country with many stiff gradients.

IN SWITZERLAND AND RUSSIA

E. Meerkamper, Davos.

Switzerland's mountain railways are famous, and here we have a scene on the Davos-Parsenn Cable Railway running between Davos-Dorf to Weissfluhsoch in the Grisons, well-known as a health-cure and holiday region. The two-coach train can carry up to 140 passengers at an average speed of 8 miles an hour.

Keystone.

European Russia is fairly well served by railways, Moscow and Leningrad being the two main centres of the railway system. So far as locomotives are concerned, the U.S.S.R. has made big strides in recent years, and here we see one of their diesel-engined trains at a station on one of the main routes.

Planet News.

SAILING BETWEEN TWO CONTINENTS

This fine ship is making the south-to-north passage of the Suez Canal, i.e., from Suez, on the Red Sea, to Port Said, on the Mediterranean. The hot desert beyond the ship belongs to Asia ; the palm-studded shore nearer the camera, to Africa. This wonderful canal, which thus divides the continents, shortens the voyage from England to the East by more than 4,000 miles. It is used by more than 12,000 vessels every year. The canal is 101 miles long (87 nautical miles) and its construction involved the removal of some 75 million cubic metres of sand. The work of improving the canal still continues.

The English Electric Co. Ltd.

THE ATLANTIC COAST EXPRESS ON ITS RUN TO THE WEST COUNTRY

For many years after the first railway was opened locomotives were driven by steam produced by coal-burning. In more recent times many experiments have been made with oil and electrically driven engines. A 1,600 h.p. diesel electric locomotive was successfully put into service on British Railways in 1947 and this type has become increasingly popular. The 2,000 h.p. diesel electric locomotive seen here draws the Atlantic Coast Express on the Southern Region of British Railways, running from Waterloo to a wide West Country area. At Exeter and again at Okehampton the train is divided and different sections go on to Plymouth, to Barnstaple, Ilfracombe and Bideford; to Bude, Wadebridge, Padstow, and Bodmin.

REPAIRING THE LINES

Topical Press.

Care of the track and of the embankments and tunnels through which the lines run is a highly important aspect of railway work. Here we see the entrance to Polhill Tunnel, at Knockholt, Kent, England, the second longest tunnel on the Southern Region system. Special track-laying equipment and all the latest devices were employed when the lines were re-laid and other repairs made. With highly-trained gangs of men the whole task was completed in three weeks.

a mileage of 14 miles, with a gauge of only 15 inches, on which run small locomotives and rolling stock, carrying passengers and goods. Then there is the Swansea and Mumbles Railway which claims to be the oldest passenger-carrying line in the world. Passenger traffic on this line began in 1807, but the carriages were horse-drawn. It first used steam in 1877, and in 1929 its 5¾ miles of track, standard gauge, was electrified. There are a number of other small railways, including those in the Isle of Man, which are outside State ownership.

When the newly-appointed Railway Executive took over British Railways in 1948 some 52,000 miles of track, 20,000 locomotives, 45,000 passenger coaches and well over two million wagons came under their control.

When Railways Began

Railways worked by steam were first used in mining, and it was their extension to other work that led to the first public goods and passenger all-steam

railway, the Liverpool & Manchester line, which was opened in 1830. The next country to have an all-steam public railway was the U.S.A., the South Carolina Railroad being opened with the locomotive " Best Friend of Charleston " in January, 1831. In 1834 Ireland's first public railway between Dublin and Kingstown was opened.

On the Continent the Belgian railway, Brussels to Malines, was opened with Stephenson locomotives in May, 1835. The Paris to St. Germain line (1837) was the first in France, and Holland's first was in 1839, with Italy in the same year, while Switzerland began in 1844.

In the Commonwealth, Canada's first railway was opened with a Stephenson-built locomotive in July, 1836, between Laprairie and St. John. The first steam-operated railway in Australia, from Flinders Street to Port Melbourne, began in September, 1854, while on the African continent the railway between Capetown and the Point (Natal) was opened in June, 1860.

SEMAPHORE SIGNALS

These were introduced on British railways in 1841 and still remain the most popular. Here we see the Standard Upper Quadrant Signals used on the North-Eastern Region lines.

British Railways.

COLOUR LIGHT SIGNALS

Since 1920 Colour Light Signals have been used where suitable. This type of colour light signal is used on the electrified suburban lines of the London Midland Region.

REPAIRING THE LINES

Topical Press.

Care of the track and of the embankments and tunnels through which the lines run is a highly important aspect of railway work. Here we see the entrance to Polhill Tunnel, at Knockholt, Kent, England, the second longest tunnel on the Southern Region system. Special track-laying equipment and all the latest devices were employed when the lines were re-laid and other repairs made. With highly-trained gangs of men the whole task was completed in three weeks.

a mileage of 14 miles, with a gauge of only 15 inches, on which run small locomotives and rolling stock, carrying passengers and goods. Then there is the Swansea and Mumbles Railway which claims to be the oldest passenger-carrying line in the world. Passenger traffic on this line began in 1807, but the carriages were horse-drawn. It first used steam in 1877, and in 1929 its 5¾ miles of track, standard gauge, was electrified. There are a number of other small railways, including those in the Isle of Man, which are outside State ownership.

When the newly-appointed Railway Executive took over British Railways in 1948 some 52,000 miles of track, 20,000 locomotives, 45,000 passenger coaches and well over two million wagons came under their control.

When Railways Began

Railways worked by steam were first used in mining, and it was their extension to other work that led to the first public goods and passenger all-steam railway, the Liverpool & Manchester line, which was opened in 1830. The next country to have an all-steam public railway was the U.S.A., the South Carolina Railroad being opened with the locomotive " Best Friend of Charleston " in January, 1831. In 1834 Ireland's first public railway between Dublin and Kingstown was opened.

On the Continent the Belgian railway, Brussels to Malines, was opened with Stephenson locomotives in May, 1835. The Paris to St. Germain line (1837) was the first in France, and Holland's first was in 1839, with Italy in the same year, while Switzerland began in 1844.

In the Commonwealth, Canada's first railway was opened with a Stephenson-built locomotive in July, 1836, between Laprairie and St. John. The first steam-operated railway in Australia, from Flinders Street to Port Melbourne, began in September, 1854, while on the African continent the railway between Capetown and the Point (Natal) was opened in June, 1860.

SEMAPHORE SIGNALS

These were introduced on British railways in 1841 and still remain the most popular. Here we see the Standard Upper Quadrant Signals used on the North-Eastern Region lines.

British Railways.

COLOUR LIGHT SIGNALS

Since 1920 Colour Light Signals have been used where suitable. This type of colour light signal is used on the electrified suburban lines of the London Midland Region.

ROUND A LOCOMOTIVE WORKS

A SCENE IN THE ERECTING SHOPS

Central Press.

This gives a general view of the erecting shops where the different parts are assembled and the locomotives built up. The photograph was taken in a Glasgow works, and some of the locomotives
being assembled here are part of a large order for the South Africa Railways. In working order
these Class 15F engines weigh, with tender, 181 tons.

IN this section we are going to tell you something about a works in which locomotives are built either for British Railways or for the railroads in other countries. There are a good number of such works in Britain, and as British engineers built many of the early railways in other continents their methods and practice are still largely followed in other lands.

A steam locomotive is a very wonderful thing. It is composed of many thousands of parts, each of which must be accurately made and securely fixed, for a locomotive is subjected to endless racketing and severe shocks. It is a travelling power-house, consuming coal and water, and producing 1,000 to 2,000 horse power, which is imparted to the wheels through pistons, rods and cranks.

Its boiler has to withstand a pressure of about two hundredweight on every square inch inside it touched by steam or water. This pressure is trying to tear the boiler to pieces, and the makers of the boiler have had to put in chains, as it were, energy sufficient to hurl the boiler miles into the air.

The Steam-tight Joints

Between the boiler and the escape pipe, which releases it up the chimney, the steam must be confined, while left free to do its work ; and this means making a great number of joints absolutely steam-tight, both where one part moves over another and where two parts are fixed together.

The great weight of the boiler and its contents, as well as that of the cylinders, is supported on a strong frame, which in turn rests on wheels of great strength. The driving wheels and the parts which turn them have to be very carefully balanced, so that the wheels may not damage the rails by hammer-like blows, or even jump off them. Wheels, axles and moving rods must be of the best design and material, for the breakage of any one of them might cause a terrible accident. A locomotive is, in short, one of those things which demands great care in its making from start to finish.

Here we are at the gates of a large works employing thousands of men in its many departments. The head offices, to which we come first, are not, so far as the work done in them is concerned, of much interest to the average visitor, for there is little to *see* there. But we must think of them with respect, for upon the men who occupy them falls the responsibility of planning, designing, considering and deciding. If these men make serious mistakes the best workmanship in the shops will be of little avail to correct them.

Let us suppose that a request for a price for fifty locomotives for a particular railway has come in, accompanied by drawings got out by the head locomotive engineer of the railway. The drawings are submitted to the costing department, and are gone through in detail. The cost of making each part has to be calculated, and on the total reckoned cost the price quoted is based, with a margin for profit. If it be a bit too high, the whole contract may be lost. On the other hand, if it has been, in error, put too low, the securing of the contract may mean a considerable loss of money. So you see that the men who do costing work must be very competent people.

The Drawing Offices

Should the works be asked to design

Central Press.

A WORKER AT THE LATHE

Every part of a locomotive is made to exact drawings and tests are made to ensure precision. In this picture we have a scene in the Vulcan Foundry at Newton-le-Willows, Lancashire. The worker is operating a big lathe which is turning the crank axle for a locomotive.

Central Press.

FINISHING THE BOILER

This photograph gives a good idea of what the boiler of a locomotive looks like before its outer covering has been fitted. When this stage has been completed a great crane will carry the boiler from the jacks on which it is now resting and place it in position on the frame which will later be put over the wheels.

as well as quote for the engines, the drawing offices get a share—and a very important one—of the responsibility. The head draughtsman's task is far from easy, and to be able to carry it out he must be a highly-trained engineer, with a thorough knowledge of mechanics, physics, the strength and qualities of different materials, price of materials, casting, forging, and all other processes carried out in the works.

He is given certain particulars, such as the greatest weight and dimensions allowed, weight to be hauled, speed of running required, fuel to be used, sharpest curves in the track, greatest length of run, and so on; and he has to design an engine that will meet all these requirements at the lowest cost to the purchaser.

In consultation with other officials he will get out the general design, which is put on paper by his assistants with the help of all the latest devices in the way of drawing apparatus. Besides drawings of the complete locomotive, there may be wanted detail drawings of cylinders, gear, boiler, etc. In any case, these will be needed before any actual manufacturing work can be done.

The original drawings are carried out in pencil, and from them tracings are made by skilled " tracers " in ink on a transparent cloth. A tracing shows the exact measurements of every part, and the positions of all holes and their distances apart. It may also be shaded in a way which enables the workman to tell at a glance the material of which a part is to be made, and on it are written "notes" giving further information in words and figures.

The tracing serves as a negative from which "working prints" are made for use in the shops, the tracing itself being much too precious to be handled by dirty fingers. Moreover, several prints are probably needed for different people to use.

If the printing is done on blue paper in the sun, the tracing paper and sensitised paper are placed together in a large frame and exposed to sunlight. The paper turns a dark blue, except under the ink lines, and when "fixed" by being washed in water it gives a "blue print," with white lines—corresponding to the black lines of the tracing—on a blue background. A great deal of use is now made also of electrical printing, a powerful arc-lamp being employed instead of sunlight. This process can be carried out at any time, and is very quick.

In the Laboratory

Another important department is the *laboratory*, wherein samples of all materials, especially metals, supplied to the works are tested for composition, hardness, toughness, strength, etc., before being allowed to enter the shops. This is very responsible work, as any bad material that finds its way into a locomotive may lead to serious accidents and loss of property and life.

In other parts of the building we find the accountants' department, where track is kept of all money owing and paid, and the wage-sheets of all the workmen employed are got out week by week; and the offices occupied by a large number of clerks and typists busy on correspondence.

Nor must we overlook the publicity department, the main duty of which is to attract business by placing advertisements in carefully selected papers and magazines, and in this and other ways keeps the public informed of

Sport and General.

WITH THE WELDER AT WORK

First-class materials capable of standing up to great strains are essential in the manufacture of locomotives. Equally important is the skill of the worker. In this photograph, taken at a Southern Region railway works, the man at work is welding the boiler ash pan for a new locomotive.

Central Press.

FINISHING THE WHEELS AND CAB

This photograph gives a scene in one corner of the erecting shops at a big railway works in Glasgow. The men seen here are putting the finishing touches on the wheels and cabs of locomotives which have been specially built for service on the Indian Railways.

changes or of special facilities which may be available.

On our way to the shops we get a peep at the stores, or the main department of them—for there probably are special storerooms or store yards scattered about the works, handy to the various shops. To be short of anything that is needed, even though it be a small item, may mean a great waste of time. The head store-keeper has to see that there is a place for everything, and that everything is in its place and in sufficient quantity.

It is a big task, keeping records of everything that comes in and goes out, and making lists showing what number or weight of any article or material is in stock at any moment. Indoors there are numberless racks and shelves filled with nuts and bolts of all sizes and lengths, screws, safety-valves, gauges, rods, parts of brakes, oil-cans, lamps, and hundreds of other things. Under sheds we find stacks of heavier goods—

steel and iron plates, angle bars, rods and bars, and perhaps timber. In a few moments we may run our eyes over thousands of pounds' worth of material.

Very likely there is a special tool-store, in which are kept supplies of every kind of tool used in the works. Close to it is the tool shop, given up to making tools, and cutting tools in particular. Here we shall see the most skilled craftsmen employed on the premises, forging, bending and sharpening the many varieties of cutters which pare or drill metal.

The Forging Shop

Heavy thudding sounds now apprise us that we are approaching the forging shop. As we enter it a furnace is being opened. Out comes a mass of white-hot steel on to a trolley. The vehicle bears it away to a steam hammer, the tup or striking part of which may weigh a ton or so, and the anvil a great deal more. A couple of smiths, pro-

STAGES IN LOCOMOTIVE BUILDING

In this photograph two workers are seen on the task of fitting the inside connecting rods to a 4-cylinder 4–6–0 type express passenger engine. The outside rods can be seen already fitted in position on the locomotive.

Photos : Sport and General.

Here the axle-box guides are being fitted to the main frames of a new locomotive at a workshop in southern England. The engine which is being built is one of a considerable number ordered for the railways of Siam.

SETTING THE VALVES

Sport and General.

A travelling crane is here seen lowering a 4–6–0 express engine on to the valve setting machine. The correct timing of the valve events on a locomotive is most important and this machine enables this to be done with the highest efficiency. The photograph was taken at the big railway works at Swindon in the Western Region of British Railways.

Topical Press.

READY FOR ITS FINAL TESTS

The locomotive has been built and various tests have been made of the different parts. Now the finished engine is being lifted into position for its final tests before being passed as ready for service.

tected from heat and sparks by masks and iron leggings, fling the steel on to the anvil, and a third man works a lever at the side of the machine.

Every movement of the lever causes the hammer to lift or come down with a bang. Bump! bump! bump! The ingot is turned about this way and that, and gradually lengthened out into a roughly circular bar which will form part of a driving-wheel crankshaft.

Bolts and Stays

Close to the hammers are rollers squeezing ingots into thin bars ; and not far from them are drop stamps forming sheets of hot metal into hollow articles. The stamp itself is shaped like the fixed die below it, but is somewhat smaller every way. It is bolted to a mass of metal weighing some tons, maybe, in guides. Every time a man pulls a chain the stamp is raised by a revolving shaft overhead. On reaching the top of its travel it is released and

falls, driving the metal further into the lower die.

Near the forge is an interesting shop given up to the making of bolts and stays. We should like to linger over the wonderful machines which form heads on bolts, cut threads on them, and turn them smooth. But there is much else to see, and we must pass on to the foundry, the chief work of which is the casting of the great cylinders, and the parts attached to them.

The pattern for a cylinder, made in the pattern shop close by, is a very complicated affair. So, too, is the mould formed from it on the foundry floor. All that we can see of it, however, is a mould enclosed by a framework having some holes in the top. Molten steel is brought up in a great ladle and poured through one of these holes till the sight of it welling up in the holes tells us that the mould is full. A few days hence the cover will be removed and the overhead crane will lift out the now hardened cylinder to have the sand cores broken out of its bore and the valve chest and steam ports.

The casting next passes to one of the machine shops, which contain a large number of great machines for turning, boring, planing, and otherwise cutting and shaping castings and other parts. Our cylinder is lowered on to the bed of a boring machine and held fast while a revolving bar, with three cutters projecting from it, passes slowly through it from end to end, scraping off metal and making the bore circular. This " roughing " cut is followed by a finishing cut, which smoothes the bore sufficiently for use. The valve chest is treated in the same way, if piston valves are used, and the cylinder then has its ends and surfaces that touch another part planed quite smooth and bored for bolt-holes.

Marked Out in Chalk

The frame of a locomotive consists of two long upright side plates, with slots in them for the axle-boxes, end plates and cross plates connecting them, and a top horizontal plate largely cut away under the boiler and where the fire-box comes. The steel sheets for the side plates measure, perhaps, 30 feet by 4 feet, and are over an inch thick.

A sheet is marked in chalk from a pattern and placed under a punching machine, which quickly stamps out wads of metal close to each other just outside the line. The " waste " is then easily broken away. Or the cutting is

Topical Press.

WHERE LOCOMOTIVES ARE TESTED

The locomotive testing station at Rugby is, it is claimed, the most up-to-date in the world. On the special roller bench seen in this photograph engines can be driven up to 120 miles per hour while stationary. The locomotive in the upper part of the picture is in position and ready to be put through all the necessary tests.

done with an oxy-acetylene flame which quickly eats a path through the metal as it is guided by a workman wearing very dark spectacles to protect his eyes from the glare.

A number of frame plates, after being softened by heating and rolled quite flat, are clamped one on the top of the other on the bed of a slotting machine. The bed of this can move to and fro, and the chisel-like tool, which makes downward strokes, can be moved sideways. The tool gradually cuts away all the rough edges outside the line. The plates are then planed on their top edges and bored for all bolts and rivets.

At the Boiler Shop

The shop in which the parts of boilers are assembled is perhaps the noisiest quarter of the works. The pneumatic riveting hammers, making hundreds of blows a minute, raise a din amid which conversation is almost impossible.

A boiler is usually built up out of nine plates. Two of them are bent into cylinders by powerful rollers and riveted together to form the barrel. The fire-box has one plate for the top and sides, to which are riveted two other plates, with turned-over edges, forming the ends. These three are of copper. The outer shell of the fire-box is of similar construction, but its plates are of steel, and its front plate has a large hole in it. The edges of the hole are turned outwards to fit over the ring of the barrel next to it.

The last plate to be mentioned is the circular one at the front of the boiler, next the smoke-box. This, like the front plate of the fire-box, is pierced with a large number of holes for the hundreds of brass or copper tubes running through the barrel from the fire-box to the smoke-box.

The fire-box and its outer shell are a few inches apart all round, to allow the circulation of water between them. At the bottom the space is closed by a cast-iron ring, and there is a similar ring round the firedoor opening. To prevent the fire-box and its shell being forced apart by the pressure of the steam, they are held together by a thousand or two stay-bolts.

Caulking the Joints

When the fire-box part is complete, it is riveted to the barrel and the tubes are inserted. Each tube is put in from the smoke-box end and expanded into the tube plates at both ends by a revolving tool with three small rollers pressing on the inside of the tube. After all joints have been " caulked " steam-tight outside with a pneumatic tool, which makes a terrible clatter, and its various fittings have been put in place, the boiler is ready for testing to a much higher pressure than that at which it will be worked.

The erecting shop is the most interesting shop of all, for here we see all the parts of a locomotive brought together.

The framework is first of all built up on low trestles. Then the cylinders are attached to it in their exact positions. A great overhead crane next brings along a boiler, all complete with its smoke-box and chimney, and lowers it into place in the frame. Gangs of men fit the driver's cab, water-tanks, pistons, cylinder covers and the running gear, and cover the boiler with a thick coating of asbestos magnesia to prevent heat escaping, and encase this in neatly fitted thin steel plates.

The engine is now lifted bodily into the air and its wheels are run forward into place. The crane then lowers it on to them. While the connecting-rods and coupling-rods are being fitted, and the valve-setters carry out the very important work of adjusting the cylinder valves correctly, the engine is painted all over and varnished. It is then ready for work.

A wheel has a cast-steel or cast-iron centre, surrounded by a rolled-steel tyre. The centre consists of a central

RAILWAY APPRENTICES

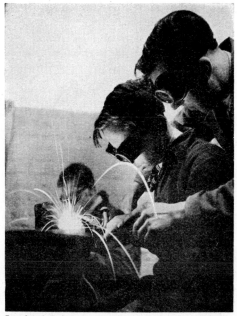

At the headquarters of British Railways Midland Region at Derby there is a school for boys where they are taught all aspects of locomotive maintenance and engineering.

In the left-hand picture the boys are learning about " smokebox arrangement." In the one above a boy is being shown by an instructor how to carry out metal-welding.

Photos : Keystone.

The course lasts one year, after which successful pupils are drafted into the works to begin apprenticeships in various technical trades. In this picture the bogie arrangements of a diesel-electric locomotive are being explained to a group of boys. The boys work 38 hours a week, two-thirds of which are spent in practical instruction.

boss for the axle, the spokes and the rim, or felloe, all cast in one piece. The axle has been turned true on a lathe, and has, near each end, a projecting " collar " to prevent the wheel being forced too far along it.

Wheels and Axles

After the wheel boss has had a hole drilled in it a trifle smaller than the axle, the centre is forced on to the axle by a hydraulic press giving a push of 50 tons to 120 tons. An axle, with both wheel centres on it, is mounted on a lathe, and the centres are turned on the outside to a diameter slightly larger than the inside of the tyres.

Then follows the interesting operation of shrinking the tyres on to the centres. A tyre is laid flat on a circular iron plate and heated by gas-jets playing on it all round. This expands it sufficiently for the wheel centre to enter it quite easily. Then the gas is turned off and the tyre shrinks, seizing the centre in a grip that nothing is likely to loosen, though as an extra precaution the two parts are further held together by screws or some other manner of fixing.

The pulling power of the locomotive is tested by lowering its driving wheels on to other wheels turning in a frame. These wheels may be connected either to a brake drum or to a wheel which drives pumps or a dynamo. The engine is hitched to a device for measuring the pull, and steam is turned on. As the brake is tightened up the engine tries to move forward, and the strongest pull of which it is capable without slipping its wheels can be measured.

Its consumption of fuel and water can also be found by letting the engine

Central Press.

FINISHING TOUCHES ON LOCOMOTIVES FOR INDIA
In this picture, taken in a well-known Glasgow railway works, the finishing touches are being given to a batch of locomotives for India. They are fitted with powerful headlights as well as " cow-catchers " as a precaution against animals straying on the line.

A LOCOMOTIVE GOES ABROAD

Fox Photos.

British locomotives run on many railways in every part of the world. In recent years orders for new engines have been heavy and with the need for our exports to be maintained at a high level, engines for overseas have often had priority over our own requirements. In this photograph the floating crane " London Mammoth " is seen at work at the Royal Docks, London, lifting heavy locomotives from the quayside to the ship which will carry them across the seas.

run against the brake for a time ; or the engine may be made to do useful work in pumping or generating electricity while its moving parts are being " run in " and tested.

The building of locomotives and the manufacture of railway equipment has been one of Britain's great industries for long years. This country was the pioneer of railways and steam locomotion and the craftsmen employed in the big railway works have traditions and standards which are steadfastly maintained.

In all parts of the world the railways were subjected to heavy strain between the years 1939–1945. There were serious difficulties in the supply of new engines and equipment. After the war heavy orders were placed in Britain for new locomotives and rolling stock of all kinds, and our home demands are just as great. The Indian railways need many new locomotives; Rhodesian railways ordered 60 engines of the Beyer-Garratt type, illustrated on another page, for early delivery. Siam and other Eastern countries were short of locomotives and equipment, and the big railway shops in Britain settled down to hard work.

Over sixty countries are mentioned in one manufacturer's list of special railway equipment. From China to Peru, from Iraq to Brazil the orders come for British locomotives, wagons, refrigerator vans, guards' vans, passenger coaches, and equipment of all kinds, and Britain's workshops continue to supply the railways of the world.

Central Press.

TESTING THE BEARINGS AND CHECK VALVES

Locomotives designed for railways in many parts of the world are built in Britain. The photograph above shows an engine almost ready for dispatch with others to Nigeria. It has been built at the Vulcan Foundry, Newton-le-Willows, and is here seen undergoing its final test in steam on a set of rollers to try out the bearings and check valves.

By courtesy of Canadian Pacific Railways.

A MODERN DIESEL ENGINE ON THE TRANS-CANADIAN RUN

Using heavy oil as fuel, the Diesel internal combustion engine was first introduced by Rudolf Diesel in 1897, and was subsequently developed in various types by many engine makers. In its modern form it has in recent years been adopted by railways throughout the world. Our picture shows the latest Diesel locomotive in service on the Canadian Pacific Railway which runs through some of the world's most spectacular mountain scenery. With over 17,000 miles of railroad, steamships sailing on the Great Lakes and across the Atlantic and Pacific oceans, as well as air services, the C.P.R. ranks as one of the great trade routes of the world.

The English Electric Co. Ltd.

A DIESEL-ELECTRIC LOCOMOTIVE HAULING "THE WESTLANDER"

The first steam-operated railway on the Australian continent ran from Flinders Street to Port Melbourne and was opened on September 13th, 1854. In the following year the first railway in New South Wales, Sydney to Parramatta, was opened, and in the century which has passed since then Australia has kept well abreast with all innovations in railway operations. Here we see one of the latest luxury trains, "The Westlander," running on the Queensland Government Railways. It is hauled by an "English Electric" 1,500 h.p. diesel-electric locomotive.

How
Steam and
Petrol
Work for Man

The
Motor Car
appears on
the Roads

THE VERY FIRST STEAM LORRY

Rischgitz.

Though we associate the locomotive mainly with George Stephenson, a road wagon propelled by steam was actually in use in the year 1763. It is still in existence in a museum in Paris and is illustrated above. Designed by a French engineer named Cugnot, the appliance consisted of a heavy timber frame supported on three wheels. In front was an overhanging copper boiler, connected with pistons and cylinders. The machine maintained a speed of four miles per hour.

FROM TRACTION ENGINE TO RACING CAR

IN or about the year A.D. 1290 the Franciscan monk, Roger Bacon, wrote in one of his works: "We shall be able to propel carriages with incredible speed without the assistance of any animal." He also prophesied the coming of the steamship and the flying machine. These prophecies have all proved correct; as also has that of Mother Shipton, a somewhat shadowy prophetess of the seventeenth century, who let it be known that "Carriages without horses shall go," and even hinted at the electric telegraph. In her prediction that:

"The end of the world shall surely come
In eighteen hundred and eighty-one."

she was, fortunately for us, less accurate.

Rather more than a century before the date assigned by Mother Shipton for the end of all things human, a French engineer, Nicholas Joseph Cugnot, put the first steam carriage on the road. It ought, perhaps, to be termed the first traction engine or steam lorry, as its purpose was to haul or carry heavy guns. The machine has—we use the present tense, because it is still to be seen in a Paris museum—three wheels, a single driving and steering wheel in front, and two other wheels at the back. Cugnot's machine attained a speed of four miles an hour, and during one of its trials charged and knocked down a wall.

This and various other little escapades caused the French military authorities to shake their heads over the invention as " dangerous to property," and this original ancestor of steam road locomotives was soon placed on the retired list.

We read that one Dallery ran a steam car in the streets of Amiens in 1780. Soon afterwards the Revolution put a stop to useful inventions in France.

From Camborne to Plymouth

Our next date is 1803. In that year Richard Trevithick, a Cornish inventor, built a steam carriage which he drove from Camborne, in Cornwall, to Plymouth, over a hilly road. The machine was taken by water from Plymouth to London, and exhibited there. But Trevithick, like many another inventor, soon lost interest in his invention, sold it for what it would fetch, and returned to Cornwall.

No further advance was made for about twenty years, and then there began a period of great activity among inventors ready to back the steam

engine against the horse-drawn stage coach. Sir Goldsworthy Gurney, a great chemist of the time, spent large sums on building steam coaches, with which he climbed the steepest hills in and around London. In 1829 he decided to test one of his machines in what we should now call a long-distance run, from London to Bath.

It is little over a century since this first of motor trips took place, so let us put back the clock 100 years and imagine ourselves in company with the daring four who occupied a private vehicle hitched on behind Gurney's steamer. We can picture what would happen to us from an account written at the time by one of Gurney's helpers.

On the Great Bath Road

We run easily enough and without the least accident down the Bath Road to Longford, where a bridge over the Camlin is being repaired. Then we have an exciting moment, for the road

Rischgitz.

AN EARLY STEAM CARRIAGE AND TRAILER

If you could have stood beside the Great Bath Road at Hounslow, Middlesex, rather more than a century ago you might have seen the above steam carriage, drawing as a trailer a handsome barouche which contained among its distinguished passengers the Duke of Wellington. Sir Goldsworthy Gurney, a great chemist of the time, was the inventor of this steam carriage, which could average fourteen miles an hour on a long journey.

IN THE EARLY DAYS OF MOTORING

Sport and General.

This photograph shows a type of motor that was built in 1902; and it says much for the car that, when more than thirty years old, it ran quite satisfactorily between London and Brighton in an annual event for pioneer motors classified as "Old Crocks."

Rischgitz.

In this illustration we see a British "Napier" six-cylindered car during trials in 1905. It covered a half mile (with a flying start and not from dead-stop) at a speed of 88·2 miles an hour. To-day some of the finest and fastest aeroplanes in the world are equipped with Napier engines.

is partly blocked by a heap of bricks, and the Bath mail is seen approaching at full speed on the other side. Our shouts to the coachman are useless, and to avoid collision Sir Goldsworthy drives his coach into the bricks, doing it some slight damage which is, however, put right in a quarter of an hour.

We reach Reading at 8.10 a.m., and leave it two hours later. Jogging along at a steady six miles an hour—Sir Goldsworthy is driving slowly to avoid giving offence to other users of the road —we enter Melksham at 8 o'clock in the evening, as dusk is falling.

There is a fair in progress at Melk-. sham and all the streets are crowded. Some stage-coach postilions, seeing our approach, begin to stir up the crowd

against the new means of transport. At first we suffer nothing worse than insulting jeers, but presently stones begin to fly, and two of our number are wounded. Sir Goldsworthy, thinking discretion the better part of valour, drives the coach into a brewery and leaves it there for the night under police protection. The next day we set out under escort for Bath, which is reached without any further incident.

Back to London

On the return trip Sir Goldsworthy takes the precaution of passing through Melksham at night, using horses instead of steam power till he is clear of the town, where the horses are unhitched. The driver now opens out the throttle to

Topical.

THE THREE-HORSED OMNIBUS

A little more than 100 years ago a man named Shillibeer introduced into the streets of London a vehicle drawn by three horses abreast, which plied between the West End and the City, picking up or setting down passengers on the way. The vehicle is seen above, and Shillibeer named it " Omnibus," a Latin word meaning " for all." To-day the word is usually shortened to " bus."

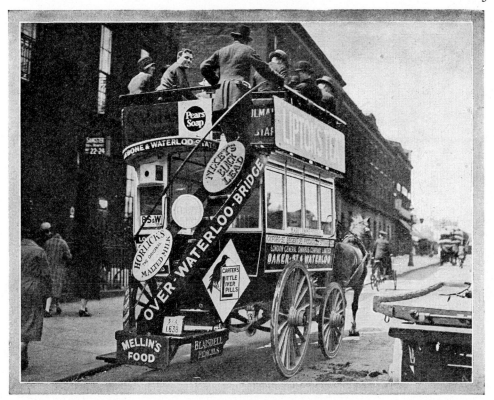

Topical.

A BUS WITH OUTSIDE SEATS

At the beginning of the present century the streets of London were thronged with buses of this type, with seats for outside passengers. These vehicles were drawn by two horses, which splashed pedestrians from head to foot in muddy weather, slipped about terribly during frost and snow, and suffered considerably in heat-waves. In those days there were many halfpenny stages.

make up for lost time. Even posting chaises are overhauled. At the foot of Devizes Hill we meet a coach, which stops to watch us mount the slope. We fly up the hill and as we reach the top we hear the loud applause of the onlookers. And so back to London.

It is an amusing fact that, on the very day when Gurney's coach ran up Devizes Hill, a mathematician published a paper in which he *proved* that no steam road carriage could possibly propel itself ! It is also interesting to note that the trip described was made in the year before that which witnessed the opening of the Manchester-Liverpool Railway, the first steam railway for passengers.

Sir Goldsworthy had several rivals,

Walter Hancock, Braythwayte, Scott Russell, Dr. Church, Messrs. Ogle and Summers and Sir Charles Dance. The last put a steam coach into service between Gloucester and Cheltenham, and in four months it ran 3,500 miles and carried over 3,000 passengers. Hancock's steam services in London traversed 4,200 miles without serious accident, and steam coaches ran to Greenwich and Windsor. In 1830 a car tested before a Special Commission of the House of Commons attained thirty-five miles an hour on the level and ran 800 miles before it required any repair.

So you see that, 100 years ago, the mechanically-driven omnibus, which we look upon as a very modern invention,

Topical.

THE MOTOR COACH OF YESTERDAY

In the days in which we live there are motor coaches running between London and Edinburgh and countless other distant points, some of the vehicles being equipped as sleeping saloons and carrying attendants who serve refreshments on the journey. Yet, less than fifty years ago, the coach illustrated above was the most up-to-date conveyance of its type and was used to take people to Ascot Races at a speed of twelve miles an hour.

was rapidly becoming a thing to be reckoned with.

Driven from the Road

But there were clouds on the horizon. The owners of stage coaches, as might be expected, were bitterly opposed to vehicles which threatened the ruin of their businesses ; and they were not above piling stones on the road to wreck their rivals. And, again, influential people were becoming interested in railways, with which also the steam coach would be a competitor. Pressure was brought to bear on Members of Parliament, and laws were passed which remained in force till 1896. Long before that they had driven all steam coaches off British roads.

If road locomotives had been backed by the public as warmly as railway locomotives, during the years 1830–50, the whole story of modern transport might have been altered. Motor 'bus services rivalling those of to-day might have sprung up, and roads been saved from the neglect which they suffered after the coming of the railway. But on the other hand, we should probably not now have our wonderful railway system. So who shall say whether or no it was as well things fell out as they did ?

The steam coach being abolished, the only road locomotives left were steam rollers and traction engines, neither of them of any interest to us nowadays, though there was a time when the passage of either was quite an exciting event in village life.

In 1878 a steam carriage was exhibited in Paris, and was followed by a series of other steam-driven French vehicles of a much handier kind than the old steam coaches. Inventors began to build small vehicles which prepared the way for private mechanical power-driven cars. One of the most interesting of them was the steam tricycle of M. Serpollet, which could easily do its twenty miles an hour. Between the two big driving wheels and behind the rider's seat was the boiler, which consisted of a coil of steel tubing, heated by a petrol burner.

Burned Internally

This kind of boiler was called the "flash" boiler, because the water squirted into it by a pump driven off the engine changed into steam in a flash; and speed was controlled by regulating the amount of water delivered by the pump.

The French steam car was on the way to being a great success when a rival appeared in the field. This was a vehicle driven by a petrol motor, which did away with the need for a troublesome boiler, as the fuel, after being expanded into gas and mixed with air, was burned in the engine itself.

As this engine has become of enormous importance to the world, we must spare just a few words for a glance at its manner of working. It may have one, two, four, six, eight, twelve or even more cylinders, but as the same thing happens in each of them, we will confine ourselves to a single cylinder. This is

Barratt.

A LONDON OMNIBUS OF TO-DAY

The evolution of the London motor omnibus is a story of steady but continual improvement. In this photograph of the latest type it will be seen that the vehicle is completely built in, with comfortable seats for both the driver and his passengers. The bus seen above is of the RTL type and carries fifty-six passengers : twenty-six below and thirty on the upper deck.

MOTOR CARS IN THE MAKING

Here we have a view in the Car Trimming Shop. Rows of power sewing machines, operated by girls, produce the leather seat covers, and internal trimming for the car.

On the Car Assembly Line seen in this photograph, the engine, suspension, steering and electric wiring are all fitted to the body which is slowly moving along on a conveyor.

Photos : Morris Motors.

In this picture we have another view of the Car Assembly Line. Here the windscreen, door lights, bonnet and radiator grill are added. All operations are accurately timed and are done as the car passes along to completion.

THE ENGINE OF A MODERN MOTOR CAR

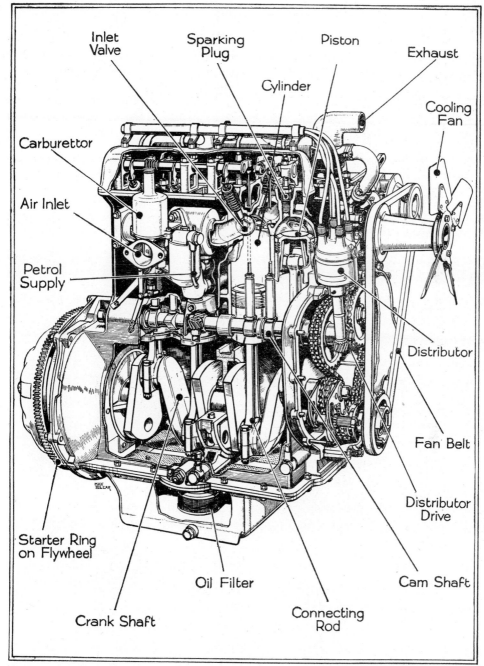

Inlet Valve   Sparking Plug   Piston   Exhaust

Cylinder   Cooling Fan

Carburettor

Air Inlet

Petrol Supply

Distributor

Fan Belt

Distributor Drive

Starter Ring on Flywheel

Cam Shaft

Oil Filter

Crank Shaft

Connecting Rod

By courtesy of " The Autocar.

In this picture we have a cut-away view of the 1½-litre Riley car engine. When the engine is working, air is drawn through the space marked " Air Inlet " and then passes through the carburettor. Here it is mixed with a very fine spray of petrol and enters the cylinder through the inlet valve. When the piston moves up to the top of the cylinder it compresses this petrol vapour and air, and, at just the right instant, a spark occurs across the points of the sparking plug. This causes the petrol mixture to explode, forcing the piston down the cylinder and so turning the engine crankshaft.

open at the bottom end, and the piston working in it is joined by a connecting rod to a crank in the crankshaft driving the gear which turns the wheels. At the top are two valves, an inlet valve and an outlet valve.

The Cycle of Operations

During the first downstroke of a cycle, or series of operations, the inlet valve opens, and the suction of the piston draws in a charge of gas and air. Before the first stroke begins, the valve has closed and trapped the charge which is severely squeezed by the ascending piston. Towards the end of the upstroke the mixture is fired by

an electric spark, and explodes, driving down the piston and giving a kick to the crank. Before the end of this stroke the outlet valve opens, and when the piston rises for the second time it pushes out the burned gases. These four operations of sucking in, squeezing, burning, and ejecting the fuel mixture happen over and over again with great rapidity as long as the engine is running.

The earliest motor cars, which appeared about the year 1884, were very queer-looking and noisy things. Their engines had only one cylinder, and their tyres were of solid rubber or iron. They chug-chugged along, making a

Central Press Photos.

A CAR THAT MADE HISTORY : THE " BLUE BIRD "

In 1931, at Daytona Beach, Florida, the late Sir Malcolm Campbell reached a speed of 245 miles an hour in his first " Blue Bird." Three years afterwards, in a later car, he attained a speed of 272 miles an hour. In 1935 the new " Blue Bird," illustrated above, raced over the Salduro sands in Utah at a speed of 301·129 miles an hour.

TWO FAMOUS RACING CARS

In this photograph we see Captain G. E. T. Eyston's 6,000-h.p. car " Thunderbolt." The car was taken to the salt flats at Utah, in the United States of America, and driven there at a speed of 359·49 miles per hour, or just under six miles a minute.

Here is the late John Cobb's world-famous Railton car which at Bonneville Salt Flats, U.S.A., attained a speed of 368·85 miles per hour and, later, 394·2 miles per hour. John Cobb was killed in September 1952 when his jet-engined boat *Crusader* sank during an attempt to beat the water speed record.

Central Press.

A RACE FOR THE INTERNATIONAL GRAND PRIX

Early in the history of motoring a concrete track was built at Brooklands, Surrey, England, in 1906–7. This famous track has now been closed, but others have taken its place. Our photograph shows the start of the R.A.C. International Grand Prix race at Silverstone, Northamptonshire. It was won by an Italian in a Maserati car.

noise which rendered a horn hardly necessary for giving warning of their approach. Very soon a second cylinder was added and the crankshaft then got a kick at every revolution, making the motion of the vehicles less jerky.

At the House of Commons

Our earliest motor-cars were built very much on the lines of the horse-drawn vehicles of the time whose place they were intended to take. They were high from the ground with a kind of box-seat for the driver. The waggonette and governess cart type of vehicle were very popular, where the passengers sat facing one another at the back of the car.

In those far-off times there were, of course, no windscreens or even canopies or hoods for the protection of passengers and driver, so that in cold or wet weather motoring was indeed an adventure only for the hardiest. The dust was intolerable, whilst ruts and pot-holes in the road made travelling most uncomfortable.

As one sidelight, the first Member of Parliament who drove into Palace Yard, Westminster, in his car was told by the policeman on duty: "Those things are not allowed in here," as though the newly-invented motor was something very disreputable.

In 1894 the editor of a Paris journal organised the first motor race, to find out what this kind of vehicle really could do. Fourteen petrol cars and nine steam cars started from Paris for Rouen, and seventeen finished the

MODERN MOTOR RACING

Goodwood, in South England, has been famed for many years as a centre of horse-racing, but another kind of racing has taken place there in recent years. In this photograph the winner of the race for midget cars is seen at the moment of victory at the Goodwood meeting of the Junior Car Club.

Photos : Central Press.

The first International Grand Prix race to be held in this country for twenty-one years took place at Silverstone, Northamptonshire, in 1948. Here we see one of the competitors driving a Talbot car travelling at speed round one of the corners of the track.

course. Crowds of spectators, cheering frantically, lined the route, and many people threw bouquets at the cars.

The Boy Chauffeur

A funny incident happened during the race. The chauffeur—that is, the stoker—of one of the steam cars signalled to the driver to stop, and when the vehicle came to a standstill he stepped off, saying that he was too hot and was going to rest in the shade of a tree. The driver's arguments were in vain, and the car would have had to abandon the race if another steam car had not lent a boy of thirteen to take the place of the disgruntled stoker.

In passing we may notice that, as the petrol car needed no stoker, the word " chauffeur " was transferred to the paid driver of a private car.

Further road races followed in France every year, and each year saw an increase in the winner's speed. In 1901 the road between Paris and Bordeaux was covered at an average speed of $53\frac{3}{4}$ miles an hour, and the fastest long-distance express in the world, running between these cities, was beaten by a full hour. Since then speeds have risen much higher still.

Motor racing became a favourite sport, even in Britain, which in 1896 had been freed from the old law requiring a road locomotive to be preceded by a red flag carried by a man on foot. Motor car engines were given first four, and then six cylinders, and cylinders were made larger, until 200 horse power was crowded under a car's " bonnet." On Brooklands track, near Weybridge, cars soon reached a maximum safe speed of 130 miles per hour.

Terrific Speeds

Attempts on speed records had then

Central Press.

A MODERN BRITISH MOTOR CYCLE

Among the latest types of motor-cycles from British workshops is this " Wooler " model. It has a 500 c.c. four-cylinder engine of patent design, is shaft-driven with shock-absorbing joint, and has a " Hardy Spicer " universal coupling.

TWO FAMOUS BRITISH CARS

Keystone.

One of the most famous small cars in the world was the Austin Seven, popularly known as the "Baby Austin." First introduced in 1922 it was later superseded for a time by the "Austin Eight," but a new "Baby" appeared in 1951. In this picture, one of the original 1922 "Sevens" (right) is seen travelling side by side with its grandson, the 1951 Austin Seven.

Rolls Royce Ltd.

Admitted to be in the very forefront of the finest cars the whole world produces, here is the Rolls-Royce Silver Wraith Six Light Saloon. Though the cars are capable of tremendous speeds, they are best known for their beautiful lines, luxurious comfort, and complete reliability. Rolls-Royce cars are manufactured at Derby, England.

to be transferred from circular tracks to long stretches of sand, on which a car could run straight for some miles.

Daytona Beach, Florida, U.S.A., has been the scene of much record-breaking, for the conditions there are almost perfect. On it, in March, 1927, the late Major Sir Henry Segrave travelled a mile at over 202 miles per hour. This was beaten the next year by another Briton, Captain Malcolm Campbell, who added a further four miles per hour; and he soon lost the record to an American, Mr. Kay Reech, who hustled his car along at 207½ miles an hour. Then in March, 1929, Sir Henry Segrave took over his " Golden Arrow," driven by a 1,000-horse power aeroplane engine and most carefully shaped, so that it should cleave the air. On this monster he dashed down the course at the terrific speed of 231½ miles an hour. Two years later, at Daytona Beach, Captain Campbell drove his car " Blue Bird " at 245·7 miles an hour; and, in 1935, he reached the velocity of 301·129 miles per hour.

This was eclipsed on Bonneville Salt Flats first by Capt. G. E. T. Eyston, who achieved 359·49 miles per hour, and then by John Cobb at 368·85 miles

per hour, and in 1947 Cobb put the world's " unlimited " record for the flying mile to over 394 miles per hour.

These records are valuable not merely from a sporting point of view, but because of the knowledge gained in devising engines and equipment to stand the strain of such severe tests. It is from the experience of the racing motorist that the manufacturer and designer learn.

When we come to the use of the motor as a labour-saving invention the result has been something in the nature of a revolution throughout the whole field of industry. New roads have had to be built to deal with the enormous increase in road transport, and for some years to come the problem of roads will be an urgent one. Even in the making of these roads the motor will have a major part to play.

In time of war petrol-driven motors and a continuous supply of oil fuel were of the utmost importance to all the combatant nations.

Where formerly infantry soldiers, often marching incredible distances, were in the forefront of the attack and formed the backbone of defence,

Sport and General.

FASTER THAN THE CAMERA'S LENS AND SHUTTER

The racing motor car is almost too much even for a high-speed camera, as this snapshot proves. The car in action is that of Captain G. E. T. Eyston during his marvellous run at Bonneville Flats, near Salt Lake City, in 1938, when a speed exceeding 359 miles per hour was reached.

CARS OF TO-DAY

Jaguar Cars Ltd.

The Mark VII Jaguar Saloon car was the culmination of five years' research and development. It was one of the outstanding successes of the Motor Show and the entire production had to be allotted to export markets for some time. Many of its features had indeed been designed to suit overseas buyers and it is easily capable of speeds of over 100 miles per hour.

Rootes Ltd.

One of the most popular of family cars is the latest Hillman Minx, seen above. At home its sales have been restricted by export demands from about a hundred different countries where it has already gained a high reputation. As with other British cars, the requirements of overseas buyers, especially in such matters as ample luggage accommodation, have been specially borne in mind.

we find now dive-bombing aeroplanes working in association with tanks that may weigh as much as eighty tons and be capable of rapid progress over the roughest country.

In Armoured Cars

To-day armoured vehicles, both light and heavy, some armed with powerful guns, have more or less taken the place of cavalry in the armies of the world. Masses of infantry are swiftly transported from point to point in lorries known in the British Army as "dragons." The guns of the Royal Artillery are drawn by motor tractors instead of spirited horses, and the sappers of our Royal Engineers depend upon the internal combustion engine in a wide variety of ways. As for the Royal Air Force, it is surely entirely dependent upon the motor for the marvellous work it is called upon to perform.

Even in the War of 1914–18 motor vehicles and a free access to the world's supplies of petrol contributed largely to the victory of the Allies, and we shall never forget the ponderous moving forts known as "Tanks" first sent into action on the Somme on September 15th, 1916. The sight of these monsters crawling slowly over hedges and ditches, spitting fire from their guns as they advanced, was probably the greatest surprise of the war for the Germans.

The All-Conquering Motor

The petrol motor has been applied to practically every kind of thing that moves on wheels. The private car has made the private horse vehicle almost a thing of the past. The motor omnibus has driven the horse omnibus entirely out of business. In London alone the motor 'buses take a million people every day to their work in the morning

By courtesy of Messrs. John I. Thornycroft & Co. Ltd.

A ROAD TRAIN FOR AUSTRALIA

The construction of the Snowy Mountains Hydro-electric stations in Australia involves the transport of indivisible units of machinery weighing up to 120 tons over mountain tracks and gravel roads. To do this two " Mighty Antar " tractors, built by Thornycroft & Co. Ltd., together with a Crane multi-wheeled trailer, were constructed, and this " road train," 131 feet long, is seen here on its road test in Britain before being sent to Australia.

THE WORLD'S LARGEST WALKING DRAGLINE

Stewarts and Lloyds.

This gigantic machine, the world's largest " walking dragline," with an all-welded tubular steel jib, is a remarkable achievement of British engineering skill and is now being used in opencast ironstone mining at Messrs. Stewarts and Lloyds' Priors Hall Quarry, near Corby, Northants. Each 60 seconds the huge bucket digs about 27 tons of earth or " overburden " which has to be moved clear of the site to get at the ironstone. The machine weighs about 1,600 tons and moves about the same amount every hour. It is driven and controlled by one man but does not move on wheels; instead it has two feet on which it walks along. The head of its tail jib is 175 feet above the ground, 5 feet higher than Nelson's Column in Trafalgar Square.

WITH THE DEFENCE FORCES

Topical.

The Centurion tanks, seen above, are now the standard tanks of the British Army, and are the best of their size in any modern army. Each weighs 50 tons when ready for action, and their fighting qualities were first demonstrated in the difficult country of Korea.

Fox Photos.

There is an Amphibian Wing in the Royal Army Service Corps, and here we have a photograph of the craft they operate. They are equally at home on land and water, and in this picture are seen entering the sea from dry land to load or unload a cargo from a ship lying well off shore.

Central Press.

TO AID THE SICK AND INJURED

Of all vehicles in use to-day the ambulance is the one in which both speed and comfort are most essential. Here we have a very modern example, a Daimler Ambulance, which has a 12 foot 6 inch wheelbase, independent suspension, a 4-litre petrol engine, and is able to carry twenty gallons of fuel in its tank.

and bring them back in the evening. Motor lorries carry heavy goods long distances; motor vans deliver parcels at our doors. Motor coaches transport tens of thousands of pleasure seekers daily from place to place, or make regular daily journeys between towns hundreds of miles apart.

We no longer see the horse-drawn fire engine, with smoke belching from its funnel, dashing down the street. A modern engine has a motor which both propels it and works its pumps.

In the mining and building industries huge machines driven by petrol engines perform the work which until comparatively recent times required gangs of men to carry out, and the huge tractors and excavators accomplish it in far less time. The site for a new building is cleared by the bulldozer; the excavator which is illustrated in these pages is capable of shifting 27 tons of earth at one bite, and it takes sixty bites an hour.

On the farm, too, the motor tractor is taking the place of the horse in many of the heavy tasks that animal has performed for long centuries past. The time has not yet come when the horse has been completely banished from the farm; quite possibly it never will be. But for some work it cannot compete with the motor tractor, and more and more farms are becoming largely dependent on their motor equipment. To-day motor tractors are employed for hauling, ploughing, reaping, drilling, and many other tasks. Men and women are still needed to operate and care for the motor, but their tasks are not so heavy and the motor tractor can accomplish far more in a day than was ever possible by hand.

It would be difficult to say how many motor vehicles there are in the world but we know that some 6,500,000 new ones have been produced annually in normal times in recent years. The greatest producing nation in this respect is the

U.S.A., and the United Kingdom comes second.

In America the motor vehicle industry now takes first place among all industries, employing over four million people, and the average person regards a car as a necessity rather than a luxury. What a change since that day in 1896 when a procession of a few dozen cars, just released from the tyranny of the " red flag " law, crawled from London to Brighton, and wise people shook their heads over the many breakdowns, saying " These motor cars will never be of any use! "

Breaking All Records

British motorists have suffered from various handicaps in the past few years owing to the economic difficulties of the post-war period. The restrictions have gradually been removed and it is hoped that new roads and improvements to old ones will keep pace with the ever-increasing traffic on the highways.

The motor-car industry has flourished throughout Britain and the Commonwealth. To prove the qualities of their cars one well-known company sent one of its stock cars to Indianapolis Speedway in the U.S.A. to attack American Stock Car Records. During its seven-day endurance test this car covered 11,875 miles at an average speed of 70·68 miles per hour.

In the course of this test the car broke every American Automobile Association record for Stock Cars between two and seven days. Altogether it established 63 records. Achievements such as these testify to the reliability of British workmanship and to the capacity of designers and craftsmen to produce machines of the highest quality.

A Shell Photograph.

A SCAMMELL " MOUNTAINEER " MOTOR LORRY

This giant motor vehicle is one of a number specially designed for use in the oilfields. A 14-ton load of steel blocks has just been piled on the skid at the back, and this skid is hauled over a roller at the rear of the body by the winch at the front. When the load has passed over the point of balance, the front of the vehicle slowly returns to the ground as the load is gradually drawn forward. The lorry is designed to operate " off the road " and under arduous conditions.

How
Steam and
Petrol
Work for Man

The Story
of the
Development
of Aircraft

Rischgitz.

THE WORLD'S FIRST POWER-DRIVEN, MAN-CARRYING AEROPLANE

December 17th, 1903, was a memorable date in the annals of aviation and also in the history of the world, for on that day a human being first flew in a heavier-than-air machine kept aloft by its own power. This actual machine is illustrated above. It was built by the brothers Wilbur and Orville Wright at Dayton, Ohio, in the United States of America.

CONQUERING THE AIR

THE conquest of the air by man has throughout the ages been in the forefront of human endeavour. The scope and freedom of birds in flight formed in itself a constant reminder and perpetual incentive; and, before the Christian Era, kites were used in China as something far more than mere toys.

Many names have come down to us to show the interest and enthusiasm there has always been in the mastery of the air. Leonardo da Vinci (1452–1519), of whom we read in our Art Section, was a genius centuries ahead of his time and his note-book drawings still exist which

show both a flying machine with flapping wings and a contraption very much like a helicopter. In the sixteenth century an experimenter named Danti constructed a glider covered with feathers and glided a short distance— until he crashed into a building. John Damian, an Italian, was another who adventured into the air in a somewhat similar manner from Stirling Castle.

Man's first successful journeys through the air were made by means of balloons. From them developed dirigible or steerable airships, eighteenth century progress in aviation being concerned almost entirely with balloons to

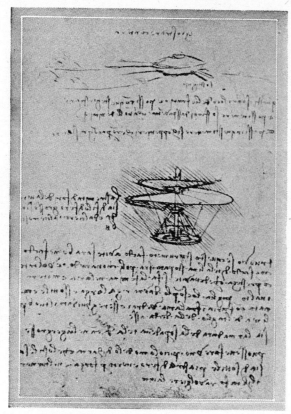

FOR THE MASTERY OF THE AIR

Rischgitz.

Leonardo da Vinci was a great genius who lived
1452–1519. He planned both an armoured car and a
flying machine, not unlike a helicopter. The above
notes and drawings were made by da Vinci.

Lilienthal in the air, carried on glider experiments and was the first to provide such a machine with wheels. His glider the " Hawk " was built in 1896. He was also the first to think of applying a petrol engine to the purpose of propulsion, losing his life before he could put this idea into effect. Meantime, in America, other trials were being carried out. A. M. Herring, a pupil of Lilienthal, and Octave Chanute, a Frenchman, built a double-deck glider on the lines of a biplane, the machine having a tail. Sir George Cayley, an Englishman, made a great name as an experimenter and earned the title of the " Father of British Aeronautics."

Step by step, these daring pioneers gathered knowledge which was of great value, and the glider must indeed be held as the introduction to power-driven aircraft. The principle of human flight was grasped by the glider-makers of the early nineteenth century, but they had not at that time a suitable prime mover or power unit with which to convert gliders into aeroplanes. The fact remains, however, that a glider is in all other respects an aeroplane and it was glider the exclusion of anything in the nature of an aeroplane, or of its true parent, the glider.

In the 'nineties of the last century, however, man in his zeal risked his life on kite-like wings to glide down the slopes of hills. Otto Lilienthal (1848–1896), a German engineer, was the first to copy the soaring flight of birds and his use of a curved wing on a glider later influenced the brothers Wilbur and Orville Wright. Lilienthal actually made some gliding flights of over 300 yards.

A young Englishman, Percy Pilcher, who had watched

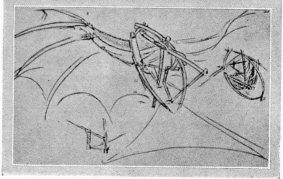

FIVE HUNDRED YEARS AGO

Rischgitz.

Here is a sketch of a flying machine by da Vinci. Man
has thought of air conquest for at least 500 years.

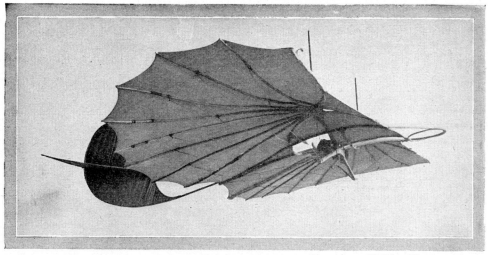

GLIDER WITH BIRD-LIKE WINGS

The Science Museum, London.

The strange looking object here depicted is the glider constructed after years of study by Otto Lilienthal, a German professor. It was formed of a pair of rigid, outstretched wings, connected to each other and to an upright tail. There was an opening between the wings through which Lilienthal thrust his head and arms. Like many another pioneer, this inventor perished whilst attempting a flight.

work that gave a full understanding of stability and control.

We come next to the astonishing work of John Stringfellow (1799–1883) —work that is not always given the prominence that it deserves. Stringfellow and William Henson built a steam-driven model aeroplane which must be considered to be the first practical flying machine of the kind we know to-day. This amazing achievement failed to gain its full appreciation simply because it was carried out only on a small scale. Had Stringfellow succeeded in his projects for building a full-scale machine and flying it, he might have held to-day the position which is rightly accorded to the Wright brothers, that of being the first men to fly in a heavier-than-air machine, on December 17th, 1903.

Balloons and Airships

Before going further with the development of heavier-than-air flying machines it may be well to consider the efforts made at various stages to ascend and travel above the earth's surface by lighter-than-air craft. On November 21st, 1783, a balloon carried human beings through the air for the first time. The balloon was a fire balloon, that is, one rendered buoyant by hot air rising from a fire at its bottom end, and was constructed by two French paper-makers, Etienne and Joseph Mont-golfier. The two aeronauts aboard—M. Pilâtre de Rozier and the Marquis d'Arlandes—made a safe journey of about five and a half miles. This aerial voyage, at a height of about 300 feet, lasted twenty-five minutes, and was the first in history.

That, however, was not the first human *ascent*. This took place in October of the same year, Pilâtre de Rozier going up alone in a captive balloon to a height of 80 feet. At that level the balloon remained for nearly five minutes, the fire, which was in a brazier slung in the aperture, having to be repeatedly stoked.

Heading for the Clouds

The hot-air balloon was soon superseded by the gas balloon. Professor Charles ascended on December 1st, 1783, from the Champ de Mars, Paris, in a small balloon filled with hydrogen, watched by a crowd of, it is said, 600,000 persons.

Great things were expected from the gas balloon, but it soon became evident that such a balloon was entirely at the mercy of the winds, and that a balloon must be self-propelling in order to be steerable, and be so shaped as to offer a minimum resistance to forward movement through the air. The first airship, or dirigible balloon, worthy of mention was that of M. Henri Giffard, shaped much like a modern airship and driven by a small steam engine. It made its initial flight on September 24th, 1852, at a speed of about 4 miles an hour in still air. The really practical airship did not, however, materialise until, in the closing years of last century, the petrol motor was applied to it. In 1898 M. Santos Dumont, a young Brazilian, launched the first of a series of motor-driven airships, termed non-rigid because they depended for the maintenance of their shape on the pressure of gas inside them.

A modification of the non-rigid is the semi-rigid airship, which has a long girder under the balloon proper to distribute the weight of the car and machinery. Some large airships of this kind have been built—especially in France and Italy—including the *Norge*, which on May 12th, 1926, carried the Norwegian explorer, Roald Amundsen, across the North Pole.

Rigid Airships

A third type of airship, the rigid type, owes its development to the German Count Ferdinand von Zeppelin. The fundamental principle of this type is that its shape is entirely independent of the condition of the gas containers. Its outer cover is stretched tightly over a framework of very light girders, which is subdivided into a number of compartments each containing an independent gas-bag. The leakage of a single bag is thus unable to influence the shape of the vessel, or to destroy its buoyancy. A further advantage is that the steering apparatus and engines can be attached directly to the hull, and many details, such as ballast, living accommodation,

Rischgitz.

ON ITS LAUNCHING CARRIAGE

Stringfellow was one of the earliest British pioneers in aviation. He built a steam-driven model aeroplane and the picture above shows the very first design for a machine having planes, which was his production. It is, of course, a triplane and the automatic launching carriage is seen. This model was exhibited at the Crystal Palace at the first Aeronautical Society exhibition in 1868.

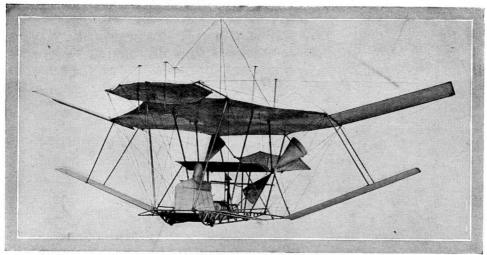

By permission of the Science Museum, London.

ONE OF THE EARLIEST FLYING MACHINES

Here is an illustration of the Maxim flying machine, which was tried at Bisley in Surrey in 1894, though the results were by no means encouraging. The machine was the invention of Sir Hiram Stevens Maxim, an Anglo-American, who is best remembered for his famous Maxim gun. As early as 1872 he prepared plans for a helicopter. He died in 1916.

etc., can be enclosed inside the envelope.

The first " Zeppelin " was launched in July 1900. It held 400,000 cubic feet of hydrogen gas. Its successors increased gradually in size until, at the outbreak of the Great War of 1914–18, they had a capacity of up to 2,000,000 cubic feet. During that war Zeppelins raided England and other countries many times, and did much damage with bombs, but so many were destroyed by storms and aeroplanes that the Germans ceased using them for offensive purposes. The most notable exploit of a Zeppelin of that time was a 5,500-mile flight from Bulgaria to Central Africa and back without landing.

Voyage Round the World

Attention then became centred on the rigid airship for both military and commercial use. Many trans-Atlantic journeys—the first of them that of the British R34—were made by them, and the German *Graf Zeppelin*, by far the most successful airship yet built, made a voyage round the world in August, 1929. This interesting vessel had a capacity of 3,708,000 cubic feet,

and was driven by five engines, totalling 2,850 horse-power. The German *Hindenburg*, 803 feet long, was the largest, highest-powered and most luxurious airship the world has ever known. With a maximum diameter of 135 feet, she carried fifty passengers and a crew of twenty-five, and reached a top-speed of 84 miles an hour, completing the Atlantic crossing from Frankfurt, Germany, to Lakehurst, New Jersey, U.S.A., in fifty-nine hours. She ended disastrously, in 1937, catching fire as she was in the act of mooring; thirty-two lives were lost. Her engines developed 4,400 horse-power, and the gas capacity was 7,070,000 cubic feet.

Two airships, R100 and R101, of 5,000,000 and 5,500,000 cubic feet capacity respectively, were constructed by the British Government. The first made a double crossing of the Atlantic; the second was destroyed by fire on French soil on October 5th, 1930, while on her way to India, with the loss of forty-eight lives, owing to buoyancy failure.

Helium Gas

In the United States the rare gas

called helium is used for inflating airships. It is the next lightest gas to hydrogen and has twelve-thirteenths of its lifting power. The fact that it also is non-inflammable renders it ideal for airship work. Two large airships, the *Akron* and *Macon*, each of 6,500,000 cubic feet capacity, were constructed for use with the United States Navy as aircraft carriers, five aeroplanes being housed in the lower part of the structure. The *Akron* had a maximum speed of 80 miles an hour, and was fitted with apparatus for condensing the water in the exhaust gases and collecting it to offset the loss of weight in fuel. This device avoided the release of the expensive helium gas to reduce buoyancy as fuel was used up.

Brought to Disaster

In spite of her practically complete freedom from fire risks, the *Akron* met with disaster on April 4th, 1933, when a violent storm drove her down into the sea off the coast of New Jersey and she sank at once, drowning all but three of her crew of twenty-seven persons. The *Macon* (84 m.p.h.) also crashed in the sea, after structural failure, in 1935; of her crew of eighty-three, eighty-one were saved.

Great Britain has abandoned construction, and in other countries the airship is regarded as less worth spending money on than the aeroplane.

Balloons, which of course came before aeroplanes, have remained in the public eye. They are put to a variety of uses. Captive balloons were employed for observation purposes during the 1914–18 war, and after the outbreak of war in 1939 they became a familiar sight in the sky as barrage balloons — also captive but without the basket for carrying observers. Attached by steel cable to a winch, their purpose in this capacity is to discourage dive-bombing by enemy aeroplanes and low-flying and machine-gunning at ground targets. They induce enemy aeroplanes to fly high. They were also used for combating the German V-1 flying bombs.

In the Stratosphere

Free balloons manned and unmanned are used for exploring in the stratosphere — the " thin " atmosphere miles above the levels in which aircraft ordinarily fly. These ascents have ranged up to over 72,000 feet, and their object is the recording of upper temperatures, wind direc-

Rischgitz.

MONTGOLFIER BALLOON ASCENT, 1783

Man first ascended into and travelled through space in a balloon constructed by the brothers Etienne and Joseph Montgolfier and heated with hot air. This old print shows the primitive heating arrangements.

Topical Press

A FAMOUS BRITISH AIRSHIP

Great Britain's airship R100, here illustrated in flight, was upwards of 700 feet in length, and was designed to travel at more than eighty miles an hour. She had no fewer than six engines, developing 4,200 horse-power. The airship was built at Howden in Yorkshire, but has long been dismantled.

tions and velocities, atmospheric pressure and so on. Two Americans, Captains A. W. Stevens and O. A. Anderson, of the U.S. Army, set up a record for an ascent of this nature in 1935, their balloon reaching a height of fourteen miles. They occupied an air-tight metal gondola attached to the balloon, reported their progress by wireless to observers on the ground, and landed again at a spot 230 miles distant from their starting point, after being in the air nearly eight hours.

Their balloon held 3,700,000 cubic feet of helium gas, and the gondola was 9 feet in diameter and carried more than twenty recording instruments. When they reached the fourteen-mile point —the limit of their ascent—the gondola was covered with ice and the outside temperature was 57° below zero. We get an idea of the real meaning of their fourteen-mile ascent when we learn that it took them over three hours to come down again.

Adrift for Eighteen Hours

Four years before those two Ameri-

cans went up, Professor Piccard made several important discoveries concerning weather and other conditions in the higher levels. He took with him Dr. Kipfer, and these two were the first ever to attain a height of ten miles above the earth. Their 6-foot globe or gondola was painted black on one side of the exterior, the idea being that when this black side turned to the sun it would capture and retain a certain amount of warmth. This appears to have been quite successful, for the inside temperature mounted at one time to an uncomfortable degree whilst many degrees of frost were recorded outside.

The aeronauts took great care that the enormous bag should be only partly inflated, to allow plenty of room for expansion of the gas as outside pressure became less with increasing height. There was no danger of the gondola bursting when the outside pressure decreased, means being provided to even-up the differences. And oxygen apparatus, to assist breathing, was carried. Eventually they made a safe landing, after drifting with changing

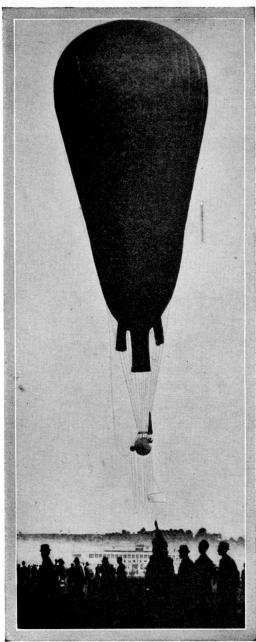

E.N.A.

TEN MILES HIGH

In the aluminium globe attached to this balloon
Professor Piccard and a companion, Dr. Kipfer,
ascended to a height of ten miles—the first ever
to do so. Careful scientific calculations were made
beforehand to eliminate as far as possible all the
risks involved in such an ascent. Their object
was to solve problems connected with the stratosphere.

winds over Germany, Austria and
Italy for eighteen hours.

Twenty-five Miles Up

Balloons with no crew have ascended as high as twenty-five miles.
Known as sounding balloons they
carry instruments for automatically
recording weather and other conditions; they can also secure air-samples
at different levels. When the gas
inside bursts the envelope (as happens
when the outside pressure falls below
a certain point) the various instruments descend unharmed, by parachute.

For none of these is any system of
propulsion required, as it is for other
types and, of course, for airships. In
that early search for means of propulsion—to get the free balloon under
some sort of control as to direction,
independent of the wind—even the
use of trained eagles and other birds
was considered !

Movable wings and a rudder were
tried by Blanchard, in 1784, and later
he experimented with oars. And
he was the first to employ a rotating
fan, which was a big stride on the way
to screw propulsion. Blanchard goes
down in history as being the first
ever to cross the English Channel
by air, which he did in a balloon,
with another aeronaut, Jeffries, in
1785.

The Wright Brothers

To return again to the history of
heavier-than-air flying machines: not
so very long ago the first authorised
biography of the Wright brothers
appeared, and in it a great deal that
was previously obscure about their
progress is elucidated. The Wrights
were working on their machines
at the time when Santos Dumont,
in Paris, was flying his small airship
and when Clément Ader had produced
a heavier-than-air machine which was
claimed to have made a flight.

Regarding the Clément Ader experi-

Charles E. Brown.

THE BARRAGE BALLOON OF THE WORLD WAR OF 1939-45
Close-up of a barrage balloon. It is attached by steel cable to a winch on the trolley and is filled with hydrogen. Grouped at a considerable height around vulnerable targets, barrage balloons discourage dive-bombing by enemy aeroplanes and low-flying and machine-gunning at ground targets and attack by flying bombs. They do not, of course, carry passengers.

ments there is still controversy. Some French engineers believe to this day that the full credit for being the first man to fly in a power-driven aeroplane belongs by right to Clément Ader. They consider that the demonstration he gave to military authorities years before the Wright brothers' famous first flights entitles him to be regarded as the chief pioneer.

There is, however, a distinction between Ader's admittedly remarkable experiments and those of the Wright brothers. The Wright brothers carried through their work to a conclusion. They continued until they could demonstrate whenever and wherever they wished that they were able to fly in a power-driven aeroplane under human control.

The verdict of the world on all these controversies is undoubtedly that the credit for being the greatest pioneers of human flight belongs to Orville and Wilbur Wright. As we have said, Octave Chanute, at the time resident in America, had been working on gliders and the Wrights described all their inventions to Chanute. Indeed, he gave public addresses concerning them in 1901 and 1902 in France.

During these two years the Wrights had been making gliding flights. Their calculations showed that they would need for power-driven controlled flight an engine lighter for its power than any then available. They were not deterred by this knowledge, though, and set about making their own unit. By modern ideas it was heavy and clumsy, weighing per horse-power more than ten times what an ordinary aero engine would now weigh, but for its day it was an outstanding achievement. The Wright machine itself into which the engine was fitted was a direct descendant of the gliders. It was a biplane and the pilot sat or rather reclined beside the engine. An interesting point here is that the engine drove two propellers. Chains were used for transmission and the propellers rotated in opposite directions.

Used in conjunction with this machine there was a special launching apparatus which had some resemblance to a catapult and was operated by a heavy weight taken to the top of a wooden tower and released, pulling behind it a rope to which a carriage on which the aircraft was put was attached. To-day it is worth noticing that that first flight which marked a point in world history was actually shorter than the run that would be taken by a fully-laden modern bombing aircraft to get off the ground. Ader's flight was said to have been made five years before, but the year 1903 is now universally accepted as the starting point of heavier-than-air aviation.

Rapid Progress

After their pioneer achievements the brothers Wright continued to work on aircraft. They built and flew many types, constantly improving on their previous performance and always remaining ahead of their rivals. It may be mentioned also that years after the first flight a dispute arose in America as to whether credit should not be given to what was called the Langley " aerodrome ". This was a heavier-than-air flying machine and it was claimed that it preceded the Wright machine in some respects. At a later date the secretary of the Smithsonian Institution recanted the claim made for Langley and so the Wright brothers gained full

Rischgitz.

A PIONEER AND HIS FLOAT SEAPLANE

This photograph shows the " waterplane " made by Samuel Franklin Cody (1862–1913). He was an experimenter whose name ranks high in aviation history. First devoting his attention to man-lifting kites, he produced a practical flying machine in 1908. He lost his life in a flying accident.

By courtesy of British Railways.

RAILWAY TRACK LAYING BY NIGHT

Continual repairs and renewals are necessary to keep the track on heavily-used railways perfectly safe. The modern method of renewing track is by building up complete units in the depot; these are conveyed to the renewal site where a crane belonging to a track-laying unit removes the old track in complete lengths and lays the new one. On the left in this picture is the track-laying unit; the compressed-air-operated winches have lowered the section of new track and the relayers are guiding it into position. On the right, the relaying ganger, carrying a standard Tilley lamp, is directing the work of the relayers, while other men to the left are waiting to do their own particular tasks in the operation

By courtesy of British Railways.

RAIL TRANSPORT IN THE SHIPBUILDING YARD

From earliest times the carrying of heavy loads over land and sea has been one of civilised man's great problems. The wheel was perhaps the first great advance, and with the use of animals for land travel and sails for water transport, great tasks were accomplished. But the most remarkable advances have been made in the past two centuries and the perfection of the steam engine began a new revolution in transport on land and sea. This painting by Norman Hepple, A.R.A., shows a scene in a shipbuilding yard, illustrating one aspect of the work behind our modern transport system: a steam locomotive is bringing material to workmen building an ocean-going ship designed to lay and repair cables that connect continent with continent.

Rischgitz.

The son of an Englishman, Henry Farman was born in France and was known first of all as a racing bicyclist. He turned his attention early to the air and built an aeroplane in 1907, being the first man to fly 100 miles. Later, he took part in flying meetings in Holland and America. With his brother Maurice, he established an aeroplane works near Paris, and we see above one of his famous machines in flight. During the First World War they built large numbers of machines for military purposes at their Billancourt factory.

credit as the unchallenged leaders in the development of heavier-than-air flight.

After the Wright brothers had demonstrated the practicability of aviation, progress went ahead at an enormous speed. Many new constructors entered the field, some of them men of remarkable originality of thought and most of them both designers and pilots. An aviator whose name ranks high was Samuel Franklin Cody (1862–1913). He was first an experimenter in man-lifting kites and made a practical flying machine in 1908. In 1911 he took part in a competition flight round Britain and his was the only British-made aeroplane to complete the course. S. F. Cody lost his life in a flying accident near Aldershot. The name of M. Louis Blériot is one that has a particular appeal to the peoples of England and France because of his first cross-Channel flight by a heavier-than-air machine in July, 1909. The other point on which he claims distinction is his early advocacy of the monoplane.

It has already been mentioned that the Wright brothers' machine was a biplane, and developments right through the war of 1914–18 and for a long time afterwards concentrated mainly on biplanes. Yet Blériot's 1909 model was a monoplane and it incorporated a number of features that were to come back into popularity just before the war of 1939.

Other names which became famous before the war of 1914–18 were those of Paulhan, Hucks, Grahame-White, Gustav Hamel, and the amazing Pégoud.

Pégoud might be said to be the inventor of aerobatics. The manner in which he risked his life in those early days of flight was fantastic and drew the rapt attention of the entire world. He leapt out of an aeroplane with a parachute, he looped the loop, he flew upside down and carried out the manœuvre afterwards called in the Royal Air Force the bunt. In fact he covered almost the entire field of aerobatics.

Topical.

FIRST ACROSS THE CHANNEL

Britain's security as an island was lost in July 1909 when Louis Blériot flew from France to England. This was the first time the Channel had been flown by a heavier-than-air machine. Here we see Blériot in his monoplane which had a 25-h.p. engine. Twenty years later he flew across again in a machine having 1,000 h.p. engines.

Rischgitz.

THE LONDON TO MANCHESTER RACE

The spring of 1910 witnessed a thrilling race from London to Manchester for a large money prize, the distance being 186 miles with one intermediate stop. The event was won by L. Paulhan (France), who is seen above with his aeroplane just before he took off again after landing at Lichfield. Paulhan was a famous aviator before the war of 1914–18.

An Upside-Down Dinner

When he came to Brooklands to display his art in England the crowds were staggered by the mastery he exercised over his aircraft. Looping the loop became a sort of craze about which everybody talked and there was even an "upside-down" dinner given in London in honour of a pilot who had afterwards imitated some of Pégoud's aerobatics. The tables were arranged with their feet pointing skywards and the menu went upside down from the savoury to the soup.

Although the immediate effect of these aerobatic displays tended to resemble that of a circus they had actually a most important and serious effect. They gradually instilled into the public mind a greater confidence in craft that were heavier-than-air. They showed people that these machines were capable of being safely handled in the most difficult circumstances and that a good pilot was never at a loss to recover control.

Those early aerobatic pilots, therefore, deserve special mention for the way in which they educated a doubting public in the control qualities of flying machines.

England had been somewhat backward in some of the early stages of the development of flying, but, soon after French and American constructors had succeeded in building successful machines, work that had been going on in England for some time past bore fruit. The first Englishman to fly in England was Lieut.-Colonel Moore-Brabazon (now Lord Brabazon of Tara). The next flight was made by a man who had designed and built his own aircraft. This was Sir Alliott Verdon-Roe and the machine was his A. V. Roe triplane. Sir Alliott had worked hard with practically no encouragement for many months, but he did eventually succeed in making fully controlled flights with complete success. Some still claim, indeed, that he was the first to make such flights in Great Britain.

One further point must be mentioned before some consideration is given to the theory of flight, and that is the part played by the great air races of the early days. They were undoubtedly instrumental in improving designs. The London-Manchester race won by Paulhan in April, 1910, and the early aerial Derbys as well as the weekend racing round the pylons at Hendon Aerodrome all contributed in some measure to the improvement of aircraft. This point is to be borne in mind when at a later

stage we come to the developments for the second world war. Here again the influence of racing will be felt and the effects of the Schneider Trophy events upon the aircraft with which Britain entered the war in 1939 noted.

Theory of Flight

Only essential facts about the theory of flight will be mentioned here because so much important history remains to be told. The aeroplane in its conventional form consists of a fuselage which corresponds to the body of a motor car and contains the crew, passengers and cargo, and the lifting and stabilising surfaces which include the wings, tailplane and elevator, the rudder, the fin and ailerons. The machine may have one or more engines which drive tractor airscrews or propellers or may produce jets.

Lift is generated by the lifting surfaces or wings by moving them through the air. If we assume a condition of

Rischgitz.

FOR THE FLIGHT TO MANCHESTER

Claude Grahame-White was one of the competitors in the great London to Manchester race of 1910 and above is seen his aeroplane being checked over just prior to the flight. Mr. Grahame-White was the first Englishman to take out an aviation certificate. He has done much for aeronautics and written many standard books on the subject.

AN EARLY VOISIN AEROPLANE

The Daily Mirror.

Colonel Moore-Brabazon (now Lord Brabazon of Tara) was the very first Englishman to fly in England, and the machine he used is illustrated here. It was of curious design and the cycle-like wheels and undercarriage are of special interest. There is neither nacelle nor fuselage as we know such parts to-day.

still air, then an aeroplane if it stopped moving would fall immediately to the ground. The whole principle of heavier-than-air flight is contained in this central fact that the movement of the aircraft through the air gives it its lift.

The way lift is obtained is by setting the wings at an angle so that as they are moved through the air they pull and press the air downwards, themselves being given an up-thrust by that process. They do, in other words, what a man does when he pushes himself up from the floor with his hands. He pushes the floor down and receives an upward " lift ".

The thrust which provides the aircraft with the movement that in turn gives it its lift is derived from the engine through airscrew or jet. So much for lift. The next point to consider is

stability. The aircraft must be balanced or directly it gets in the air it will either tend to dive into the ground, to climb vertically or to turn over on its side. The balance is achieved by arranging the wings and other surfaces in appropriate positions about the centre of gravity.

Other aids to stability are the angle of the wings, that is the slight angle they make with the horizontal which can sometimes be seen when an aeroplane is flying directly towards one, and the angles of the tailplane and the main-plane. The fin also plays its part in giving stability by a weathercock action similar to that of an ordinary weathercock on a steeple.

Control comes from the elevator, the rudder and the ailerons. The rudder plays a part somewhat like that of a ship, but, for turning, an aeroplane must be banked as well, this banking being brought about with the ailerons. The elevator controls the attitude of the machine about its lateral axis.

It has already been said that the earliest aeroplanes were mostly biplanes but that a few progressive pioneers like Blériot had shown that the monoplane could be a highly efficient type of machine. When the war of 1914–18 broke out the biplane was in the ascendant. The French had a few monoplanes such as the Moranes, which were afterwards to do good service, but the British Royal Flying Corps was mainly equipped with biplanes.

The War of 1914–18

The early years of the war saw these military machines used almost entirely for reconnaissance. Here and there attempts were made to use them for bombing and in an extremely crude form for fighting, but they were conceived mainly as the eyes of the army. Their performance varied, but a fair average would give a top speed of about eighty or ninety miles an hour and a duration of two to three hours with extremely restricted weight-lifting qualities.

As the war proceeded and as both sides introduced more and more aircraft air fighting began to develop. At first it took place between machines armed with rifles or even revolvers and one case is recorded of a pilot throwing his field glasses at the enemy machine. Then came the fixed forward gun and this was an important stepping stone in air-war development.

We will not enter here into the controversy as to exactly who was

Central News.

IN FLIGHT AT WEMBLEY PARK

The name of A. V. Roe (Sir Alliott Verdon-Roe) stands very high indeed in the annals of British aviation. The machine he favoured at first was a triplane and one of these models is here seen in flight piloted by Sir Alliott at Wembley Park, near London. Sir Alliott worked for many months before he could achieve successful flights.

Rischgitz.

A " PUSHER " FIGHTER BIPLANE

In the picture above, taken at Beauval on the Western Front, we see a de Havilland single-seater fighting biplane of the " pusher " type in which the pilot sat with the engine behind him. These machines were used quite successfully against German Fokker monoplanes early in 1916. Note what aerodromes and hangars were like in the war of 1914–18.

responsible for this invention. It first appeared in the form of a gun fixed on the fuselage of a small manœuvrable aeroplane. On the blades of the airscrew in front of the gun were fitted deflector plates so that if bullets happened to hit the blades they did not break the airscrew. A later and better form consisted of an interrupter gear which stopped the gun from firing at the critical moment when the airscrew blades were passing its muzzle.

This invention immediately conferred upon the small manœuvrable machine an exceedingly high fighting quality. It was able to shoot down the clumsier aircraft that were being used for reconnaissance and for gun spotting, and it transformed the whole air battle situation all along the western front. Reconnaissance machines, if they were to continue working, had to be given protection and that entailed introducing other small manœuvrable machines with these fixed guns.

The Fokker was the type used by the Germans with fixed forward firing guns and it did great slaughter among British aircraft. The British reply, however, though it was tardy, was effective. It took two forms, first the de Havilland 2 and F.E.8, and second the Sopwith Pup and subsequent types. The D.H. 2 was a pusher. The pilot sat out in a nacelle right in front of the machine and the engine was mounted behind him. It was a biplane and the tail had to be mounted on tail booms because it was a pusher.

The object of this arrangement was to give a full field of fire in front of the pilot. Armed with a Lewis gun he was able to turn it about in any direction he wished in the forward hemisphere. The D.H. 2 proved very successful and immediately put some slight check on the Fokkers. It was improved upon in speed and climb by the Sopwith Pup which was an ordinary tractor biplane of very small size and light weight with one Vickers gun fixed to fire forward in the line of flight controlled by an interrupter gear. The Sopwith Pup had a speed of over 100 miles an hour and could climb some 19,000 feet. It was in addition highly manœuvrable and able to turn in small circles.

After the Pup, which proved extremely successful in coping with the German fighters, came the Sopwith Camel and the Sopwith triplane. Aircraft of French origin included the Nieuport and various Moranes.

Whilst this development of the fighters was going on bombers were being increased in size and in weight-carrying capacity. The de Havilland 4 was a fast high-flying biplane bomber and the Handley Page 0/400 a twin-engined machine which had for its time unusually good weight-lifting qualities.

It was largely with the Handley Page 0/400 that the technique of night bombing began to be developed by the Royal Flying Corps, a technique later taken up, extended and amplified by the Royal Air Force in the second world war. Bombing in fact came increasingly into the picture in 1914–18 as the battles proceeded and statements were made by the great commanders of those days, including Field Marshal Foch, about the power and efficiency of air bombing, statements which proved remarkably wise and far-sighted and which had an almost equal validity under the changed conditions of the second world war.

The first world war ended with Britain possessing an air force with a total of 22,000 aircraft, over 3,000 of them in the first line. Peace, however, brought with it many problems, among them that of turning over the aircraft to civil uses.

Although there had been before the first world war attempts at running air mail services and other air lines, nothing really substantial had been achieved. Now a vigorous effort was made to establish air lines and postal services. We look back and see the mistakes

Peckham.

THE DE HAVILLAND MOTH MINOR

When flying clubs became popular in this country, the de Havilland Company designed and built that most notable aircraft the Moth biplane. Above is depicted the later Moth Minor monoplane, which had an engine of 90 h.p. The Moth series included many other models, among them the Leopard Moth and the Tiger Moth service trainer much used in 1939–45.

SEAPLANE AND FLYING-BOAT

Charles E. Brown.

The famous Schneider Trophy races were for seaplanes and the event was instituted before the war of 1914–18. The idea of the contests was to develop sea-worthiness as well as speed, Britain, America and Italy being the chief contestants. Eventually the Trophy was won outright by Great Britain in 1931, but the machine seen above carried off the honours in 1927.

Photographic News Agencies.

This is a photograph of the Bristol, the Boeing flying-boat which earned a great reputation for comfort and air performance. One of those purchased from the U.S.A. by British Overseas Airways, this machine had four engines and there was standard accommodation for sixty-six people, including the crew. During their period of Atlantic service the Boeings were the largest passenger flying-boats in the world.

of those days more clearly now, but we must also recognise the great enthusiasm and energy of those pioneers.

Organisers of commercial aviation had available large numbers of aircraft which were totally unsuited to civilian operation. They could not hope to design and build new aircraft economically. Service machines were to be bought cheaply from the Government, which was anxious to dispose of them. New types would have cost large sums and taken a long time to make.

These pioneers of civil flying therefore did the best they could by converting the bombers into civil transport aircraft. A London-Paris air line was opened, using a variant of the de Havilland bomber. A night mail service was run to Cologne. Various other services were started with varying results.

It was an heroic struggle against odds, but gradually these air services failed for one reason or another and the time came when government assistance had to be asked in order that British civil aviation should continue to function at all.

Other countries were going through similar difficulties and they had most of them arrived at a similar conclusion, namely, that a governmental subsidy was necessary in order to keep civil flying in existence. Our own Government realised some of its obligations and sought to do what it could to keep things going. In Britain a competition for civil aircraft was held under the

Central Press.

FOR LONG DISTANCE PASSENGERS AND MAILS

British Overseas Airways controls a vast system of air transport throughout the world and many of its largest services were instituted with flying-boats such as the British-built *Castor*, depicted above. The photograph was obtained at an English terminus, and we see how passengers were taken to and from the shore by launch.

New York Times.

THE WORLD'S LARGEST NAVAL FLYING-BOAT

Here is illustrated the Mars, at the time of its launching the world's largest flying-boat, during a flight at Baltimore. The craft weighs 70 tons and has a wing span of 200 feet. She is capable of flying from America to Europe and back non-stop. Top speed is over 300 miles an hour.

ægis of the Air Ministry. Many of the great war-aeroplane firms entered this competition. The Sopwith Company, Supermarine, Westland, Bristol, and Handley Page were among them ; but, although the winners in their various classes were remarkably good machines for their day, there still seemed trouble in placing them into service in any large numbers. Indeed, it began to be recognised that a long-term policy was essential if British commercial aviation was to keep going.

Meanwhile other branches of civil aviation were in difficulties. Private flying was almost non-existent. The light aeroplane which had been glibly promised during the first world war did not make its appearance ; or, if it did, did not command public sympathy and support.

The Second Phase

After this decline of aviation which resulted from the war of 1914–18, there came a gradual revival. It coincided with the establishment of flying clubs, with the creation of Imperial Airways Limited as a government-subsidised company, and with the formation of a number of other small air line companies.

The flying clubs, which owed their existence partly to Air Vice-Marshal Sir Sefton Brancker, one of the greatest men British civil aviation has ever had as its leader, and partly to Sir Philip Sassoon, who was then the Under-Secretary of State for Air and himself the owner of a private aeroplane. The clubs aimed at giving cheap and safe flying to as many people as possible, and another government-sponsored competition was held at Lympne, in Kent, to stimulate the design and production of a suitable machine. Quite independently the de Havilland Company had weighed up the position with marked accuracy and designed and built that notable aircraft, the de Havilland Moth.

It is fair to say that the success of the light aeroplane club movement was in large measure due to the success of the Moth. It was a small, cheap, safe aeroplane which was easy to fly and it immediately earned the approval and confidence of vast numbers of pilots. There then came the period of air pageants, small race meetings, and private flying of all kinds.

The pageants were held at aerodromes all over the country and often attracted enormous crowds of people. The races were almost equally successful and accomplished their purpose in improving the aircraft and showing the public in general what could be done with them.

Meanwhile commercial aviation gradually began to find its feet. Imperial Airways Limited, under a progressive management, ordered the biggest air line machines ever contemplated at that time. They were known as the Handley Page 42 class and were, for their day, immense biplane air liners, each with four engines and capable of offering to the passengers a degree of comfort which had never before been thought possible in aircraft.

Between London and Paris

On the London-Paris route these huge machines, although slow, earned considerable popularity. Their comfort was quite exceptional for the time. Their cabins were quiet and spacious.

Then came the Short Empire flying-boats ordered under the same management with Mr. Woods Humphery as managing director. These flying boats bring us in aviation development to the eve of the second world war. They were certainly the finest commercial aircraft to be produced before 1939. Produced for the great Empire routes inaugurated by Imperial Airways, they worked successfully on these routes right up to the outbreak of hostilities. All the time they built up their reputation for trustworthiness, speed and comfort. They were a triumph for British engineering.

The remaining years before the outbreak of the second world war marked a period in which development

E.N.A.

TO CROSS THE ANDES MOUNTAINS

This air-liner is just about to leave an American airport for its long journey over the Andes range of mountains carrying mails and passengers to Chile. Known as the Cordillera, the Andes have an average height of 14,000 feet, with summits up to 20,000 feet.

FACING THE ATLANTIC OCEAN

Captain Kingsford-Smith, the Australian airman, held a great place as a pioneer of long-distance flights. Above is his monoplane *Southern Cross* a few minutes after the take-off from the beach at Portmarnock, near Dublin. Dawn has just broken and New York is the airman's objective. This flight took place in the summer of 1930.

suddenly accelerated in almost dramatic fashion.

On the service side the Royal Air Force gave its pageants, which were afterwards called displays, at Hendon every year. Tens of thousands of people flocked to these remarkable demonstrations of air power. They saw the latest machines doing amazing aerobatics and engaging in mock combats which gave them some hint of the tremendous aerial fights that might take place if ever the world were again plunged into war. On the civil side the light aeroplane clubs were flourishing as never before. Their membership was growing day by day. They were using hundreds of aircraft where before they had used tens. Further, they were being added to and supported by numerous gliding clubs which had sprung up in various parts of the country.

The world seemed to have gone aviation mad. Great flights were accomplished by individual pilots such as Amy Johnson, James Mollison, and that supreme exponent of long-range flying, Sir Charles Kingsford-Smith.

The Atlantic, which had been the scene of Britain's great air success of 1919, when Sir John Alcock and Sir Arthur Whitten Brown made the first direct flight across this ocean in a Vickers Vimy aircraft with two Rolls-Royce engines, was now the scene of further astonishing achievements. It was flown in each direction and at successively higher speeds. It was flown by big machines and by light aeroplanes.

Flying the Atlantic

Many good pilots were lost during the Atlantic flying craze, but none can doubt that the effect of the successive flights repeated at shorter and shorter intervals was to impress upon people that aircraft were gradually reaching the stage of being able to conquer the vast ocean spaces. Pre-war aviation worked up to its climax with the great air races, the Schneider Trophy contests, the MacRobertson England-Australia event, and the England-South Africa race. Nothing like these sporting events had ever been seen before.

The Schneider Trophy races were held every other year and had been instituted before the war of 1914–18. They were for seaplanes and were intended in their original state to develop sea-worthiness as well as speed, but they later turned into speed events, pure and simple. Britain, America, and Italy were the greatest contestants and they fought vigorously for victory every time the race was held. The rules proclaimed that three successive wins gave the trophy to the victor in perpetuity so that the race would cease. In 1927, the Royal Air Force undertook to send a team to represent Britain to Venice where the race was being held. Thus, a prodigious festival of speed took place over the placid waters of the Lido before the most expensive and luxurious hotels in Europe.

Flight-Lieutenant S. N. Webster, in a Supermarine Napier seaplane, won this event at a speed of 281.656 miles an hour. 1929 saw the race being held over the waters of the Solent in Great Britain. Again victory went to the Royal Air Force, Flying Officer Waghorn being the victor at 328.63 miles an hour. 1931 saw the supreme climax of speed when Flight-Lieutenant J. Boothman tore round the triangular course at an average speed of 340 miles an hour and concluded the series by winning the trophy outright for Great Britain. Ever since it has stood in the Royal Aero club as a tribute to the work of the designers and pilots who took part in these events.

The winning aircraft in the last two races were Supermarine seaplanes fitted with Rolls-Royce engines; and, as is well-known, they were the starting point from which the famous Vickers-Armstrongs Spitfire fighter was developed. They were designed by Mr. R. J. Mitchell and represented the best that had until then

Doughtys.

THE BLACKBURN BLUEBIRD

This is the Mark 4 type of the Bluebird aeroplane, a machine which had side by side seating and enjoyed a period of popularity in the flying clubs before the outbreak of the World War in 1939.

been accomplished in the way of high-speed single - seat aircraft.

It must be mentioned also that during the last of this series of races Flight-Lieutenant George Stainforth set up for Britain a world's speed record of 407 miles an hour.

All these events made people far more interested in aviation. Articles were written and books came out seeking to interpret what would be the result of aeronautical progress in the event of another great war breaking out. Terrible pictures were painted of capital cities laid in ashes by immense bombing raids and descriptions given of terrific battles fought in the skies by vast air fleets.

Charles E. Brown.

A MOSQUITO BOMBER

One of the most versatile aircraft ever produced is the de Havilland Mosquito bomber, the fastest in service during the last war. It is fitted with two Rolls-Royce Merlin engines and made its first appearance in 1940. Our photograph shows a P.R. (photographic reconnaissance) Mosquito, Mark 16, in flight.

Prelude to War

The Royal Air Force was still small, though public opinion had at last awakened to the fact that Great Britain was an island only in relation to surface transport and that the barriers to invasion constituted by the sea were now less complete. Blériot's Channel flight of 1909 was recalled as the first practical indication that the isolation of the British Isles no longer existed.

We turn now to the structure of the Royal Air Force as it was at the outbreak of the World War of 1939–45. The Force contained three important operational commands, Bomber Command, Fighter Command and Coastal Command. The Army Co-operation side was less fully developed though subsequently an Army Co-operation Command was formed. Plans were also laid whereby units could be taken from these Commands to form special forces which would be sent overseas in the event of Britain being called to go to the aid of France.

As will be seen, the Command structure was the backbone of the Royal Air Force organisation. In particular, Fighter Command under Air Chief Marshal Sir Hugh Dowding, as he then was, though he later became Lord Dowding, had been working intensively upon defence arrangements. Dowding had seen that a tremendous responsibility might suddenly be placed upon his shoulders. He had realised that if Germany went to war against the Allies once again she might try to smash Britain by all-out aerial attack. He therefore worked incessantly to prepare to meet such an onslaught.

The amazing invention of radio-location, primarily the work of Sir Robert Watson-Watt, was applied to Fighter Command's special strategy for meeting air attack from the skies. It conferred the enormous advantage of giving early information of the approach of enemy aircraft. The whole length of the coast of Great Britain could be watched by this astonishing new instrument both by day and by night, and this enabled Sir Hugh Dowding to dispose his fighter aircraft to meet the attacks.

Not long before war broke out an exercise was held in which Royal Air Force bombers made mock assaults upon London and Fighter Command sought to intercept these attempts. The results seemed satisfactory. The number of interceptions was high and few of the bombers got through without having to fight.

Lockheed Aircraft Corporation.

A LOCKHEED CONSTELLATION PASSENGER AEROPLANE

Carrying 43 passengers by day, with sleeping accommodation for 34, the Lockheed Constellation is used on a number of long distance air services between America and Europe. Our illustration shows the Constellation 'plane which flies a regular schedule between Rio de Janeiro and Paris and London, via Natal and Lisbon, at an average speed of 300 miles an hour.

"Aeronautics."

THE "VISCOUNT"—THE WORLD'S FIRST PROPELLER-TURBINE AIR-LINER

When the Vickers-Armstrongs "Viscount" aeroplane came into service with the British European Airways Corporation in July, 1950, it was the world's first propeller-turbine air-liner to fly on regular passenger routes. It brought a new conception of comfortable travel by air for those going to and from the continent of Europe. The "Viscount" is fitted with four Rolls-Royce Dart gas turbine engines, driving air-screws, and these are noted for their freedom from vibration and their low noise level, features which are greatly appreciated by all passengers. The cruising speed is between 280 and 300 miles an hour, according to circumstances. Many airline companies, including Trans-Australia Airlines, have ordered "Viscount" machines for their passenger services.

THE BRISTOL "BRITANNIA" OF BRITISH OVERSEAS AIRWAYS

Powered by four Bristol Proteus turbo-propeller engines, each of which gives 3,780 horse-power, the Bristol "Britannia" is the latest addition to the fleet of air-liners in service with the British Overseas Airways Corporation. In use on the regular routes it is capable of carrying a hundred passengers from London to Cairo in six hours. The "Britannia" has a wing-span of 142 feet and a total weight of 155,0co pounds. When larger long-range versions of the "Britannia" come into production, the engines will be more powerful and a later variant of the Proteus engine will give a shaft horse-power of 4,150.

Flight.

THE PERCIVAL MEW GULL

With its 200 h.p. engine, this proved to be a first-class aeroplane for skilled and experienced pilots interested in racing. It is really a high-speed racing machine and is not to be confused with the Percival Gull, which is essentially a touring aircraft.

The World War of 1939-45

At this period the anticipated storm broke. In 1939 Germany struck at Poland; and, as had been predicted, air power played a dominant *rôle*. The German bombers launched their first massive attacks on the city of Warsaw; and, although the Polish fighters strove heroically, they could not hold them off. Britain was immediately involved in the war and there arose a feeling of tension which was largely the result of knowledge that air attack might come at any moment and that the Navy, which had provided a certain shield for so many centuries, was no longer complete in itself.

The first bombing attack launched by the Royal Air Force was afterwards known as the Kiel raid and it evoked great enthusiasm, though in the light of subsequent events it must be held to be a mere incident. In France the Advanced Air Striking Force and the Air Component were set up alongside the French Army and French air force,

the first to launch bombing raids on the enemy, the second to work mainly in collaboration with the ground forces.

Then came the dramatic sweep of the German armies across Europe. The Advanced Air Striking Force found itself almost powerless to check the enemy's activities and the Air component was in a similar position. Where air battles took place Allied fighters proved themselves as good as any and better than most, but they could not stem the onrush of the mighty power of the Reich.

The Dunkirk evacuation was the next stage and then for the first time Royal Air Force fighters were able to slow the Germans. They bravely held up some kind of canopy over the British and French forces during the historic evacuation. They fought incessantly and managed in face of well-nigh insuperable difficulties to enable the men to be carried home without crippling casualties.

The scene now moves to Britain

during the period when she stood alone against the whole might of the enemy. Air assault on a gigantic scale was daily expected; and, in August, 1940, it came. The Luftwaffe sent out immense fleets of bombing aeroplanes escorted by fighters with the deliberate intention of striking down the might of Great Britain.

At this stage arrived the opportunity for Sir Hugh Dowding and his Fighter Command to test the devices, the organisation and the training on which they had worked so hard in the years of peace. Fighter Command was a small force, but it was equipped with magnificent aircraft and well-trained pilots, and its spirit was high.

The Vickers-Armstrongs Spitfire, whose creation we have already discussed, and the Hawker Hurricane were the two machines which had to ward off the immense onslaught, both of them powered by the Rolls-Royce Merlin 12-cylinder, liquid-cooled engine. Each of these aeroplanes had eight machine guns mounted in the wings and they

were the most powerful, and the quickest climbing and best fighting aircraft anywhere in the world. It was well that they were, for they were to face the most prodigious problem ever presented to so small a force of fighting pilots.

The great German air fleets set out. They approached the coasts of England. Radio-location functioned according to plan. The numbers, height and course of the aerial armada were flashed to Fighter headquarters. Sir Hugh Dowding, repeating in earnest exactly the same series of operations that he had practised in peace time, sent up his squadrons. The Battle of Britain had begun and a period of intense air fighting supervened.

The results are well known and stand to the undying credit of our gallant airmen. No German formation had a clear run over Britain. Every one was challenged and often shattered by the repeated fighter attacks of the Hurricanes and Spitfires. The German pilots soon began to fear the British

Associated Press.

A WATER-BASED JET FIGHTER

The first water-based jet fighter in the world was the SR/A1, built by Saunders-Roe. It is seen here taking off for a trial flight from the River Medina, Cowes, Isle of Wight. The aircraft has a speed of over 500 miles an hour and carries four 20 mm. cannon. For the protection of shipping round our coasts this type of aircraft would be particularly useful.

BRITAIN'S FIGHTER AIRCRAFT

So vast is the area of sky to be covered by the airman in modern fighter aircraft that human vision is of little use. Because of this more elaborate and bulky radar equipment has to be carried to overcome the " vision barrier." The Delta wing makes this possible, and the new Gloster GA5 Javelin all-weather fighter made its first appearance towards the end of 1952.

Photos : Central Press.

In this photograph Britain's new two-seater all-weather fighter, the De Havilland 110, is seen in flight. It is powered by two Rolls-Royce Avon axial-flow jets, and has flown many times at a speed greater than sound. This aircraft combines high speed, a very high rate of climb, and splendid manœuvrability at extreme altitudes, with all the practical equipment required by a modern fighter.

14—2

machines. The morale of the invaders began to waver.

Enemy losses mounted at a prodigious rate. In the Battle of Britain more than 1,700 German aircraft were shot down, and hundreds of others were damaged, some beyond repair. Hitler's pilots decided they had had enough. Their attacks tailed off, but the slowing of th's phase only meant that they were preparing something more. Actually, they were making ready for the night assault. With this they hoped to escape the attentions of our fighters and to be able to inflict decisive damage on our big cities and ports. Here again history records the result. At first the German bombers were able to work their will almost unchallenged. Anti-aircraft fire was inadequate, the arrangements for night fighting were not sufficiently advanced technically to enable the enemy's bombers to be found and attacked at night.

Great Britain underwent a difficult time during which considerable damage was done to many famous cities, including London. At no time, however, was there any wavering among the civil population, which stood up to the assault and worked with all its might to get ready for the counter blows which it knew would eventually be launched.

After this the war centre shifted to Libya and North Africa where there had been many movements and innumerable attacks. In this field aviation played its part in collaboration with the armies, and British commanders devised methods of achieving an even

Charles E. Brown.

A FAMOUS TWO-SEATER SAILPLANE

Here you see a sailplane in the course of a flight. It has two side-by-side seats and proved itself capable of astonishing performances. The picture shows Lieutenant W. E. Murray and Mr. J. S. Sproule in *Falcon III*, when in 1938 they set up a duration record for gliders by remaining in the air for 22 hours, 13 minutes and 35 seconds and returning to the point of their departure.

THE MASTERS OF THE SKY

Central Press.

This striking photograph shows Hurricane fighters of the " United Provinces " Squadron on patrol. These aircraft were provided by the people of the United Provinces of India and can here be seen flying in echelon well above the clouds. The pilots of these machines were British, Australian, Canadian and Polish.

closer co-ordination of air and land than the German commanders had achieved during their early successes in the Low Countries and France.

War in the Pacific

Air collaboration with sea forces had not been developed so highly as air collaboration with land forces, though the blow struck by the Fleet Air Arm on the Italian Fleet in Taranto was an historic occasion. Next an attack by the Japanese on American naval units in Pearl Harbour (December 7th, 1941) brought America into the war and there was ushered in a period in the Pacific struggle when aeroplanes and naval vessels combined their efforts brilliantly.

It was here that the tremendous air-sea battles of Midway Island and the Coral Sea were fought between fleets which attacked one another mainly with the aid of aircraft, most of them ship-based. The United States Navy set a high standard in this new type of sky fighting.

Torpedo bombers played an especially prominent part in this work. They had always been known by naval authorities to be a potentially powerful weapon, but they had not been proved sufficiently in combat to enable their value to be assessed with any certainty. The Royal Navy had only Fairey Swordfish and later the Fairey Albacore. Both these machines were biplanes, regarded as being somewhat out of date in their general structure.

The Americans, however, introduced the Grumman Avenger which was later

Central Press.

THE WONDERFUL PICK-A-BACK PLANE

This picture, taken from another aeroplane flying alongside, shows the Short-Mayo composite aircraft in mid-air. The upper component is mounted on the wings of the larger component and launched when a suitable height has been reached. This system of launching enables a bigger load to be carried when taking-off.

TRAINING NAVAL PILOTS

Central Press.

However experienced an airman may be, he needs special training to become proficient in landing on the decks of aircraft carriers at sea. Here such training is in progress, a space being marked out on the ground to represent the deck of the ship. Thus, as the Seafire pilot comes in to land the deck control officer signals to him information about his approach. Under the British-American system of signalling the " batsman " is telling the pilot that he is " coming in too high."

JET AEROPLANES

Graphic Photo Union.

A new record was set up in February, 1951, when the English Electric Co.'s Canberra B2 tactical bomber made a non-stop Transatlantic flight from Aldergrove, Northern Ireland, to Gander, Newfoundland, in 4 hours 40 mins. Later in the same year, it reduced this time by 18 minutes. The Canberra flew at a height of more than 40,000 feet and carried a crew of three.

Central Press.

At the display given by the Society of British Aircraft Constructors at Farnborough airfield, the world's first Delta jet bomber made its initial public appearance. This huge Avro 698 Delta-wing aircraft marks another dramatic step forward in the progress of British aviation and will influence both combat and civil aircraft.

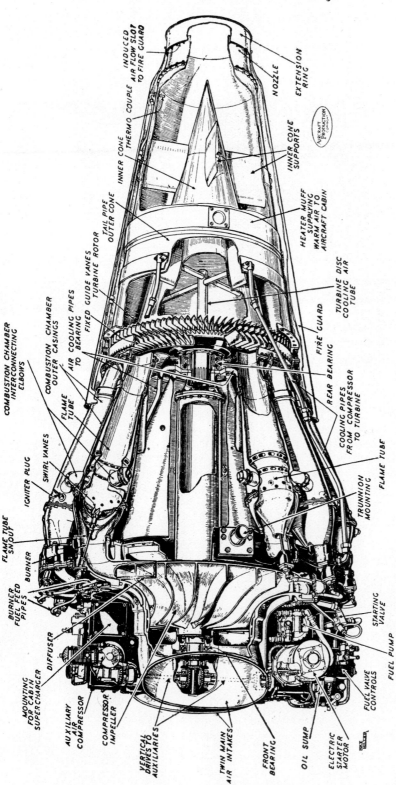

NOZZLE

EXTENSION RING

THERMO COUPLE

INDUCED AIR FLOW SLOT TO FIRE GUARD

INNER CONE

INNER CONE SUPPORTS

TAIL PIPE OUTER CONE

HEATER MUFF SUPPLYING WARM AIR TO AIRCRAFT CABIN

TURBINE ROTOR

FIXED GUIDE VANES

TURBINE DISC COOLING AIR

AIR COOLING PIPES TO BEARING

FIRE GUARD

COMBUSTION CHAMBER OUTER CASINGS

REAR BEARING

COMBUSTION CHAMBER INTERCONNECTING ELBOWS

FLAME TUBE

COOLING PIPES FROM COMPRESSOR TO TURBINE

FLAME TUBE

SWIRL VANES

IGNITER PLUG

FLAME TUBE SNOUT

TRUNNION MOUNTING

BURNER

BURNER FUEL FEED PIPES

STARTING VALVE

MOUNTING FOR CABIN SUPERCHARGER

DIFFUSER

FUEL PUMP

AUXILIARY COMPRESSOR

COMPRESSOR IMPELLER

FUEL VALVE CONTROLS

VERTICAL DRIVES TO AUXILIARIES

TWIN MAIN AIR INTAKES

FRONT BEARING

OIL SUMP

ELECTRIC STARTER MOTOR

Reproduced by permission of "Aircraft Production."

THE POWER UNIT OF A JET-PROPELLED AEROPLANE

Jet-propelled aeroplanes in this country were the invention of Air Commodore Sir Frank Whittle of the R.A.F., the first patent being taken out in 1930, though it was not until 1941 that the first successful flight was made. Our illustration shows the de Havilland Goblin II turbojet unit which is fitted to the Vampire jet-plane. Fuel is supplied by a constant-stroke Dowty pump, an automatic control spilling excess fuel back to the tank at altitude. Speeds of over 750 miles an hour have already been made with jet-planes, and machines that reach a thousand miles an hour are within the bounds of possibility.

Photographic News Agencies.

THE AVRO YORK

In this official photograph we are shown the Avro York, which is the civil transport version of
the famous Avro Lancaster bomber. The fuselage has been specially re-designed for the carrying
of passengers and freight ; a third, central, tail fin has been added. The wing span of this
machine is 102 feet and its overall length 78 feet.

ordered by the Royal Navy. This was
a monoplane of reasonably good performance which carried a short, fat
21-inch torpedo internally stowed and
was capable of a fairly high speed and
rate of climb. The Americans used this
machine with great success in the
Pacific, and it showed that torpedo
carrying need not cripple an aircraft.
In this region also Australian Beauforts
and later Beaufighters were active.
It was not until after the war that the
idea of the single-seat high performance

torpedo carrier was introduced by the
Royal Navy.

Fleet fighters also underwent rapid
development as a result of the stimula-
tion of the Pacific war. The Grumman
Wildcat, as the United States Navy
called it, was successful as a fighter, but
it was still found that there was scope
for higher performance. The Fleet Air
Arm, therefore, put into train a series
of experiments with the highest per-
forming landplanes. The Hurricane
was worked successfully from decks and

Charles E. Brown.

THE SANDRINGHAM PASSENGER FLYING-BOAT

Our photograph shows the civil version of the famous Sunderland flying-boat which did such
valiant service during the last war. Powered by 4 Bristol Pegasus radial engines, the Sandringham, as this civil machine has been named, has luxurious accommodation for 24 passengers
by day and 16 by night.

ONE OF OUR FASTEST FIGHTER AIRCRAFT

Hawker Aircraft Ltd.

It was our fighters such as the Spitfires and Hurricanes that saved Britain in the early days of the last World War. For the latest fighter, the Hawker P.1067, seen above, it is claimed that it is superior to the U.S.A. Sabre and the Russian MIG–15. It has wing-root intakes for the Rolls-Royce Turbojet.

standardised as the Sea Hurricane for use on aircraft carriers. Then the Vickers-Armstrongs Spitfire was flown successfully from a carrier. Under the name of the Seafire it was introduced into the Fleet Air Arm at about the time of the North African landings in 1943. The Seafire had the characteristics of the landplane Spitfire, though it carried slight additional weight for arrester hooks and the like. Jet fighters were not flown from carriers until after the war. The Vampire figured in the early trials.

With the introduction of the Seafire as a standard ship-borne aircraft the Fleet Air Arm made a rapid advance in the performance of its machines. The United States had played an important part in these improvements. American aircraft had shown the way for the take-off of heavily-laden medium bombers from carriers. This was on the occasion of the attack upon Tokyo on April 18th, 1942, which was led by Major-General Doolittle. In this attack North American Mitchell B.25 bombers were used and they started from American aircraft carriers at a great distance from Tokyo.

The Bombing Assault

The year 1942 closed with all attention focussing on the Pacific region. It was there that the great battleships *Prince of Wales* and *Repulse* were sunk by Japanese torpedo-carrying aircraft. After this success, however, the Japanese forces made progress at a gradually decreasing rate and attention tended to swing back again to the western front. In this area the Royal Air Force Bomber

Command was building up and gradually increasing the weight of its blows.

In 1942, under Air Chief Marshal Sir Arthur Harris, a series of raids had been launched on Cologne and other German cities with more than 1,000 bombers in each attack. Those raids, although not in themselves so powerful as the numbers would suggest, marked the turning point in the bombing technique of the Allied nations. A greater proportion of the total national effort in Great Britain was turned to the manufacture of bombers and by February and March of 1943 Bomber Command disposed a powerful force mainly comprised of four-engined machines which it immediately began to use to the best advantage.

The year 1943, as we look back upon the air war, stands out as the period in which massive cascade or concentrated raids were brought to their highest pitch of military efficiency. In these raids large numbers of aircraft were brought into operation on the target within a short space of time. Total bomb loads of 1,500 tons and more were delivered on a given spot in fifty minutes or less.

Planning and Achievement

In order to do this very great advances had to be made in the whole technique of marshalling the aircraft, sending them off, and controlling their movements in the air. Bomber Command tackled all these problems successfully and by June of 1943 was launching a sequence of attacks whose power had never before been attained.

The spring and summer were devoted mainly to raids upon the Ruhr, which was regarded as the industrial heart of Germany and the place from which a very large proportion of German military output came. During these attacks the dam-bursting raids on the Mohne and Eder dams were made by a force led by Wing Commander Gibson who later received the Victoria Cross for this daring work.

These attacks were made by a special means which had been developed entirely for the purpose of dam bursting. The aircraft were Lancasters and they made their attacks from a low level and placed their special mines on the water faces of the dams so that the structure was breached and the water poured through. These dam-bursting raids were among the most remarkable technical and operational achievements of the whole of the first four years of the war. The technical problem was one of immense complexity and its solution high testimony to the competence of British engineers.

Towards the end of 1943 the power of the Luftwaffe appeared to be on the wane. While the attacks upon Germany by Bomber Command increased in fury and the weight of bombs delivered went up at a rapid rate, the German air force contented itself with occasional minor raids usually on coastal places. It seemed completely incapable of hitting back on anything like the same scale as the Allies. Meanwhile United States forces helped to build up the weight of Bomber Command's offensive with their daylight attacks. The atomic bomb was not used against Germany, only against Japan; but it calls for an entirely new approach to the whole subject.

The history of the second World War, therefore, contains a picture of air development pressed forward at a high rate, but mainly concentrated upon military results.

Undoubtedly a great deal of technical information was obtained during the war which might otherwise have taken a much longer time before it had been brought to light. Much of this information, however, was restricted to military matters and had no wider application.

In many ways civil flying had to make an entirely fresh start in 1946. It had not gained much from the feverish war developments.

The war of 1914–18 saw the lighter-than-air craft making several attempts

FLYING ROUND THE WORLD IN FOUR DAYS

Associated Press.

The first non-stop flight round the world was made in 1949, when an American Air Force Superfortress B-50, named *Lucky Lady II*, landed safely back at Carswell Airfield, Fort Worth, Texas. The photograph above shows the aeroplane landing on its return. During the flight the plane was re-fuelled four times in the air. Over 23,000 miles were flown in two hours less than four days.

to challenge the supremacy of the heavier-than-air craft. In other words, the airship, and especially the large rigid vessel of the Zeppelin type, showed signs of being able to be turned into a military weapon of an importance at least equal to that of the heavy bomber. The end of the war of 1914-18, however, did not see the airship so well placed.

In the years of peace that followed, Great Britain decided that the value of the airship was still a matter of doubt and that it would be worth while instituting a series of full-scale experiments in order to test its qualities further. The big airships R100 and R101 were therefore built and they made a number of flights. The Atlantic was crossed and plans were laid for airship services covering the entire British Commonwealth, mooring masts for these immense vessels being set up in Great Britain, Egypt, Canada and

elsewhere. There was a period during which the airships showed promise, but gradually they made fewer useful flights and their value was more and more urgently challenged by those who believed that the aeroplane or the heavier-than-air craft would in all cases prove to be the superior craft.

The disaster to the R101 in France during the early part of a journey it was to have made to Egypt and India finally tipped the scales and the construction of large airships was abandoned in Great Britain.

The non-rigid type of airship had proved itself useful in the war of 1914-18 for anti-submarine patrolling, but it also had made small progress in relation to the meteoric advance of the heavier-than-air craft. When the second World War broke out America decided to use the small non-rigid airship for coastal work, but Great Britain did not employ such machines.

Topical Press.

A BUTTERFLY-TAIL NAVAL FIGHTER

Fastest and most powerful naval fighter in the world is the Supermarine 508 which is seen in flight in the foreground of the photograph above. The picture also shows the so-called " butterfly tail " which has not been used before on high-speed aircraft. Unlike the Supermarine Swift, which can be seen in the background, the Supermarine 508 does not have swept-back wings.

In fact, in this country, in the second World War the only use of the non-rigid lighter-than-air craft was for balloon barrages. These were designed mainly to check the activities of low flying and dive-bombing aircraft and made their appearance at vulnerable points.

The Future of Aviation

The survey of aeronautical history that has been undertaken in the foregoing pages illustrates the remarkable speed of advance made since the first flight by the Wright brothers in 1903. No science has ever before shown an equal rate of progress. It may be that that rate is still to be continued for a number of years to come and that we shall see in the near future amazing new developments in aviation. Work now in progress on jet propulsion and on various forms of rocket drive supports this view.

On the other hand, we have to accept it that there may be a period of reduced rate of progress. Many fresh inventions have swept forward during the early stages at an astonishing pace and then tailed off to a gradually decreasing speed of development.

In size of machine, in speed, in range, and in weight-carrying the aircraft of the future are undoubtedly going to make enormous strides ahead of anything so far seen. The Martin Mars flying-boat weighs about 70 tons, but there is no reason yet discernible which would prevent flying-boats of more than twice this weight being built and successfully flown. The immense Hughes Hercules has indicated the prospects and the Saunders-Roe SR-45 flying-boats will establish them. Land-planes also are bound to increase in weight, though here there may be a check on size increases before there is a check on the size increases of flying-boats. The Bristol Brabazon at 127 tons was lighter than the Saunders-Roe flying-boats which will weigh 140 tons.

The limits of land aerodromes and the difficulties of providing sufficiently lengthy firm runways for very large machines make it less desirable to increase the weight of landplanes beyond certain points than flying-boats.

In speed considerable progress was made during the second World War, but again a warning should be uttered against the commonly accepted idea that war stimulates speed progress far more vigorously than does peace. The fact is that the peace years between the two wars brought into being a more rapid rate of progress than the war years themselves. We may see in the years of peace a more rapid advance with jet and rocket driven machines than anything that occurred in the war. At the outset of hostilities the Vickers-Armstrongs Spitfire in its early form was credited with a speed of 367 miles an hour at its rated altitude. By the end of 1943 service aircraft were flying with a speed in level flight of slightly over 400 miles an hour. At this same time speeds of over 500 miles an hour were visualised. Over 600 miles an hour was achieved by the Meteor fighter before the end of 1945, and speeds of more than 750 miles per hour were being attained by the end of 1953. The speed of sound has been exceeded.

Power units were going up in size and output. From the engines of approximately 1,000 horse power in the early days of the war units giving nearly 2,000 horse-power were available by 1943, and units giving considerably more than this were well advanced in development. Experiments in Italy with the Caproni-Campini jet-propelled aircraft, for instance, had shown that jet propulsion might offer remarkable

Saunders-Roe Ltd.

A GIANT FLYING-BOAT AS A TROOP CARRIER

This giant flying-boat, the 140-ton Princess, was constructed at Cowes, Isle of Wight, by Saunders-Roe Ltd. She can carry 200 troops a non-stop distance of 3,500 miles, and has a cruising speed of 380 miles an hour. Two other flying-boats of the same class were completed by 1953, but the lack of suitable engines made it necessary to keep them temporarily out of commission.

advantages over the ordinary reciprocating petrol engine for high altitude
operations. A possibility, therefore,
that in the future the jet-propelled
machine would attract increasing attention and might in the end, and for
certain special duties, oust the machine
powered by a piston engine, grew to a
certainty.

In the matter of range there had
been steady progress during the war,
but again not the sensational progress
that had been associated with record-
breaking achievements. The world's
long distance record achieved by the
Royal Air Force in 1938 of 7,158 miles
was a special case and it was not
expected that normal aircraft carrying
either a bomb load or a commercial load
would be able to repeat it for many
years to come. It did, however, set a
standard which commercial aircraft
strove to equal. Theoretical considera-
tions suggested that a maximum range

of 6,000 miles was about the limit with
normal design and normal methods, but
all engineers were agreed that means
could be employed whereby this range
might be markedly increased. It is
worth noticing that during the latter
part of 1943 bombing raids were made by
United States aircraft on targets which
entailed a round trip of 2,500 miles. In
fact, all the indications were that the
barriers would be overcome and
that range also would be gradually
extended.

High flying was expected to be seen
in the World War of 1939–45 to a much
greater extent than was actually the
case. The Germans produced the
Junkers 86 high altitude aircraft with a
diesel type engine and it appeared once
or twice over Great Britain and also in
Egypt. This machine was specially
designed for sub-stratosphere operations. The Royal Air Force had large
numbers of machines which were operat-

Air Survey Co.

AN AERIAL VIEW OF LONDON AIRPORT

London Airport is the largest in Britain and is situated at Heathrow, near Hounslow, Middlesex.
This photograph, taken from the air, gives an excellent idea of the staggered parallel runways
angled to the prevailing winds, a system which adds greatly to the safety of the airport. The
construction of the airport began in 1946. Eventually it will be possible to control the movement
of 100 aeroplanes an hour here.

Australian News and Information Bureau.

TAKING-OFF FOR THE SYDNEY-VANCOUVER FLIGHT

This photograph shows one of the British Commonwealth Pacific Airline's 4-engined high-altitude 'planes taking-off from the Mascot (Sydney) Kingsford-Smith Airfield. The 'plane was making the first flight from Sydney across the Pacific to Vancouver, Canada. As it taxied across the runway, the 'plane passed the Constellation aircraft (the tail of which can be seen in the picture) used on the Sydney-London service. B.C.P.A.L. no longer exists as a separate airline.

ing at a great height, especially those belonging to the Photographic Reconnaissance Units, but they were none of them in the true sense stratosphere aircraft.

It was always expected that bombing attacks would be made by one side or the other with aircraft flying in the stratosphere and having pressure cabins for the crews. This method seemed to offer a chance of evading both anti-aircraft fire and fighter opposition. The difficulties of lifting really useful loads to heights of much more than 45,000 feet, however, and of carrying them long distances at these heights proved more obstinate than had been thought and in consequence the stratosphere bomber was slower in appearing on the battle-front than had been expected.

Commercial aviation was often in the minds of the designers of military aircraft and of their operators. Indeed, some bombers, such as the Lancaster, were converted during the war into commercial machines. The York was one adaptation of the Lancaster and seemed to offer excellent qualities as a transport aircraft. The Americans produced a number of transport aircraft intended for the carriage of troops and supplies, but capable also of being quickly converted into commercial machines.

The view gained ground as the war proceeded that commercial flying would occupy an important place in the world activities of the future and, in consequence, all the nations paid a great deal of attention to the development of machines and methods which would be useful for establishing their air lines after the war.

Aviation has shown in the past a remarkable capacity for development and for rapid progress. There is no sign as yet that it is reaching the limits of its capacity in these respects. Indeed, there seems to be little doubt that world transport of the future will be dominated by air lines and by air transport.

Some Uses of Parachutes

Parachutes, originally designed for life-saving, served other and startling purposes. Germany used them for dropping magnetic mines into the sea from seaplanes and for scattering huge bombs on land. Parachutes have also been used to drop food, ammunition and medical supplies to troops cut off from the usual source of supplies, and to civilians isolated by snow-drifts or impassable roads.

One very useful purpose to which the aeroplane is put is for surveying country otherwise inaccessible, the aeroplane flying at a constant height on parallel but overlapping courses, the photographer taking a series of overlapping pictures which, when pasted together, form a complete mosaic of the district surveyed. In war-time aerial photography is employed for mapping enemy territory, taking pictures of aerodromes, docks and railway junctions and other points vulnerable to bombing, and for spotting troop movements and gun positions.

One of the most remarkable feats of air transport was that undertaken by the British and American authorities in Germany at the time when all surface transport from Western Germany into Berlin was brought to a standstill owing to a disagreement between the Eastern and Western Occupying Powers. The " Berlin air lift " was quickly organised and for a long period during 1948–9

Chas. E. Brown.

FIRST OF BRITAIN'S FOUR-JET BOMBERS

Britain's first four-jet bomber, the Valiant, is powered by four Rolls-Royce Avon engines. It is claimed that this machine, which is now in production for service with the Royal Air Force, is even faster than the Canberra and it has an even longer range and carrying capacity. The machine made its first flight in public towards the end of 1951.

Australian News and Information Bureau.

AN AUSTRALIAN-BUILT AIRCRAFT UNDER TEST

Australia is rapidly developing a highly-efficient aircraft industry, and various types of machines, both for the Services and for civilian use, are now in production. In this photograph an Australian-built Lincoln aircraft is showing its paces in a test flight made at a special display held at Fishermen's Bend, Melbourne, Victoria.

many thousands of tons of food and raw materials were flown into the city. For all practical purposes Berlin was under blockade, but the success of this " air lift " rendered it ineffective. Air transport had triumphed.

In Australia and New Zealand transport by aircraft for passengers and goods is developing on a big scale. To keep pace with the demand for machines Australia is building up her own aircraft industry.

Aeroplanes are also used for the transport of gold from the mines of Africa and elsewhere, returning with cargoes of machinery, mails, food and other supplies, completing in hours journeys which formerly, in some cases, occupied weeks. Trappers and fur-hunters of Canada can send their goods and themselves travel by 'plane where once dog-teams dragged sledges over frozen wastes. Day-old chicks travel in large consignments by air, and perishable choice fruits and flowers reach markets hundreds of miles distant in perfect condition.

Fire Patrols and Shoal Spotters

Medical supplies urgently required are rushed by air from one end of the earth to the other in response to an S.O.S., and air ambulances are always available. Fire-patrols keep watch from the skies over valuable timber-lands in America and Canada; and machines equipped with special spraying apparatus fly low over crops infested with destructive insects and scatter clouds of powder deadly to the pests. Fishing fleets employ a scouting aeroplane to " spot " big shoals and report their position to the headquarters of the fleet.

AIRCRAFT WHICH MADE HISTORY

Specially drawn for this work.

In these three pages we have a pictorial record of the development of aeroplanes from the beginning of the century : 1. Wright Bros.' aeroplane, first controlled flight, 1903. 2. Blériot's Channel flight, 1909, 3. Fabre : the first seaplane to fly, 1911. 4. Curtis : world's first flying-boat, 1912. 5 and 6. The Sopwith " Camel " and S.E.5—famous fighters of the First World War. 7. Vickers " Vimy," first trans-Atlantic aeroplane flight (Alcock and Brown, 1919), and first flight to Australia (Ross and Smith, 1919). 8. Avro " Avian," first light 'plane flight to Australia (Hinkler, 1927). 9. Ryan monoplane, Lindberg's Atlantic flight (3,600 miles), 1927. 10. Supermarine S.6B, 407.5 miles per hour, 1932 speed record.

A RECORD OF PROGRESS

Specially drawn for this work.

From 1920 onwards records were being regularly set up and broken. 11. Breguet aeroplane : world's distance record (Costes and Bellonte, 1929). 12. Dornier Do. X, carried 100 passengers, 1929–30. 13. "Vega," first round the world flight (Post and Gatty in 8½ days, 1933). 14. H.P. Liner of 1932 : the last of biplane lines. 15. Houston "Westland" : flight over Everest, 1933. 16. "Comet," · England to Australia (Scott and Black, 1934). 17. Tiger Moth (D.H.) : the popular club and training machine. 18. Boeing 299 : first U.S.A. four-engined bomber, 1934 (developed into "Fortress" during Second World War). 19. British flying-boat, "Caledonia" : start of trans-Atlantic service. 20. Russian monoplane : first flight over North Pole (Moscow to California).

MODERN CONQUERORS OF THE AIR

Specially drawn for this work.

Faster machines and a wide variety of types have been among recent developments. 21. "Rota," last and final development of Autogiro, 1923–39. 22 and 23. Hawker "Hurricane" and Supermarine "Spitfire," two famous types of the Battle of Britain, 1940. 24. "Sunderland" flying-boat, long distance anti-submarine patrol of Second World War. 25. Gloster "Meteor" jet aeroplane, 1943–44. 26. Westland Sikorsky S.51, Helicopter, 1947. 27. American Bell X-1, first aircraft to fly faster than sound, 1948. 28. Hawker N-7/46, jet aeroplane, 1948. 29. Vickers "Viscount," first turbo-propeller liner, 1950. 30. Bristol "Britannia" air-liner, 1954.

CIVIL AVIATION

Airspeed.

AN AIR-LINER OF THE ELIZABETHAN CLASS

This aircraft, formerly known as the Ambassador, has been re-named Elizabethan, and this class is
very popular on the various continental routes of British European Airways. Its high wing permits
a good view for everyone on board and up to 47 passengers can be carried in its pressurised cabin.
Its cruising speed is 270 miles an hour.

THE peaceful transport of passengers and goods has been, since the beginning, one of the aims of aviation. It has been an aim which has been partly frustrated by two world wars. In 1913 a beginning had been made to the work of showing that aircraft would eventually be able to fulfil useful rôles for the carriage of mails, passengers and freight. The first World War checked these developments and switched the development of aircraft towards military objectives.

Between the two wars aircraft had made much progress in proving their peaceful capabilities. The London-Paris passenger service, then the services over greater distances and finally the Empire air mail scheme whereby all first-class mail for places within what was then still known as the British Empire, went by air without surcharge, were examples of what was being done.

Passenger aircraft increased in size from the converted bombers of World War I to the remarkable Empire flying boats which remain to this day among the finest commercial aircraft ever built. The operating companies had a difficult time, for there was free competition and the costs of running services were already high. Many companies were formed and many failed. Eventually government assistance was granted to the company known as Imperial Airways Ltd.

This assistance, however, was conditional upon the company striving to make its services pay their way. With its Short Empire flying boats Imperial Airways made rapid progress towards a state of financial self-sufficiency. It had a good safety and punctuality record and it energetically developed the main airlines which linked the Commonwealth.

But its work was criticised on the grounds that it was not as advanced as the work of the companies of other countries. Imperial Airways were sometimes compared unfavourably with the services of K.L.M. and it was held that the aircraft used by the British line were not fast enough. The consequence was the decision of the government of the day to substitute for Imperial Airways a Corporation over which fuller control could be exercised and to grant it a higher rate of subsidy.

Aircraft for Private Flying

This was the condition of British commercial flying at the outbreak of the Second World War. Meanwhile private and club flying had made extremely rapid progress and the United Kingdom was among the leading countries of the world in the matter of its private pilots and flying clubs.

After World War I the government had decided to stimulate experiments in the design of a cheap, low-powered aircraft for personal use. It inaugurated, therefore, under the auspices of the civil aviation department of the Air Ministry (for at that time there was no separate Ministry of Civil Aviation), a series of competitions which were held at Lympne and were designed to encourage economical and safe flying.

Many extremely interesting small aircraft emerged from these competitions and some of them showed high efficiency. Nevertheless, they were not destined to find popular favour and neither the winners of the competitions, nor any of the other aircraft which were entered for them, achieved the world-wide use and renown of the de Havilland Moth.

The Moth had been developed independently, the reasoning of Captain Geoffrey de Havilland being that the government competitions demanded too low a margin of engine power. He believed that the public would like and would be ready to buy a small aircraft rather more robust and rather more highly powered than those called for by

BRABAZON I TAKES THE AIR

Topical Press.

Brabazon I, the largest air-liner in the world, was first planned in 1943 and production began in 1945. Not until 1949 was the building of this giant aircraft finally completed. It is seen here just after taking off for its first flight from Filton in September, 1949. In 1953, after much valuable information had been gleaned, the whole Brabazon project was abandoned and the first and only aircraft of the series was dismantled.

A VICKERS VIKING PASSENGER AIR-LINER

This is a medium size transport aircraft which came into extensive service in Europe after the 1939–45 war. It was the first air-liner to be flown with turbo-jet engines, an experimental version being tried with two Rolls-Royce Nenes. With these jets the Viking achieved a top speed of 667 kilometres (415 miles) per hour.

the rules of the official competitions. He proved right. The Moth was the foundation of an immense personal and club flying movement in Great Britain.

The people in this movement began to show the world what the small aircraft was capable of when skilfully handled. This was the period of the pioneer flights, often made by men and women who had learned to fly at one of the clubs. It was found that with an aircraft with an engine of only about 150 horse-power, two people could go half-way round the world and do so at speeds never before dreamed of as being possible.

A Race to Australia

This was also the period of rallies, meetings and pageants. They were held in all parts of the country and often drew immense crowds. Air races, competitions of all kinds, aerobatic flying and parachute jumping were included in many of the programmes. Air racing was in its prime. The King's Cup race, held every year, was an event which drew large entries and many spectators at the starting and finishing points. The Aerial Derby had been popular at first but began to decline and was not being held by the time of the outbreak of the Second World War.

Greatest of the civilian air races was the MacRobertson Trophy race between England and Australia. It was won by Scott and Campbell Black in a de Havilland Comet specially designed for the event, and incorporating many of the features which later made the Mosquito military aircraft famous. Even more significant than the Comet's victory was the second place obtained by the Dutch pilots Parmentier and Moll, for this was the first notable public appearance of an aircraft that was later to be known everywhere as the Douglas Dakota.

At the outbreak of World War II, therefore, civil aviation was making rapid headway. In both the commercial and the personal flying fields there were many aircraft, many new ideas, many new services. Yet once again war was to set back the civil aviation clock. Once again there was the period during which the entire effort of the aeronautical community was directed to military ends. Private and club flying stopped; the airlines were set to military tasks.

Britain's Fresh Start

When the Second World War was over, in 1945, civil aviation was less well placed to recover than it was in 1918. The only way in which Britain could obtain a large system of airways was to offer heavy subsidies. So the three Corporations, British Overseas Airways, British South American Airways and British European Airways were formed, as State concerns, with a monopoly of scheduled services in the United Kingdom and with the taxpayer to meet their deficits.

With some converted military aircraft and some American aircraft they re-established the commercial lines pioneered by Imperial Airways. The Atlantic services and the services to Australia and New Zealand and other parts of the Commonwealth were started. But there were heavy losses, amounting during the early years to about £10,000,000 a year.

How Helicopters Developed

Meanwhile private and club flying remained unsubsidised and made little headway. The flying charges were too

Copyright.

FOR SHORT RANGE TRANSPORT WORK

Originally designed and built by the Miles Company, the Marathon, seen above, was taken over by Handley Page. It is a short range transport, intended to fulfil all the safety requirements of the International Civil Aviation Organisation. At present it has four de Havilland Gipsy Queen engines, giving a total of 1,320 horse-power, but it may later be fitted with turbo-prop engines. Top speed is 370 kilometres (230 miles) per hour.

SPEED AND COMFORT IN TRAVEL

Topical.

The world's first jet air-liner services were actually inaugurated by the B.O.A.C. early in 1952 with the Comet aircraft, after several long-distance records had been set up in test flights. Here we see the Comet on its arrival at Khartoum airfield, with Sudanese policemen passing by.

B.O.A.C.

Every device which will add to the comfort of the passenger is embodied in the furnishing of modern aircraft used for long distance travel. In this photograph is seen the interior of a Comet air-liner, now in regular service with the B.O.A.C.

Keystone.

THE NEW BRISTOL HELICOPTER

An important milestone in the history of British helicopter development was passed in 1952, when
the new twin-engined Bristol 173 helicopter successfully carried out its first flights. It is designed
to carry 10 to 13 passengers or 2,500 lb. of freight over medium or short distances.

high at the clubs to encourage large and active memberships and personal flying diminished.

Gallant attempts were made by the Ultra Light Aircraft Association to point a way whereby private and club flying costs might be brought down by the use of low-powered engines.

While the Corporations were developing their lines with the aid of the taxpayer, and while private and club flying was in abeyance, helicopters were being developed. They seemed to offer a means of avoiding the difficulties of finding the space needed for ordinary aerodromes near cities and they also seemed well suited to work such as crop dusting—or the spreading of insecticidal powders on growing crops. The Post Office also believed that they might be of value for the final delivery of mails in outlying districts.

Helicopter development therefore went forward rapidly. The British Fairey Gyrodyne successfully passed flying trials and set—in 1948—an international speed record of 200 kilometres an hour. The Bristol company produced their new helicopter and at the end of 1948 the Cierva Air Horse and Cierva Skeeter both began their flying trials, two entirely novel kinds of helicopter, one large, the other small. The latest helicopter, the Bristol 173, will carry 10 to 13 passengers and it is expected that in the next few years these machines will lead to considerable developments in air transport services between town and city centres, as well as to the big airports.

By this time civil aviation came within the province of two ministries, the Ministry of Civil Aviation and the Ministry of Supply. New aircraft and engine construction was the responsibility of the Ministry of Supply, as well as research, while the operation of aircraft and the maintenance of aerodromes was the responsibility of the Ministry of Civil Aviation, which was amalgamated with the Ministry of

Transport in 1953. At first it was not permitted for even the State airline corporations to order their aircraft direct from the makers; they had to place their orders through the Ministry of Supply; but this arrangement was later altered to allow direct orders to be placed.

Technical Advance

When peace came in 1945 the general tendency was towards higher speeds and greater ranges. Technical interest had been excited by the remarkable German work with jet-driven aircraft and with rockets, just before the end of the war. The consequence was that a great deal of research attention was devoted to studying the extreme possibilities of speed and height and range. The stratosphere air-liner, with pressure cabin, driven by turbo-jets, and cruising at over 400 miles an hour, was the aim of much development work. And designers were even looking forward to more remarkable achievements.

The great 127 ton Brabazon air liners were designed to carry 100 passengers non-stop between London and New York. Only one Brabazon was built, and this was demolished when, in 1953, it was decided not to proceed with the original plans for these giant aircraft.

The world's first turbo-prop engined air-liner, the Vickers Viscount, proved during its testing flights in 1948 and 1949 that this form of power unit offered great silence and smoothness in the running while at the same time giving a good air performance. The turbo-prop is not so admirable for high speeds as the plain jet, but it is claimed to possess certain economic advantages. The Viscount was designed to carry anything from 36 to 48 passengers and its top speed when it first appeared was 350 miles an hour. It has a

"Aeronautics."

REFUELLING AIRCRAFT WHILE FLYING

Both the United States Air Force and the United States Navy have adopted the British system of air fuelling. By this means the range of a fighter or bomber can be considerably increased. In this photograph three American fighters are being fuelled simultaneously from a single tanker aircraft. The tanker trails fuel lines, each of which carries at its end a funnel shaped coupling. The pilot of the receiving aircraft guides a rigid tube into this coupling and fuel flows automatically until he breaks off by slowing down.

Copyright.

FOR FEEDER LINE SERVICE

Most modern of the medium-sized feeder line aircraft is the de Havilland
Dove. It has a retractable tricycle undercarriage and braking air-
screws. Its two de Havilland Gipsy Queen engines give a maximum
speed of 338 kilometres (210 miles) per hour. Ten passengers are
carried with a crew of two.

pressurised cabin so
that the passengers
are protected from the
reduced pressure and
lack of oxygen at
height.

Meanwhile a new
and advanced design
of turbo-jet air-liner
was being built at the
de Havilland works.
This is the jet-engined
Comet, a large
passenger aircraft
which has now demon-
strated its capacity
and is in regular service
on B.O.A.C. routes to
Africa and the Far
East. This aircraft
relies on plain jets,
without airscrews.

The piston engine
will continue to be of
value in small aircraft
and in some kinds of
middle and small sized
transport aircraft; but
in the large air-liners
the gas turbine, either
driving an airscrew or
driving directly by
means of a jet, is
certain in the end to
oust other means of
propulsion.

Refuelling In Flight

Among the other
technical possibilities
are rocket drive and
refuelling in flight.
Rocket drive has great
uses for military pur-
poses because,
although a rocket has
a very small duration,
it can develop an
enormous thrust dur-
ing that brief period.
It thus comes about
that among military

Keystone.

THE BRISTOL BRITANNIA AIR-LINER

Powered by four Proteus turbo-props, the Bristol Britannia air-liner can carry fifty passengers on long distance oceanic travel or over a hundred on shorter flights. A number of these new air-liners are being built for the B.O.A.C. This photograph was taken at Filton Airfield, Bristol.

aircraft, the highest rates of climb have been done by rocket driven machines.

But because of its lack of duration the rocket is not suitable for civil aircraft except in one way, and that is as a take-off assister. Rocket assisted take-off has already been used in freight carrying and it may eventually come into use for passenger carrying. It gives the advantage of a quick take-off and a rapid initial climb when the aircraft is fully loaded. The pilot touches off the rockets, which may be mounted under the wings, at the start of the taking-off run.

A danger period for all aircraft is at the take-off and during the initial climb. When the aircraft is heavily loaded this danger is at its greatest. But the extra thrust given by rocket attachments which weigh little can reduce this danger. Flight refuelling can give similar results. It can permit an aircraft to take off light and to receive its full load of petrol after it has climbed to operating height.

Extended tests of flight refuelling on the Atlantic run were made during 1948 by British South American Airways and by British Overseas Airways. In these instances the object of refuelling in flight was rather to extend the range of the aircraft than to permit it to take-off light. The passing of the fuel from the tanker aircraft to the operating aircraft while the latter remained on course was done without any difficulty or trouble. Both the United States Air Force and the U.S. Navy have adopted air refuelling to extend the endurance of their aircraft. They use the fuelling method developed in Britain.

Speed increases are certain in the future, and also increases in the operating height of aircraft. Payloads are likely to go up as well either by the use of flight refuelling or by rocket assisted take-off or some other means such as a further lightening of structure weight by the use of new alloys. Commercial aviation will greatly extend its scope.

The future of private and club flying in the United Kingdom is more difficult to foresee. Greater freedom for private pilots and lower costs are the needs.

To Make Air Travel Easier

It is possible that collaboration between European countries, such as France and Britain, might enable the cost of personal flying to be reduced. France has produced some successful low-powered engines and the air touring conditions in France are better than in Britain. The Royal Aero Club reported in 1949 that the previous year had seen an increase in the number of air tourists going to the Continent in their own aircraft.

Since the Second World War French designers have taken a pre-eminent position in the field of small, low-powered jet aircraft. While Britain and America were developing ever more powerful jet engines for very fast fighters and bombers the French aircraft industry saw the opportunities presented by the jet engine for light sporting aircraft and trainers.

A series of simple and comparatively cheap engines was developed by the Turboméca company for aircraft of this type, and with their aid two companies built trainers for the French government. These are light aircraft with a maximum speed of 400 miles an hour, and capable of carrying light machine guns, bombs, rocket projectiles and other equipment for the training of jet pilots.

Both the American and British air forces decided to follow the lead given by the French, but in the early stages at least they are being forced to turn to France for engines since their own industries have not worked on the lower powered units.

France has also developed small jet-driven private aircraft, and has been followed by Italy in this field. Once the high fuel consumption of jet engines is overcome, their reliability and low maintenance costs may help to revive private flying which has proved too expensive for all but a very few wealthy enthusiasts.

It was in December, 1903, that the first aeroplane flight, of less than a minute's duration, was made. In the fifty years that have gone by since then the amazing progress which has been made in the story of man's conquest of the air has far exceeded even the wildest dreams of those early pioneers.

"Aeronautics."

A SMALL JET AIRCRAFT TRAINER

Since the Second World War France has specialised in the development of small jet aircraft and has taken the lead in this field. The Morane Saulnier Fleuret trainer shown here has a maximum speed of about 400 miles an hour. It is powered by two Turboméca jet engines. The instructor and his pupil sit side-by-side.

ROCKET FLIGHT

Associated Press.

FASTER THAN SOUND

The possibilities of rockets, both as a practical aid in aviation as well as in more adventurous spheres, are considerable. An experimental American aircraft, the Bell X1, seen in the photograph above, was the first piloted aeroplane to fly faster than sound. It was powered by a rocket burning oxygen and alcohol, and the duration of its flight at full power was 2½ minutes.

ROCKETS are familiar to everyone as the most impressive of the fireworks with which Guy Fawkes night is celebrated every year.

Since the earliest known rockets made by the Chinese some 800 years ago until the present century, they had been nothing more than a simple form of entertainment, although one or two attempts were made to use them for military purposes. Then in the Second World War they had a growing military importance, culminating in their use by the Germans to rain down explosives on London.

These rockets were the German V2s, and they opened the eyes of the world. Such a missile, consisting of rocket motor, guiding devices and explosives, weighed 12 tons at the start of its flight and took off straight upwards from a concrete base. As it climbed it turned towards its target 200 miles away. The flight of these rockets was very much like that of a high-thrown cricket ball, but on a very much grander scale. The flight to a target 200 miles away took about five minutes.

Before the V2s, smaller rockets had been used by the forces of Britain, America, Russia and Germany for a wide variety of purposes. The main advantage of the rocket for firing shells is that it has no recoil. When a shell is fired from a gun, there is a strong backward force on the gun and its mounting, and a special buffer is fitted to absorb this shock. Further, the gun has to be firmly staked to the ground. Even a rifle gives a certain kick when fired and, if not properly held, can bruise the shoulder of the firer. But a rocket can carry a large shell with it when it is fired and gives no recoil at all. No buffer is necessary and it is fired from a simple tube open at both ends.

Such firing tubes for small rockets can be held on a man's shoulder, and are very much cheaper and quicker to make than guns with their precise breech mechanism and rifled barrels of finest quality steel, which require skilled work and special machinery.

Because of their cheapness, rockets were often used in place of guns, notably by the Russian army, when factories could not make guns quickly enough. In England they were used to augment the anti-aircraft guns defending big cities against raiding bombers. In Russia they were used in place of field artillery in battles on the ground.

By using rockets, aeroplanes were able to fire heavy shells without having to carry heavy guns and without requiring any special strengthening to resist the " kick " of the large gun. On the ground, rocket fire was used against tanks. The light weight of the rocket-firing apparatus meant that troops could be provided with an anti-tank weapon when they would not have been able to carry bulky anti-tank guns.

A Rocket Range in Australia

After the Second World War the military importance of rockets was everywhere understood, and experimental work was urgently begun by governments, especially those of Russia, Britain and the U.S.A. For this work large open spaces were required. They were easily found in America and Russia, but in the smaller area of the British Isles no uninhabited areas of sufficient size were to be found, and it was therefore decided to make a rocket range in southern Australia.

The firing point of this rocket range is at a place called Woomera, about 200 miles north of the city of Adelaide. It is expected that some rockets fired from Woomera may land 3,000 miles away. Since Australia itself extends only some 1,900 miles westward from Woomera the last part of their flight will be over, and into, the Indian Ocean.

Much laboratory work must be done in conjunction with the actual firing of rockets on the range, and for this purpose a scientific base associated with the range has been established at Salisbury, a suburb of Adelaide.

Supporting the work in Australia are scientists in Great Britain at the Ministry of Supply and in the factories of the aircraft manufacturing companies.

Guarded statements in the House of Commons and elsewhere have made it clear that British defence policy is turning more and more towards " guided weapons." By this is meant a whole variety of missiles not fired from guns, but usually rocket-driven. Some of them may have jet engines, but the simpler rocket motor will be more popular.

Among British rocket motors developed for aircraft use are the de Havilland Sprite, which gives two tons of thrust, and the Armstrong Siddeley Snarler, which gives one ton of thrust. Both these units use liquid fuel.

The main rocket-testing ground of the U.S.A. is at White Sands, New Mexico, where much work has been done to improve upon the German V2 rocket and where new American designs are tried out. In March of 1949, it was announced that a rocket fired from White Sands had reached a height of 245 miles. This was achieved by making a two-stage rocket, consisting of a V2 carrying a smaller rocket. The V2 does not normally go higher than 100 or 110 miles, but when it had reached its maximum height the smaller rocket was automatically fired and continued on its own. This method of firing rockets in stages, so that the earlier stages give the last one a flying start, is a very important one for one special use of the rocket, that of making a voyage through space from the earth.

A Voyage to the Moon

The importance of the rocket to man's dreams of voyaging to the planets has been realised for many years, but it was not until after the First World War that serious experiments were begun to find out how to build a rocket which might overcome the force of gravity. The best of this work was done in Germany

British Official Photo.

In recent years experiments with radio-controlled rockets have been carried out in this country at Aberporth on the Cardiganshire coast and on a bigger scale at the Woomera range in Australia. Our photograph shows a British guided rocket fired at Aberporth. The initial boost motors at the rear of the missile fall off later.

by a small body of enthusiasts and it was their work which eventually led to the V2.

Although the amount of work done on the practical development of interplanetary rockets differed between one country and another, a great deal of thought was given to it in all countries. Societies were formed so that those interested could get together and talk their ideas over. In England the one important society for this purpose is the British Interplanetary Society. Members of such societies have considered carefully all the problems that can be foreseen in escaping from the earth by rocket and have established, by the most proper and authoritative calculations, in what circumstances such voyages would be possible.

Their calculations show that a voyage to the moon, or to any other of the planets, is quite feasible in every respect, and could be undertaken with present-day knowledge of rockets. The un-fortunate drawback is that although it is now quite possible it is too expensive.

Facing the Problems

To see why it is too expensive now and how it may be made less expensive in the future it is best to analyse the problems of interplanetary travel one by one.

The first and greatest obstacle is gravity which gives the property known as weight. A rocket-propelled vessel for the 250,000 mile journey to the moon and back might weigh as much as 100 tons. If it is to leave the earth this 100 tons must be lifted to a very great height indeed. The force of gravity actually decreases the farther one goes from the earth, growing less and less but never disappearing altogether. On the other hand, the gravity of the moon would increase as one approached, until it was greater than that of the earth, when the ship would tend to fall naturally toward the moon. This would happen

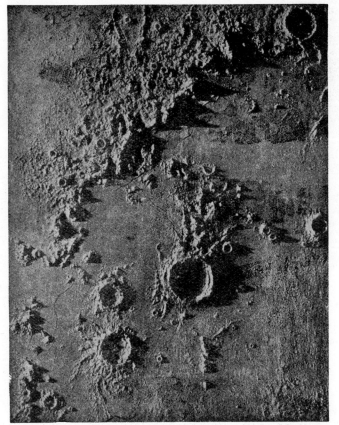

By permission of Messrs. John Murray.

WHERE THE SPACE FLYERS HOPE TO LAND

The Moon will be the first objective of interplanetary travel since it is very much nearer the Earth than any other heavenly body, and its small gravitational attraction makes it a useful starting-point for longer journeys. This photograph of an accurate model of the Moon shows typical lunar mountains.

gravity cannot pull it back and it is free to fly on through space until it comes within the influence of the gravitational attraction of another body, such as the moon.

Whether it is the moon or some other planet, there is a problem of gravity on arrival that is almost as great as that at the departure. It would not do for the rocket to crash down upon the moon and all its occupants to be killed. It must land in a controlled fashion. To do this it would be turned end for end during the period of its free flight so that it was approaching the moon tail first. Then, at a pre-calculated time, the rocket motor would be started at a suitable power to act as a brake. Losing speed steadily, the ship could arrive on the moon with a gentle bump and stand upon its tail end, in just that attitude in which it

toward the end of the journey, about 20,000 miles from the moon.

To escape from gravity does not mean that the rocket motor must be kept going continually for the whole of the journey. A more economical way is to run the motor at a very high power for a short time until a certain speed is attained. This speed is known as the " escape velocity," and in the case of an escape from the earth it is a little more than 25,000 miles an hour—a speed which would cover the distance from London to Paris in a little more than half a minute. When the rocket has reached this speed, the earth's

prepared for its original departure from the earth.

The fact that there is no atmosphere on the moon makes the use of parachutes for landing impossible.

The turning of the space ship while flying through space would be achieved with the aid of small auxiliary rockets mounted near one end or the other of the space ship and discharging sideways. The adjustment of rocket power to guide a great space ship would call for considerable piloting skill, and many local experiments would first have to be made in manœuvring near the earth and in landing upon it, before a moon voyage could possibly be attempted.

On the other hand, a rocket could be sent to the moon without a human crew, but simply to crash down upon it and mark its arrival in some way, say by a bright explosive flash which could be seen from the earth, or by scattering some white powder over a large area to make a distinguishing mark. By this means many problems would be avoided, and a good deal of useful information could be obtained. Indeed, the first flight to the moon may be of such a type since it would be prudent to send an un-manned missile first to confirm all the calculations which have been made.

In the case of a manned flight to the moon there are problems of providing sufficient food and water on the flight, and of providing enough oxygen for the crew to breathe, both during the flight and on their arrival at the moon. These have been considered and calculations have been made of every essential for the flight. There is not sufficient space here to mention all of them, but the most important and the greatest in bulk weight is the fuel for the rocket motor.

The exact weight of fuel required for any rocket voyage depends upon the efficiency of the fuel itself. Different fuels have different efficiencies—they do not all give off the same amount of energy for the same amount burned. If one must use a fuel that can liberate only a small amount of energy, a greater quantity of it must be carried. This also means more weight to be lifted off the earth against the attraction of gravity, so that it is doubly bad.

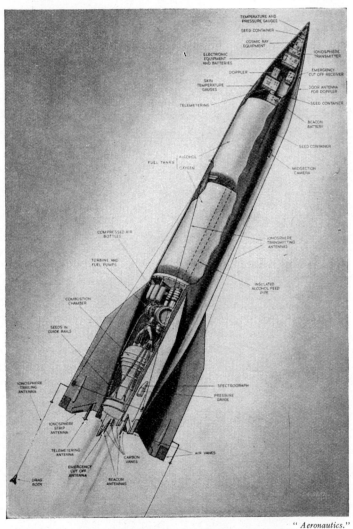

" Aeronautics."

TRANSFORMED FOR PEACEFUL PURPOSES

Some of the V2 rockets used in the Second World War were later used for experimental purposes in the U.S.A. This drawing shows clearly the arrangement of fuel tanks and the combustion chamber. In war the nose of the rocket would have carried explosives. In peace it carries instruments from which records of the atmospheric conditions 100 miles above the earth can be obtained.

British Interplanetary Society.

A STATION IN SPACE

Rocket power makes possible the establishment of space-stations. The station seen here would use the sun's heat to supply energy for warming its inhabitants, as well as for operating radio apparatus and driving necessary machinery. The sun's heat would be collected and focused by the large mirror seen here, behind which would be the crew's quarters.

including the fuel tanks themselves, is clearly not possible. The only answer to this problem is to use a two- or three-stage rocket. In a two-stage rocket, for example, the space ship proper would be carried on the front of a larger rocket and given a good start on its journey. A height of 250 miles has been reached in America with a two-stage rocket. A small WAC Corporal was carried to about 100 miles by a Viking and then continued for another 150 miles under its own power.

But the best solution to the problem rests with an improvement in the fuel. Atomic energy holds the answer. The inner forces of the atomic nucleus have been released in the atomic bomb, and they have been released more slowly for the generation of electric power by steam turbines. When atomic power can provide heat for a rocket motor as other fuels have done in the past, the fuel problem for interplanetary flight will be solved.

Unfortunately, the types of fuel which have so far been used have been able to give only rather low supplies of energy. If one of the best modern fuel combinations were used (the burning together of oxygen and hydrogen) as much as 120 tons of fuel would be needed to take a one-ton space ship to the moon and back. But to accommodate that quantity of fuel in a ship which weighs only one ton, including all the parts of the rocket, the crew, their food and equipment, and many other things,

The extension of man's powers of travel beyond the confines of the earth does not only point to other planets.

It will also be possible to establish bases in space, either stationary or moving relative to the earth. Such bodies will neither fall to earth nor fly away into space because they will be restrained by the combined effects of gravity and centrifugal force. Gravity will be tending to pull them to earth, centrifugal force will be tending to throw them outwards. A stone whirling on the end of a string is an example of centrifugal force. The faster it travels, the more it tends to fly out. If the string is released the stone will fly off on its own. But the string retains it and the pull of the string is like the pull of gravity. These forces are the very ones that keep the sun and all its planets, including the earth and the moon, in their regular paths. An artificial satellite is just another heavenly body provided by mankind, but conforming to the same laws as all other heavenly bodies.

It can be arranged that such a satellite will take the same time to complete the full circle of its course as the earth takes to turn round once— 24 hours. Then the satellite will remain over the same place on the earth and to the earth-bound people will appear stationary.

For Television and Weather

A natural question is " What can be the use of such space-stations ? " There are several uses to which they can be put. In the first place such stations would probably be of great use to interplanetary rockets as refuelling points or for changing crews and the like. Secondly, they have a use for the transmission of television. Television waves on earth can travel only a limited distance, because unlike longer wireless waves they travel in straight lines and cannot follow round the curved surface of the earth. But three space stations could receive and re-transmit television programmes so as to cover the whole world.

Thirdly, from a space-station, weather observers would have the best possible view of the clouds forming on earth on which to base their forecasts which are of such great importance to farmers, sailors and airmen. A fourth possibility is that space-stations could be in the form of large groups of mirrors to reflect the sun's light down to earth, giving the effect of a full moon every night. In addition, a space-station would be the ideal place for carrying out many scientific observations of the universe and its behaviour.

The Working of a Rocket

What is it that pushes a rocket that soars into the sky ? The answer is gas pressure.

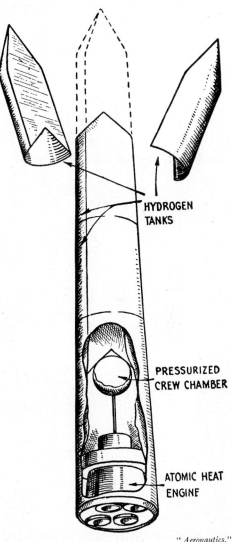

HYDROGEN TANKS

PRESSURIZED CREW CHAMBER

ATOMIC HEAT ENGINE

" *Aeronautics.*"

PLAN OF A MODERN ROCKET

Atomic energy may help to solve the problem of fuel, but other solutions may be required. Liquid hydrogen would be used in this type of rocket, with an atomic power plant for heating purposes. Empty fuel tanks would be discarded on the journey.

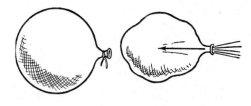

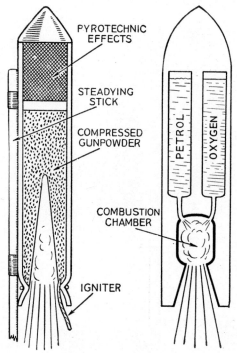

PYROTECHNIC
EFFECTS

STEADYING
STICK

COMPRESSED
GUNPOWDER

PETROL   OXYGEN

COMBUSTION
CHAMBER

IGNITER

Specially drawn for this work.

ROCKETS OLD AND NEW

On the left is seen the ordinary " Guy Fawkes "
stick rocket, while on the right is a more modern
type with liquid fuel. In this latter type the gas
results from the burning of the fuel and pressure
from combustion temperature. An ordinary
balloon can be used to illustrate the principle of
rocket motion. When the neck is tied the
balloon is stationary, but when air is allowed to
escape rearward the balloon moves in the
opposite direction.

In a powder-burning rocket of the
kind used on November the Fifth, the
fuel, or powder, is held in a cardboard
container and is ignited by a slow-
burning fuse—" the blue touch paper."
When the powder burns it creates a
large volume of gas and this volume is
further increased by the heat of the
burning. The volume of gas is many

times greater than the original volume of
powder, so that a great pressure is
developed. This pressure exerts itself
upon the cardboard container, tending
to burst it, and, indeed, it would do so
if it were not for the fact that a way of
escape is provided at the rear.

Because the gas can escape rearward
no backward pressure is exerted upon
the container. Pressure is exerted sideways, of course, but the pressure at
any side is exactly balanced by the
pressure on the other side, so that
no movement is caused. But between
the front and rear of the container
there is an unbalance of pressure which
drives it forward. The well-known law
that every action must have an equal
and opposite reaction is illustrated here.
A certain force drives a large volume of
gas out of the container and an equal
force reacts against the container itself.

It can be seen that the working of a
rocket will continue in a vacuum since
the pressure of air is not necessary to
the process. In fact, the slight pressure
at the atmosphere is a hindrance, since
it slows the escape of gas.

Modern rockets burn many different
types of fuel, liquid or solid, and their
combustion chambers are made of
special steel to resist high temperatures,
for the higher the temperature attained,
the greater the gas expansion and the
greater the pressure developed.

Special cooling devices have to be
incorporated so that the high temperatures of these motors shall not
become dangerous; separate motors are
installed to pump the fuel more quickly;
radio and navigational instruments are
provided, and as rockets grow bigger
and travel farther they become more
complicated. But the principle of rocket
propulsion remains as simple as the
propulsion of our un-tied balloon.

Where directional control is needed
at very high altitudes the air is too thin
to be effective upon external control
surfaces, and vanes of graphite or some
other heat-resisting material must be
set in the exhaust stream.

How
Steam and
Petrol
Work for Man

Ships
Big and Little
And How
They Are Built

P.-A. Reuter Photos.

THE " CARONIA," A MARVEL OF GRACE AND SPEED

The 34,000-ton Cunard White Star liner, *Caronia*, seen in the photograph above, was one of the largest ships to be built in any country in the world in the first few years after the war. She was truly described as " a marvel of grace and speed " when she sailed on her maiden voyage from Southampton to New York in January, 1949.

OCEAN GREYHOUNDS AND RIVER WHIPPETS

THE very word "ship" conjures up pictures of many kinds. Of Vikings, pirates, buccaneers ; of coral islands and treasure islands ; of sea fights, Nelson and the Spanish Armada; of explorers feeling their way into unknown seas ; of trade, tall Indiamen and tea clippers ; of storms, icebergs and waterspouts ; of clanging ship-yards and busy docks ; of captains and pilots ; of shipwreck, lifeboats and salvage. One could lengthen the list into pages.

In the Trade Winds

The fascination of the ship will never die. The ship is too closely bound up with our history and our very existence to cease to interest. The picturesqueness of the " tall ships " with their mountains of billowing canvas has passed away almost entirely, but the modern ship, driven by power inside herself, is still in the main a thing of beauty, and one of the finest products of man's art.

The application of steam to ships, rather more than a century ago, brought about an enormous change in navigation. It practically converted the seas and oceans into vast plains over which vessels might move in any direction, regardless of wind and currents, holding to a course continuously for days, or even weeks, on end. The length of a voyage was now not a question of favouring wind, adverse wind, or no wind at all, but more or less the quotient of a simple division sum, in which the distance to be travelled was divided by the speed of the ship. The calm belt of the " doldrums," wherein ships might lie motionless for weeks, became a help instead of a hindrance ; and if the trade winds no longer gave so much assistance when astern, they impeded far less when a ship had to face them.

To-day a voyage from England to Australia is a matter of four or five weeks ; in the times of sail it might occupy as many months, perhaps a year.

You may have thought, some time or other, how convenient it would be if there were " no more sea," and the oceans were turned into level plains, over which we could drive huge motor vehicles at full speed whithersoever we wished. The idea looks attractive at first sight. But if turned into fact we might have reason to regret it. For the big ship, moving through a medium which wears her hardly at all, and supports her perfectly, can carry goods in large quantities more cheaply than can anything on wheels.

Brunel's Great Ships

The day of the big steamship began with the launching of the *Great Britain* in 1843. At the time she was regarded as a giant ship, with her length of 322 feet, beam of 51 feet, and displacement of about 3,000 tons. She is especially interesting as being one of the earliest *iron* steamships, and the first vessel designed for the Atlantic trade that was propelled by a screw. Though she ran aground on her first trip, and was got off only with great difficulty, she remained in service for many years between Liverpool and Australia.

Her designer, Isambard Kingdom Brunel, who is also remembered as the engineer

British Thomson-Houston Co. Ltd.

TO PROPEL A GREAT LINER

The huge mass of machinery shown above is one of two propelling motors in a P. & O. turbo-electric ship. These two motors work together or independently, energy reaching them from a turbo-generator. Broadly, in a ship equipped for electrical transmission of power, oil fuel works the turbine engines, which turn a dynamo. So current is created which operates the propelling motor illustrated.

Cunard S.S. Co. Ltd.

SCENE IN STOKEHOLD OF AN OIL BURNER

When an ocean liner is propelled by oil instead of coal, the grimy stokers are not required, and we have instead a stokehold such as the one depicted above. Here the work is carried on by a mere handful of men who have only to watch pressure gauges and adjust the valves that admit oil into the furnaces in the form of spray. We should remember also that oil fuel requires less space in a ship than coal.

who laid out the Great Western and other railways, and built the wonderful bridge at Saltash, near Plymouth, took on himself the planning of a truly mammoth ship, the *Great Eastern*. This remarkable vessel was 693 feet long, and 83 feet wide. At full load she displaced over 27,000 tons of water. She had two sets of engines, one working paddles 56 feet in diameter and the other a screw propeller. Apart from her size, she was a very notable ship, for her design included several new features which shipbuilders have made use of ever since. Among them were her double bottom and the division of her hull inside into separate watertight compartments by bulkheads, that is, upright metal divisions, running lengthwise and crosswise.

A " White Elephant "

She was launched on the Thames after many unsuccessful attempts, in 1858, and made her first trip to New York in 1860. Two years later, while nearing New York, she scraped over some rocks, and would have been lost but for her double bottom. The outer skin of this was ripped open for a distance of 80 feet, but the inner skin held, and the ship arrived safely in port without any of the passengers knowing how near they had been to disaster.

The *Great Eastern* was ahead of her time, and a sad " white elephant " to her various owners. Yet she proved herself a complete success so far as design was concerned and her great bulk enabled her to lay, in 1865, the first Atlantic cable to give perma-

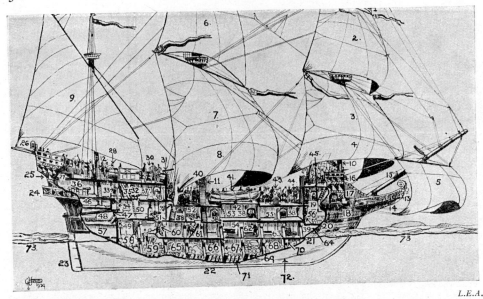

L.E.A.

A GALLANT OLD-TIME SAILING SHIP

Here is a section of a sailing ship of other days. The various compartments, sails and parts are
described in our table below, by means of which you can follow the key numbers.

SAILS

1. Fore Top-gallant.
2. Fore Topsail.
3. Fore Course.
4. Fore Bonnet.
5. Spritsail.
6. Main Topsail.
7. Main Course.
8. Main Bonnet.
9. Mizzen.

MASTS

10. Fore.
11. Main.
12. Mizzen.

HULL

13. Figure Head.
14. Beak.
15. Bowsprit.
16. Fore Castle.
17. Cathead.
18. Anchor.
19. Upper Gun Deck.
20. Lower Gun Deck.
21. Orlop Deck.
22. Keel.
23. Rudder.
24. Quarter Gallery.
25. Half (or sometimes called Quarter) Deck.
26. Stern Lantern.

DETAILS ON HALF DECK

27. Lockers.
28. Master giving directions to Steersmen on Deck below.

29. Great Skylight.
30. Officers.
31. Demi - Falcon (a small gun).

DETAILS ON UPPER GUN DECK

32. Officers' Cabins.
33. Helmsmen.
34. Whipstaff (for steering).
35. Main Staircase from Half Deck.
36. Great Cabin.
37. Main Capstan.
38. Guns.
39. Break in the Deck.
40. Night's Head.
41. Boats Stowed.
42. Great Hatch.
43. Jeer Capstan.
44. Members of Ship's Crew.
45. Galley Fluepipe.
46. Officers' Stores.

DETAILS ON LOWER GUN DECK

47. Tiller.
48. Gunners' Store.
49. Break in the Deck.
50. Crew's Space.
51. Lower Main Capstan.
52. Members of Crew asleep on the Deck (no hammocks were then in use).
53. Ladder to Upper Gun Deck.

54. Great Hatch Opening.
55. Base of Jeer Capstan.
56. Galley.

DETAILS OF ORLOP DECK

57. Lazaretto.
58. Beer Store.
59. Magazine.
60. Protected Magazine Lantern.
61. Young Members of Crew carrying powder to the Guns.
62. Cables, Spare Spars, etc.
63. Hatch Covers.
64. Crew's Space.

HOLD

65. Flour, etc.
66. Fresh Water in Barrels.
67. Diagonal Bracing characteristic of Elizabethan ships.
68. General Stores, Cargo, etc.
69. Ribs and Main Timbers.
70. Cross or Athwartship Timbers.
71. Ballast, largely consisting of stones.
72. Outer Planking diagrammatically cut away to show interior.
73. Water Line.

ON BOARD THE QUEEN MARY

Here is one view of the lounge in the *Queen Mary*, furnished in the most exquisite taste and dignity and offering to those privileged to use it great spaciousness together with an atmosphere that is completely restful. Few of the stately homes of England have rooms so comfortably ornate as this lounge.

Photos: Stewart Bale.

If you have never travelled by a crack ocean liner you will find it hard to realise the luxury of these modern floating cities which offer to their passengers all the spacious comfort of a magnificent hotel. Here, for example, is the restaurant of the *Queen Mary* with the tables set for a meal.

British Thomson-Houston Co. Ltd.

THE ENGINE CONTROL ROOM

If you regard the officer in charge of a liner's engines as the " driver," he would be found in an apartment such as that illustrated above. Orders from the bridge would reach him by telegraph and he would operate the control levers to give full speed ahead, half-speed, slow, reverse or stop.

In Oriental Splendour

The iron ship gave way to the *steel* ship in 1873 or thereabouts, and at the same period shipbuilders began to turn out mail and passenger ships giving a reasonable amount of comfort to those aboard. When Charles Dickens crossed the Atlantic in 1842, in the old *Britannia*, he wrote of her saloon as being "a gigantic hearse with windows in the side." It was left to her successors to come up to the advertisements of her as "furnished in than Oriental

nent electrical communication between Britain and America. Fifty years had passed after her launching before another ship of equal size entered the water.

For many years steamships carried sails to help their rather weak engines, and to fall back on should the engines go wrong—as not infrequently happened. But the time came when the reliability and power of engines made sails a mere encumbrance, and they were practically abolished, though masts were still used for signalling and other purposes, and a sail or two might be stowed away in case of special emergencies.

a style of more splendour."

Along with greater comfort came greater speed. In 1893 the Cunard liner *Campania*, driven by engines of 30,000 horse-power, and twin screws, averaged 22 knots, and was the first of a long series of Atlantic " ocean greyhounds " designed to keep the voyage from England to New York within a compass of a week. During the opening years of this century England lost the speed record to Germany, who launched three large 23½-knot liners. (A knot, it should perhaps be mentioned, is a speed of about 1⅐ statute miles per hour.) All

TO THE SOUTH AND THE FAR EAST

This fine vessel is the *Capetown Castle*, one of the largest liners of the Union-Castle Company. She was built at Belfast in 1938 and is a twin-screw motor ship, 734 feet in length and 82 feet in width, 27,000 tons gross. Equipped with every luxury, she carries 292 first class and 499 cabin class passengers.

Above we see one of the latest P. & O. liners, the *Stratheden*, a vessel of nearly 24,000 tons, 640 feet in length and 82 feet in width. She was launched in 1937. The P. & O. is one of the oldest steamship companies, having been founded in 1835. Its trade is largely with Egypt, India, the Far East and Australia. This picture was taken at Malta.

PAINTING THE FUNNELS

The men here seen make one think of flies round a jam jar, but they are actually engaged in the important task of applying the familiar red paint to the lower parts of the funnels of a Cunarder. Each man is supported by ropes and occupies a swinging seat known as a " bosun's chair."

these ships had magnificent piston engines, expanding the steam in three or four stages in successive cylinders. But a great rival was in the field, the steam turbine, invented by Sir Charles Algernon Parsons.

The Steam Turbine

The Parsons marine turbine has inside it a long hollow drum mounted on a shaft. Rows of blades stick out from the drum, and the gaps between the rows are filled with rows of similar blades projecting from the casing and almost touching the drum. The steam enters at one end of the drum and works its way along through the blades. It gives the first row of drum blades a sideways push, as a wind pushes the sails of a windmill. Having passed through these, its direction has been changed, and if it then struck the next row of moving blades it would tend to stop them. So it has first to pass through a row of fixed blades, which turn it in the right direction for striking the next row of moving blades. And so on over and over again. To allow for the expansion of the steam, the space between drum and casing increases gradually and the blades are made longer. A turbine may have

SHIPS TO·DAY AND YESTERDAY

Fox Photos

The Cunard White Star liner, the *Queen Mary*, was the first of the two "Queen" sister ships, the largest vessels afloat. Compared with the *Queen Elizabeth*, the *Queen Mary* has three funnels instead of two, her total length is 10 ft. less, and she is nearly 4,000 tons less gross tonnage. The first Cunarder, *Britannia*, carried 200 passengers; both the *Queen Elizabeth* and *Queen Mary* carry over 2,000 passengers as well as a crew of more than 1,200 to run the ship and attend to the needs of all on board.

A SHIP OF THE ANCIENT NILE

At least 5,000 years before the birth of Christ the Egyptians are known to have made use of boats, and the above picture of a vessel sailing on the Nile is based on carvings found in the Temple of Del-el-Bahari. The great blocks of granite used in the building of the Pyramids are known to have been brought from Assouan by water, and the ships so employed must have been of considerable size, though the marvel of how such great weights were handled and transported still remains.

FROM THE VIKINGS TO EAST INDIAMEN

In the seventh and eighth centuries the world's greatest mariners were the Norse Vikings, who probably discovered America before Columbus. A Viking ship is seen above.

From the seals of very old towns we can reconstruct a ship such as those which sailed the seas around the English coasts in the thirteenth century. The anchors were kept on the two platforms.

Drawings specially prepared for this work

Here we have a drawing, based on a picture in the British Museum, of an English merchant ship about the year 1675 in the reign of Charles II. Compared with the warships of the period the merchantmen were only lightly armed.

The East India Company had its own fleet of merchant ships, and in the days when pirates flourished the East Indiamen were armed for defence. In the drawing above, the lower row of ports are dummies to deceive an enemy.

A SAILING SHIP THAT RECALLS PAST GLORIES

Long after the steam engine had revolutionised travel on land and sea the sailing ships flourished, and in the middle of the nineteenth century the famous "Tea Clippers" made records on their voyages from China to England. There are still a few gallant sailing-ships carrying their cargoes across the Seven Seas, and in this photograph we have a modern sailing-ship, the *Archibald Russell*, in full dress.

The early steamships still carried sails and the engines turned paddle-wheels as seen in this picture of the *Great Western*. She was among the earliest examples of an Atlantic liner, was 236 ft. in length, and could steam at the rate of nearly 10 land miles an hour. She made her first crossing from Queenstown to New York in sixteen days in April 1838.

Drawings specially prepared for this work

Designed by the famous engineer, Isambard Brunel, the *Great Eastern*, seen above, was built in 1858 and was the largest steamship built to that date. She had two sets of engines, one turning paddle-wheels 56 ft. in diameter and the other a "screw" or propeller. As a passenger ship she was not a success, but was later employed to lay the first Atlantic cable.

BETWEEN BRITAIN, AUSTRALIA AND NEW ZEALAND

Shaw Savill & Albion Line

The oldest shipping line in the trade between Great Britain and New Zealand is the Shaw Savill and Albion Line. They brought the first consignment of frozen meat to England in 1882. Our photograph shows the quadruple-screw motor vessel *Dominion Monarch*, of 27,155 tons, which does the voyage from England to New Zealand in 35 days, calling en route at South African and Australian ports.

Orient Line

Built at Barrow-in-Furness by Vickers-Armstrong, the Orient liner *Orcades* was completed in November 1948 and is the largest and fastest ship on the Australian run. A twin-screw turbine-driven vessel, the *Orcades* can carry 1,555 passengers with a crew of 617, as well as mails and cargo. The voyage from London to Melbourne has been reduced from 36 to 27 days.

SAILING IN SOUTHERN SEAS

Union Castle Line

In 1853 the Union Steam Collier Co. came into being, while nine years later Donald Currie founded the Castle Line to carry goods between Liverpool and Calcutta. These two companies shared the transport of the South African Mail and eventually joined together in 1900 as the Union Castle Line. The "Castle" tradition has continued and here we see the R.M.S. *Pretoria Castle*, a vessel of 28,705 tons.

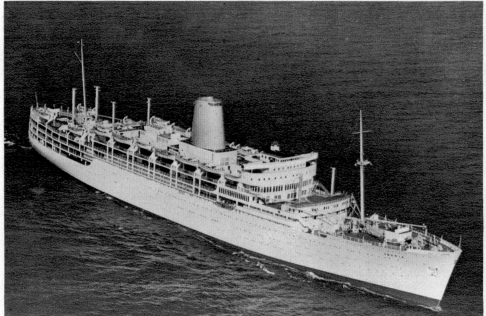

P. & O. Line

The P. & O. liner *Iberia*, built in the famous Belfast shipyards of Harland & Wolff Ltd., sailed on her maiden voyage to Bombay, Colombo, and Australian ports in September 1954. Fitted with every modern device and navigational aid to ensure comfort and safety for 1,400 passengers and 711 crew, the *Iberia* is over 718 ft. long and has a service speed of 22½ knots.

OIL TANKER AND FISHING TRAWLER

The transport of highly inflammable petrol from distant oilfields has brought into existence a special type of ocean-going vessel known as the "tanker," with its engines astern and special ventilators from the storage holds. Most of the great oil companies now have fleets of these vessels which are generally about 12,000 tons. Our picture above is of the Shell tanker *Dromus*.

In this photograph we have one of the latest and most up-to-date fishing trawlers, built by Messrs. Cochran & Co., of Selby, Yorkshire, for the Rinovia Steam Fishing Co., Ltd., of Grimsby, on the east coast of Britain, at a cost of £100,000. It is fitted with Radar to assist in navigation and from the wireless room the skipper can contact by microphone any part of the ship.

some hundreds of thousands of blades.

The advantage of a turbine is that it turns smoothly and evenly at high speeds, being in perfect balance. All the world's fastest ships, including almost all warships, are now driven by turbines, which are connected to the propellers direct, or drive them through gearing. By the use of gearing the propeller is made to turn much more slowly than the turbine, and better results are obtained at moderate speeds.

A Floating City

After the turbine had been tried successfully on some small vessels, it was applied to ocean steamers. In 1907 the splendid sister ships, *Mauretania* and *Lusitania*, 762 feet long, and each equipped with four turbines giving 65,000 horse power and driving four propellers, were put into the Atlantic service, and attained a speed of over 25 knots. Their speed remained unbeaten by merchant ships till 1929, when the German liner *Bremen* averaged about 28 knots for the crossing. In June, 1935, however, this record was beaten by the French liner *Normandie*, whose speed averaged 30 knots. From 1938 until 1952 the *Queen Mary* held

Nautical Photo Agency.

LIFE-BOAT DRILL AT SEA

Every passenger on an ocean liner is allotted to a special boat station at the start of a voyage, and all precautions are taken to ensure that in the event of danger everything will work smoothly and quickly. Our photograph shows boat drill on board the New Zealand Shipping Co's vessel *Rangitiki*.

SHIPS WITH A NEW LOOK

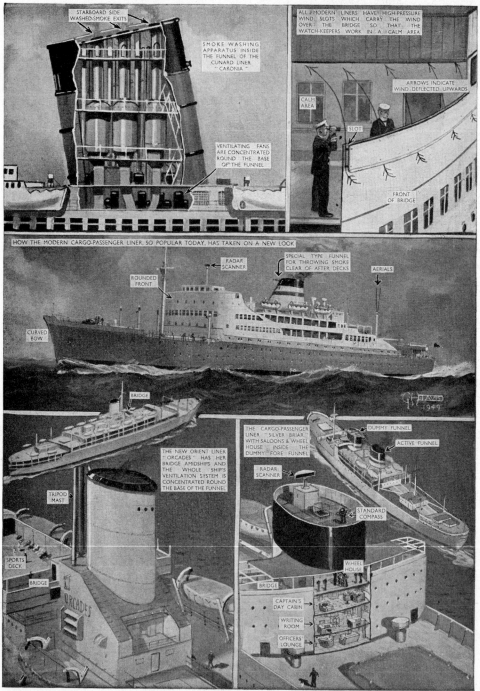

STARBOARD SIDE WASHED-SMOKE EXITS

SMOKE WASHING APPARATUS INSIDE THE FUNNEL OF THE CUNARD LINER "CARONIA"

VENTILATING FANS ARE CONCENTRATED ROUND THE BASE OF THE FUNNEL

ALL MODERN LINERS HAVE HIGH-PRESSURE WIND SLOTS WHICH CARRY THE WIND OVER THE BRIDGE SO THAT THE WATCH-KEEPERS WORK IN A CALM AREA

ARROWS INDICATE WIND DEFLECTED UPWARDS

CALM AREA

SLOT

FRONT OF BRIDGE

HOW THE MODERN CARGO-PASSENGER LINER, SO POPULAR TODAY, HAS TAKEN ON A NEW LOOK

RADAR SCANNER

SPECIAL TYPE FUNNEL FOR THROWING SMOKE CLEAR OF AFTER DECKS

AERIALS

ROUNDED FRONT

CURVED BOW

BRIDGE

THE NEW ORIENT LINER "ORCADES" HAS HER BRIDGE AMIDSHIPS AND THE WHOLE SHIP'S VENTILATION SYSTEM IS CONCENTRATED ROUND THE BASE OF THE FUNNEL

THE CARGO-PASSENGER LINER "SILVER BRIAR" WITH SALOONS & WHEEL HOUSE INSIDE THE DUMMY FORE FUNNEL

DUMMY FUNNEL

ACTIVE FUNNEL

RADAR SCANNER

STANDARD COMPASS

TRIPOD MAST

SPORTS DECK

BRIDGE

ORCADES

WHEEL HOUSE

BRIDGE

CAPTAIN'S DAY CABIN

WRITING ROOM

OFFICERS' LOUNGE

Specially drawn for this work.

Many new ideas have been adopted in recent years to add not only to the speed of passenger and cargo ships but to increase the comfort of passengers and crews as well as the over-all efficiency of the ships themselves. Some of these innovations are illustrated and explained above. In addition to the use of welding on a large scale for the hulls, the adoption of duralumin and other lightweight metals for funnels and superstructures has become general.

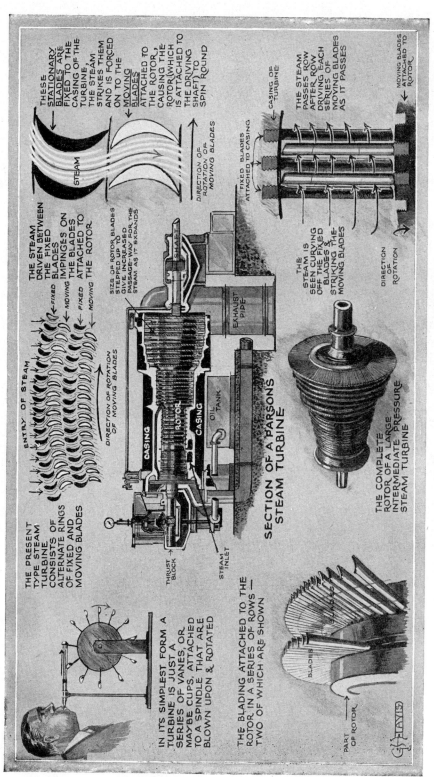

THESE STATIONARY BLADES ARE FIXED TO THE CASING OF THE TURBINE. THE STEAM STRIKES THEM AND IS FORCED ON TO THE MOVING BLADES

THE STEAM DRIVEN BETWEEN THE FIXED BLADES IMPINGES ON THE BLADES ATTACHED TO THE ROTOR

MOVING BLADES ATTACHED TO THE ROTOR, CAUSING THE ROTOR (WHICH IS ATTACHED TO THE DRIVING SHAFT) TO SPIN ROUND

STEAM

DIRECTION OF ROTATION OF MOVING BLADES

FIXED
MOVING
FIXED
MOVING

CASING OF TURBINE

THE STEAM PASSES AFTER ROW DRIVING EACH SERIES OF MOVING BLADES AS IT PASSES

FIXED BLADES ATTACHED TO CASING

MOVING BLADES ATTACHED TO ROTOR

THE PRESENT TYPE STEAM TURBINE CONSISTS OF ALTERNATE RINGS OF FIXED AND MOVING BLADES

ENTRY OF STEAM

SIZE OF ROTOR BLADES STEPPED UP TO GIVE INCREASED PASSAGE-WAY FOR THE STEAM AS IT EXPANDS

SHAFT

DIRECTION OF ROTATION OF MOVING BLADES

CASING

ROTOR

CASING

EXHAUST PIPE

OIL TANK

THE STEAM IS SEEN CURVING OFF THE FIXED BLADES & STRIKING THE MOVING BLADES

DIRECTION OF ROTATION

THRUST BLOCK

STEAM INLET

SECTION OF A PARSON'S STEAM TURBINE

THE COMPLETE ROTOR OF A LARGE INTERMEDIATE PRESSURE STEAM TURBINE

IN ITS SIMPLEST FORM A TURBINE IS JUST A SERIES OF VANES, OR MAYBE CUPS, ATTACHED TO A SPINDLE THAT ARE BLOWN UPON & ROTATED

THE BLADING ATTACHED TO THE ROTOR IN A SERIES OF ROWS — TWO OF WHICH ARE SHOWN

BLADES

PART OF ROTOR

Specially drawn for this work.

THE ENGINE THAT GAVE US FASTER STEAMSHIPS

In this series of pictorial diagrams you obtain a very clear idea of how a steam turbine engine works, imparting to the propeller shaft a motion that is never jerky, but always even as well as swift. The propeller shaft is carried into the turbine engine and coupled to a rotor, from which thousands upon thousands of blades protrude. Steam playing forcefully upon the blades sets them spinning round so that they turn the motor, and so the propeller. The blades are ranged in larger circles as steam expands.

17—2

Central Press.

A STREAM-LINED FUNNEL

The single stack of one of the latest liners, the 28,000 tons Orient Line *Orcades*, is stream-lined. Just forward of this monster funnel can be seen part of the navigating bridge.

saloons, wonderfully decorated; their electric lifts, swimming baths, gymnasiums, shops and gardens; their wonderful array of lifeboats, handled by ingenious gear for dropping them overboard; their bridges, replete with every possible aid to navigation; their great boiler rooms, filled with rows of enormous boilers; their engine rooms, with the huge but almost silent turbines; and the vast array of auxiliary machinery for ventilating, lighting, heating, lifting, steering, and what not.

Oil Fuel on Fast Ships

But we may note specially that no coal will be found in or near the boiler rooms, for on these fast ships coal has been replaced by oil as fuel. The old *Mauretania* originally burned 1,000 tons of coal a day, and she had to have 6,000 tons of it aboard when she left port. The change-over to oil has effected a great saving of room, as a smaller weight of fuel is carried, and oil can be stored in spaces—such as the double bottom —not suitable for coal bunkers.

The oil is pumped or blown into the furnaces in the form of a spray, which burns with a fierce heat, and gives off practically no smoke. Instead of a large gang of perspiring stokers shovelling coal, a boiler room now needs only a few men to watch gauges and adjust valves controlling the oil and water; and the very dirty process of coaling a ship has been replaced by " oiling " from shore tanks or lighters, which needs little labour and causes no discomfort to crew or passengers.

the Atlantic record, but the new American liner, *United States* (53,330 tons), set up a new record, just over 10 hours less than the *Queen Mary's* record, in July, 1952. The new record-holder is driven by steam turbines driving the shafts through reduction gearing, which is customary in big ships.

The largest ship in the world is the *Queen Elizabeth* (83,673 tons), launched in 1938. She is nearly 4,000 tons bigger than the *Queen Mary*, and during the war carried over 800,000 troops across many thousands of miles of ocean.

We have not time to describe these beautifully-shaped ships in detail. We can merely refer to their numerous decks, the uppermost of which towers many feet above the sea; their palatial

But coal is beginning to invade boiler rooms again, though in the form of fine dust, which can be blown into the furnaces in the same way as oil. Since powdered coal is cheaper than oil in countries which do not produce petroleum, and as a fuel has some of oil's advantages, we may see its use expand greatly before we are much older.

With air transport becoming a serious rival of the shipping industry, everything is being done to perfect sea travel.

All of the oil fuel that comes aboard ships is not burned in furnaces. Much of it finds its way direct into the cylinders of great engines, in which it is mixed with air and burned explosively, like petrol in a motor-car engine.

The motor ship is progressing by leaps and bounds. If we seek for the reason why, we find it in the great saving of fuel and space. More power is got from a ton of oil, and the absence of boilers gives room for more cabins or holds. In recent years an almost

equal tonnage of motor ships has been built as the tonnage of steamships. The list of large motor liners now includes several ships of between 20,000 and 30,000 tons displacement, with speeds exceeding 20 knots.

Systems in Rivalry

The engines used are much like steam marine engines in general appearance. Many of them have six cylinders, with pistons acted on in both directions by the explosions. Air is drawn into a cylinder and compressed by the piston to a pressure of about 400 pounds to the square inch, by which time it has become very hot. A small quantity of oil is then sprayed into it, and the heat causes it to fire at once and produce an explosion which moves the piston. At first these big engines gave a good deal of trouble, but they are now

Orient Line.

THE LAST LINK WITH SYDNEY

The gang-planks are about to be raised and the last moorings slipped as the Orient liner R.M.S. *Orcades* departs from its wharf at Pyrmont, Sydney. Thousands of paper streamers still join friends and relatives on board with those on the wharf who have come to bid them *bon voyage* as they sail for England, some 12,000 miles away.

BETWEEN AUSTRALIA AND BRITAIN

Autotype Co.

Here we see the S.S. *Gothic*, a vessel of 15,902 tons belonging to the Shaw Savill Line. This ship was refitted in 1953 for the Royal Tour to New Zealand and Australia. H.M. the Queen and the Duke of Edinburgh embarked on the *Gothic* at Kingston, Jamaica, at the end of November and reached New Zealand shortly before Christmas Day.

Orient Line.

Completed early in 1954, the Orient passenger liner *Orsova* has been described by her owners as "the ship of shapes to come." She has no masts, a funnel like an inverted flower-pot, and an all-welded hull, and she created a record in post-war construction. With accommodation for 1,498 passengers she will be able to take 12,000 people to and from Australia and Britain each year.

LINERS OF THE EAST AND WEST

Australian News and Information Bureau.

The photograph above was taken at the pier of Port Melbourne in Australia, and shows the departure of the 23,000-ton British liner *Orion*. This magnificent vessel belongs to the Orient Steam Navigation Co., a well-known Line which was founded in 1877. The ships of this Line sail between London, the Far East and Australia.

Royal Mail Lines Ltd.

Here is a picture of R.M.S. *Highland Vessel*, a ship of 14,200 tons belonging to the Royal Mail Steam Packet Co. More than a hundred years ago this company was running a service of paddle steamers from Falmouth to the West Indies and it developed great interests in the many ports of South America.

In this drawing of the Cunard White Star *Caronia*, one of the largest ships to be built in any country in the world since the end of the Second World War, the arrangement of the different decks, rooms and cabin is shown. The key to the various numbers marked on the drawing is as follows: 1. Anchor Cables 2. Cargo Hatch; 3. Derricks; 4. Observation Lounge; 5. Navigation and Radio Officers' Accommodation 6. Captain and Officers' Accommodation; 7. Bridge; 8. Wheel House; 9. Chart Rooms, etc.; 10. Gyro Compartment; 11. Radar House; 12. Corridor; 13. Radar Instruments; 14. Crow's Nest; 15. Tripod Mast; 16. Starboard, 45-ft. Motor Launches; 17. First-class Lounge; 18. Fans; 19. First-class Cabins; 20. Engineers' Ward Room; 21. Verandah Café; 22. Theatre; 22a. Wireless Masts; 23. Lido 24. Swimming Pool; 25. Open Terrace; 26. Docking Bridge; 27. Cabin Class Deck; 28. Port Anchor 29 and 29a. First-class Cabins; 30. Entrance; 31. Private Suites; 32. Cabin Class; 33. Cabin Class Open Space; 34. Crew Accommodation; 35. First-class Cabins; 36. Entrance Stairs and Lifts; 37. First-class

Illustrated London News.

abins; 38. Officers' Mess; 39. Cabin Class Rooms; 40. Entrance (Aft); 41. Open Space; 42. Crew's
ccommodation; 43. First-class Accommodation; 44. Entrance Stairs and Lifts; 45. Forward Restaurant;
6. Plate Room; 47. Fruit Storage Room; 48. Cold Rooms; 49. Kitchens; 50. Plate and Cutlery Rooms;
1. Private Dining Rooms; 52. After Restaurant; 53. Entrance, Stairs, Lifts, etc.; 54. Second-class
ccommodation; 55. Stewards' Quarters; 56. Crew's Quarters; 57. Engineers' Accommodation; 58.
angway; 59. Petty Officers' and Laundry Workers' Mess; 60. Cabin Accommodation; 61. Shop;
2. Hospital; 63. Stores Entrance; 64. Cabin Class Accommodation; 65. Stewards' Accommodation;
6. Gangway; 67. Grocery Stores; 68. Cabin Accommodation; 69. Cargo and Stores; 70. Stores;
1. Linen Stores; 72. Auxiliary Machinery; 73, 73*a*, 73*b*. Fuel Tanks; 74. Turbo-Generators; 75. Boiler
ooms; 76. Engine Room; 77. Stores; 78. Gymnasium; 79. Domestic Water Tanks; 80. Port Propeller;
81. Water-line.

made as reliable as steam engines. In most cases they drive the propellers direct. What is called electrical transmission is also used, as on some steamships. The engine turns a dynamo, and the electricity generated is sent to an electric motor which turns the propeller. For low speeds one engine may be connected electrically with two or more propellers, and give the others a rest, thus saving fuel.

It is early yet to say whether the motor ship will put the steamship " out of business," for steam engineers are making a good fight with turbines and very high pressure steam. We may well believe that there will be plenty of room for both motor ships and steamships.

Motor-driven Flyers

Mention of the motor ship reminds us of another kind of craft driven by

internal combustion engines—their very small sisters, the motor-boats. Though only a few yards long, some of them can run even a liner off its legs in the matter of speed—on calm water. We refer to boats built specially for racing.

These are called hydroplanes, or skimming-boats, and their bottoms are shaped into more or less flat, sloping steps. As the boat gathers speed, the upward pressure of the water on these steps or planes forces her out of the water until at last she is scuttering along the top of it with but a small part of her hull submerged. The power needed to lift her up in this way is much smaller than that which would be required to drive her at the same speed *through* the water.

In Plumes of Spray

When a boat of this kind is given engines of great power she puts up

Isle of Man Steam Packet Co. Ltd.

BOUND FOR THE ISLE OF MAN

One of the most popular passenger steamship services in the United Kingdom is that running between Liverpool and the Isle of Man. The Isle of Man Steam Packet Company, first known as Mona's Isle Co., began in 1830, and since then it is estimated that the Company's ships have carried over 60 million passengers between Liverpool and Douglas. The S.S. *Mona's Queen*, seen above, is the fourth to bear this name and is the latest of the I.O.M. fleet. With a speed of 21 knots she can carry 2,500 passengers.

General Steam Navigation Co. Ltd.

HOLIDAY-MAKERS ABOARD THE " ROYAL DAFFODIL "

London's river has its own pleasure craft including various sea services. Here is the twin-screw motor-vessel *Royal Daffodil* which can carry 2,073 passengers and has a speed of 21 knots. The *Royal Daffodil* sails from Gravesend during the summer with passengers for Margate, but also calls at Southend. From Margate the vessel takes a cruise along the French coast, returning to Margate and Gravesend.

astonishing speeds. The record is over 141 miles an hour—more than two miles a minute. This was made by the late Sir Malcolm Campbell in a vessel driven by enormously powerful engines which revolved the propeller at terrific speed. In the distance a boat travelling " express " appears like a mere dot between two great curving plumes of spray thrown right and left from under her.

In time of war boats of this kind, called Coastal Motor Boats— or C.M.B.'s for short—are used as torpedo boats. They drop a torpedo over the stern ; and, before it can catch them up, get out of its way, leaving the torpedo to speed onwards to its mark. Nothing afloat is able to out-strip them in fairly calm water, as they can spurt at forty-six miles an hour.

Water-buses on the Thames

The Thames is the home port of many great ships and to the Port of London as well as to the docks nearer the mouth of the Thames come passenger ships and cargo vessels from all the countries of the world. There was a time, however, when the Thames was famed as " the silent highway " for people who wished to travel from the City to Westminster or to places farther west. In the sixteenth century more than 3,000 watermen found employment with their small craft in carrying passengers from one point to another along London's river.

With the improvement of the roads and of better means of transport this trade died down. In recent years, how-ever, there has been a revival of the passenger-carrying craft, though the oars have given place to the motor engine. A number of these ply for hire in much the same way as the motor-buses in the streets, picking passengers up at stated points and conveying them to different landing-places between Putney and the Tower of London. More than half-a-million people made use of these motor-vessels in 1948, and in the following year bigger and speedier water-buses came into service. Even larger craft, capable of carrying 250 passengers, have been designed. These water-buses reached the peak of their popularity during the Festival of Britain year, but more recently their use has become mainly confined to pleasure trips.

In the gallant service of the Royal National Life-boat Institution the motor-propelled boat has brought a tremendous advance. Because of the tempestuous seas, the motor itself is housed in a water-tight compartment, and it is calculated that two motor boats are the equivalent of five rescue vessels pulled by oars or propelled by sails. Speed alone often makes possible a saving of life that could not otherwise be attempted, and the motor life-boats live in angrier seas than oared craft dared to face.

A1 at Lloyd's

Two aspects of the business of shipping should be mentioned here: Lloyd's is a name that is bound to crop up whenever the talk is of ships, and most of us have used the expression " A1 at Lloyd's," meaning something which is 100 per cent. fit.

Planet.

A RECORD-MAKING MOTOR-BOAT

Here we see a modern version of the speed-boat, the 300 h.p. motor-boat *Pucico*, in which Carlo Leto, a well-known Italian speed-boat racer, set up a world record for this particular class. It travelled at 139·150 kilometres per hour.

CAR FERRY AND RIVER CRAFT

Cars and double-decker buses can be carried comfortably on board the newest and biggest car ferry vessel, the *Lord Warden*, which went into service between Dover and Boulogne in the summer of 1952. It can carry 1,000 passengers and 120 cars.

At one time the Thames was famed as London's " silent highway," but with improved streets and transport the passenger-carrying craft practically disappeared. In recent times a revival has taken place, and our photograph shows the *Prefect*, a pleasure craft running on the Thames.

Lloyd's Register of Shipping is a separate organisation from Lloyd's, the corporation of marine underwriters which has its headquarters in Leadenhall Street, London. The offices of Lloyd's Register are in Fenchurch Street, London. In nearly all cases every fair-sized ship built in this country is watched by a surveyor of Lloyd's Register at every stage of her progress. If everything is satisfactory the surveyor gives the ship certain letters and figures which are her passport with regard to insurance, chartering, or any other business. An iron or steel-built steamer which is first-class in every respect is classed as 100 A1. " A " relates to the hull; the " 1 " refers to the equipment, and the " 100 " indicates the standard of perfection she attains.

The society has surveyors in most British ports and throughout the world. *Lloyd's Register* is a very large book and the only one of its kind that includes every ship of every country of over 100 tons except certain sailing vessels belonging to countries in the Far East.

Lloyd's, the underwriters, are mainly interested in the insurance of ships, though other risks are also insured. This corporation dates back to 1688 when business men interested in shipping met at the coffee house of Edward Lloyd. It was from these meetings that the great organisation of underwriters interested in the insurance of ships and their cargoes gradually developed. To-day, Lloyd's is the great centre of shipping insurance and has a system of shipping intelligence which is the most complete of its kind in the world.

Fox Photos.

AN HISTORIC MOTOR-BOAT THAT MADE MANY RECORDS

The motor-boat seen here at speed is the famous *Blue Bird* which made history in the years just before the war. It was the property of the late Sir Malcolm Campbell and the photograph was taken on Lake Maggiore during an attack on the speed record. This was in 1937 when a speed of 129 miles per hour was attained. On Lake Hallwil, Switzerland, Sir Malcolm created the record of 132·86 miles per hour, and, later, reached a speed of 141·74 miles per hour.

WONDERFUL TOPS WHICH STEER SHIPS

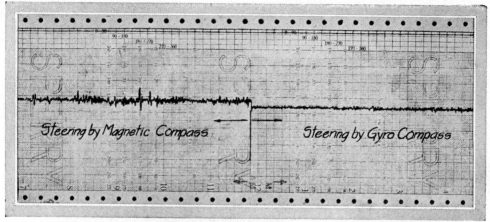

Sperry Gyroscope Co. Ltd.

OLD AND NEW WAYS OF STEERING SHIPS

For the steering of ships a wonderful new compass has been brought into use within comparatively recent times. It works on the principle of a top or gyroscope, and the above diagram is the actual record of the course taken by a vessel at sea. The wavy, jerky course first shown marks the period when a magnetic compass was employed. In the second course we see that the ship was steered by gyro without the slightest variation to left or to right.

THE statement that a top can either steer or steady a ship may seem rather hard to believe. So perhaps it had better be explained that the word " top " must not be taken too literally. The devices of which we are going to write are, however, dependent on whirling bodies like tops; and they make use of the forces which keep a top upright when spinning.

Imagine yourself on the bridge of the good ship *Scientia*, a fine liner of 20,000 tons, fitted with all the latest aids to navigation. Having been given the run of the bridge by the captain, you are sure to peep at the compass in the binnacle. As you watch the circular card with all the points of the compass marked on it, you may perhaps wonder where the magnets guiding it are. In this case, however, there is no need to do so, for the compass you are looking at is no more directed by magnetism than a farm cart is moved by steam.

By Gyroscopic Compass

What *does* hold it with its big arrowhead turned due north is an arrangement of heavy discs revolved at a great speed by electricity. As long as they are running—and they will continue to do so for a long time even after the current driving them has been cut off—that card will do its work correctly.

The gyroscopic compass—a rather formidable name, but it is the one by which it is known—is quickly replacing the magnetic compass, though that old and faithful servant of seamen is still carried aboard to fall back on should anything go wrong with the " gyro." The truth is that the magnetic compass suffers from certain faults, and gives a good deal of trouble. It is liable to be badly upset by masses of iron or steel brought near it. Even when working at its best it seldom points true north, being attracted by the magnetic poles, which are many miles away from the geographical poles of the earth.

You will be interested to learn another thing about the " gyro." The spinning device itself is not on the bridge, but somewhere far below. It controls cards besides that on the bridge, sending out electric currents which make the " servant " cards copy the movements of the " master " exactly.

The Iron Steersman

So much for the compass. But we have not yet done with its spinning apparatus, since the captain draws your attention to the fact that the helmsman, instead of being at the wheel, is standing some distance away looking out of the wheelhouse window. For the moment his services are not needed, as the steering of the big ship has been handed over to a gyroscopic device. The captain has laid out a certain course straight ahead and ordered the automatic steersman to " make it so." Should the ship deviate from it the least bit to port or starboard, the gyroscope switches current into the steering control, and the rudder brings the ship's head back to the right line. This seems marvellous enough, but to do justice to the " iron steersman " one must add that it steers a straighter course than a human being could do.

Should you go into the chart-room you will perhaps see there an apparatus at work tracing a line on a moving ribbon of paper to show any deviations from the course set ; and another which marks on a chart the course taken by a ship during a voyage. Both of these machines are controlled by the gyroscopic compass gear.

A Top that Fights Waves

There is quite a heavy sea on, and the *Scientia* might be excused for rolling heavily. But despite the big waves on her beam she is remarkably steady, and with one's eyes shut one would imagine the sea to be almost calm.

Sperry Gyroscope Co. Ltd.

THE MASTER GYRO-COMPASS

The gyro-compass itself, here illustrated, is kept in a special chamber well down below decks in the ship and away from heat and dirt. Inside the apparatus is a large top with a disc, weighing 50 lb. or more and spinning some thousands of times a minute. By means of electrical current the gyroscope can assume control of the steering of a ship.

Specially painted for this work.

THE "QUEEN ELIZABETH," LARGEST SHIP IN THE WORLD

In July, 1840, the first Cunarder sailed from England on her maiden voyage to provide the first regular mail and passenger steam service between Europe and America. That early voyage took 17 days, and ever since the trans-Atlantic liners of the Cunard White Star Line have maintained the service. The ships have steadily increased in size, speed and comfort, culminating in the "Queen Elizabeth," the largest ship in the world. She was launched on September 27th, 1938, at Clydebank in Scotland by Her Majesty Queen Elizabeth (now the Queen Mother). With a gross tonnage of 83,673 and with her 200,000 h.p. engines, a speed of more than 30 knots can be developed, enabling this ship to cross the Atlantic in four days or less.

N.P.K. v, p. 272.

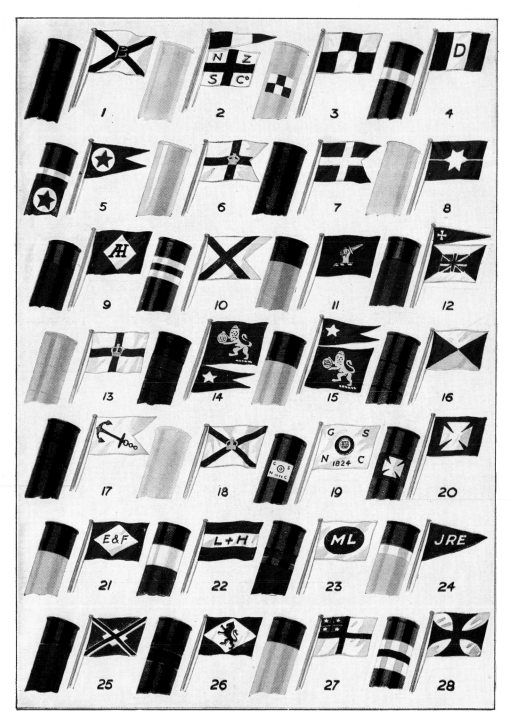

SHIPS' FUNNELS AND HOUSE FLAGS

1. Booth. 2. New Zealand Shipping Co. 3. Canadian Pacific. 4. Donaldson. 5. Blue Star. 6. Elder Dempster. 7. British & African Steam Navigation Co. 8. Aberdeen & Commonwealth. 9. Blue Funnel. 10. British India Steam Navigation Co. 11. Bibby. 12. Glen Line. 13. Orient. 14. Cunard White Star—Cunard ships. 15. Cunard White Star—White Star ships. 16. P. & O.—cargo ships, black funnels; passenger ships generally have buff funnels. 17. Anchor. 18. Royal Mail Steam Packet. 19. General Steam Navigation Co. 20. Houlder. 21. Elder & Fyffe. 22. Lamport & Holt. 23. Manchester Line. 24. Ellerman. 25. Union Castle. 26. Clan. 27. Shaw, Savill & Albion Line. 28. Harrison Line.

A NEW FRIEND FOR SAILORS

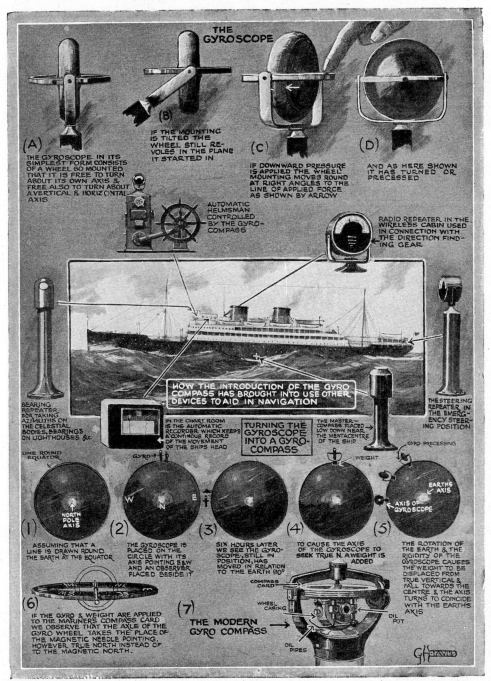

Specially drawn for this work.

For centuries mariners have placed dependence upon the magnetic compass, which always points to the north, though seldom " true north," but this occupant of the binnacle has now to a large extent been replaced at sea by the gyroscopic compass. Such an instrument, whose workings are explained in our pictorial diagram, is made after the principle of a spinning top and can steer a straighter course than a human being.

A visit to a chamber below decks will clear up the mystery. In it is a huge " top " with a disc, weighing 50 tons or more, spinning some thousands of times a minute. You cannot see it, for it is enclosed in a strong casing. The casing has stout pins projecting from its sides to port and starboard, like the trunnions of a big gun, and these fit into sockets bolted to the ship's beams. When a wave comes along and begins to heel the ship over, an electric motor tips the casing forwards or backwards. The top inside resents this treatment, and does its best to turn the ship over towards the wave. The two forces pretty well balance, and the roll is nipped in the bud. Every wave is met in the same way, so the ship is unable to do more than heel over very slightly and therefore is very steady in the roughest of weather.

Sperry Gyroscope Co. Ltd.

A QUARTERMASTER IN IRON

The appliance here illustrated is known to sailors by the familiar name " Metal Mike." It is the Sperry Single-Unit Gyro-Pilot, and is really an iron quartermaster or helmsman that does not grow tired or make any mistakes, but will stand on watch week in and week out. Once the course is set this mechanical device will steer a ship even better than would be the case if a sailor had charge of the wheel.

Harland and Wolff Ltd.

TAKING THE WATER FOR THE FIRST TIME

The launch of a big ship from the yard by the river where the massive hull has slowly taken shape is a thrilling moment for all who watch her. Here we see the 28,700 tons *Edinburgh Castle*, built for the Union-Castle Line, taking the water for the first time from the Musgrave Yard at Harland and Wolff's Belfast shipbuilding works.

MANY years ago the great writer on matters of art, John Ruskin, pronounced a ship to be the most honourable thing made by the combined labours of men. It needed so much forethought, judgment, patience and skill to bring it into being. He was writing of wooden ships, of a size and tonnage that would seem small nowadays. We can hardly doubt, however, that his opinion would still hold good could he watch the building of one of the huge steel ships which furrow the oceans to-day.

It is not granted to many people unconnected with the actual construction or handling of ships to enter a big ship-yard. This is, perhaps, a pity. We all admire a finished ship as she ploughs through the water, but our admiration must be greater than it otherwise would be if based on some knowledge of the manner in which she grew out of a huge number of metal parts.

The story of the making of a ship falls into three parts : the designing of her ; the construction and launching of her hull ; and the equipment of the hull when afloat with engines, boilers, auxiliary machinery, gear of all kinds, and internal fittings. The third is a very much longer business in the case of a passenger ship than in that of a simple cargo-carrier.

Designing a Ship

Very few merchant ships are exact duplicates of any other ship. So we may assume that in most instances the building of a ship cannot begin until very complete sets of drawings have been prepared by naval draughtsmen. These are drawn very carefully to scale. They show not merely the shape of the hull at different levels, and as it would appear if cut through at points equal distances apart, both lengthwise and crossways, but the size and position of every part that will be built into the hull. And, in addition to the hull drawings, there will be another set covering all her machinery and other appointments ; while a passenger vessel will demand yet a third series dealing with the fittings of saloons and cabins.

The " lines " of a ship, that is, her external shape, decide how easily she will travel through water. When a fast vessel is being projected, her designers sometimes make a wax model from provisional drawings and have this towed through a testing tank which may be compared to a huge swimming-bath several hundred feet long.

The cord towing the model is attached to delicate instruments which register the speed and resistance. From the figures so obtained one can reckon the power needed to drive the full-sized ship at the desired speed. If the results are not satisfactory, the shape of the model is altered until the

designers get it right. For very large ships it may be even worth while to make a model big enough to be driven by its own engines. It is far cheaper to alter the model than the ship itself; and a slight change of shape at this stage may mean a great saving of fuel later on.

As soon as the ship's lines have been fixed finally, the draughtsmen can go ahead with the detail work.

In a Shipyard

A shipyard is a vast factory, necessarily close to the water's edge. In most cases it will be found on one bank of a river, wide enough to give plenty of room for launchings. In one part of the water-front are the slipways on which the hulls of ships are built. In another are the fitting-out berths.

Sport and General.

THE KEEL-PLATE IN POSITION

In the building of a ship the first part of the framework to be laid down is the keel or great backbone, from which spring the ribs in pairs. Here you see the keel-plate of a ship which has just been " laid " or bolted together on massive baulks of timber in the shipbuilding yard. The ship is built on a slope to make launching possible.

MODELS FOR THE TESTING TANK

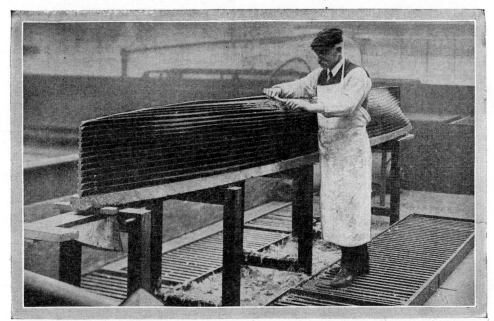

Shipbuilders find it insufficient to carry out their work even from carefully prepared scale drawings, and very often a wax model of the projected vessel is made. Here you see such a model in the course of being " dressed " by an experienced craftsman. Sometimes quite a small alteration in the shape of the boat brings a great increase in speed.

Photos: Cunard White Star.

Models are thoroughly tried out in a testing tank, such as the one here illustrated. The cord towing the model is attached to delicate instruments which register the speed and resistance to the water. By this means the power needed to drive a real ship can be worked out. It is at this stage that the different experts who designed the vessel can check their calculations.

A SHIP BEGINS TO GROW

Harland and Wolff Ltd.

The ship is beginning to take shape, and in this photograph it will be seen that the side framing is almost complete; the deck beams are being erected and the plating of the double bottom and the decks is now being carried out. Somewhere else men are already at work on the engines though it will be months before these will be required.

AS THE WORK PROGRESSES

Harland and Wolff Ltd.

The ship has advanced a stage further, and the beams and deck plating are now being erected. In the shops near at hand workmen are preparing all the material required for the completion of the hull. The number of different trades which eventually contribute to the building of a big ship is astonishingly large.

Round about slipways and berths are the various shops needed for working metal, wood and other materials. They contain many wonderful machines for cutting, planing, bending, punching and drilling steel plates and beams. It would be interesting to watch these at work, but we are here concerned rather with the assembling than the making of parts.

The shops, be it noted, are arranged on an ordered plan, so that materials and parts shall be passed through them with the least possible amount of carrying. And the works are traversed in all directions by railway tracks, along which parts are transported from shop to shop, or from shop to slipway or berth.

The hull of a ship is a steel box of curious shape. It is, in fact, an enormously strong girder, designed to withstand terrific strains tending to bend it upwards, downwards and sideways.

We may divide its parts into three groups: the skeleton or framework; the skin or outer plating; and the internal divisions. The last are made up of horizontal decks and upright bulkheads.

The chief member of the framework is the great backbone, the keel and centre girder, running right along the ship, and having the stem bar rising from it at the far end and the stern frame attached to the rear end. From this spring at intervals the ribs or frames, in pairs, those of a pair being of exactly the same shape and in line with each other on opposite sides. The frames are held together by beams, called longitudinals, running lengthwise at different levels, and by horizontal beams carrying the decks.

L.E.A.

TO KEEP THE SHIP ON THE RIGHT COURSE

In this picture we see the stern of one of the fine steamers of the Canadian Pacific Company, a vessel of some 42,000 tons. Workmen are busily engaged in fixing the gigantic rudder in position, aided by an elaborate system of scaffolding. Note the starboard propeller.

FIFTY=FIVE TONS OF RUDDER

Sport and General.

The rudder which is being hoisted into position in this picture is of a somewhat different shape from the one seen on the previous page. The exact shape is necessarily dependent on the design of the stern of the vessel. This ship is an Atlantic liner and its giant rudder weighs some 55 tons, yet by means of mechanical equipment the great ship is steered with no more difficulty than a small motor-car.

When Bent to Shape

The outer skin of the hull is made up of a great number of steel plates riveted to the frames. The plates of a very large ship may weigh up to 4 tons each and be 40 feet long. They are arranged in strakes, or courses, corresponding to the courses in a brick wall. Alternative strakes touch the frames and are overlapped along the edges by the intermediate strakes. In order to fit snugly against certain parts of the framework, some of the plates have to be bent very exactly to shape, and every plate has to have rivet holes punched in it to come exactly over holes in the framework or other plates next it. This means a great deal of measurement and marking.

The frames are very deep over the flat part of the ship's bottom, and are covered with plating inside as well as outside, thus forming what is called a double-bottom, which gives extra protection to the part of the hull most likely to be damaged. The double-bottom can also be used for holding water ballast, fuel oil, etc.

The decks are riveted to the deck beams and sides of the ship. The upright partitions, called bulkheads, divide the hull into a number of water-tight compartments, and both strengthen it and reduce the danger of sinking if the ship springs a leak or sustains damage to her plates.

The framework, sides, bottom and decks of a ship give it great stiffness in all directions, and they are kept in their proper positions by the members of the framework. So much for the general arrangements of the hull's parts.

On the Slipway

A ship is built on a great flat floor of concrete or wood, called a slipway. This

Sport and General.

A DRILL FOR TURBINES

Holes in a plate are easily punched, but for many classes of shipbuilding work the drilling of metal becomes necessary. In this picture we see a turbine engine being fashioned to the shape required by the engineers by means of a colossal drilling machine.

Harland and Wolff Ltd.

ALMOST READY FOR THE DAY OF THE LAUNCH

Here we have a ship in the last stages before the day when the launching ceremony will take place and she will slide down the slipways to the deep waters. This particular vessel is the *Thorshavet*, a whale factory ship, and the photograph shows the stern aperture which is a special feature of such a vessel.

falls towards the water on a slope of about half-an-inch to the foot. Now, the hull of a big ship may weigh 15,000 tons to 20,000 tons when it is ready for launching. If the floor sank at any point during construction, the results would be disastrous. So the whole area of a slipway is made quite safe by driving thousands of piles into the ground. The tops of these carry great cross-timbers, which are covered with concrete or thick planks, forming an immovable floor.

In a few instances a slipway is roofed over, though most slipways are open to the air. But whether closed in or open, a slipway is well provided with powerful cranes, commanding the whole of it, which lower plates and beams into the places where they are wanted and support them till they are fixed. The cranes come in useful also for suspend-ing the riveters and the heavy tools these operatives use.

The lowest part of the ship, the keel, does not rest on the slipway itself, but on piles of blocks, the keel blocks, laid at intervals along the centre line of the floor. To prevent the hull toppling over, and to distribute the weight, two more rows of blocks are laid parallel to the keel blocks, one on each side of them and 20 feet or 30 feet away. This arrangement gives the workmen room in which to move about beneath the hull.

The hull of a ship is held together by an enormous number of rivets. One great liner, for example, had four million rivets in her and they weighed 700 tons. The outside of a hull is rough, on an orderly pattern, with rows of rivet heads. Every rivet on the outside of a ship must be perfectly watertight, and

A SHIP IS LAUNCHED

Central Press.

The most important function during the building of a ship is her christening and launching.
Usually the ceremony of christening the ship is performed by a lady who makes a speech wishing the
vessel good fortune on her voyages, names her, and breaks a bottle of wine across the bows just
before the vessel is released to slide down the well-greased ways to the water. Our picture shows
the New Zealand Shipping Co.'s motor-vessel *Rangitane* entering the water just after her launching
by the Duchess of Gloucester at the Clydebank yard of John Brown & Co.

is carefully inspected after being put in place.

Whenever possible, the closing of a rivet, that is, the forming of a head on it, is done by a hydraulic riveter, which exerts a squeeze of 30 tons to 40 tons, and does its work neatly in a few seconds. In some places, however, the operation is done with hand hammers or light mechanical hammers using compressed air. A riveting hammer makes a terrible din, so that a slipway is hardly the place for a person suffering from disordered nerves !

Could we shorten days into minutes, we should see the framework growing as if by magic, while a small forest of scaffold poles is erected on each side of the hull to support working platforms.

Then we should see the slipway invaded by the plating gangs and the bottom and sides quickly covered by plates. Then decks and bulkheads would appear in the interior, and at last the ship's hull would be complete.

Launching a Ship

To get a true idea of the size of a ship, as of a locomotive, one needs to view it from ground level. When in the water a ship has from 20 to 40 feet of her hull out of sight below the water-line. Here on the slipway we see her full stature, towering 50, 60 or 70 feet above us, and making the men who built her seem the merest pigmies.

The hull of a big ship is about the largest and heaviest thing that has to be moved in one piece. Getting it into

New York Times.

A LINER AT HER FITTING-OUT BERTH

A ship is launched when the hull is complete, but there are many months of work to be done before she is ready to sail the seas. The floating hull is taken round to the fitting-out berth after the launch, and here giant cranes lift the engines, boilers and funnel into position. In this photograph the *Caronia* is seen at her fitting-out berth at John Brown's shipyard, Glasgow.

the water is anxious work, requiring months of preparation.

On each side of the keel is built a wooden slide, 5 feet or 6 feet broad, running out into the water on rows of piles. The two " standing ways," as these slides are named, must be perfectly straight and parallel to one another. On them, up to the bottom of the ship, the " sliding ways " are built. These rise into massive structures, the " cradles," at bow and stern, where the ship's sides draw together.

The sliding ways contain hundreds of wooden wedges, in pairs. One wedge of a pair lies on its fellow, and their ends project on either side of the way. In order that the ship may slide freely, the standing ways are greased with tons of tallow and soft soap.

It is impossible to launch the ship till her weight has been taken off the blocks on which she was built. When the day of the launch approaches, hundreds of workmen, armed with heavy hammers and wielding them in time together, strike the heads of the wedges and drive them in, forcing the cradles upwards. The vast bulk of the ship is now borne by the sliding ways and a number of shores, and the keel blocks and other blocks can be removed. On the actual day of the launch the shores are knocked away, and the ship is prevented from moving only by a number of enormous triggers.

The great moment has now arrived. The person—usually a lady—appointed to name the ship breaks a bottle of wine on her bows and presses an electric button. Hydraulic rams release the triggers and the ship begins to move.

Central Press.

PREPARING FOR THE COMFORT OF PASSENGERS

While she lies at her fitting-out berth the ship is a veritable hive of industry. Engineers and other technicians are busy down in the depths of the ship. Carpenters and joiners, upholsterers and decorators, as well as many other craftsmen, are busy in the various rooms and cabins. The photograph above shows the scene in one of the smoke-rooms of the *Caronia* when workmen were making it ready for the maiden voyage.

AN AIRCRAFT CARRIER IS LAUNCHED

Harland and Wolff Ltd.

In this photograph we have another view of a launch and of another very different kind of vessel taking to the water after completion of the massive hull. This is an aircraft carrier, built at the great shipbuilding yards of Messrs. Harland and Wolff in Belfast. The picture was taken just after she had been released and is seen on the point of entering the water.

She quickly gathers speed, but as she slides stern-first into the water she is "kept in hand" by heavy drags, which come into operation one after another. The effect of these has been calculated so exactly that she fetches up within a few yards of the spot where she ought to stop, while the parts of the sliding ways and cradles fall apart and cover the surface of the water. The huge berth that she has left looks strangely empty now.

Fitting Out the Hull

Immediately after the launch tugs take the floating hull round to the fitting-out berth, where she will remain while giant fixed or floating cranes, able to play with weights of 100 tons or more, lift her engines or turbines, boilers and funnels aboard. For months she is in the hands of engineers, electricians, painters, plumbers, glaziers, upholsterers, decorators, and a host of other craftsmen. And then at last she is ready for her trials.

Her engines are tested by running them for twenty-four hours or forty-eight hours continuously while she is still tied up in dock. If everything is all right, she is allowed to show her paces in the open sea. Then follows the cleaning and painting of her bottom in dry dock, after which she is ready for her official trials. These include steaming over a course where the distances are clearly shown by landmarks.

Once these tests have been passed to the satisfaction of all the experts concerned, the ship proceeds to what will be her home port, and is ready to load up for her maiden voyage. A great many people are interested, and not a few are even a little anxious about this first voyage of a new ship. However careful everyone has been there is always the vague possibility of some weak point revealing itself under the stress of this first voyage.

Generally speaking, however, any faults have been discovered during the final stringent tests, and the ship has been passed 100 A1 by Lloyd's surveyors. A maiden voyage is usually in the nature of a happy christening party, the first chapter in a long and useful life on the great oceans.

Central Press.

WHERE PASSENGERS WILL DINE

In this photograph is seen a view of one of the several restaurants on the *Caronia* before completion. In the foreground workmen are fixing an electrically-heated dumb waiter, while in the background a glazier is at work on one of the mural panels which decorate the walls.

By permission of George Harrap & Co., Ltd.

THE SWORD EXCALIBUR

Many writers have been inspired by the legends of King Arthur and his Knights of the Round Table. When Arthur had lost his sword he met the Lady of the Lake, as depicted in this painting by Rowland Wheelwright. In the middle of the lake an arm rose, holding a sword, and the Lady bade him row out in a barge. It was in this manner that King Arthur became owner of the magic sword Excalibur. When at last he was stricken in battle he commanded that the sword be thrown into the lake, where it was caught by a hand and vanished.

Specially painted for this work.

ROBIN HOOD AND HIS MERRY MEN

Robin Hood, legendary hero of many stories and ballads, was the chief of a band of outlaws, among whom were Little John and Friar Tuck. With his companions, Robin Hood lived in Sherwood Forest, robbing the rich to give to the poor, and fighting only when attacked. There was probably some historical basis for the legends associated with this philanthropic outlaw, and many theories have been put forward as to his identity.

Fable,
Myth
and
Legend

Tales
of
Brer
Rabbit

Specially drawn for this work.

In *Uncle Remus : His Songs and Sayings*, Joel Chandler Harris told the Negro folklore tales of Brer Fox and Brer Rabbit, now world-famous. Some of these stories are re-told here.

BRER RABBIT AND BRER FOX

ONCE upon a time Brer Rabbit and Brer Fox met one another in the wood, and Brer Fox thought Brer Rabbit looked very plump and tender.

Brer Rabbit didn't go too near Brer Fox, for he didn't trust him at all.

"Heyo, Brer Rabbit!" called Brer Fox. "Come over here and have a talk with me. I was seeing Brer Bear yesterday and he said what a pity and a shame it was that we didn't live lovingly together."

"Well, that may be so," said Brer Rabbit. "Perhaps you'd like to come round to dinner with me to-morrow, Brer Fox? We haven't got a feast, but we can give you something."

"Thank you," said Brer Fox. "I'll be right along."

Next day Brer Rabbit got a fine dinner ready. He was just putting it on the table when one of the little rabbits came running in.

"Oh, ma! Oh, ma!" she cried to old Mrs. Rabbit. "Mr. Fox is a-coming, he's a-coming!"

Then Brer Rabbit took his little rabbits by their ears and sat them down in a row. He and Mrs. Rabbit waited for Brer Fox—and they waited and they waited.

"Dinner's a-spoiling," said Brer Rabbit at last. "Where's Brer Fox got to?"

He went to the door and looked out to see—and what did he see sticking out from round the corner of his house but the tips of Brer Fox's ears! Brer Fox was there waiting for Brer Rabbit to go out and look for him—then he meant to catch him and run off with him.

"Oho!" said Brer Rabbit quietly to himself. He slammed his door, and then he and his family sat down to the fine dinner and ate it all up.

Now next day Brer Mink came round to Brer Rabbit's house.

"Brer Fox says he's very sorry he didn't come to dinner with you yesterday, but he was ill. He says will you please come and have dinner with him to-day," said Brer Mink.

"Tell him I'll be right along," said Brer Rabbit, with a twinkle in his eye.

So, when dinner-time came, Brer Rabbit washed his paws and brushed himself, and then he set off for Brer Fox's house. When he got near he heard somebody groaning, and he peeped in at the open door.

He saw Brer Fox sitting in a rocking-chair wrapped up in red flannel, looking very weak. Brer Rabbit took a good look all round, but he couldn't see any dinner. All he saw was a saucepan on the table, and close to it a carving knife.

Then Brer Rabbit guessed that Brer Fox was going to try and get him for dinner.

" Heyo, Brer Fox," he said. " What have you got for dinner ? "

" Chicken," said Brer Fox.

" Have you got any calamus root to eat with the chicken ? " asked Brer Rabbit. " I just can't eat chicken unless it's well-seasoned up with calamus root. I'll go and get some, Brer Fox. You just sit there and wait for me."

Off went Brer Rabbit, and as soon as he was outside he went and hid himself among some bushes nearby, and

Specially drawn for this work.

Brer Fox was sitting in a rocking-chair, looking very weak.

watched to see what Brer Fox would do.

When Brer Rabbit had gone out of the door Brer Fox jumped out of his chair, flung off his red flannel, and crept behind the door so that he could jump on Brer Rabbit when he came back again.

But Brer Rabbit could see all he was doing and he chuckled to himself. By and by he shouted out to Brer Fox:

" Oh, Brer Fox! I'll just put the calamus root on this tree stump. You'd better come and get it whilst it's fresh! "

And with that Brer Rabbit galloped off home!

BRER RABBIT AND THE TAR-BABY

ONE day, after Brer Rabbit had tricked Brer Fox with the calamus root, Brer Fox got a mighty fine idea. He got some tar, mixed it with turpentine and made a funny-looking figure that he called a tar-baby.

He took the tar-baby and put it in the middle of the road. Then he went and hid himself in a bush not far off and waited to see what would happen.

Pretty soon along came Brer Rabbit, lippitty-clippitty, singing at the top of his voice, just as saucy as a jay-bird. Brer Fox lay low and didn't make a sound. Brer Rabbit pranced along till he saw the tar-baby—and then he stood still in surprise.

" Good morning," said Brer Rabbit to the tar-baby. " Nice weather this morning."

The tar-baby said nothing, and Brer Fox lay low.

" How are you feeling this morning ? " said Brer Rabbit.

Brer Fox winked to himself and lay low. The tar-baby stared at Brer Rabbit and said nothing.

" What's the matter with you ? Are you deaf ? " said Brer Rabbit to the tar-baby. " Because if you are I can shout louder."

Specially drawn for this work.

When Brer Fox heard Brer Rabbit coming along the road he hid in a bush. "Good-morning," said Brer Rabbit to the tar-baby. "Nice weather this morning."

The tar-baby stayed still and Brer Fox lay low.

"You're stuck-up, that's what you are," said Brer Rabbit.

Brer Fox chuckled deep down inside himself, and the tar-baby said nothing.

"I'm going to teach you how to talk to respectable folks," said Brer Rabbit fiercely. "If you don't take off your hat and say how-do-you-do to me, I'm going to give you a good whipping."

The tar-baby stayed still and Brer Fox lay low.

Well, Brer Rabbit kept on asking the tar-baby how he was and the tar-baby kept on saying nothing, till at last Brer Rabbit drew back his paw and hit the tar-baby blip! on the side of the head. But his fist stuck and he couldn't pull it away, because the tar held tight.

"If you don't let go of my paw I'll hit you with my left one," said Brer Rabbit, in a temper. With that he lifted up his left paw and hit the tar-baby another blow. Well, that paw stuck too, and there was Brer Rabbit with both his fists held tight in the tar. The tar-baby stayed still and Brer Fox lay low.

"Let me loose before I kick the stuffing out of you!" shouted Brer Rabbit. But the tar-baby just stared at him and did nothing at all.

Then Brer Rabbit kicked the tar-baby with his right foot, and that stuck too. Then he kicked with his left foot, and that stuck as well. All this time Brer Fox lay low, though he kept chuckling deep down inside himself every time Brer Rabbit hit the tar-baby.

"If you don't let me loose, I'll butt you with my head," said Brer Rabbit to the tar-baby. But the tar-baby held on fast, and so Brer Rabbit suddenly butted him with his head, and that got stuck too.

Then Brer Fox got up and wandered out from beneath his bush, looking as if butter wouldn't melt in his mouth. He walked up to Brer Rabbit and the tar-baby and had a good look at them.

"Heyo, Brer Rabbit," he said. "You look sort of stuck-up this morning!"

Then Brer Fox rolled on the ground and laughed till he could laugh no more.

"I expect you'll take dinner with me this time, Brer Rabbit," said Brer Fox, when he had stopped laughing. "I've got some calamus root and all, so you've got to come. I think I've caught you this time, Brer Rabbit. Maybe I haven't, but I *think* I have! You've been going round saucing me a long time now, but you won't do it any more."

Brer Rabbit listened and said never a word. He couldn't move at all, because he was stuck fast to the tar-baby.

"You're always somewhere that you've got no business to be," said Brer Fox. "Who asked you to come and talk to the tar-baby? Nobody in the world.

Specially drawn for this work.

Brer Fox caught Brer Rabbit by the hind legs and flung him right into the very middle of the bramble-patch.

You just walked up to the tar-baby and began hitting and kicking and butting as hard as you could. Well, there you are, all nicely stuck up, and there you'll stay till I get a bonfire going. I think I'll roast you for my dinner."

Then Brer Rabbit began to talk in a very humble voice.

" I don't care what you do with me, Brer Fox," he said, " so long as you don't fling me into that bramble-patch over there."

" It's too much trouble to light a fire," said Brer Fox. " I think I'll hang you instead."

" Hang me as high as you please," said Brer Rabbit. " But please, please, Brer Fox, don't fling me into that bramble-patch over there."

" I haven't any string," said Brer Fox, looking in all his pockets, " so I can't hang you. I think I'll drown you instead."

" Drown me just as deep as ever you please," said Brer Rabbit. " But all I ask you is—*don't* fling me into that bramble-patch, Brer Fox."

" There isn't any water near," said Brer Fox, looking all round. " So I think I'll skin you alive-o, Brer Rabbit!"

" Skin me," said Brer Rabbit. " Go on, skin me, Brer Fox. You can do anything you like to me so long as you don't fling me into that bramble-patch over there."

Well, Brer Fox wanted to hurt Brer Rabbit just as much as ever he could, so he thought he *would* fling him into the bramble-patch, as he seemed so afraid of it. So he caught him by the hind-legs and flung him right into the very middle of the bramble-patch. Then he hung round to see what was going to happen to Brer Rabbit.

There was a great dust and a flurry —and nothing else happened. Brer Fox looked to see where Brer Rabbit was—and then he heard someone calling him. He turned round to see who it was, and what did he spy far away up the hill, sitting cross-legged on a tree-stump, but old Brer Rabbit, combing the tar out of his hair with a wood chip!

Then Brer Fox knew that Brer Rabbit had tricked him again, and he could hardly stand up for rage.

" I was born and brought up in a bramble-patch, Brer Fox!" yelled Brer Rabbit. " Born and brought up in a bramble-patch!" And with that he hopped off as lively as a cat on hot bricks!

HOW BRER RABBIT RODE BRER FOX

BRER Rabbit and Brer Fox had some great friends, Mrs. Meadows and her girls. One day, when Brer Rabbit went round to see them, they began laughing at him and asked him if he had met many tar-babies lately.

"Brer Fox told us all about it," said the girls. "Oh, Brer Rabbit, you must have looked mighty funny."

"What do you want to listen to Brer Fox's silly tales for?" asked Brer Rabbit. "Why, don't you know that Brer Fox was my daddy's riding-horse for thirty years? Yes, ma'am, for thirty years and maybe more."

With that Brer Rabbit raised his cap, said good-bye and went off with his head high in the air.

Next day Brer Fox came calling on the Meadows, and they told him what Brer Rabbit had said. Brer Fox gnashed his teeth and looked very angry.

"Ladies," he said. "Brer Rabbit doesn't know how to speak the truth. But I'll fetch him along here, and I'll make him say he was wrong about my being his daddy's riding-horse, sure as I sit here." And off marched Brer Fox, straight for Brer Rabbit's house.

When he got there, Brer Rabbit had bolted his door fast, for he was expecting Brer Fox. Brer Fox knocked, blim, blam! Then Brer Rabbit shouted:

"Is that you, Brer Fox? Well, you just go and fetch the doctor to me. I ate some parsley this morning and it didn't agree with me. You fetch me the doctor, for I'm feeling mighty queer."

"I've come to fetch *you*, Brer Rabbit," said Brer Fox. "There's going to be a party up at Mrs. Meadows. All the girls will be there."

"I'm too sick to come," said Brer Rabbit.

"No, you're not," said Brer Fox. "Besides, the party will do you good."

"No, it won't," said Brer Rabbit. "I'm much too sick."

"You come along with me," said Brer Fox. "I'll help you along."

"I can't walk," said Brer Rabbit. "I feel much too ill."

"I'll carry you," said Brer Fox.

"How?" asked Brer Rabbit.

"In my arms," said Brer Fox.

"You'll drop me, I know you will," said Brer Rabbit.

"No, I won't," said Brer Fox. "Come along, Brer Rabbit, open your door, and let me right in."

"Well, I'll come if you carry me on your back," said Brer Rabbit, after a bit. "But I won't come if you carry me in

Specially drawn for this work.

Brer Fox marched off to Brer Rabbit's house and knocked on the door.

your arms. I don't like the thought of that, Brer Fox, and that's the truth."

"Well, all right, I'll carry you on my back," said Brer Fox.

"You'll have to get me a saddle," said Brer Rabbit. "I can't ride without a saddle."

"Well, I'll get one, then," said Brer Fox. "And I'll get a bridle too, for you to hold on by."

"Then I'll go with you," said Brer Rabbit. "You just go and get that saddle and bridle, Brer Fox."

Of course, Brer Rabbit knew quite well that Brer Fox meant to get him to Mrs. Meadows' and then tell her and the girls just what he thought of him for telling untruths—and Brer Rabbit made up his mind to trick Brer Fox. He washed himself and brushed himself,

Specially drawn for this work.

Brer Fox leapt in the air and then began to gallop over the ground.

and by the time Brer Fox came along with a saddle and bridle on him, he was looking just as smart as smart.

Brer Rabbit mounted on Brer Fox's back and they ambled off. Soon Brer Fox felt Brer Rabbit lift up one of his feet.

"What are you doing, Brer Rabbit?" he asked.

"Just pulling up my stockings," said Brer Rabbit. Then in a little while Brer Fox felt him lifting up the other foot, and he asked him again what he was doing.

"Just pulling my bootlace tight," said Brer Rabbit. But all the time, my goodness me, Brer Rabbit was putting on a pair of sharp spurs, and when they got near to Mrs. Meadows', where Brer Fox meant Brer Rabbit to get off, so that they might walk into the house together, Brer Rabbit clapped his spurs into the sides of Brer Fox's body and made Brer Fox nearly jump out of his skin.

He leapt in the air and then began to gallop over the ground as if a hundred dogs were after him, and as soon as he slowed down a bit, Brer Rabbit spurred him again.

They flew past the Meadows' house and all the girls sitting in the garden saw them go by and stared in surprise. Then Brer Rabbit made Brer Fox go back again and rode through the garden gate. He leapt off Brer Fox, tied him up to the post, and then walked up to the girls and Mrs. Meadows, as proud as you please.

"Ladies," he said, "perhaps you remember that I told you Brer Fox was the riding-horse for our family. He is slower now than he was, but he isn't so bad if I spur him up a bit."

Then Brer Rabbit gave a slow sort of grin, and the girls began to smile. Mrs. Meadows praised up his pony, and poor Brer Fox, tied up to the post, had to stand and listen to it all, grinding his teeth in rage to think that he had let Brer Rabbit play him such a cunning trick.

Specially drawn for this work.

Brer Fox ran wild. He jumped and he bucked, he shouted and he capered, but no matter what he did, he couldn't shake Brer Rabbit off his back.

BRER FOX CATCHES BRER RABBIT

BRER Rabbit sat a long time with the girls and Mrs. Meadows, and at last he said he must be going. So he bade them good-bye, and went out to the post where he had tied Brer Fox. He jumped on to his back and rode off.

Brer Fox said nothing at all. He just galloped off and kept his mouth shut tight. Brer Rabbit knew what Brer Fox was thinking, and he began to feel rather scared. Brer Fox trotted on till he got out in the lane, and then he just ran wild.

He yelled and he roared, he jumped and he bucked. He snorted and he

Specially drawn for this work.

Brer Fox ran so fast that he nearly caught Brer Rabbit.

capered, he stood on his hind legs and then he stood on his front ones. He was trying to fling Brer Rabbit off his back! But he might just as well have tried to get rid of his own shadow. Brer Rabbit stuck on his back, and every now and again clapped the spurs into Brer Fox's side so that Brer Fox snorted in rage.

Brer Fox tore the grass to bits and he jumped so high and so often that he nearly snatched his own tail off. But no matter what he did, he couldn't seem to get Brer Rabbit off his back. Then Brer Fox threw himself down on the ground and began to roll over and over.

That unsettled Brer Rabbit in a shake of a duck's tail, and he fell off Brer Fox's back at once. But he was off through the bushes in a twinkling, and Brer Fox set out after him.

Brer Fox ran so fast that he almost caught Brer Rabbit, and if Brer Rabbit hadn't just had time to slip through a hole into a hollow tree, that would have been the end of him. The hole was too small for Brer Fox to get into, so he lay down outside to get his breath and to plan what to do.

While he was lying down there, Brer Turkey Buzzard came flapping along, and seeing Brer Fox lying there, he flew down to him and took a good look at him.

"Poor old Brer Fox, he's dead, and I'm so sorry," said Brer Buzzard, shaking both his wings.

"No, I'm not dead," said Brer Fox. "I've got old Brer Rabbit in this hollow tree, and I'm going to get him this time if it takes me till Christmas!"

Brer Buzzard peeked into the hole, and sure enough Brer Rabbit was there.

"Look here now, Brer Buzzard," said Brer Fox. "I'm a-going to get an axe to chop this tree down. Will you stay here and watch the hole, to see that Brer Rabbit doesn't get out of it?"

Brer Buzzard was quite willing, and he took up his stand by the hole, while Brer Fox ran off to get an axe.

By and by, when all was quiet, Brer Rabbit began to scramble about in the tree, and presently he shouted out:

"Brer Fox! oh, Brer Fox!"

Brer Fox was gone and Brer Buzzard said nothing. Then Brer Rabbit shouted as if he was mad.

"Brer Fox! You needn't talk unless you want to! I know you're there! All I want to say is that I wish old Brer Turkey Buzzard was here!"

Then Brer Buzzard tried to talk like Brer Fox.

"What do you want with Brer Buzzard?" he said.

"Oh, nothing much," said Brer Rabbit. "Except that there's the fattest grey squirrel in this hollow tree that ever I saw, and I guess Brer Turkey Buzzard would like to have him for his dinner."

"But how could Brer Buzzard get him?" said Brer Buzzard, feeling excited.

"Well, there's a little hole round on the other side of the tree," said Brer Rabbit. "And if Brer Buzzard was here he could stand by the hole whilst I drive the squirrel out."

"Drive him out, then," said Brer Buzzard. "And I'll see that Brer Buzzard gets that squirrel for sure!"

Then Brer Rabbit began to scramble about inside the tree, and squawk, and made such a to-do as if for all the world he was trying to drive something out. Brer Buzzard rushed round to get the squirrel—and just as he got to the other side of the tree Brer Rabbit dashed out of the hole this side and set out for home.

Well, Brer Buzzard heard him go and he guessed he'd been tricked. But he had promised Brer Fox to stay there till he came back, and he thought he would stop and see what Brer Fox did. Before long up galloped Brer Fox with an axe over his shoulder.

"How is Brer Rabbit getting along?" he asked Brer Buzzard, with a grin.

"Oh, he's all right," said Brer Buzzard. "He's very quiet though. Perhaps he's taking a nap."

"Then I'm just in time to wake him up," said Brer Fox, and he flung off his coat and took the axe in his hands. Then he began to chop down the tree. Pow! went the axe, and pow! Brer Fox laid to with a will, and all the time he chopped, Brer Buzzard danced round him and shouted loudly.

"Oh, he's in there, Brer Fox; he's in there, for sure!"

And every time a chip of wood flew up into the air, Brer Buzzard would dodge it, and shout still more loudly.

"Here's in there, Brer Fox. I heard him squeak. Oh, he's in there, for sure!"

Well, Brer Fox lammed away at that tree until soon he had got it almost cut in half. Then he had to stop to get his breath, and suddenly he saw Brer Buzzard laughing at him behind his back. Brer Fox stared at him—and then he guessed that Brer Buzzard was tricking him somehow.

But old Brer Turkey Buzzard kept on dancing around and yelling out, "He's in there, Brer Fox. He's in there; I saw him, yes I did!"

Then Brer Fox pretended to peep into the hollow tree.

"Come here quickly, Brer Buzzard!" he said. "Look and see if this isn't Brer Rabbit's foot hanging down."

Brer Buzzard came stepping up and stuck his head into the hole. And no sooner had he done that than Brer Fox grabbed him. Brer Buzzard flapped his

Specially drawn for this work.

"Brer Rabbit's in there for sure!" shouted Brer Buzzard, while Brer Fox chopped at the tree

Specially drawn for this work.

Brer Buzzard squawked in delight and rose in the air. "Do you want me, Brer Fox?" he cried. "Come and catch me, then!"

wings, and struggled hard, but it wasn't a bit of use. Brer Fox had got him tight, and he held him down on the ground.

"Let me alone, Brer Fox," squalled Brer Buzzard. "Look out! Brer Rabbit will get out of the tree if you don't watch. Go on with your chopping. You've nearly got the tree down and you'll soon get to Brer Rabbit."

"I've got you," said Brer Fox. "And I guess I shan't get Brer Rabbit this day. What have you tricked me for, Brer Buzzard?"

"You let me alone, Brer Fox," said Brer Buzzard. "Let me go home. My old woman is waiting for me and my dinner will be ready. Brer Rabbit's in the tree, I tell you."

"Look here," said Brer Fox, pointing to a blackberry bush. "There's a bunch of Brer Rabbit's fur on that prickly branch. He's gone that way, Brer Buzzard, so don't you tell me any more stories."

Then Brer Buzzard knew he couldn't deceive Brer Fox any longer, and he told him all that had happened.

"Well, if Brer Rabbit isn't the worst rapscallion ever I saw in my life!" said Brer Fox, in a rage. "But see here,

Brer Buzzard, I left you here to guard that hole, and I left Brer Rabbit in that hole. I come back and I find you at the hole and no Brer Rabbit there. Well, I'm going to pay you out," said Brer Fox. "I'm going to fling you on a bonfire and burn you."

"If you do that I'll fly away," said Brer Buzzard.

"Well, then, I'll settle you right now," said Brer Fox, and with that he grabbed Brer Buzzard by the tail and was just going to dash him to the ground when all the tail feathers came out in his hand! Brer Buzzard squawked in delight and rose into the air.

"It's the time of year I moult, Brer Fox!" he said. "All my tail feathers come out now! Do you want me, Brer Fox? You come and catch me then! Yes, you come and catch me!"

Then Brer Turkey Buzzard sailed away in the air, and left Brer Fox sitting down below, feeling mighty cross!

BRER RABBIT AND BRER TERRAPIN

ONE day Brer Rabbit and Brer Terrapin set off together to go to Mrs. Meadows and the girls. They were asked in, and Brer Rabbit sat down on a chair. But Brer Terrapin was so small that he was too low on the floor and not high enough on a chair. So Brer Rabbit picked him up and set him on the mantelpiece, and Brer Terrapin sat up there, very proud indeed.

Then they all started talking, and the girls told Brer Rabbit that they thought he rode his horse, Brer Fox, very well indeed, for they had not forgotten how Brer Rabbit came galloping up a few days before.

"Well, I'd have ridden him over this morning," said Brer Rabbit, leaning back in his chair, "but he was a bit lame. I'm afraid I shall soon have to sell him and buy a better horse to ride."

Then Brer Terrapin spoke up.

"Well, Brer Rabbit," he said, "if you sell Brer Fox, you sell him to some-one far away, because he's been living here too long already. He's a rude fellow, Brer Fox is. Do you know what he said to me yesterday?"

"You don't mean to say he was rude to *you*, Brer Terrapin!" said the girls.

"Yes, he was," said Brer Terrapin. "He shouted out to me, 'Hallo, you crawling old slowcoach!' What do you think of that, ladies?"

"Oh my!" said the girls. "What a rude fellow Brer Fox is to call respectable people like you such dreadful names, Brer Terrapin."

Then everyone began to talk about Brer Fox, and nobody had a good word for him—and all this time who should be standing outside the door listening but Brer Fox himself! He got in a terrible rage when he heard what they said, and suddenly he rushed into the kitchen and made a grab at Brer Rabbit.

Everyone jumped up in a hurry, and Mrs. Meadows and the girls screamed in fright. Brer Terrapin tried to see what was happening, and he leaned so far over the mantelpiece that he fell right off—blip! He fell bang on to Brer Fox's head, and Brer Fox fell down in a faint. When he opened his eyes again, he saw nobody in the room at all. The girls were gone, Brer Terrapin was gone and Brer Rabbit was gone too.

Brer Rabbit had jumped up the chimney, Brer Terrapin was under the bed, and the girls were out in the garden. Brer Fox looked round, and then he felt the big bump on the back of his head where Brer Terrapin hit him. He wondered where Brer Rabbit had gone to—and then suddenly he heard a sneeze—hucky-chow! It was Brer Rabbit up the chimney. The smoke

Brer Rabbit picked up Brer Terrapin and set him on the mantelpiece.

and the ashes had got up his nose and made him sneeze.

"Oho!" said Brer Fox. "You're up there, are you? Well, I'm going to smoke you out, if it takes me all day! I've got you this time, Brer Rabbit."

Brer Rabbit didn't say a word.

"Aren't you coming down before I build up a mighty big fire?" asked Brer Fox. Brer Rabbit still said nothing. So Brer Fox went out and got a heap of firewood. When he came back he heard Brer Rabbit laughing.

"What are you laughing at?" he asked.

"Can't tell you," said Brer Rabbit.

"You'd better tell me," said Brer Fox.

"Well, I'm laughing because someone's gone and put a box of money up here in the corner of the chimney," said Brer Rabbit.

"I don't believe you," said Brer Fox.

"Well, look up and see," said Brer Rabbit. So Brer Fox went to the fireplace and looked up the chimney. That was just what Brer Rabbit was waiting for! He scuffled about in the soot with his feet, and down fell a whole cloud over Brer Fox! It got into his eyes and he couldn't see a thing!

He rushed out into the yard to wash his head under the pump, and Brer Rabbit came down the chimney. He went to say good-bye to the girls, and they were most surprised to see him.

"How did you make Brer Fox go away?" they asked.

"Oh, I just told Brer Fox that if he didn't go home like a good boy, I'd give him a good whipping," said Brer Rabbit.

"My, but you're wonderful, Brer Rabbit!" said Mrs. Meadows and the girls. Then off went Brer Rabbit, waving his cane and twirling his whiskers —but he kept a sharp eye for Brer Fox, you may be sure!

BRER RABBIT RAISES A DUST

ALL the animals were fond of visiting Mrs. Meadows and the girls, for they had plenty of fine things to eat at the big house.

When there was chicken hash for dinner up would come Brer Fox and Brer Possum, and when there were fried greens or fresh lettuce old Brer Rabbit would pop his head in at the door.

"Now this won't do," said Mrs. Meadows to the girls. "We're being eaten out of house and home. You must stop these visitors coming."

"Oh, we can't do that!" said the girls. "They would think us so rude."

Specially drawn for this work.

Brer Fox went off and told Brer Rabbit, Brer Bear, Brer Possum and the rest what they had to do
if they wanted to visit Mrs. Meadows.

Specially drawn for this work.

Brer Rabbit shuffled along in Brer Coon's old slippers. The others all laughed at him, but he took no notice at all.

But Mrs. Meadows wouldn't give way, so the girls had to think of some plan to stop all the creatures coming, and it had to be a plan that wouldn't offend them.

"Let's tell them that we're only allowed to have one visitor each week," said one of the girls at last, "and as we can't choose who it is to be, they must decide it themselves by seeing who can knock dust out of the big flint rock that stands down the road."

"But nobody can knock dust out of a rock!" said the other girls.

"Of course not," said the first one. "So if none of them can do what we say, none of them can come to meals, and we shan't offend any of them!"

Well, the others thought that was quite a good idea, and when next Brer Fox came to the house they told him about this and sent him to tell the others.

So off he went and told Brer Rabbit, Brer Bear, Brer Possum, and the rest what they had to do if they wanted to visit Mrs. Meadows and the girls any more.

They all said they could knock dust out of the rock as easy as winking, but old Brer Rabbit, he didn't say a word. He knew there wasn't much dust to be got out of hard flint rock. So he crept off by himself to a cool place to do some thinking, and he puzzled his brains to know how he could get dust out of that rock.

By and by he grinned, jumped up and clicked his heels together, and then set out for Brer Coon's house. He knocked at the door and Brer Coon opened it.

"Will you lend me your slippers?" asked Brer Rabbit. "I've got blisters on my feet, and I want some nice big shoes so as to make my feet easy."

Well, Brer Coon didn't mind doing that. He gave Brer Rabbit a pair of big old slippers, and Brer Rabbit went away whistling like a blackbird.

When Saturday evening came all the animals went up to Mrs. Meadows. There was Brer Fox, Brer Coon, Brer Wolf, Brer Bear, Brer Terrapin, Brer Possum, and all the rest. At first Brer Rabbit didn't turn up, and everyone wondered where he was—but after a bit

Specially drawn for this work.

Brer Rabbit took hold of the hammer, lifted it in the air, and jumped high with it, coming down with a bump and a bang. The ashes in his slippers filled the air with dust and made everybody blink and cough.

he shuffled along in Brer Coon's old slippers.

And what made him late? Why, he'd been to the ash-bin and filled his slippers full of ashes!

As soon as the others saw him, they began to laugh at him for wearing such big slippers, but Brer Rabbit, he took no notice at all.

Then Mrs. Meadows and the girls took the animals down the road to where the big flint rock stood. Mrs. Meadows carried a large sledge-hammer to strike the rock.

" Now," she said, when they were all in front of it, " each of you can have three blows at the rock, and the one who gets most dust out of it shall be the one to come to meals every week. Here, Brer Fox, you have first turn."

Brer Fox took the big sledge-hammer, raised it high in the air, and brought it down on the rock—*blim!* No dust flew out at all. Then Brer Fox drew back, and down came the hammer again—*blam!* Still no dust came. Brer Fox looked mighty wild, rubbed his hands together, took a fresh hold on the hammer, and brought it down with a big swing on the rock—*kerblap!* But still no dust flew !

Well, that was his three turns gone, and he had to give up the hammer to someone else. Brer Possum took it, and tried his best to raise some dust from the rock, but he couldn't. Then

Brer Bear tried, and wasn't he astonished to see that his great blows made no dust at all!

One by one all the animals had their turn except Brer Terrapin, who said he had a crick in his neck. Last of all it was Brer Rabbit's turn. He took hold of the hammer, lifted it up in the air, and jumped high with it, coming down with a bump and a bang on the rock.

The ashes flew out of his slippers in a cloud! Brer Fox began to sneeze, and Mrs. Meadows and the girls began to cough and splutter.

Again Brer Rabbit jumped high in the air and brought the hammer and his heels down on the rock together, filling the air with dust and making everyone blink and cough. And once again he hit the rock and dust flew high!

And every time he hit and jumped he shouted out : " Stand farther off, ladies! Here comes the dust!"

Nobody knew that it was just the ashes from his slippers, and what a fuss the girls made of Brer Rabbit for being so strong!

" Well, he must come to meals every week," said Mrs. Meadows. " Brer Rabbit knows how to raise the dust, sure enough! "

With that all the other animals pulled long faces and went home, except old Brer Rabbit, who went off with Mrs. Meadows and the girls—but he took care to kick off Brer Coon's slippers first and hide them in his pocket!

BRER RABBIT DOWN THE WELL

ONE day, Brer Fox, Brer Rabbit, Brer Bear, Brer Wolf, and a whole lot of others were clearing the ground for planting out potatoes. The sun was very hot, and Brer Rabbit began to get tired of working so hard. He didn't like to say so, because he was afraid the others would call him lazy.

But soon he gave a shout and began hopping about as if he were in pain.

" I've run a thorn into my hand! " he yelled. " I must go and get it out."

With that off he ran to find a nice quiet place to rest in, for, of course, he hadn't any thorn in his hand at all.

After a while he came across a well with two buckets hanging on a rope. One bucket was at the bottom of the well and the other was at the top. They worked on a pulley, and when one came up, the other went down.

" That looks cool ! " said Brer Rabbit, " and cool I expect it is! I guess I'll get in this bucket and have a nap."

And with that in he jumped, but he had no sooner got himself in the bucket than his weight began to take it down the well, bringing the other bucket up as it went.

Brer Rabbit was scared to death when he felt the bucket going down, and he shivered and shook with fright. He knew where he came from, but he didn't know where he was going! Soon he felt the bucket hit the water, and then it stayed still. So did Brer Rabbit, because he didn't know what was going to happen next!

Now Brer Fox always kept an eye on Brer Rabbit, and when he saw him run off, Brer Fox crept after him to see where he was going. He guessed Brer Rabbit was up to something or other, and he wanted to see what it was.

Well, Brer Fox saw Brer Rabbit come to the well and stop, and then he saw him jump into the bucket—and, lo and behold, he went down out of sight! Brer Fox was so astonished that he couldn't believe his eyes!

He sat there in the bushes and tried to make out what Brer Rabbit was doing, but he couldn't make head or tail of the business.

" Old Brer Rabbit must keep his money down there! " he said at last. " Or if it isn't that, well, he must have discovered a gold-mine! And if it isn't that, well, I'm just going to see what it *is*! "

He crept a little nearer to the well and listened, but he could hear nothing at all. He crept nearer and nearer, but still he couldn't hear a sound. By and by he peeped right over the edge.

Specially drawn for this work.

Brer Fox saw Brer Rabbit jump in the bucket—and lo and behold, he went down out of sight !

There lay Brer Rabbit in a bucket at the bottom, scared out of his wits, frightened to move in case the bucket tipped over and spilled him into the water. Suddenly he saw Brer Fox looking down at him.

" Heyo, Brer Rabbit! " shouted Brer Fox in surprise. " Who are you visiting down there ? "

" Who ? Me ? " said Brer Rabbit. " Oh, I'm just a-fishing, Brer Fox, that's what I'm doing. I said to myself it would be nice to surprise you all with a dish of fishes for dinner, and so here I am, and here are the fishes! "

" Are there many fish down there ? " said Brer Fox in astonishment.

" Lots of them, Brer Fox. Scores and scores of them. The water is just alive with them. Come down and help me haul them in," said Brer Rabbit.

" But how can I get down there ? " asked Brer Fox, longing to get some fish.

" Jump into the bucket, Brer Fox," said Brer Rabbit. " It will bring you down all safe and sound."

Well, Brer Rabbit talked so happily and sweetly that Brer Fox was quite taken in. He jumped into the bucket at once and he went down, because he was heavier than Brer Rabbit. His weight pulled up the bucket where Brer Rabbit sat, and they passed one another half-way, much to Brer Fox's surprise.

Just as they were passing, Brer Rabbit pulled a funny face and sang out :

" *Good-bye, Brer Fox, take care of your clothes,*
For this is the way the old world goes,
Some go up and some go down,
You'll get to the bottom all safe and sound ! "

When Brer Rabbit got to the top he jumped out of the bucket and galloped off to the folk that owned the well.

" There's a fox down in your well muddying up your drinking-water! " he cried.

Then back he ran to the well and leaned over the top, shouting a warning to old Brer Fox, who was shivering and shaking in the bucket at the bottom.

" *Here comes a man with a great big gun—*
When he hauls you up, you jump and run ! "

cried Brer Rabbit, and off he went into the bushes.

Well, soon the man came along with a gun to shoot the fox. He pulled on the rope to get him up to the top, and as soon as the bucket neared the edge of the well, out jumped old Brer Fox and was off into the hedge before the man could pick up his gun!

In about half an hour Brer Rabbit and Brer Fox were back in the clearing, working as if they had never heard of any well or bucket, except that every now and then Brer Rabbit burst out in a laugh, and Brer Fox gave a mighty dry grin !

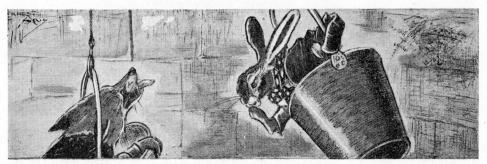

Specially drawn for this work.

" Goodbye, Brer Fox ! Take care of your clothes," sang out Brer Rabbit as the buckets passed each other.

Fable,
Myth
and
Legend

Tales
for
Nursery
Folk

Specially drawn for this work.

" Peepo, I'm ashamed of you," said the Fairy Queen, who chanced to stop just then. " If you
don't get your cottage clean and neat before a week is over, I shall punish you."

PEEPO AND THE MAGIC BRUSH

PEEPO lived in Cuckoo Cottage at the end of Wishing Village. He was the laziest little pixie in the kingdom, and his cottage was always untidy and dirty.

One day the Fairy Queen came by, and she chanced to stop at Cuckoo Cottage for a drink of water. When she saw how dirty it was, she was very angry.

" Peepo, I'm ashamed of you," she said. " If you don't get your cottage clean and neat before a week is over, I shall punish you."

Peepo trembled, and promised that he would. But day after day he got up late, and the cottage was just as dirty as ever. The pixie at last made up his mind to go and buy a sweeping-brush, so off he ran to the village.

Now, on the way he passed old Mother Dumble's, and he peeped in at her kitchen window, for he was a cheeky little fellow ; and there he saw a sight that made him stay still for

quite five minutes, without making a sound.

Mother Dumble was sitting on a chair, and standing in front of her was a sweeping-brush. It had a very long handle, and was painted bright blue. As Peepo watched, Mother Dumble waved her hand three times, and said:

" Whilst I am sleeping,
  Brush, do the sweeping! "

At once the brush set to work all by itself. It swept over the floor most carefully, and when it had finished the kitchen, it went into the parlour, and Peepo heard it sweeping there. Mother Dumble was fast asleep, and didn't see the pixie looking into her kitchen, in the greatest astonishment.

Peepo went on his way with his hands in his pockets.

" If only I had a brush like that," he said, " my work would soon be done! "

When he got to the market, there

Specially drawn for this work.

On his way to the village Peepo passed old Mother Dumble's and looked in at her kitchen window.

wasn't a brush to be bought, so Peepo had to go back home again without one. As he passed Mother Dumble's he looked in at her window once more. She was still asleep, but the brush was leaning against the wall by the window, quite still. It had finished its work.

Then a naughty thought came into Peepo's mind. He would borrow the brush without asking Mother Dumble, and use it to get his cottage clean! Then he would take it back again, and put it in its place without her knowing.

So he took it and ran home with it. He shut his door, and sat down. He put the sweeping-brush in front of him, and did just as he had seen Mother Dumble do.

He waved his hand three times, and said:

> " Whilst I am sleeping,
>   Brush, do the sweeping! "

At once the brush set to work, exactly as it had done in Mother Dumble's cottage. It swept up the dust and crumbs on the dirty floor, and put them in a neat pile in the corner, ready for Peepo to take away. Then it started on the little bedroom, and did its work there.

The pixie didn't go to sleep. He was much too excited and pleased. He sat and watched the brush, and rubbed his hands for joy to see his work done without any bother.

Soon the brush had finished sweeping up all the dust, for there were only two rooms in Peepo's little cottage.

" Now you can stop," said Peepo in a pleased voice. " I'll take you back to Mother Dumble's."

But, dear me, the brush *wouldn't* stop! It went on sweeping! And because there was no longer any dust for it to sweep up, it began to sweep up the furniture !

Clatter, clatter went the chairs as the brush swept them into a corner. Crash went the table as the brush swept it off its legs. Bang went the stool.

PEEPO SETS THE BRUSH TO WORK

Specially drawn for this work.

Peepo waved his hand three times and said the magic words. At once the brush set to work. It swept up the dust and crumbs on the dirty floor and put them in a neat pile in the corner.

"Stop, stop!" cried Peepo. "You mustn't do that! Stop, I tell you! You'll break all my furniture!"

But nothing he could say would stop that magic brush. It piled everything into a corner, and then went into the bedroom and began doing the same thing there. The pixie ran after it and tried to catch hold of it. But it gave him such a hard whack on his knuckles that he ran from it in pain, howling and crying.

"Oh, oh! What shall I do? It won't stop, it won't stop!" he sobbed.

When the brush had finished sweeping up the furniture, it started sweeping up Peepo himself! It suddenly pounced on him, and swept him right off his legs. Down went Peepo with a dreadful bump, and was swept into the corner. But he was up again in a minute, and ran away. Then the brush swept him into the corner again. Up leapt the pixie, flung open the door, and ran off to Mother Dumble's to ask for help.

The brush followed him all the way, sweeping him off his feet whenever it could. Mother Dumble was standing at her gate when he came panting up, and she laughed and laughed and laughed.

"Well, Peepo, so it was you who took my brush!" she said, when at last she stopped. "I can see you've been well punished!"

"Make it stop!" begged Peepo, with tears running down his cheeks.

"Brush, come here!" cried Mother Dumble. The brush at once came to her hand and stayed quite still.

"Now, Peepo, I expect your cottage is all upside-down," said Mother Dumble, "and you'll have to set to work to put it right again. Let this be a lesson to you, and just mend your lazy ways, or I'll send my brush after you again!"

Peepo dried his eyes, and went back to Cuckoo Cottage. He *did* have to work hard to get it right again, but the Fairy Queen was very much pleased with it when she saw it.

"I'll never be lazy again," thought Peepo, "and I'll never borrow things without asking, either!"

I'm sure you will be glad to know that he never did!

Specially drawn for this work.

Peepo ran off to Mother Dumble's to ask for help, but the brush followed him all the way, sweeping him off his feet whenever it could.

BOO=BOO AND HIS TAIL

Specially drawn for this work.

Boo-Boo the Guinea-pig found Frisky the Squirrel curled up asleep in a tree and wakened him.
" I should advise you to go to Hush-Hush the Owl," said Frisky. " He has a very sharp beak
and perhaps could help you."

BOO-BOO was a guinea-pig, and he lived in a nice little hutch in Billy-Boy's garden. Billy-Boy loved him, and always took his friends down to see Boo-Boo.

But the guinea-pig used to be frightened when he sometimes heard Billy-Boy say: " Hold him up by his tail, and see what happens! "

Billy-Boy's friends never did hold Boo-Boo up, but the guinea-pig was so afraid they would that he used to go into the corner of his cage and hide there. Then Billy-Boy's friends laughed and went away.

One day Boo-Boo decided to go and have his tail cut off, for then no one could ever hold him up by it. He tried to see if he had a big one, but he was so fat that he couldn't see round himself.

That night the little guinea-pig slipped out of his hutch, and ran off. He went to Prickles the Hedgehog, who was snuffing about in a ditch.

" Prickles," he said, " will you do something for me ? "

" What do you want ? " asked Prickles.

" Please could you cut my tail off ? " begged Boo-Boo. Prickles stared at him, and shook his head. Then he began to laugh.

" What are you laughing at ? " asked Boo-Boo.

" Just something I thought of," said Prickles. " Why don't you go and ask Frisky the Squirrel to see to your tail for you ? He's got a fine one himself, and I'm sure he'd do what he could for yours."

So Boo-Boo ran off to Frisky the Squirrel. He found him curled up asleep in a tree, and wakened him.

" Frisky," he said, " will you do something for me ? "

" What do you want ? " asked Frisky sleepily.

" Please could you cut my tail off ? " begged Boo-Boo. Then Frisky stared

Specially drawn for this work.

Prickles the Hedgehog shook his head and then began to laugh. "What are you laughing at?" asked Boo-Boo.

hard at Boo-Boo, and suddenly began to laugh.

"What are you laughing at?" asked Boo-Boo in surprise.

"Oh, nothing," said Frisky. "Just my thoughts. Well, I haven't got any scissors, Boo-Boo, so I can't do anything for you. I should advise you to go to Hush-Hush the Owl. He has a very sharp beak, and perhaps he could help you."

So Boo-Boo left Frisky, who was still laughing, and went to where Hush-Hush the Owl was watching for mice by the buttercup field.

"Hush-Hush," he said, "will you do something for me?"

"What do you want?" asked Hush-Hush in surprise.

"Please could you cut my tail off?" begged Boo-Boo. Then Hush-Hush stared hard at Boo-Boo, and laughed loudly.

"What are you laughing at?" asked Boo-Boo.

"Nothing, nothing," said the Owl, still laughing. "I'm afraid I can't cut your tail off, Boo-Boo. Why don't you go and ask Chack the Jackdaw? I believe he has a pair of bright scissors in his nest that he stole from somewhere."

Boo-Boo thanked him, and ran off again. It was not long before he came to the old barn where Chack had his big nest. He had stuffed it into a hole in the roof, and Boo-Boo had to run up the rafters to get to it.

"Chack," said Boo-Boo, "will you do something for me?"

"What do you want?" asked Chack.

"Please could you cut my tail off?" begged Boo-Boo. Then Chack the Jackdaw began to caw and laugh merrily. He took a pair of scissors from his nest and held them in his right foot.

"I got these from a lady's garden," he said. "I love bright things, don't you, Boo-Boo? I have a silver pencil, too, and a thimble. But I like the scissors best of all. Turn round and I will cut your tail off."

HUSH-HUSH THE OWL

Specially drawn for this work.

" Please could you cut my tail off? " begged Boo-boo the Guinea-pig. Hush-Hush the Owl stared hard and laughed loudly. " I'm afraid I can't cut your tail off, Boo-Boo," he said. " Why don't you go and ask Chack the Jackdaw? I believe he has a pair of bright scissors."

"But what are you laughing at?" asked Boo-Boo. "Everyone seems to be laughing to-night, and no one tells me why."

"Oh, never mind," said Chack, looking serious all in a moment. "Now, where's that tail of yours?"

Boo-Boo turned round nervously, as though he was feeling a little frightened.

"Will it hurt?" he asked.

"Not a bit!" said Chack. Then snip-snip went his scissors.

Boo-Boo turned round again, this time in amazement.

"Why, I didn't feel anything at all!" he said. "It didn't hurt a bit. Where is my cut-off tail?"

Then Chack laughed more than ever.

"Oh, Boo-Boo!" he said. "You'll make me die of laughing, really you will! You're the silliest little guinea-pig I've ever seen! Don't you know that *no* guinea-pigs have tails?"

Boo-Boo listened in great astonishment. Then he went very red from his toes to his ears, and ran off. Oh, to think that he had made everyone laugh at him like that, all because he hadn't known that no guinea-pigs have tails.

"What a silly little fellow I am!" he thought as he crept back into his hutch. "I'll never be afraid again when Billy-Boy tells his friends to hold me up by my tail!"

And, of course, he never was!

Specially drawn for this work.

Chack the Jackdaw took a pair of scissors from his nest. "Turn round and I will cut your tail off," he said to Boo-Boo.

TIPTOE'S MAGIC PAINT

Specially drawn for this work.

" How pleased the King would be to see his grey parrot a lovely red! " thought Tiptoe the Fairy.
That night with light strokes of her brush she painted the parrot red from the top of its head to
the longest feather in its tail.

THE Queen of Fairyland was in the middle of her spring-cleaning. She was having lovely wall-papers in her palace rooms, and everywhere there was fresh new paint.

" I would like a set of furniture painted a nice warm red to match the wall-paper in the kitchen," she said one day. So the painters showed her all the reds they had.

But none of them would do. They were not the right colour at all.

" There's a little fairy who has just painted her garden gate exactly the colour you want," said one of the painters at last. " She is called Tiptoe, and lives about five miles away. Shall I fetch her, your Majesty, and tell her to bring you the paint? "

" Yes," said the Queen. " Go at once, please, and say I shall be very much delighted if her paint is the shade I want."

So Tiptoe was fetched. She brought her paint-pot with her, and, sure enough, it was exactly the colour that the Queen wanted—not too dull, nor too bright, but just right.

" This is splendid! " said the Queen. " How do you make it, Tiptoe? "

" I use a little of the red sunset, some of the reds of the autumn trees, stir them up with a little moonlight, and add a spell of my own," answered Tiptoe proudly.

" Well, it's very good," said the Queen. " Now, would you like to give it to the painters to use, or would you rather paint the furniture yourself? "

" I'll paint it myself," said Tiptoe, who was very proud of the way she could decorate things. So she began working hard at the furniture, and soon had it all looking really beautiful. Everyone praised her, and then she began to boast. Soon she was vain and spoilt, and no one liked her.

" Isn't my paint a lovely colour? "

Tiptoe said day after day. But when the palace folk tired of saying that it was, and took no more notice of her, she grew cross.

" I'll just show everyone what I can do! " she thought. So one night she slipped out of her room and went to the stables where the Queen's lovely pink and gold carriage was kept.

And what do you think that naughty little fairy did? Why, she painted the wheels red! You can imagine how dreadful the carriage looked when she had finished. Pink and gold and red! No wonder the coachman thought his eyes had gone wrong the next morning when he saw it!

Nobody thought that it was Tiptoe who had done such a naughty thing, and when that little fairy saw how cross everyone was, she said nothing.

A little while after this, she happened to pass by the parrot that belonged to the King. It was a grey one with a few red feathers. Tiptoe couldn't help thinking how lovely it would be if, instead of being grey, the bird was red all over.

" How pleased the King would be to see his grey parrot a lovely red! " she thought. " He would praise me very much and say that my paint was the prettiest colour he had ever seen! "

That night she slipped out of her room again, and went to where the parrot was sitting asleep on its perch. With light strokes of her brush she painted it red from the top of its head to the longest feather in its tail.

Then she slipped upstairs again, and waited eagerly for the next morning.

But, dear me! When the King saw that his splendid bird had turned red in the night, he was terribly worried.

" What has happened to dear old Polly? " he said to the Queen. " She must be ill. Just see, my dear, she has changed colour in the night! Whatever shall we do about it? "

" Send for the bird-doctor," said the Queen. So he was sent for, and came in a great hurry, for he had never in all his life heard of a bird that turned red in one night.

He looked at Polly carefully and then smelt her feathers.

" Madam," he said to the anxious Queen, " your parrot is not ill. Some mischievous person has painted her red."

" Good gracious! " cried the Queen. " But whoever would be naughty enough to do that? "

Tiptoe was listening, but she was afraid and said nothing. She crept away and hid herself.

One of the palace painters came and bowed to the Queen.

" Your Majesty," he said, " I think perhaps Tiptoe has done this, for no one else has paint exactly that colour."

" Call Tiptoe," said the Queen, frowning. So Tiptoe was called, and told to go to the Queen. She went, and when she saw the frown on her Majesty's face, she began to tremble.

Specially drawn for this work.
Tiptoe the Fairy was fetched to the Royal Palace. She brought her paint-pot with her; and, sure enough, the colour was exactly what the Queen wanted.

SCOLDED BY THE QUEEN

Tiptoe the Fairy, under suspicion of having painted the King's parrot, was summoned to the royal apartments. When she saw the frown on the Queen's face, she began to tremble. "You can go away from Fairyland," said her Majesty.

THE FLIGHT FROM FAIRYLAND

Specially drawn for this work.

A little brown bird who was flying by happened to notice the tired Fairy and flew down to her.
"Climb on to my back," he said kindly. Tiptoe thanked him and did so. Then the bird flew
off with her and soon passed the borders of Fairyland.

"Did you dare to paint the King's parrot?" asked the Queen sternly.

"Yes," said Tiptoe. "And I think he ought to be pleased that his parrot is such a lovely colour now, for there is no other red so pretty, I'm sure."

"You're a vain little creature," said the Queen. "When will you learn that a colour which is good for kitchen chairs is horrid for carriage wheels, or parrots? I am ashamed of you. If you had come to say you were sorry, I would have forgiven you. But, instead, you speak quite rudely. You can go away from Fairyland, and take your paint with you."

Then Tiptoe began to cry, but it was of no use. She had to go. She took her paint with her, and began the long walk to the far-away gates of Fairyland. Soon she became very tired, and sank down.

But the Queen's servants would not let her rest. "You must be out of Fairyland by sundown," they said sternly. So she had to go on again.

Then a little brown bird who was flying by happened to notice the tired elf, and flew down to her.

"Climb on to my back," he said kindly.

Tiptoe thanked him, and did so. He flew off with her, and soon passed the borders of Fairyland and came to our country.

"Where are you going?" he asked. Then Tiptoe began to cry, and told him that she didn't know.

"You shall come to my nest for the night," said the little brown bird. "You will be warm and comfortable there. You can tell me your story when we arrive."

So he took her to his nest and listened to her tale.

"I'm sorry now for what I did," she said. "I know I was naughty and vain. I don't know what I shall do here, for I can't do any work except painting."

"I've got a fine idea!" said the bird excitedly. "I think that paint

Specially drawn for this work.

Next morning Tiptoe began her work and soon the little brown bird had a beautiful red breast and was very proud of himself.

Specially drawn for this work.

Tiptoe the Fairy was very busy and very happy. She wanted nothing better than to be with the little birds who loved her.

of yours is a lovely colour. Do you think you could paint my breast with it? I'm always being mixed up with those common little brown sparrows, but if I had a bright red breast, everyone would know me."

"Oh, I'd love to do that," said Tiptoe. "You've been so kind to me, and I really could make you look lovely."

So next morning she took her paint-pot and stirred the paint up well. She murmured some magic words over it, and it began to glow brightly. Then she took a clean paint-brush and dipped it in. The little brown bird stood in front of her and fluffed out his chest feathers.

Tiptoe began to paint them. How they shone in the sunlight! The fairy painted each feather very carefully, and took great pains, for she was very grateful to the little bird who had helped her so much.

Very soon the brown bird had a beautiful red breast, and was very proud of himself indeed. He went to look at his reflection in a bright puddle, and sang with delight. Then he flew off to tell his friends, and soon they all came to be painted too.

Tiptoe was very busy and very happy. She painted all day long, and at night she cuddled up in the nest and went to sleep. Soon she forgot to be lonely, and wanted nothing better than to be with the little brown birds, who loved her. But she was never vain again, for she had learnt her lesson.

Don't you think Tiptoe's paint is a lovely colour? You must have seen the birds she paints, for they are robin redbreasts.

Tiptoe's busiest time is in the autumn, for then she is at work all day painting the breasts of the new baby robins. They are born with brown breasts you know—and I expect you've often wondered how they get their lovely red waistcoats in the autumn. Well, now you know!

Fable,
Myth
and
Legend

A Story
from the
Arabian
Nights

Specially drawn for this work.

" Have a care, master! " cried Aladdin. " Help me out of the cave first and you shall have the lamp." Then the magician lost his temper and stamped and shouted in rage.

ALADDIN AND THE LAMP

ONCE upon a time there was a poor youth called Aladdin. He was taking his mother's washing home one day when a magician stopped him.

" Will you help me ? " he asked. " I want to get a lamp from a cave, and the entrance is too small for me to pass through."

Aladdin went with the magician and soon slipped into the cave. " Put this ring on your finger," said the magician, handing him a curious gold ring. " That will keep you from harm. Go along the narrow passage, and at the end you will find a large room. In the middle is an old lamp. Bring it to me, and I will reward you well."

Aladdin ran down the passage and came to the room in which the lamp stood. He picked it up, and went back to the magician. The man was so impatient to have it that he tried to snatch it out of Aladdin's hand.

" Have a care, master! " cried the youth. " You almost sent me flying to the ground. Help me out first, and you shall have the lamp."

Then the magician lost his temper and stamped and shouted in rage. All at once the cave entrance closed up, and Aladdin was left standing in the darkness. The magician stared in horror, for he knew he had lost the lamp.

Aladdin was frightened. He sat down and waited, but nothing happened. Then he idly rubbed the ring that the magician had given to him.

BANG! A cloud of smoke appeared, and when it had cleared away Aladdin saw a genie standing in front of him, bowing low.

" I am the slave of the ring," said the genie. " Command me and I will obey! "

" This is splendid ! " thought Aladdin when he had recovered from his amazement.

"Take me home," he commanded. In a trice the slave lifted Aladdin up and whirled him through the air. Aladdin shut his eyes, and when he opened them, there he was at home, whilst his mother looked at him in surprise.

Swiftly he told her all that had happened, and showed her the lamp.

She took it and began to rub it in order to clean it.

CRASH! An even bigger genie stood in front of them, bowing.

"I am the slave of the lamp," he said. "Command me and I will obey."

"Oh, Aladdin!" said his mother, "we can have anything we want!" She turned to the genie. "Bring fine food, beautiful clothes, and a sack of gold," she commanded.

In a moment slaves appeared with dishes of food, and others laid down splendid garments at the feet of Aladdin and his mother. A big black slave brought the bag of gold.

"Aladdin, with this slave of the lamp at our command, we can be wealthier than the Emperor himself!" cried the woman. "Let us send sacks of gold and jewels to the Emperor to-day, and ask for the hand of Princess Badroul-Badour, his daughter, so that you may marry her and become a prince!"

Aladdin rubbed the lamp.

CRASH! The slave appeared and bowed low.

"Take a hundred sacks of precious stones to the Emperor and tell him they are from Aladdin, who asks him for the hand of the princess," said the youth.

That day the Emperor was amazed to see a hundred slaves appearing before him, with sacks full of rubies, diamonds, sapphires and other precious stones. He heard the message Aladdin sent him, and smiled in delight.

Specially drawn for this work.

Aladdin's mother took the lamp and began to rub it in order to clean it. CRASH! Almost immediately a genie stood in front of them, bowing. "I am the slave of the lamp," he said. "Command me and I will obey."

HOW ALADDIN LOST HIS LAMP

Specially drawn for this work

The Princess fetched the old lamp that Aladdin always had by his bedside and gave it to the man who had come down the street with a tray of brand-new lamps. At once the man shouted with delight, rubbed the lamp and vanished. He had come to win back the Magic Lamp.

"This man would make a splendid husband for my daughter," he said. "Go slave, and tell him that if he will build a beautiful palace for the princess and give her twice as much as he has sent me to-day, I will let him marry her."

The slave took the message and told Aladdin. At once the youth commanded the palace to be built and the sacks to be sent. The next morning the Emperor was amazed to see a marvellous palace glittering opposite his own, and to observe two hundred slaves appearing, each with a heavy sack of precious stones.

"My daughter shall marry this rich man to-day!" cried the Emperor. So the wedding was hurried on, and that night Aladdin slept in his new palace with the beautiful princess by his side.

They were very happy together until one day when a dreadful thing happened. Aladdin was away, and an old man came down the street with a tray of brand new lamps.

"New lamps for old! New lamps for old!" he shouted.

"Here is a strange thing!" thought the princess. "I wonder if the old man means what he says? I will try him."

She fetched the old lamp that Aladdin always had by his bedside and gave it to the man. At once he shouted with delight, rubbed it, and vanished! He was the magician, and had come to see if he could get the magic lamp.

Specially drawn for this work.

The genie appeared and bowed low, ready to receive commands. At once Aladdin was lifted up and rushed through the air to the desert.

The next thing that happened was strange and frightening. Aladdin's palace suddenly rose into the air and flew away to the middle of a desert! The magician had commanded the slave of the lamp to take it there. He meant to marry the princess himself, and so punish Aladdin for taking the lamp.

When Aladdin arrived home, he was horrified to find no palace there. He sat down on a stone in despair, and then suddenly remembered his ring. He rubbed it hard.

BANG! The genie appeared and bowed low.

"Take me where my palace is," commanded Aladdin. At once he was lifted up and rushed through the air to the desert. He was set down before the door of his palace.

Aladdin rushed up the steps and ran to the room of the princess. He was just in time to hear the magician say: "You shall marry me, lovely lady, whether you will or no!"

At once he pounced on the magician and swept off his head. Then he turned to his princess and took her into his arms.

"Take us back again to our own land," he commanded the slave of the lamp, who appeared as soon as Aladdin rubbed it. In a trice the palace stood in its rightful place, and everything was as it had been before.

Fable,
Myth
and
Legend

Tales
from
Hans Andersen
and Grimm

Specially drawn for this work.

The duckling came from the biggest egg of the lot and ran about. " What a big ugly thing! "
thought the mother duck. " It is a dirty grey, and not nearly so pretty as the others."

THE UGLY DUCKLING

A MOTHER duck once sat on a brood of eggs. One by one they hatched, and pretty yellow ducklings came out. At last only one egg was left.

" I wish this egg would hatch," said the duck. " It is the biggest of the lot, and I am so tired of sitting."

As she spoke, it hatched. The duckling came out and ran about.

" What a big ugly thing! " thought the mother duck. " It is a dirty grey, not nearly so pretty as the others."

Nobody liked the ugly duckling. All the ducks in the yard pecked it, and even its mother told it to go away, for she was ashamed to own such a big ugly creature as one of her brood of ducklings.

The little girl who came to feed the birds kicked it. " Go away, you ugly creature! " she cried. " Let the pretty little ducklings feed by themselves."

The ugly duckling was sad, and made up his mind to fly away. He flew over the fence, and soon came to a great moor where the wild ducks lived.

Soon the wild ducks came to see him. " What sort of duck are you ? " they asked. " You are surprisingly ugly. Keep to yourself and do not try to go with us."

" I will not go with you," promised the duckling humbly. He flew away from them, and came to two wild ganders.

" How ugly you are! " said one of the ganders. Then it started with fear for there came the sound of shot-guns. The two ganders rose into the air, and at the same moment there came the bang-bang of a gun. They fell dead to the ground near the frightened duckling.

Then hunting-dogs came rushing up to take the dead ganders. The duckling put his head under his wing and trembled. A great dog ran up to him and sniffed at him. Then he ran off again, and the duckling looked round.

Specially drawn for this work.

A strange feeling came over the ugly duckling. He felt as if he really must go and swim on the water. When he told the hen and the cat this they were amazed.

" It is a good thing for me that I am ugly! " he said, " for even the dog did not like to bite me."

When evening came the duckling flew off again. A fierce storm blew up, and the poor creature, terrified, came to a tumble-down hut. He slipped through a crack in the door and found himself in a tiny room.

An old woman lived there with her tom cat, Sonnie, and her hen, Chicka-biddy-Shortshanks.

In the morning the old woman saw the duckling. She was short-sighted, and thought he was a fat duck strayed from somewhere.

" Ho, ho! " she said, pleased. " Now I shall have duck's eggs for tea! "

But of course the duckling laid no eggs. He did not have a very good time, for the cat and the hen were very vain creatures and looked down on the ugly duckling.

" You can neither lay eggs like me, nor purr like the cat," said the hen. " What use are you, I should like to know? "

The duckling said nothing. He sat in a corner of the room and moped. Suddenly a strange feeling came over him. He felt as if he really must go and swim on the water.

When he told the hen and the cat this, they were amazed.

" You are mad! " said the cat. " I hate the water, and so does Chicka-biddy-Shortshanks. Since we are the cleverest animals in the world, you may be sure that we know what is good and what is not."

The duckling stayed no longer. He ran out and flew away. Soon he came to a stretch of water, and he was very happy to see it. He flew down to it and dived and swam to his heart's content. If only he had not been so ugly, he would have been quite happy, but he could not bear to be slighted.

Soon the autumn came, and over the water flew a flock of beautiful white birds, so dazzling that the ugly duckling could scarcely bear to look at them. They were swans. How the duckling loved them, and how he longed to go with them, for he was very lonely ; but he felt sure they would peck him if he even ventured to call to them.

When the winter came, the poor little duckling was frozen into the ice. He would have died there if a peasant had not come by and broken the ice with his shoe. He took the cold bird home to his wife, and she warmed it and brought life to it again. Then two children came to play with the duckling, and frightened him.

He flew up to the ceiling of the room and then down again. He fell into the milk-pan and upset it. He tumbled into the butter-tub, and then into the flour barrel. How queer he looked then, and how angry the woman was with him! In a fright the duckling flew out of the door and away.

When spring came he felt more cheerful. He found that his wings were stronger, and he flew away over the hills. Soon he came to a beautiful garden, in which lay a lovely lake surrounded by green trees. The duckling flew down to it.

Suddenly he saw three glorious white swans swimming towards him. The duckling at once felt frightened and unhappy.

" They will hate me because I am so ugly," he thought. " What shall I do? I am too ugly to live! I will go to these royal birds and beg them to kill me, for I am no use to anyone."

So he swam to them and begged them to kill him. He bent his head down upon the water and waited for them to strike.

But what was this he saw reflected in the clear water? Could it be his own reflection? Surely not! The duckling looked in amazement, for he saw, not an ugly grey duckling, but a beautiful white swan!

Then the other swans swam up, and they stroked him with their beaks and welcomed him, so that the duckling was happy and proud.

Soon some children came to feed the swans. They threw bread and corn upon the water, and suddenly the youngest of them cried out in surprise:

" Oh, see! There is a beautiful new swan with the others to-day! He is the loveliest of them all! "

The old swans bowed their heads to

Specially drawn for this work.

What was this the duckling saw reflected in the clear water? He looked in amazement, for he saw, not an ugly duckling, but a beautiful white swan!

the new one, and he was so happy that he hid his head under his wing. Then he drew it forth again and rustled his dazzling white wings.

" I am no longer the ugly duckling! " he cried. " I am a swan, beautiful and happy! "

THE HARDY TIN SOLDIER

Two street boys ran up and found the tin soldier. They made a paper boat and set him upright
in it. " Sail him down the gutter! " they cried. So the little boat went sailing away.

ONCE upon a time there were five-
and-twenty tin soldiers. They
were very splendid in their red
and blue uniforms, and each of them
shouldered his gun and looked straight
before him.

A little boy had them for his birth-
day. He took them out and stood
them on the table. They were all
exactly alike except the last one, for
instead of two legs, he had only one.
But he stood just as straight on his
one leg as the others did on their two.
The one-legged soldier looked straight
in front of him, and he saw a fine
castle, made of cardboard. In front
of it was a little lake made of glass,
and pretty wax ducks were swimming
there. At the door of the castle stood
a lovely lady. She was a tiny doll,
dressed in white, with a scarf of blue
ribbon over her shoulder. She wore a
red rose, and the soldier thought she
was the daintiest little creature that
he had ever seen.

She was a dancing doll, and one of
her legs was lifted so high behind her

that the soldier could not see it. He
thought she had just one leg like
himself.

" If only she could be my wife! " he
thought. " But she is too grand, for
she lives on a fine estate and I only
live in a box."

Now, one morning the little boy put
the tin soldier on the window-ledge.
Soon the window blew open, and the
soldier fell out. Down he went, and
stuck head foremost in a crack of the
pavement. The little boy ran out to
look for him, but could not find him.

Soon the rain fell, and the soldier
got wet. Two street boys ran up and
found him. They made a paper boat
and set him upright in it.

" Sail him down the gutter! " they
cried. So the little boat went swirling
down the gutter. The tin soldier was
frightened, but he stood bravely there
and looked straight in front of him.

Suddenly the boat rushed into a
drain, and everything became dark.
Then a great rat ran up and snapped
at the soldier.

CAUGHT BY A FISH

Specially drawn for this work.

The tin soldier's paper boat was so heavy with water that it was sinking. Soon it sank and the canal closed over the soldier. But at that very moment along came a fish and snapped at him. He was swallowed and went down the fish's throat. How dark and narrow it was inside.

"How dare you come into my drain!" cried the rat. "I'll have you, I will!"

But the stream became stronger, and carried the boat safely away from the rat. It was getting near the canal, and the soldier was afraid when he heard the rushing of the water where the drain entered the canal through a big round pipe.

His paper boat was so heavy with water that it was sinking. The tin soldier still stood upright, and showed no fear, but he was dreadfully frightened, for only his head was now above the water. In another moment, he thought, he would be drowned.

Then with a swirling rush he was swept into the canal. The boat sank, and the water closed over the tin soldier. But at that very moment up came a fish and snapped at him. He was swallowed, and went down the fish's throat.

How dark and narrow it was in the creature's body. The brave tin soldier lay there, never moving, and no one would have known how afraid he was, for he still looked straight before him.

The fish suddenly began to make some strange movements, and then lay quite still. A long, long time passed, and suddenly there came a flash, and lo and behold! the soldier saw daylight again.

The fish had been caught, taken to market, sold, and brought into a kitchen. The cook had sliced open the fish and found the little tin soldier safely tucked up inside. How surprised she was!

"Why, here is a tin soldier!" she cried, in amazement. "I will take it to the children."

She ran upstairs and showed the children what she had found. "Take him," she said, smilingly. "He is quite a hero."

One of the boys shouted for joy, and took the soldier.

"Why, he is the one I lost this morning!" he cried. "I should know him again anywhere, for he has only one leg! What a brave fellow he is, to be sure! He tumbled from the window, got into the canal, was swallowed by a fish, and then brought back here again!"

"He is a real hero," said another boy. "Do not put him back into the box. Let him live in the castle with the little dancing doll! They would be quite good friends."

The tin soldier's heart began to beat fast. To live in the castle with the little doll he loved so much! What good luck was his!

The little boy put him in the castle with the doll, and a very fine couple they made, standing there each on one leg.

The dancer was delighted to have such a hero beside her, and when night came she made him tell her his story. She was never tired of hearing it, and he was never tired of telling it, and he must have told the tale of his adventures a hundred times over.

The little tin soldier was happier than he had ever been before. He stood proudly in the castle, his gun on his shoulder, looking straight before him.

THE DONKEY'S BAND

Specially drawn for this work.

The cock crowed till he nearly burst, the cat meaowed loudly, the dog barked and growled fiercely and the donkey brayed. It was the funniest band that ever was heard. Then the creatures burst in at the window and fell upon the robbers.

THERE was once a donkey who was turned away by his master because he was old and could no longer work hard.

"This is bad luck," said the donkey to himself. "What can I do now?"

He trotted along the road and made up his mind to go to Bremen.

"They have a splendid town band there," he said. "Perhaps they will let me join it, for I have a fine loud bray."

On the way he met a dog limping along the road, and spoke to him.

"Where are you going?" he asked.

"I don't know," replied the dog. "I am old and my master says he will get rid of me. So I am running away from him, as you see."

"Come with me," said the donkey. "I am going to join the town band at Bremen. Your growl and your bark ought to do well in the band."

So the dog went with the donkey. Soon they saw an old cat sitting by a wall, looking miserable. They asked her what was the matter.

"I am sad because my mistress is so unkind," said Puss. "I can no longer catch mice as I used to do, and my mistress says she will have me drowned."

"Come with us," said the donkey. "We go to join the Bremen town band, and I am sure your meaow would be welcome there."

So the cat went with them. Soon they came to a cock, who was standing on a gate, crowing loudly.

"What is the matter?" asked the donkey.

"I am telling my mistress what I think of her," said the cock angrily. "For many years I have crowed every morning to tell her the dawn is here, and what do you think she means to do this evening? She is going to have me killed and cooked!"

"Come with us," said the donkey. "We are going to Bremen to join the town band. Your crowing will be greatly welcomed."

So the donkey, the dog, the cat and the cock all went along together. When night came they saw a farmhouse near by, and went up to it. The donkey put his head through the window and saw a band of robbers sitting at the table, eating.

"We will frighten them away!" said the donkey gleefully. "Get on my back, all of you, and when I give the signal, make as much noise as you can."

So the dog jumped up on the donkey's back, the cat climbed on to the dog's back, and the cock flew up to the very top and stood on the cat. Then when the donkey gave the signal, the cock crowed till he nearly burst, the cat meaowed loudly, the dog barked and growled fiercely, and the donkey brayed his very loudest. It was the funniest band that ever was heard.

When they had finished, they burst in at the window and fell upon the robbers. The men had been terrified when they heard the donkey's band, and when they saw the animals at the window, they shouted with terror and fled away.

The hungry beasts ate everything on the table, and then lay down to sleep for the night. The donkey found some straw in the yard, and lay down on that. The dog stretched himself out on a mat behind the door. The cat sat by the dying fire, and the cock flew up into the rafters.

When the robbers heard nothing more one of them crept back to the house. He went into the room and found a candle. Thinking to light it from the embers of the fire, he went towards the hearth. The fire was out, but he saw the two gleaming eyes of the cat, and thought they were live embers. So he poked the candle at them to light it.

The cat gave a screech and scratched his face. The robber fled in terror. He fell over the dog at the door, and was bitten in the leg. Then he tumbled on top of the donkey in the yard, and the furious animal kicked out with his back legs and sent the robber flying head-over-heels yards away.

Just as he was picking himself up the cock awoke in the rafters and began crowing loudly. That frightened the robber still more, and he fled back to his comrades, terrified.

" What's the matter ? " they asked. " What did you find ? "

" Oh," said the robber, " it was dreadful. At the fire was sitting an old witch, whose two eyes gleamed horribly. She nearly scratched my face to pieces. I turned to run and at the door was a strong man with a dagger. He stabbed me in the leg. Look, you can see the wound he made. I ran into the yard and, dear me, there was a great savage monster who smote me so hard that I went head-over-heels and nearly broke my neck. Up in the rafters sat a judge and all the time he shouted: ' Bring the rogue to me! Bring the rogue to me! ' "

The robbers were full of fear when they heard all this, and ran away, never to come back. The animals watched them go, and then made up their minds to live in the house for the rest of their lives and make it their own.

They did so, and spent many happy years of peace and comfort there.

Specially drawn for this work.

The donkey was furious. He kicked out with his back legs and sent the robber flying head-over-heels yards away.

RAPUNZEL AND THE PRINCE

The woman was so happy with her dear little baby that she forgot all about her husband's promise to the witch. But one day the old crone came and walked off with the crowing baby.

THERE was once a poor woman whose house overlooked a witch's garden. In the beds there was some lovely lettuce, green and crisp. The woman saw it, and longed for some.

"Husband," she said one night, "I must have some of the lettuce from that witch's garden. Go and get me some."

The man climbed over the wall and picked a handful. But, just as he was climbing back again, the witch came out and caught him.

"Oho!" she said. "What robber is this? I will turn you into a frog."

"Have mercy!" begged the frightened man. "My wife longed for a salad and sent me to get a lettuce."

"I will let you go if you promise to give me the first baby that is born to your wife," said the witch.

The poor man had to consent, and then the witch let him go. When he told his wife what he had promised, she was very sad.

Some time after this a dear little baby came to the woman, and she was so happy with it that she forgot all about the witch. But one day the old crone came and took it. She walked off with the crowing baby, leaving the poor woman crying and sobbing.

The baby grew into a beautiful girl. She was so lovely that the witch was afraid some one would steal her. So she built a tower in the depths of a wood, and put the girl into it.

The maiden was called Rapunzel, which is the witch-word for lettuce. She was a happy girl, even though she saw no one but the witch and knew nothing of the world.

The tower she was in had no door, and only one small window at the top. No one could enter and steal her, and the witch was content.

Every day at sunrise and sunset she came to visit Rapunzel. She brought her food and drink. But how did she get into the tower?

When she arrived at the foot, she called to the maiden, and Rapunzel looked from the window.

"Rapunzel, Rapunzel, let down your
    hair
    That I may climb without a
      stair!"
cried the witch.

Then Rapunzel let down her glorious
silken hair. It was in two plaits, and
was so long that it reached from the
tower window to the ground. It was
bright gold, and shone dazzlingly in
the sunlight.

The witch took hold of it and climbed
up, hand over hand, till she reached
the window. Then she sprang inside
and gave Rapunzel what she had
brought.

Now, one day a prince came riding
by that way, and came to the strange
tower. He heard a sweet voice singing
a song, and looked around to find out
who it was. But he could see no one.

"Perhaps the maiden whose voice I
hear is in the tower," he thought. So
he rode around it to find the door.
But there was none.

As he was riding away, much puzzled, the prince saw the old witch
coming in the distance. He thought
that perhaps she might have something
to do with the tower, so he hid himself
and watched. He heard her call out to
Rapunzel to let down her hair, and in
great surprise saw the witch climb up
the maiden's plaits.

"So that is the way in!" thought
the prince.

He waited until the witch had gone,
and then he softly went to the foot of
the tower.

"Rapunzel, Rapunzel, let down your
    hair
    That I may climb without a
      stair!"
he called.

At once Rapunzel let down her plaits
again, and the prince felt them come
tumbling against his cheek, soft and
sweet-smelling. In a trice he climbed
up and leapt into the maiden's room.

She was frightened and ran into a

Specially drawn for this work.

The Prince hid himself and watched closely. He heard the old witch call out to Rapunzel to let
down her hair; and, in great surprise, saw the witch climb up the maiden's plaits.

HOW RAPUNZEL LOST HER TRESSES

" Oh, you wicked girl," said the witch. " I will cut off your hair and then you can let no one in at all! " So the old crone took a knife and snip-snip! Rapunzel's beautiful hair fell on the floor. The maiden was terrified and shrank into a corner.

Specially drawn for this work.

The witch let down the two plaits that she had cut off the maiden's head. The Prince climbed up and leapt into the room.

corner, for never had she seen anyone before but the old witch. But the prince soon comforted her, and told her so many wonderful stories of all that went on in the world, that she forgot her fears and listened eagerly.

He climbed down her plaits and went away before the witch came again. He promised to return as soon as he could, and he kept his word. Every day he came to see Rapunzel, and soon she loved him very much. The prince loved the maiden too, and begged her to run away with him and marry him.

"But how can I escape from here?" she said. "I cannot climb down my own plaits!"

"I will bring you some silken threads each day," said the prince, "and you shall weave them into a strong rope."

So every day he brought her silken threads, and Rapunzel hid them, and little by little wove them secretly into a rope.

All went well until one evening when the maiden was putting out her plaits for the witch to climb up.

"I wonder why you are so much heavier than the prince!" she said.

"What!" screamed the witch in rage. "Has a prince been visiting you? Oh, you wicked girl, I will cut off your hair, and then you can let no one in at all!"

She took a knife and snip-snip! Rapunzel's beautiful hair fell on the floor. The maiden was terrified and shrank into a corner.

"Now we will go to sleep," said the witch. "I shall stay here to-night, Rapunzel, and when your prince comes, he will be surprised to find someone else here besides you! I will turn him into a toad!"

The witch fell asleep before Rapunzel did. Then, swift and silent, the maiden took out her rope of silk and tied it to a nail. She threw it out of the window, and then slid down it safely. Once on the ground, she ran off, eager to find her prince and warn him of his danger;

but she could not see him, and soon was lost.

Meanwhile, the prince had arrived at the tower.

"Rapunzel, Rapunzel, let down your hair
That I may climb without a stair!"
he called.

The witch awoke, and quickly she let down the two plaits that she had cut off the maiden's head. The prince climbed up and leapt into the room. Then he saw the wicked old witch and cried out in fear. In a trice he turned to the window to climb down the plaits again, but lost his hold and fell.

He fell into some thorn bushes, and although he did not hurt himself, the thorns scratched his eyes and blinded him. The witch saw this and laughed in delight.

The prince went wandering through the wood, blind and helpless. As morning dawned he heard a sweet singing somewhere near by, and knew it to be the voice of his beloved Rapunzel.

He made his way to her and called to her. She was full of joy to see her own prince, but sad that his eyes were blind. Softly she kissed them—and lo and behold! they were healed of their hurt, and the prince could see!

"My own Rapunzel!" said the prince, looking on the maiden with gladness. "Your love has given me my sight once more. But what have you done with your glorious hair?"

"Alas!" said Rapunzel, "the witch cut off my plaits and used them to trap you with. But let us not weep, my prince. We are happy."

"Come," said the prince, taking her hand. "We will follow this path through the wood, and soon we shall come to the high road that leads to my father's palace."

Then happily they went together to the palace and were married that same day. They soon forgot about the old witch, and lived happily ever after.

Specially drawn for this work.

Rapunzel was sad that her Prince's eyes were blind. Softly she kissed them and once again the Prince could see!

HANSEL AND GRETEL

Specially drawn for this work.

As soon as his parents were asleep Hansel slipped out of the cottage and picked up as many of the pebbles as his pockets would carry.

ONCE upon a time there dwelt near a large wood a poor wood-cutter, with his wife and two children, whose names were Hansel and Gretel. The children were step-children, for their own mother had died.

A famine came over the land, and the poor man could not find food enough for his family. "What will become of us?" he said. The step-mother cruelly answered, "Let us take the children to the wood and leave them there. We have no food for them in the house."

The father of the children was very sad when he heard this, for he felt how cruel it was to do such a thing.

Now it so happened that the children heard what their cruel step-mother had said. Gretel began to cry, and said to Hansel, "What will become of us?" "Do not cry," said Hansel, "I will soon help you."

As soon as the parents were asleep, he got up, put on his coat, unbolted the door and slipped out. Outside the door were some pebbles, and Hansel stooped down and picked up as many as his pockets would carry. He then went back again.

The next morning, before the sun arose, the wife went and woke the two children. "Get up, you lazy things," she said. "We are going to the forest to chop wood." She gave each of the children a piece of bread, and they all set out.

Now as Hansel walked along, he dropped very quietly, every now and then, one of the pebbles he had in his pocket so that he and his sister could find their way home again.

When they all reached the middle of the wood, the wicked step-mother told the children to collect some twigs and make a fire to keep themselves warm. This they did, and a bright, cheerful fire was lit. The children were then told to lie down by the fire and get warm while the father and his wife went into the forest to chop wood. But they did not mean to chop wood. They only said so in order to escape from the children.

Warm but weary, Hansel and Gretel soon fell asleep. When they woke it was dark, and Gretel began to cry. "How shall we get out of the wood?" she sobbed. Hansel tried to comfort her by saying, "Wait a little while till the moon rises, and then we will quickly find the way."

The moon shone forth, and taking his sister's hand, they both followed the shining pebbles which Hansel had dropped. All night they walked, and at last they reached their father's house. The father was delighted to see them. But the step-mother was not. She scolded them for sleeping so long in the wood, pretending it was their fault.

Again a famine came over the land and the family were starving as before. "We must send the children farther into the wood this time," said the step-mother.

Luckily the children heard her this second time. So Hansel got up in the night to pick up some more pebbles. But lo! his step-mother had locked the door.

In the morning the children were given a slice of bread each as before, only it was a smaller slice. And as they went along Hansel cleverly dropped his slice, crumb by crumb, on the ground, so that he and his sister should find their way home again.

This time a bigger fire was lit and the children again fell asleep. Hansel did not fear, because he was thinking of the crumbs strewed along the way. When the moon shone, the children got up and began to walk homewards. But where were the crumbs? There were none to be seen, because thousands of birds had been flying about in the woods and had picked them all up.

Hansel kept on saying to Gretel, "We shall soon find the way." But they did not. They walked the whole night and all next day, yet could not get out of the wood.

At last, worn out and hungry, they lay down under a tree and fell fast asleep. When they awoke, they still walked on. Suddenly they saw a beautiful snow-white bird sitting on a bough and sweetly singing. It soon leapt off, and, spreading its wings, flew away to a cottage and perched on the roof. It was a curious cottage. It was made of bread and cakes and the window-panes were made of clear sugar.

"We will go in there," said Hansel, "and have a glorious feast. I will eat a piece of the roof and you can eat the window. They broke off pieces and began eating. Then a sweet voice called out, "Tip-tap, tip-tap, who raps at my door?" But the children went on eating.

Just then the door opened, and a very old woman, walking on crutches, came out. Hansel and Gretel were very frightened, but the old woman said, "Ah, my dear children, come in and stop with me, and no harm shall befall you."

A good meal of milk and pancakes, with sugar, apples and nuts was spread on the table, and in the back room were two nice little beds with white covers. Hansel and Gretel laid down on the beds and fell fast asleep.

Specially drawn for this work.

Hansel took Gretel's hand and by the light of the moon they followed the shining pebbles which Hansel had dropped.

Specially drawn for this work.

The door opened and a very old woman came out. "Ah, my dear children," she said, "come in and stop with me, and no harm shall befall you."

The old woman at first treated them kindly, but she was really very wicked, and only built the bread-house to entice children in and treat them cruelly and to eat them.

All her cooking was done in a big oven, and one day she told Gretel to get into the oven to see if it was hot enough. But Gretel was too sharp for her and said she did not know how to do it. The wicked old witch then put her head into the oven to show Gretel how to do it.

Quick as thought Gretel gave her a push right into the oven and banged the door.

And that was the end of the wicked old witch. As soon as the oven door was bolted Gretel ran to tell her brother of all that had happened.

"Oh, Hansel, Hansel," she cried. "We are saved! The old witch is dead and we are free."

Hansel ran to her and they danced together for joy, kissing each other again and again.

What did the children do then? They went all over the house and found in it pearls and precious stones in every corner.

"These are better than pebbles," said Hansel, putting as many into his pockets as they would hold.

"I'll take some, too," said Gretel, and she filled her apron with as many of the precious stones as she could carry.

"Now we must get out of this forest," said Hansel. "We must find our way home again."

They walked together for two long hours, and then came to a large piece of water.

"We cannot possibly get over this," said Hansel, "I can see no bridge at all."

"And there is no sign of a boat, either," said Gretel, "but there swims a white duck. I will ask her to help us over;" and she sang—

" Little Duck, good little Duck,
Gretel and Hansel, here we stand;
There is neither stile nor bridge—
Take us on your back to land;
Take us on your strong white back,
Take us to the other shore."

So the duck came to them, and Hansel sat himself on, and bade his sister sit behind him. "No," answered Gretel, "that will be too much for the duck; she shall take us over one at a time."

This the good bird did, and when they reached the other side safely, they came to the wood they knew so well. Presently they saw the smoke from a chimney, and at last they could see their father's house.

Then they began to run and, bursting into their house, they fell on their father's neck. He had not had one happy hour since he had left the children in the forest. And the children's step-mother had died and their father was living alone.

Gretel shook her apron, and the pearls and precious stones rolled out upon the floor. Hansel also threw down one handful after another out of his pocket.

Then all their sorrows were ended, and they lived together in great happiness ever afterwards.

Specially drawn for this work.

The good little duck carried Hansel and Gretel over the water one at a time.

THE GOOSE THAT LAID THE GOLDEN EGGS

THERE was once a man who owned a wonderful goose. This bird laid a golden egg each day, and the man began to get rich.

" I shall soon be able to buy myself a great house and dress in silk," said the man to himself. " I wish the goose would lay two eggs a day instead of one, then I could buy my house more quickly."

But the goose laid no more than her one egg every day. Soon the man became impatient.

" I will kill the goose! " he said. " Then I shall get all my wealth at once, and need not wait any longer to buy my house."

So he took an axe and killed the goose, expecting to find untold wealth inside. But he found nothing, not even a golden egg.

" How foolish I am! " he cried. " I shall never be wealthy now, for I have killed the goose that laid the golden eggs! "

Specially drawn for this work.

The goose laid a golden egg each day and the man began to get rich. " I shall soon be able to buy myself a great house," said he.

THE FOX WHO LACKED A TAIL

ONCE upon a time there was a fox who lost his tail in a trap. He looked so queer that all the other foxes laughed at him.

He did not like this, so he made up his mind to pretend that it was a fine thing to be without a tail.

" Ho, you foxes! " he cried. " Why do you not cut off your ugly, heavy tails, and go free like me ? Tails are no longer fashionable ; and, besides, they may be caught in traps! Cut them off, I say! "

The foxes listened and smiled.

" We see through your trick! " they said. " You wouldn't tell us to cut off *our* tails if you hadn't lost your own! "

Then they all ran off to their holes, and left the silly fox to himself.

Specially drawn for this work.

The fox who had lost his tail in a trap looked so queer that all the other foxes laughed at him. He did not like this, of course.

THE LION AND THE MOUSE

A MOUSE once ran over a sleeping lion and awoke it. With a roar the great beast clapped his paw on the trembling mouse, and vowed to eat it. "Let me go," begged the mouse. "Perhaps one day I can serve you, great master."

"How can a tiny thing like you serve *me*?" said the lion scornfully, but he let the little creature go.

A week later the lion was caught in a hunter's net. Turn and twist as he might, he could not get free. Suddenly the little mouse came running up.

"Lie still, master!" he cried. "I can free you!"

The lion lay still, and the tiny animal gnawed at the knots of the net with its sharp teeth. Soon there were great holes, and the lion freed itself with ease.

"Thank you, little mouse," said the lion gratefully. "Never did I think that a little thing like you could ever be of service to me!"

Specially drawn for this work.

"Lie still, master!" cried the little mouse, running up to the helpless lion. "I can free you!" So the tiny animal gnawed at the knots of the net.

THE FOX AND THE CROW

A FOX once saw a crow with a fine piece of cheese in her beak. He was hungry, so he resolved to get it.

"What a beautiful bird you are!" he cried to the crow. "How your feathers shine, and what a lovely tail you have. I am sure you must have a beautiful voice to match your body. Will you not sing to me, and let me hear it?"

The crow was flattered. Never before had anyone spoken to her in such a way. Not once in her life had a single compliment been paid to her. She opened her beak and gave a harsh croak. The cheese fell down, and the fox pounced upon it and ate it. Then off he ran, laughing at the foolish crow, who had fallen a victim to his cunning words.

Specially drawn for this work.

The crow opened her beak and gave a harsh croak. The cheese fell down and the fox pounced upon it and ate it. Then off he ran, laughing.

Specially drawn for this work

The shepherd boy was terrified and shouted:
"Wolf! Wolf!" at the top of his voice
But no labourers came to help him.

THE ASS IN THE LION'S SKIN

THERE was once an ass who found a lion's skin. He put it on and went into the fields and woods to terrify all the animals he met. They ran away from him, and the ass was mightily pleased.

"I will now frighten my master!" he said. So he went to meet him, and brayed loudly to terrify him. But the man saw the ass's long ears sticking out, and knew him at once. When he heard him bray, he took a big stick and ran to the ass.

"Here is a fine beating for you!" he said as he laid about the silly animal. "Those who pretend to be what they are not, thoroughly deserve to be well punished!"

THE SHEPHERD BOY WHO CRIED "WOLF!"

THERE was once a shepherd boy whose duty it was to guard the sheep on the hillside. If a wolf came he was bidden to shout: "Wolf! Wolf!" so that the labourers in the fields near by could come and drive it off.

The boy was foolish, and often cried "Wolf!" when there was none, to make the labourers leave their work for nothing. This made them angry, but the boy would not stop his foolishness, and caused them to come running to him many times a week.

Then one day a wolf really did come. The boy was terrified, and shouted "Wolf! Wolf!" at the top of his voice.

But no labourers came to help him. "It is only that foolish boy playing tricks with us again," they said. "There is no wolf!" So they went on with their work and paid no attention to his cries.

The wolf killed and ate many lambs, and when the boy's master knew, he beat him well.

"It is your fault!" he said. "You have so often called 'Wolf!' for nothing that no one believes you when you tell the truth!"

Specially drawn for this work.

The donkey brayed loudly to terrify his master, but the man saw the ass's long ears sticking out and knew him at once.

THE DONKEY IN A LION'S SKIN

Specially drawn for this work.

The ass put on the lion's skin and went to frighten all the animals he met. They ran away from him and the donkey was very pleased. " I will now frighten my master! " he said,

THE DOG AND HIS SHADOW

A DOG once stole a piece of meat and ran off with it. He chanced to run over a stream, and looking down into the water, saw his own reflection there.

"Ho!" he thought, stopping, "there is another dog there with an even bigger piece of meat than mine! I will get it!"

He dropped his own piece, and leapt into the water. Of course, there was no dog there, and the greedy animal not only could not find the other dog's meat, but lost his own as well, and so had to go without.

Specially drawn for this work.
The dog chanced to run beside a stream; and, looking down into the water, he saw his own reflection there.

Specially drawn for this work.
Every time the hungry calf tried to eat a wisp of hay the dog snarled and sent him away.

A DOG IN THE MANGER

A DOG once lay down in a manger full of hay. A calf came into the shed, and being very hungry, tried to eat the hay.

The dog leapt up at once, and began snapping at the frightened calf. Every time the hungry animal tried to eat a wisp of hay, the dog snarled and sent him away.

"What a selfish creature!" said the calf to his companions. "He cannot eat the hay himself, and yet he will not let me eat it either. I have no liking for this dog in the manger."

And the calf was surely right!

Fable,
Myth
and
Legend

Tales
from
the
Norse

Specially drawn for this work.

The god Thor set out to go to Giantland. With him were the god Loki and his servant Thialfi.
They travelled far; and, when night came, looked about for shelter.

THOR AMONG THE GIANTS

ONCE upon a time the god Thor set out to go to Giantland. With him were the god Loki and his servant, Thialfi. They travelled far, and when night came they looked about for a shelter.

Suddenly Thor came upon a spacious hall, of which the door, which was as wide as the house itself, stood open.

"Let us lodge here for the night," said Thor. So they went in and looked round. There were five small rooms opening off the wide hall, but all of them were empty. Thor and his companions ate their supper in the hall, and lay down to sleep.

But they could not rest, for strange noises kept them awake. Never had Thor heard such loud mutterings, such thunderous snorts. The whole earth trembled with them, and even the house in which they were lying shook from roof to floor. Thor leapt up and went out to see what made the noise. But he could find nothing.

In the morning he and his companions went out into the forest, and there, lying on the ground, Thor saw a most gigantic man, a giant whose breath swayed the topmost branches of the trees.

As he looked at the great giant, the monster awoke and arose. From his mountainous height he looked down at Thor, and his eyes were like blue lakes.

"What have you been doing with my glove?" he said, and picked up the house in which Thor and the others had lain for the night. The five small rooms were the fingers and thumb, and the great hall was the mouth of the glove.

"I would have you know that I am going to Giantland to fight the giants," said Thor. Then, raising his hammer, Miölnir, he flung it straight at the giant's broad white forehead.

"Ah," said the giant, "did a leaf touch me?"

Specially drawn for this work.

Raising his hammer, Thor flung it straight
at the giant's broad, white forehead.

Thor's hammer returned to his hand
(for so it always did when he threw it),
and once again he hurled it at the
giant.

"I think an acorn must have fallen
on my head," said the giant, with a
smile.

The hammer returned to Thor's hand
a second time, and again he flung it
with all his strength. This time the
giant laughed loudly.

"Was that a feather that a bird
dropped on to my face?" he asked.
Then he slung his wallet on his shoulder;
and still laughing, walked off.

Thor and his companions set out on
their way once more. Before the sun
had set, they came to a vast barren
plain, on which stood a gigantic city,
whose walls were so high that Thor
could not see the tops of them. The
gates were closed, but the three travellers slipped through the bars.

Soon they came to the chief building
of all. They entered, and found themselves in an immense banqueting hall.
A table stood in the midst, and around
it, seated on stone thrones, were grim,
stony-looking giants.

Thor went up to the chief and
greeted him.

"Ho, little mannikin," said the
giant, "so you are the famous god
Thor? It is the rule here that none
shall sit down to eat until he has
performed some wonderful feat. Let
us see what you can do!"

Then Loki came forward and bowed.

"I am most famed for eating," he
said. "I will challenge any one of
your followers to a match, and I
warrant I will eat more than he
does!"

The giant king called to a thin
yellow-faced man, called Logi. A
large trough of meat was set in the
middle of the hall, and the two, Loki
and Logi, set to work. In a few
minutes each met the other in the
middle of the trough! Never before
was seen such eating.

But while Loki had eaten meat

alone, Logi had eaten bones, trough and all. So the giants decided that Logi had won.

Then Thialfi, Thor's servant, offered to run against any of the giant's followers. So the king called a slender lad called Hugi to him. The goal was fixed and the two started running.

Thialfi ran like the wind, but Hugi ran so swiftly that he reached the goal and then overtook Thialfi half way along the course! The giants nodded their great heads, and said that Hugi had won.

" Now, god Thor, what will *you* do ? " asked the king.

" I will try a drinking-match with any one of you," said Thor.

So a great drinking horn was brought and set before Thor.

" Drink from this," said the giant. " We say it is well-drunk if the horn is emptied at one draught. Some men take two draughts, but only the weakest take three."

Thor took a deep draught and put the horn down again. To his surprise it seemed almost as full as before. He drank again, and this time set it down thinking he had emptied it. But it was still nearly as full, and Thor became angry. He took a third pull and drank till his breath failed him; but even then he saw that only a small part of the contents had gone. Then he vowed he would try no more.

" See," said the giant king, pointing to a large cat that had come into the hall. " Try your strength with the cat, god Thor. Can you lift her from the ground ? "

Thor ran to the cat and strove to lift her. But he could only manage to get one of her paws from the ground, and in disgust gave up his attempt.

" You are but a little fellow," said the king, with a smile.

" Little I may seem to you! " cried Thor. " But who is there that would dare to wrestle with me ? "

" Wrestle ? " said the king. " Well,

Specially drawn for this work.

Thialfi ran like the wind, but Hugi ran so swiftly that he reached the goal, and then overtook Thialfi half-way along the course.

if you must try your strength at wrestling, mannikin, I will call in the old crone, Elli. You shall wrestle with her."

The crone came. Thor did not want to wrestle with her, for she was old and bent. But he could not help himself, for she suddenly leapt at him and threw him to the ground. Thor struggled hard and put forth all his strength, but it was of no use. The old crone was stronger than he was, and Thor was defeated. The giants laughed loud and long to see him.

"You are well vanquished," said the king. "Now come, Thor, we do not want to see any more of your so-called feats of strength. Sit down to meat with us."

Thor sat down with as good a grace as possible, for he was puzzled and sore at heart. He and his companions spent the night in Giantland, and in the morning bade their friends goodbye and set forth once again.

The king came to the gates with them, and Thor, looking up at him, suddenly saw that he was the giant whom he had found sleeping in the forest.

"Fare thee well," said Thor. "I am grieved to think that I acquitted myself so poorly in Giantland, for I know you will all account god Thor to be a man of little worth."

"Not so," said the giant. "I would never have let you enter my city, god Thor, if I had known your fearful strength. But now that you are safely outside, I will tell you of the tricks we played you:

"When you hurled your hammer at me in the forest, I should have been killed if I had not quickly placed a mountain between myself and you. Your hammer cleft three great ravines in it, which you will see as you go forth. Then when Loki and Logi sat down to eat at the trough, Loki did indeed eat like hunger itself. But

Specially drawn for this work.

Thor did not want to wrestle with Elli, for she was old and bent. Suddenly the woman leapt at him and threw him to the ground. The crone was strong and Thor was defeated.

THOR AND THE GREAT HORN

Specially drawn for this work.

Thor took a deep draught. To his surprise the horn seemed almost as full as before. He drank again, and this time thought he had emptied it. But it was still nearly as full, and Thor became angry. He took a third pull and drank till his breath failed him; but even then he saw that only a small part of the contents had gone.

Specially drawn for this work.

Thor ran to the cat and strove to lift her. But he could only manage to get one of the animal's paws from the ground.

Logi was Fire, and therefore ate up meat, bones and trough too. Who could hope to eat like Fire?

"When Thialfi ran against Hugi, he stood little chance, for Hugi was none other than my thought, and what speed can ever equal Thought? As for you, god Thor, your strength made me tremble, for when you drank from the great horn, you nearly emptied the sea! The other end was in the ocean itself, and when you come to the waters to-day, you will see how far out is the tide because of your great draught.

"What appeared to you to be the cat, which you tried to lift, was none other than the great serpent Jörmungand which encircles the world, and which, by my spells, I had changed into the cat. When you lifted one paw from the ground, there were earthquakes, and we trembled at your might. Nor must you be ashamed that you could not wrestle with the old crone, Elli. For she is Old Age, and never in this world has there been a man who could conquer Old Age!

"Now go, god Thor, and come here no more, for you are too mighty a man, and we shall trick you with other enchantments if you show your face here again. Be sure we shall never allow you to defeat us!"

The giant finished speaking and looked mockingly at the god, who was listening in anger. Thor felt his wrath rising in him, and he grasped his hammer Miölnir tightly. Then, as he heard the giant's scornful laughter, he raised it and shouted loudly.

"Once more do I, the god Thor, challenge you!" he cried in a mighty voice. "This time, oh King, you shall not trick me so easily!"

But he spoke to the empty air. The giant king had vanished utterly. The city disappeared to, and Thor and his companions found themselves alone in the midst of a vast, empty plain.

BALDER THE BRIGHT AND BEAUTIFUL

BALDER was the best-loved god in the lovely city of Asgard. He was very beautiful, and his face was so bright that everyone loved to look upon it. Not only gods, but men and women, and even the stony giants of Giantland, loved him and wished him well.

One day Balder had a dreadful dream. He awoke and put his hand to his heart, for he felt as if a shadow were there, dark and heavy. He arose and went to his mother, Frigga, where she sat on her throne, and lay down at her feet.

"What is the matter?" she asked him.

He put her hand over his heart, and she felt the shadow there. Her face grew pale, and she sprang up in alarm.

"It is the shadow of death!" she cried.

"If I must die, then I will die bravely," said Balder, his bright face clouded.

"Nay!" said Frigga. "You shall not die. I will make everything in the world promise not to hurt you, then you cannot be slain."

Without a moment's pause she sent out her commands. "Let everything come to me and promise not to hurt Balder the Bright and Beautiful," she said.

Then all things of the world came to her to promise. Stones and metals, trees and flowers, birds and beasts, illnesses of all kinds. They bowed before Frigga and gave her their promise, vowing never to hurt Balder.

Then the Queen of Asgard smiled, and she was happy again, though Balder still felt the shadow heavy about his heart.

"You are safe, my beloved son," said Frigga. "Fear no more."

When the gods knew that nothing could hurt Balder, they thought of a new game. They went to the green outside the city and stood Balder in the midst of it. Then they threw their spears at him, struck at him with swords, and smote him with staves.

But nothing could hurt him! The spears glanced away, the swords slipped and the staves broke. Balder stood smiling in the midst, feeling no hurt and no pain. Stone and metal were keeping their promise to Frigga.

Loki came up to see what the gods were doing. He was an evil god, jealous of the love that everyone bore Balder. He wondered if anything could hurt the smiling young god, and determined to find out. So, disguising himself as an old woman, he went to the palace to see Frigga.

She greeted him kindly, thinking he was a poor old dame, and they talked together for some time. Loki told

Specially drawn for this work.

Balder went to his mother Frigga and put her hand over his heart, so that she felt the shadow there. Her face grew pale and she sprang up in alarm. "If I must die, then I will die bravely," said Balder.

how he had passed by the green and seen the gods hurling weapons at Balder, who was hurt by none.

Frigga smiled with pleasure.

"Everything has promised not to hurt him," she said.

"What, everything?" cried Loki.

"Well, almost everything," said Frigga. "I forgot to ask the mistletoe to promise. It grows high in the big apple tree outside the palace, and I overlooked it. But it is so small and weak that I am sure it could not hurt Balder, so I have not asked it to promise."

Loki's eyes gleamed when he heard this. He bade Frigga good-bye and left the palace quickly. He made his way to the apple tree outside the palace and climbed it. He broke off a piece of the mistletoe and fashioned it into a short but strong stave. Then, changing himself into his own shape, he hurried to where the gods were still playing with Balder.

Near the laughing gods was standing Hödur, the blind twin brother of Balder. He was sad because he could not join in the game, but as he was blind, he could not see to throw anything at his brother. Loki spied him and went up to him.

"I see you are left out, Hödur," he whispered in his ear. "Here is a stave for you to throw at Balder. I will guide your arm. Throw your hardest, for nothing can hurt your brother."

Hödur took the stave. Then, with Loki guiding his arm, he threw with all his strength. The stave struck Balder on the heart and pierced it. With a cry the beautiful god fell to the earth and lay still.

The gods ran to him in horror, but they could do nothing. Balder the Bright and Beautiful was dead.

Then with sad and tearful faces the gods returned to Frigga and told her the dreadful news. Round Asgard went the whisper: "Loki did it! It was he who killed Balder."

Loki was nowhere to be found. Bitterly did Hödur repent that he had

Specially drawn for this work.

Disguised as an old woman, Loki, the evil god, went to the palace to see Frigga. She greeted
him kindly, thinking he was a poor old dame, and they talked together for some time.

thrown the stave, and angrily did he
call for Loki to come forth. But the
evil god remained well hidden.

Odin was full of grief when he saw
his beloved son lying dead. He looked
round at the assembled gods.

" Who will go down to Helheim, and
beg Hela, Queen of the Dead, to give
up our beloved Balder ? " he asked.

" I will! " cried brave Hermod, and
he stepped forward.

" Go, then! " said Odin. " Bring us
back your news with the best speed
you may."

Hermod saddled his horse, and swift
as lightning galloped off. Down and
down he went, for the road to Helheim
is a slanting one. Dark it was, and
very cold, but Hermod did not
once falter. He thundered over the
noisy river that flows betwixt the
living and the dead, and rode on
until he came to the barred gates of
Helheim.

He dismounted, tightened his saddle-
girths, and remounted. Then, spurring
his horse madly, he leapt over the
great gates at one bound. Then he

stood where no living man had ever
stood before.

He rode on through the City of the
Dead until he came to the palace of
Hela, the Queen. He sought the
banqueting hall, and there, with Balder
at her right hand, sat the dreadful
ruler.

" Sit down and sup with us," said
Hela in her far-away voice. " We
have an honoured guest, as you see.
Balder has come to join us."

Hermod sat down and ate the
strange meal with them. Then, afterwards, sitting on a purple-draped
couch, he spoke with Balder. The god
wished to give him messages to take
back to Asgard, but Hermod would
not listen to them.

" You will be back among us soon,"
he said. " Then you can give your
messages yourself."

Soon Hermod went to speak to Hela.

" Let me take Balder back to
Asgard," he besought her. " The great
All-Father Odin has sent me, for
everyone loves Balder."

Hela laughed a thin, distant laugh.

"If that is so," she said, "let everything weep for him. If everything sheds tears for Balder, he shall return. But if only one thing refuses to weep, then he shall remain with me."

Hermod leapt upon his horse with joy. "All things will weep willingly!" he cried. "I go to take your message."

Swiftly he rode out of Helheim, and galloped up the long dark road to Asgard. The gods were all waiting for him, and when they heard his message they were glad.

"Everything will weep!" they cried. "For all things and all people love Balder the Beautiful!"

Straightway the gods themselves began to weep bitterly. Frigga sent out her messenger maidens, the Valkyries, bidding them to go everywhere in the world, and tell all things and all men to weep.

The maidens flew off, and soon all men knew of Balder's death and shed tears of sorrow. Even the stony giants wept too. Then the Valkyries told their message to the sea, to the fields and hills, to the marshes and mountains. Everything wept. Not even a stone was there that did not ooze out a tear for the dead god.

Then Odin went to fetch Balder. Everything wept, and he himself had tears in his one good eye. The other he had given long ago in exchange for wisdom. Down the rocky road to

Specially drawn for this work.

Odin was full of grief when he saw his son lying dead. He looked round at the assembled gods. "Who," he asked, "will go and beg Hela, Queen of the Dead, to give up our beloved Balder?"

A MESSAGE FROM THE KING

Hermod went to speak to Hela the Queen. "Let me take Balder back to Asgard," he besought her. "The great All-Father Odin has sent me, for everyone loves Balder." Hela laughed a thin, distant laugh. "If that is so," she said, "let everything weep for him."

Helheim he went, eager to fetch his best-beloved son back to all his former happiness.

On the way down, he came to a dark and noisome cave. At the entrance sat an evil-looking crone, whose long black hair hung in tails around her wrinkled face.

She peered at Odin as he came, and laughed to see him stumble on the stony path.

"Do not laugh, witch," said Odin. "Do you not know that Balder is dead? Has not the message reached your ears? If all things weep, he will come back again to us. Weep bitter tears, old witch, wail loudly! You are the only one who does not weep."

But the evil old woman cackled all the more.

"I will not weep for Balder!" she said. "You and his many friends shall not have him back! He shall stay in Helheim!"

Odin looked at her in despair, but nothing he could say would make her weep. Then, with a last long laugh, she leapt up and ran as fast as she could go down to Helheim, disappearing in the dark mists.

Then Odin knew who the witch was. She was no other than wicked Loki, who had hidden away and disguised himself as the old crone. The All-Father turned away with a heavy heart.

Hela's voice came to him from the walls of Helheim.

"One has not wept," she said mockingly. "Helheim must keep its own, for my wishes have not been obeyed. Return whence you came, Odin, and mourn for Balder."

Sadly Odin went back to Asgard, and bitterly did he mourn for the bright and beautiful god. But Balder was not lost for ever. There came a day, long after, when he returned, and great was the happiness in Asgard then.

Specially drawn for this work.

On his way along the rocky road Odin came to a dark and noisome cave. At the entrance sat an evil-looking crone, who peered at Odin as he came. "I will not weep for Balder," she said.

Fable,
Myth
and
Legend

Tales
from
the
Greek

Specially drawn for this work.

Midas fell upon his knees before the god and begged for the Golden Touch. "Grant that every-thing I touch may be turned to gold," he pleaded. "Then I shall be the richest man in the world, and the happiest."

THE KING WITH THE GOLDEN TOUCH

THERE was once a king called Midas, who loved gold more than anything else in the world. He spent most of his time in the treasury counting his riches and fondling his precious stones.

One day, wandering in the palace grounds, he met an old man called Silenus, a friend of the god Bacchus. Silenus was lost, and had no idea where he was. Midas took pity on the old man and led him safely back to Bacchus.

The god was delighted to see his friend again, and thanked Midas.

"Ask me any boon you wish and it shall be granted," said Bacchus.

Then Midas fell upon his knees before the god, and begged for the Golden Touch.

"Grant that everything I touch may be turned to gold," he pleaded. "Then I shall be the richest man in the world, and the happiest."

"The richest, certainly, but not the happiest," said Bacchus. "Your wish is granted, Midas. To-morrow morning at sunrise you shall have the Golden Touch."

Trembling with excitement and joy, the king went back to his palace. He could hardly wait for the night to come. When he lay down, he found that he could not sleep, so anxious was he for the dawn to arrive.

At last the rays from the rising sun

357

Specially drawn for this work.

The little Princess cried bitterly to see her doll changed to gold. "Hush, child," said King Midas, "she is prettier than she was."

came slanting through the eastern windows. Midas stretched out his hand and touched the sheet. It turned to shining gold!

"I have the Golden Touch!" cried the king in joy. Up he sprang and began to touch everything around him. Chairs, tables, carpets, vases, curtains, all became gold. Hurriedly the king dressed himself. His clothes turned to heavy gold as he put them on, and they seemed very heavy. But little he cared for that—were they not precious gold?

He went to the dining hall, and saw his breakfast being prepared. His little daughter was not yet down, so he passed out into the garden. The roses were beautiful, but Midas thought they would be even more lovely if he changed them to gold. So he touched them, and at once they stood stiff and scentless on their branches, as yellow as the sunshine itself.

The king was happy. He went once more into the dining hall, and on his little daughter's chair saw her doll. Thinking to prepare a splendid surprise for his child, he touched the doll, and in a trice it had changed to gold.

A minute later the little princess came into the hall, crying.

"The roses in the garden are dead," she sobbed. "They have lost their lovely colours and scents, and are yellow and stiff. I loved them, and I am sad."

Then she saw her golden doll, and snatched it up with a scream.

"Oh, what has happened to my doll?" she cried. "She is changed."

"Hush, child," said King Midas. "Can you not see that she is made of gold? She is prettier than she was before."

But the little princess would not be comforted. She cried bitterly to see her doll so changed. The king frowned and began his breakfast. But what was this! Every time he tried to eat or drink anything, it changed at once to gold!

The bread became hard and yellow. The fish changed to solid metal. The honey was uneatable. In horror, Midas stared at the food. Did this mean he was to starve?

The little princess saw that her father was miserable, and she ran to him. The king took her into his arms and kissed her. In a moment she was stiff and heavy—turned to shining gold!

Then indeed did sorrow come to Midas. What was gold compared to his little daughter? There she stood, a small golden statue.

Midas began to weep bitterly, for he saw that he had been very foolish. Bacchus had been right; gold did not bring happiness. The Golden Touch had brought the king misery, and since he could not eat, he must die of starvation.

Midas ordered his carriage and drove off to beseech Bacchus to help him. The carriage turned to gold, and the horses wondered at the sudden weight. Soon the king leapt out and entered the house of the god.

"Take away the Golden Touch," he besought him. "I cannot bear it."

"I thought you would find you were wrong!" said Bacchus. "Go to the River Pactolus at sundown and bathe there. You will find the Golden Touch has gone as soon as you come from the waters."

Impatiently the king waited for sundown. At last it came, and he hurried into the river. As he came forth from the water after bathing, he felt as if a great load had been lifted from him. He raised his hand and touched a white flower on a tree. It remained white! The Golden Touch was gone.

Then swiftly the king filled an ewer with water from the river and threw it over his little daughter. In a trice she changed back to her sweet self.

Soon nothing remained to show that he had had the Golden Touch—save only the sands of the river, which had turned to gold beneath his feet, and have remained so to this day.

Specially drawn for this work.

The King came forth from the water after bathing. He raised his hand and touched a white flower on a tree. It remained white!

THE STORY OF MERCURY AND ARGUS

Specially drawn for this work.

There was a quarrel between Jupiter, King of Heaven, and Juno, his Queen. Juno was jealous of a river nymph, called Io; and, to save her from the Queen's anger, Jupiter changed the maiden into a pretty white heifer.

LONG, long ago, when Jupiter was King of Heaven and Juno was his Queen, there was a quarrel between them. Juno was jealous of a river nymph called Io, and to save her from the Queen's anger, Jupiter changed the maiden into a pretty white heifer.

But Juno felt certain that the heifer was really Io, and she resolved to have her watched. So she called Argus the Watchman to her. This man had a hundred eyes, and even when he was asleep they were not all closed. At least two were always open.

"Watch the heifer for me," commanded Juno. "See that she does not escape."

So all day long Argus kept watch. Io's brothers and sisters, who lived near by, came to pat the pretty creature though they did not know it was their own sister. Then one day poor Io, longing to make herself known to them, scraped her name in the dusty earth with her foot. "I O" she wrote, and then her family knew her to be Io.

Argus saw this and took her away to a distant hillside. Then, sitting down by the cool hedge, he set himself to watch her even more closely.

Jupiter was sorry for Io. He did not dare to change her back into her own shape whilst Argus was watching, but he longed to get her away, for he saw that she was unhappy.

He called Mercury, his messenger, to him.

"Go to Argus the Watchman, and see if you can send him to sleep, so that all his eyes close at once," he commanded.

So Mercury flew off. When he came near to Argus, he changed himself into a shepherd. Then, taking a shepherd's pipe in his hand, he strolled along the hedge towards the watchman, playing a merry tune.

Argus was glad to see someone, for his work was lonely and dull. The shepherd sat down by him and talked. Then he played again on his pipe— not merry tunes this time, but soft,

THE MAN WITH A HUNDRED EYES

Specially drawn for this work.

Mercury changed himself into a shepherd and strolled up to Argus the Watchman. The shepherd sat down by Argus and talked. Then he played soft, sleepy melodies on his pipe so that soon some of the watchman's eyes closed.

Specially drawn for this work.

Poor Argus had all his hundred eyes taken from him and Juno put them into her pea- cocks' tails.

sleepy melodies that caused Argus to yawn.

Soon some of the watchman's eyes closed. Mercury played more softly. He was glad to see quite half the eyes of Argus shut tightly. He put aside his pipe and began to tell stories. They were long, droning tales, dull and hard to follow. Argus listened and felt sleepier than ever. The sun was hot and the air was heavy. The watchman longed to sleep.

One by one his eyes closed. At last all were shut, save two. These twinkled brightly and Mercury thought despair- ingly that they would never shut. He took up his pipe again, and played such a dreamy tune that Argus could no longer keep awake. His last pair of eyes closed, and he was fast asleep!

Swiftly and silently Mercury ran to Io. He took her to Jupiter, who quickly changed her back into her own shape and sent her happily to her family.

Soon Juno saw here there, and ran to see whether the heifer was still being guarded by Argus. She looked around but it was not in the field. The god- dess gave a cry of anger, for she knew that in some way Jupiter had taken the heifer and changed her back into her own shape once more. And now, where was Argus?

Juno found him under the hedge, fast asleep in the hot sunshine, his eyes tightly closed. Never had the goddess known all his hundred eyes to close at once, and she was amazed and angry.

In great wrath she awoke him.

"You have lost the heifer!" she said in anger. "She has been stolen away whilst you slept. Of what use to you are your hundred eyes? I shall take them away from you and give them to my peacocks."

She kept her word. Poor Argus had all his hundred eyes taken from him, and Juno put them into her peacocks' tails. There they are to this day, as you will see when next you look at a peacock.

PHAETON AND THE SUN=HORSES

Specially drawn for this work.

Phaeton scarcely heeded his father. He leapt into the chariot, shook the reins and drove off. The horses galloped at headlong speed into the sky, and people looking upwards said: " The Sun has risen ! "

THERE was once a little boy whose father was Apollo the sun-god. His mother was a mortal woman and lived alone with her son in a country village. She often showed Phaeton, the boy, the golden sun-chariot in the sky, which, she told him, was his father's.

Phaeton told the other children this, but they laughed at him in scorn.

" We do not believe you," they said. " If Apollo really is your father, why does he not come to see you ? "

Phaeton was unhappy when the children scorned him. He ran to his mother and begged her to let him go and visit his father. His mother agreed, and he set out on the long journey to the palace of the sun-god.

At last he arrived there and walked boldly in through the gleaming doors. Apollo was seated on a throne at the end of the great hall. He wore a crown so dazzling that Phaeton could not bear to look at it, for it blinded him.

Apollo saw the boy, and took off his crown so that the child might come nearer.

" Who are you ? " he asked, for the boy was handsome and his body was strong and beautiful.

" I am your son," said the child proudly. " Do you not know me, father ? "

Then Apollo knew his son, and held out his arms to him. Gladly Phaeton went to them, and soon he was seated on the sun-god's knee, telling him all that the children of the village had said.

" Dear child," said Apollo fondly, " ask me anything you would like, and you shall have it. You shall show these children that you are indeed my son."

He clasped the boy closer, for he was glad to see him. Phaeton looked into his father's face and asked his wish.

" Father," he said, " let me drive your great sun-horses to-morrow. Then my playmates will indeed know that I am your son ! "

" No, no ! " cried Apollo. " Ask me anything but that ! My horses are strong and wild, and only my hand can calm them. You would be dashed to death, my son."

" You promised to grant me any-thing I asked," said Phaeton. " A god cannot break his word, oh, my father. But do not fear—I am a strong youth, and will drive your horses well for you."

So the boy spoke in his foolishness. Little did he know the wildness of the great sun-horses. Apollo grieved when he heard the youth beseeching him. He could not break his word, but he knew that no child could hope to hold the sun-horses.

The next morning, when Dawn had opened the doors of the sun-palace, the horses were led to where Apollo waited for them. Phaeton waited by him, eager to take the reins.

" Drive in the middle way," said Apollo gravely. " Do not go too high, nor too low."

Phaeton scarcely heeded him. He leapt into the chariot, shook the reins, and drove off. The horses galloped at headlong speed into the sky, and people looking upwards said: " The sun has risen! "

But soon the horses knew that Apollo was not driving them, for the boy was light and small, and the chariot was not kept steady, but was tossed about from side to side. The horses took fright and began to leave the middle way of the sky.

They plunged down towards earth, and with fire streaming from their nostrils scraped against the mountain-tops. They scorched them, and then went lower still. Rivers dried up in the dreadful heat of the sun-chariot, and men and women shrank in fear, thinking that the end of the world had come. So near did the chariot go to the earth in Africa that the people there were burned black, and have remained so to this day.

Phaeton was frightened, for he knew he could not manage the horses. His hair was on fire, and the boy did not know what to do. Then the wild steeds leapt up towards the stars and galloped among them, mad with fear.

Specially drawn for this work.

Phaeton's mother often showed the boy the golden sun-chariot in the sky which, she told him, belonged to his father. He begged her to let him go and visit his father.

Phaeton pulled on the reins in despair, but the fierce horses paid no heed. The boy tried to remember their names, so that he might call to them—but he could not think of even one, so frightened was he.

Higher and higher rolled the chariot. Now there were stars all around, and Phaeton gazed in fear. So strange was the sight that the boy suddenly loosed his hold on the reins and sank down upon his knees. He buried his face in his hands and groaned. How came he to have thought that such a lad as he could manage animals as fierce as these?

The horses felt the reins loosen, and more and more madly they galloped among the bright stars. The chariot rocked to and fro, and Phaeton was nearly flung out.

Then Jupiter, the King of Heaven, saw the sun-chariot lost among the stars and gazed in amazement. Why should the god Apollo drive there?

Then he saw that it was no god driving the horses, but a youth, who could no longer even hold the reins. Jupiter grew pale, for he knew that unless something were done swiftly, the whole world would perish.

He called for a thunderbolt, and when this was brought, he hurled it straight at the thundering chariot. It struck Phaeton full on the shoulder, and with a despairing cry he fell headlong out. Down he fell to earth, like a shooting star, his hair blazing. The River Eridanus swallowed him up, and he was drowned.

Then the god Apollo whistled loud and long to his horses, and cried out to them. They heard his stern voice and piercing whistle, and wheeled about in the sky. Then swiftly they galloped betwixt the stars and returned, panting and fearful, to their master. The god leapt into the chariot, and took hold of the reins. Then he drove the horses into their stable, and darkness descended upon the earth full six hours too soon.

"Alas for Phaeton!" said Apollo, with tears in his bright eyes. "Never again shall any other hand but mine take the reins of the wild sun-horses!"

Specially drawn for this work.

Phaeton arrived at the palace of the sun-god. He walked boldly in through the gleaming doors and saw Apollo seated on a throne. "Who are you?" asked Apollo. "I am your son," said the child proudly.

ECHO AND NARCISSUS

ONCE upon a time there lived a beautiful nymph called Echo. She was a great chatterbox, and was very fond of having the last word. One day she spoke rudely to Juno, the Queen of Heaven, and a curious punishment fell upon her.

"You are too fond of talking," said Juno angrily. "You are so anxious to have the last word that you forget to be polite. You must be punished. In future you shall never speak except to repeat the last words of other people, and unless someone bids you show yourself, you are not to come forth from your hiding place. Now go to the mountains, and let me see you no more."

"No more," repeated Echo sadly, and went away to the mountains.

Yet at first she was happy enough in the lovely woods on the hillsides of Greece, nor was she alone. She found other beings like herself there with whom she could sport and dance despite the disability she suffered because of the orders she had received as part of her punishment imposed by Juno.

In the woods there were the tree-spirits called Dryads, as well as the fountain spirits known as Naiads, little mischievous fauns, half-boy and half-goat. There was, too, the great Pan, lord of all wild birds and beasts, and having a sweet voice and music-making hands.

But to Echo he was ugly because although his body was like a man's, his legs were those of a goat and he had the horns of a goat.

This wood god fell in love with Echo, but she scorned him, and his sweet music as he played his pipes brought no pleasure to her. And presently Echo wandered away from the dancing Naiads and pined for her old companions in the court of Jupiter and Juno from which she had been banished.

For a time she kept in hiding among the rocks and bushes. When she saw hunters coming merrily by, she longed to talk with them, but alas ! she could only repeat their last words. She could say nothing that she wanted to tell them. All that she could do was to repeat the last words they spoke.

Then one day, as she sat sorrowfully by herself, she saw a beautiful youth coming up the mountainside. He was called Narcissus, and was glorious to look upon. His hair curled thickly about his head, his eyes were as bright as the morning dew, and he was as strong and graceful as a god. Echo fell in love with him at once and longed to speak to him.

Specially drawn for this work.

As a punishment for having spoken rudely to Juno, the Queen of Heaven, Echo was sent into the mountains; and, in the words of the Queen, she must " never speak except to repeat the last words of other people."

Specially drawn for this work.

All that day Echo walked unseen near Narcissus and peered out at him from bushes and from behind rocks.

She determined to follow him, and hoped that perhaps he might hear her footsteps and call her to him. She knew that she must not show herself until she was bidden to come forth.

All that day Echo walked unseen near Narcissus, and peered out at him from bushes and from behind rocks. He began to feel that someone was near him, and at last he called out.

" Who is there ? " he cried.

" There ! " said Echo, repeating his last word.

" Why do you hide ? " asked Narcissus.

" Hide ! " answered Echo.

" Come out to me here ! " cried Narcissus, puzzled.

" Here ! " said Echo gladly, and she came from her hiding place as she had been bidden.

The nymph ran to Narcissus, and would have flung her arms around his neck, but he pushed her roughly away. He cared for no one but himself, for he was vain and conceited. He would not look at Echo's pleading eyes. He thought she mocked him when she repeated his last words, and he was angry with her.

" Go away ! " he said roughly, and turned to a lovely pool that lay near-by, for he was thirsty.

Echo could only answer, " Away ! " and go back to her hiding place. She had no words to tell Narcissus of her broken heart, nor could she explain why it was that she could only repeat his last words. As she sadly glided away, she wished with all her heart that the vain youth might fall in love himself; and, in his turn, be scorned. Then he would know how sad she felt, and would perhaps be sorry for her.

Narcissus thought no more of the sad nymph. He lay down by the crystal-clear pool to drink. And then, in the shadowy depths, he saw a beautiful face looking up at him. The eyes were bright and very lovely, and the hair curled thickly round the white brow. Narcissus thought that a beau-

tiful water-nymph was gazing up at
him, and he was delighted.

He did not know that it was simply
his own reflection looking back at him
from the water. In those days there
were no mirrors, and people only knew
what they looked like from the crooked
reflections in their shining battle-
shields. Narcissus had never seen himself clearly, and he did not recognise
his own face now. He was certain
that it was some lovely nymph, and he
fell in love with her face at once, even
as Echo had fallen in love with his.

He called aloud to the nymph in the
pool and begged her to come to him.
He saw her lips move as his did, and
he stretched his arms out into the
water. At once the reflection was
broken, and Narcissus saw that the
face was gone. He waited until the
water was still again, and then once
more saw the lovely face.

All day long he lay by the side of the
pool, begging the nymph to come out
of the water and sit beside him. When
she would not, he was sad. At night,
when the moon rose and lighted up
the water with its cold beams, Narcissus
was still there. He peered into the
pool and saw the beautiful face looking
up at him again.

Day after day Narcissus lay by the
water, and begged the nymph to love
him. He did not once guess that she
was only his own reflection. He forgot
to eat, and very soon he grew pale and
weak. It seemed to him that the
nymph in the pool grew pale too, and this
made him sad. But nothing he could
say or do would make her leave the pool.

Echo kept near him all the time,
sighing when Narcissus sighed and
echoing his sad words. She was sorry
now that her wish had come true, and
would have unwished it if she could.

She could not bear to leave him yet
she was afraid to show herself. All
that she could do was to echo his last
words.

Soon Narcissus died, for he had not
left the pool once since he had first

Specially drawn for this work.

Narcissus began to feel that someone was
near him. " Who is there ? " he cried.
" There ! " said Echo, repeating his last word.

seen the lovely face. When the gods saw the lovely youth lying dead by the water, they were sorry for him, and changed his beautiful white body into a flower. You know it well—it is the lovely white narcissus, which, when it grows beside a pool, bends over to look at itself, even as the youth Narcissus did long years ago.

Echo was full of sadness when Narcissus died. She looked lovingly at the white flowers that grew by the pool, and touched them sorrowfully.

"Never shall I come forth into the world again!" sighed the nymph. "For sorrow of Narcissus I will hide myself away in the mountains. None shall see me again—only my voice shall men hear, repeating always their last words."

Then Echo slipped away among the hills. All day long she was alone, sorrowing for Narcissus. She ate nothing, and soon faded away to a shadow. Longing to die, she wandered into the lonely places among the mountains, far from the haunts of her former companions. There, brooding over her sorrow, she pined away until nothing remained but her lovely voice.

The gods were displeased at what they thought was her lack of proper pride, and they condemned her to haunt the rocks and caverns and lonely places, her voice repeating the last sounds she heard. This voice we hear still, calling mournfully among the hills—but never does it say anything save our last words. When we shout loudly, and our cry comes back, we stop and say: "Hark! Do you hear the echo?"

But the nymph herself we shall never see.

Specially drawn for this work.

ECHO AND NARCISSUS BY THE POOL

Echo kept near him all the time, sighing when Narcissus sighed and echoing his sad words.

Fable,
Myth
and
Legend

Tales from
the Iliad
and
the Odyssey

Specially drawn for this work.

Paris, the shepherd lad, looked on the three goddesses. Then he held out the apple to Aphrodite, and eagerly she took it with a mocking glance at the other two. Then all three vanished into the night. The shepherd had won one friend, but had made two enemies.

THE SHEPHERD PRINCE OF TROY

LONG ago there lived a shepherd lad called Paris. He dwelt on a hill-side, tending his sheep. He was very fair to look upon and was strong and sturdy.

One night something strange happened to him. He was lying down guarding his sheep, when a bright light shone out beside him. In amazement, he leapt to his feet. In the midst of the shining light was Athene, the great goddess of wisdom!

As he gazed upon her in awe, another goddess appeared beside her, Hera, the lovely Queen of Heaven. Then a third goddess shone dazzlingly in the midst, and Paris fell upon his knees. It was Aphrodite, the rosy goddess of Love.

" Rise up, Paris," said Hera. " We have come to thee for judgment. This golden apple, which I now give into thy hand, belongs to the fairest of us three. Look well upon us, and choose. If thou choosest me, I will give thee great power and endless might."

" Choose me and I will give thee wisdom," said Athene.

Then beautiful Aphrodite smiled on the dazzled shepherd lad and spoke in her turn.

" Give the apple to me," she said, " for am I not the fairest? If thou wilt give me the apple, I will make thee a prince, and thou shalt have the loveliest woman in the world to be thy wife! "

The shepherd looked on the three goddesses. Then he held out the apple

24—2

to Aphrodite, and eagerly she took it, with a mocking glance at the other two. Then all three vanished into the night. Paris had won one friend, but had made two enemies.

Aphrodite kept her promise to the shepherd. When he went down to the City of Troy to take part in the sports there, he defeated everyone but the eldest son of the king. Then suddenly a strange cry was heard, and Cassandra, the king's daughter, pointed to Paris.

" See! " she cried to King Priam. " Is not this shepherd lad thine own long-lost son, he who was put out on the hills when a babe ? See how like he is to thee, oh king! Surely he is thy son ? "

Paris listened, startled. Cassandra's words were true. He was indeed the king's own son. When a babe, he had been left on the hillside by a slave, and a bear had found him and tended him with her own cubs. He had grown up thinking himself to be but a poor shepherd lad.

Now life was altogether different for him. He was made a prince, and very royal he looked in his splendid clothes. King Priam made much of his new son, and everyone honoured him.

Soon Priam gave him a fleet of ships and sent him voyaging to Greece. Paris sailed off proudly, happy to be in command of so many fine galleys. He came in due time to Sparta, where King Menelaus held court with his beautiful wife, Helen.

Menelaus welcomed the handsome young prince and bade him stay at Sparta. Helen welcomed him also, and the youth stayed with the royal pair, honoured and praised by all.

But he repaid Menelaus ill for his kindness. Helen was so beautiful that Paris fell deeply in love with her, and she with him. Never had there been so lovely a woman as this queen, and the goddess Aphrodite, remembering her promise to Paris, caused her to forget her loving husband and to agree to all that the prince said.

" Fly with me," begged Paris. " Leave Sparta, and thy husband, and come to

Specially drawn for this work.

One night when Paris was lying down and guarding his sheep a bright light shone out beside him. In the midst of the light was Athene, the goddess of wisdom.

Specially drawn for this work.

Cassandra, the King's daughter, pointed to Paris. " See! " she cried to King Priam. " Is not this shepherd lad thine own long-lost son, he who was put out on the hills when a babe ? See how like he is to thee, oh king! "

my galleys. We will sail to Troy, and there thou shalt be my wife and be worshipped by all."

Helen consented, and when Menelaus had gone on a long journey, she fled away with Paris. Forgotten was her honour, forgotten her husband and little daughter. She loved the handsome young prince, and thought only of him.

King Priam of Troy was angry when he heard what Paris had done, for he knew that there would be war. But when he saw Helen's beautiful face, he consented to fight for her.

When Menelaus returned to Sparta and found that his lovely wife had fled with Paris, he was mad with anger. He vowed that he would win her back again, and straightway sent messages to his friends to come and help him fight against Troy.

All the Greek kings and princes heard his call and answered it. They came to his aid, bringing men and ships in plenty—men for fighting and

ships to take them across the purple seas to Troy.

The men that came were heroes whose names were well-known and much feared. There was mighty Achilles, whose awful strength was feared by all his enemies, and against whom none could stand in battle. There was the giant-like Ajax, whom none could equal in courage. There was Diomedes the brave, and Patroklus the courageous friend of Achilles. Nestor came, he whose counsel was wiser than any other's, and Odysseus the cunning, whose mind was full of guile.

Agamemnon was the chief, for he was a powerful king and a very strong and mighty warrior. Under his command all the princes stood, trusting him and obeying his behests. Thousands of men embarked in the galleys lying in the harbours of Sparta, and at last the day came when Agamemnon gave the command to set forth over the sea to Troy.

The Trojans heard of this mighty

Specially drawn for this work.

"Fly with me," begged Paris, and Helen consented. Forgotten were her husband and little daughter. She loved the handsome young Prince, and thought only of him.

Specially drawn for this work.

Paris and Helen and the people of Troy lined the city walls and watched the great fleet drawing into shore. They marvelled when they saw what hosts of men had come to do battle with them.

army, and many were the hard words sent after Prince Paris as he walked through the streets of the city. But none spoke against the lovely Helen.

As soon as the Trojans saw the great fleet coming over the sea, they made fast the gates of Troy, and every man took up his arms. Hector, son of the king, was made the chief, for he was brave and bold.

The people of Troy lined the city walls and watched the fleet drawing into shore. It was a brave sight, but the Trojans feared to see so many ships. Never had such a fleet sailed against them before, and the men of Troy marvelled when they saw what hosts of men had come to do battle with them.

Ship by ship the Greeks drew in. Soon the galleys lay in lines by the shore, and the men landed, glad to stretch their legs once more. A great camp was made, and many fires began to burn, the black smoke streaming out against the deep blue sky. The plain between the city of Troy and the sea was bright with shining armour, and the Trojans wondered to see it.

Then began the great Siege of Troy. The battles that were fought there resounded down the ages, and even to-day we seem to hear the shouts of the mighty Achilles, the clash of armour and the groans of the fallen. Not only men fought in these battles, but gods and goddesses too. Aphrodite fought for the Trojans, but Hera and Athene fought for the Greeks.

Mighty were the battles and great were the deeds done. Most daring of all were the deeds of brave Diomedes, and of these you shall hear.

DIOMEDES THE BRAVE

Specially drawn for this work.

" Quick, Diomedes," cried the charioteer, "let us fly." "I will not fly," said the brave Greek,
grasping his shield tightly. " I will stay here and slay them."

MANY were the brave deeds done at the Siege of Troy. Both Trojans and Greeks acquitted themselves well, but few equalled the daring of bold Diomedes, for he fought not only with men, but with the gods themselves.

It came to pass that on a day when chariots thundered towards each other across the plain, Diomedes stood beside his charioteers, his helmet flashing brightly. His war-cry rang out loudly, and both Greek and Trojan marvelled to hear it. Athene the goddess was with him, for she loved brave men.

When he came near to the foe, Diomedes sprang from his chariot and faced them. A Trojan chariot came by bearing two famous warriors, and one of them, seeing Diomedes standing there, threw his spear at him. It glanced over his shoulder and missed him.

Diomedes turned and straightway hurled his spear at the Trojan. It struck him on the chest and he fell dead to the ground. His brother at once leapt down and fled away, fearing to be slain also. Diomedes sprang into the splendid Trojan chariot and drove it to his men, bidding them keep it for him till after the battle.

Into the fight went Diomedes once more, raging like a torrent in springtime, so that none could stand against him. A great archer, called Pandarus, saw him, and resolved to slay him. Swiftly he fitted an arrow to his bow and shot it. It struck the Greek, and in a trice his corselet was dabbled with red blood.

" Ho! He is hit! " shouted Pandarus loudly in triumph. " See, Trojans, here is the mightiest of the Greeks wounded and about to die! "

Diomedes descended from his chariot and spoke to his charioteer.

" Take this stinging arrow from my shoulder, I pray thee! " he said. At once the driver did so, and Diomedes clapped his hand over the wound to stop it bleeding.

" Oh, Athene! " cried the Greek in pain, " bring me to the man whose arrow smote me, I beseech thee! "

Soon Diomedes sprang once more into his chariot and rushed against the Trojans. He slew many mighty warriors and fought like a lion.

Æneas, one of the captains of the Trojan force, son of Aphrodite, saw Diomedes dealing death, and blazed with anger.

He went to Pandarus the archer, he who had wounded Diomedes, and spoke scornfully to him.

" Art thou not famed for thy bow ? " he asked. " Why, then, dost thou not loose an arrow and slay this raging Greek ? "

" Once have I struck him with an arrow and his corselet was crimsoned," answered Pandarus. " But still he rushes on his enemies more like a god than a man ! "

" We will go together in thy chariot and fight this mad Greek," said Æneas. " Mount, Pandarus, and I will drive thee near to him. Then shalt thou hurl thy spear at him and stay him in his fighting."

Pandarus leapt into the chariot, taking his strong spear with him. Æneas shook the reins and the mighty horses thundered through the hosts towards Diomedes. That brave warrior was standing near his charioteer, who cried out in fear when he saw the chariot bearing down upon them.

" Quick, Diomedes ! " he cried. " Let us fly to our chariot, for here come two mighty Trojans, Æneas and Pandarus."

" I will not fly," said Diomedes, grasping his shield tightly. " I will stay here and slay them ! If I am victor, see that thou takest their horses, for they are beautiful, and I would have them for mine."

The Trojan chariot thundered near, and Pandarus flung his spear straight at Diomedes. It smote his shield and pierced it.

" He is hit, he is slain ! " cried Pandarus in triumph. But Diomedes laughed scorn-

fully. He sent his spear at the archer, and it struck him and slew him at once. Down he fell from the chariot, his armour clanging. The lovely horses plunged in fear, but Æneas reined them in. Then he sprang down and planted his great legs across the archer's dead body; and, like a mountain lion, stood there to defend it.

Diomedes saw a huge stone lying near him, so heavy that two men could scarce lift it to-day. He picked it up with ease and flung it swiftly at Æneas. Down fell the brave Trojan, and everything went black around him. Diomedes ran at him to slay him, but the goddess Aphrodite, mother of Æneas, picked him up from the ground and bore him away from his foe.

Diomedes ran after her and smote

Specially drawn for this work.

Diomedes stood beside his charioteer, his helmet flashing brightly. His war-cry rang out, and both Greek and Trojan marvelled to hear it.

her on her snow-white wrist. She dropped Æneas with a cry and fled. Another god seized the Trojan and was carrying him away to safety, when bold Diomedes sought to prevent him. He could not see the god who held Æneas, but fiercely he struck at the place in which he thought the rescuer stood.

Suddenly a great and terrible voice thundered out:

"Beware, beware, thou bold Greek! Thou art warring with a god!"

Diomedes dared no more and drew back afraid.

Then came many gods and goddesses down to the battle, and warred with one another and with the Greeks and Trojans, some on one side and some on the other. Men held off in fear, for they knew the gods were among them and dreaded to meet them.

Soon Athene sought for Diomedes, and found him wiping the blood from one of his wounds.

"Why art thou afraid to join the battle?" she asked.

"I fear nothing," answered Diomedes, "but when the gods fight, wise men look on."

"Come with me and thou shalt fight the god Mars," said Athene eagerly. "He is leading the Trojans now, and I would have him punished. Leap into thy chariot, oh Diomedes, and I will myself drive thee to him."

Specially drawn for this work.

Diomedes descended from his chariot and spoke to his charioteer. "Take this stinging arrow from my shoulder," he said bravely.

Diomedes obeyed her, and fiercely she drove the chariot towards the god Mars. Mars turned to meet the Greek, and cast his great spear at him. Then would Diomedes have been slain outright, but Athene deftly caught the weapon and twisted it aside, so that the point glanced away from him and the spear fell harmlessly to the ground.

"Now hurl your weapon at Mars!" commanded Athene. "I will guide it, and you must put forth all your might."

Then Diomedes lifted his spear, and with all his strength flung it at the threatening god. Athene guided it, and it pierced Mars in the thigh, wounding him sorely.

The war-god let forth such a fearful cry of anguish that it sounded like a hundred thunderclaps. Then, with his hand pressed to his wounded side, he swept from the battlefield up to the sky, and men, watching him, likened him to a great storm cloud.

For a space the battle paused, for all men were full of amaze and terror to see the wounded god, and to hear his dreadful cry.

But soon the fight went on, and once more weapons gleamed brightly in the sun. And on every lip was the name of Diomedes, brave Diomedes, who stayed not his hand for men or gods.

Specially drawn for this work.

Mars the war-god let forth such a fearful cry of anguish that it sounded like a hundred thunder-claps. Then he swept from the battlefield up to the sky; and men, watching him, likened him to a great storm cloud

THE WOODEN HORSE OF TROY

Sinon, the Greek who had been left behind to deceive the Trojans, was discovered hiding under the horse. He was dragged forth and questioned. " What is this horse that the Greeks have left behind ? " the Trojans asked him.

FOR ten long years the Siege of Troy went on. Sometimes the Trojans defeated the Greeks and drove them back towards the sea, and at other times the Greeks drove the Trojans into their city.

Then spoke Odysseus, the wily Greek.

" If we cannot take Troy by force, let us take it by cunning," he said. " Here is my plan: Let us tell Epeios, the clever builder, to build us a great wooden horse. Inside it we will put our bravest warriors. Then we will burn our camps, enter our ships, and pretend to sail away, leaving behind us the wooden horse.

" By it we will leave a traitor, and he shall tell the Trojans we have gone away, and that the horse is an offering to the great goddess Athene. Then they will drag it into their city, and in the midst of the night, the warriors inside shall open the gates, and set fire to Troy. We, in our ships, will come stealing back again, and will slay every Trojan in the city! "

This plan was carried out. Epeios set to work to build a great horse. It was a gigantic monster, and in its eyes and ears were set red and green stones. The Trojans watched the horse being built, and were puzzled to know what it was.

When it was finished, Odysseus spoke again.

" Who will enter the horse with me ? " he asked.

Then Menelaus sprang to the side of the wily Odysseus. Diomedes followed, he who had fought with gods. Then many other brave warriors joined the daring band, and soon they all climbed into the wooden horse. Epeios, who knew the secret of the opening and shutting of the door, climbed in the last of all and fastened the entrance. Then it was barred outside. The wooden horse was ready!

Soon the Greeks set fire to their camps, and when smoke and flames rose into the sky, they entered their black ships and sailed away, with bold Agamemnon at the head.

The Trojans, who were watching from the walls, were amazed. "The Greeks fly!" they cried in joy. "They have gone! Now we may live in peace!"

They poured out of the city and ran across the plains to the burning camps of the Greeks. They went up to the great wooden horse and gazed at it in amazement.

"What is this?" they cried in wonder. "Why have the Greeks left behind such a strange monster?"

Then Sinon, the Greek who had been left behind to deceive the Trojans, was discovered, hiding under the horse. He was dragged forth and questioned.

"What is this horse that the Greeks have left behind?" the Trojans asked him. At first Sinon pretended that he would not tell, but when they beat him, he delivered his false message.

"This horse was built by the Greeks in honour of Athene," he said. "They wished her to bring home their ships in safety. They wanted to sacrifice me to her, but I escaped and hid beneath the horse, from whence they did not dare to drag me. Thus they left me behind, thinking that I would meet my death from you, oh Trojans!"

"But why did they make the horse so large?" asked the Trojans in wonder.

"They were afraid that if they did not, you would drag it into your city," said Sinon. "Then they knew that Athene would be angry, and would send a storm to destroy their ships. Therefore they built the horse of such a size that it could not enter the gates of Troy."

The listening Trojans believed Sinon.

"Let us break down the city walls and pull the horse into the city!" they cried. "Then will Athene follow after the Greek ships in anger, and destroy them! We need no walls now that the Greeks are gone!"

The foolish Trojans breached their

Specially drawn for this work.

The foolish Trojans breached their walls and began to drag the great wooden horse within the city. On went the horse and at last was within the city of Troy.

Specially drawn for this work

Softly Sinon went to the roof of a building to look over the sea.
He saw what he wanted. The Greek fleet was stealing silently
back over the waters to Troy. The single light at the poops of
the ships was the signal.

commanded King Priam. "Our enemies are gone, and we can sleep in peace to-night."

Then the Trojans began to feast, and laughter and merriment sounded throughout the town. The soldiers inside the horse heard the feasting and longed for the night to come, for they were tired of keeping silent and still.

At last night came. The Trojans, weary with their feasting and merry-making, lay asleep in their houses. No one was on guard. All was silent and dark.

Only Sinon was awake. Softly the traitor went to the roof of a building to look over the sea. He saw what he wanted. The Greek fleet was stealing silently back over the waters to Troy! One single light hung at the poops of Agamemnon's ships, the signal to Sinon of the Greeks' return.

At once Sinon turned and ran down to the silent city. Swiftly he made his way to the gates and flung them open. Then as swiftly he ran to the wooden horse and unbarred the entrance.

Epeios undid the secret door and flung down a rope. One by one the hidden Greeks, weary with their long stillness, slid to the ground. They went to join the hosts of Agamemnon who were pouring in at the gates of Troy. In a trice the city was theirs!

Sinon ran from house to house with

walls and began to drag the great wooden horse within the city. It rumbled over the plain, and the warriors inside trembled for fear the Trojans should hear the clash of their armour. But the enemies were too full of joy to heed anything. On went the horse, and at last was within the great City of Troy itself.

"Let us feast and make merry!"

a torch, and soon flames sprang up, roaring hungrily. Smoke poured into the streets and startled Trojans awoke and sprang up in alarm.

What was this? Fire! Fire! They ran to the doors, and there they saw the fierce Greeks with swords in their hands, ready to slay without mercy. The wretched Trojans were between fire and death.

Cries and groans filled the air. Buildings crashed to the ground. The Greeks were everywhere, slaying and burning, and many a brave Trojan warrior met his death before he knew what was happening. Temples flared to the sky, and the strong city walls broke and fell.

When the night was over, Troy was no more. The Trojans were slain, the Greeks were victorious. Rejoicing, they entered their ships once again, this time to sail away in earnest.

King Menelaus found Helen wandering in the burning streets. She

Specially drawn for this work.

Sinon, the traitor, ran from house to house with a torch and soon flames sprang up within the city, roaring hungrily. Smoke poured into the streets and startled Trojans awoke and sprang up in alarm.

looked so sad and sorrowful to see the dreadful ruin she had caused that he took her into his arms and bore her in safety back to his ship. She sailed away with him to Sparta, where once again he made her his lovely Queen.

Thus ended the long Siege of Troy, and greatly did the departing Greeks rejoice.

Proudly they turned their galleys towards Greece, and sailed away over the purple sea. For many a long year had they been far from home, and many a hero lay on Trojan soil, never to return. But vengeance was done, Troy was burnt, and the lovely Helen was once more to rule her court in Sparta.

Up to the heavens streamed a black pillar of smoke—all that was left of the brave town of Troy.

POLYPHEMUS THE ONE=EYED GIANT

Specially drawn for this work.

Odysseus and his companions fled into the darkest corner of the cave and crouched there in fear.
Driving his flocks before him and carrying a bundle of tree-trunks over his shoulder was a
monstrous giant.   In the middle of his forehead was a gleaming red eye.

WHEN Troy was no more, and the Greek ships sailed proudly away, Odysseus, he who had commanded the building of the Wooden Horse, turned his ships towards Ithaca, his rocky kingdom.   On they sailed over the sea, whilst the Greek captain thought longingly of his lovely wife awaiting him.

When the ships had sailed for some days, they came to a misty island. Odysseus did not know it, but since he wanted to get fresh meat, he commanded his ships to stay in the harbour there whilst he and twelve others landed.

The land he had come to belonged to the Cyclops.   These were great giants, with one red eye set in the middle of their foreheads.   Fierce they were and cruel, merciless to men who were cast up on their island.

Odysseus knew nothing of this.   He bade his men bring with them a goatskin of red wine, so that they might give it in exchange for meat. Then he and his company landed on the shore and made their way inland.

Soon they came to a great cave, overhung with laurel.   Outside there was a sheep-fold, walled in with stone and tree-trunks.   Sheep and lambs lay there, looking at the men with startled eyes.

"See," said one of the men, "here are sheep.   Shall we not take what we want and go, for there is none to hinder us?"

"Not so," said Odysseus.   "We will wait for the owner's return and beg him to give us what we wish, in exchange for our goatskin of wine."

The men entered the cave and looked round it.   It was very high, and up the sides were piled great cheeses. On shelves stood bowls of whey, so large that Odysseus marvelled.

He and his men sat down and waited.   They kindled a fire and ate of the cheeses.   The day passed and the evening came.

Suddenly there sounded a thunderous noise of tramping feet, and Odysseus looked towards the cave's mouth, wondering who was coming.   When he saw, he leapt to his feet in horror. He and his companions fled into the darkest corner of the cave, and crouched there in fear.

Driving his flocks before him into the cave came a monstrous giant.   In the middle of his forehead was a gleaming red eye, shining like a red-hot coal. Over his shoulder he carried a bundle of tree-trunks, which he had brought for firewood.   He flung them down with such a crash that Odysseus was nearly deafened.

The giant kindled a great fire.   When

the flames rose high and lighted up the darkest corners of the cave, he caught sight of the trembling men. Then he cried out in a voice like the roaring of a torrent, and said:

"Who are ye that come to the cave of Polyphemus, and what would ye ask of him?"

Odysseus took courage and answered boldy.

"We are Greeks driven from our course in our voyage from Troy. We have come to beg for meat."

"Where lies your ship?" demanded the giant.

Odysseus knew well that if he told the truth, Polyphemus would at once arise and go forth to destroy his fleet. So he answered cautiously.

"I have no ship," he said. "It is wrecked, and I and my twelve companions escaped by swimming."

Polyphemus spoke no more. He made a sudden dash at the men, seized two, and ate them. Then he lay down to sleep. Odysseus was horrified, and took his sword to kill the cruel monster. But even as he lifted his weapon, he paused.

He remembered the great stone at the entrance of the cave. How would he and his men get out if the giant were killed? The stone was too heavy for them to move. Another plan must be thought of. Odysseus replaced his sword, and sat down to think.

In the morning Polyphemus took two more men and ate them. Then he went forth with his flocks, setting the great stone at the mouth of the cave once more, so that Odysseus and his men were imprisoned.

Then the wily Greek told the others of his plan. "Take one of the tree-trunks," he commanded, "and sharpen it to a point. Then I will harden it in the fire. When the giant lies asleep to-night, I will drive it into his one eye and blind him."

His men did as they were commanded.

Specially drawn for this work

The giant seized two of the men and ate them. Then he lay down to sleep. Odysseus was horrified, and took his sword to kill this cruel monster.

Odysseus put the point into the fire and let it harden. Then he waited for the giant to return.

At nightfall Polyphemus entered with his flocks. Once again he took two men and devoured them. Then, as he was lying down to sleep, Odysseus came to him. He carried in his hands a bowl of the red wine he had brought with him, and he begged Polyphemus to drink it.

The giant gulped the draught down and licked his lips in joy.

"Now, that was a drink fit for the gods," he said. "In return for that, oh Greek, I will eat thee last of all. What is thy name?"

"My name is No-man," answered Odysseus, craftily, for he did not wish Polyphemus to know who he was.

The giant fell asleep, and snored heavily. Odysseus beckoned to his frightened men, and they helped him to thrust the sharpened tree-trunk into the fire, and so made it red-hot; then they drove it fiercely into the monster's one eye, burning it out.

The giant leapt to his feet in pain and began yelling and howling. Odysseus and his men hid away and the monster could not find them, for he was blind. His friends soon heard his yelling and came in alarm to help him.

"Polyphemus, what ails thee?" they cried. "Is anyone harming thee?"

"No-man is harming me!" cried Polyphemus. "No-man has blinded me!"

"What dost thou mean?" cried the giants in astonishment. "If no man is hurting thee, then why dost thou cry like this and wake us from our sleep? Thou art mad!"

They went away and left the giant alone. He sat down at the cave entrance and waited till day. Meanwhile, Odysseus had been busy. He bound three rams together and tied a man underneath the middle one. He did this for each of his six men and then bade them wait until the giant let the flock out of the cave, when the rams would run off in safety with them.

Last of all he chose for himself one beautiful ram, very large and shaggy. He hauled himself underneath the surprised animal, and taking hold of his long fleece, hung there tightly,

Specially drawn for this work.

Odysseus carried in his hands a bowl of red wine and begged Polyphemus to drink it. The one-
eyed giant gulped the draught down and licked his lips in joy.

Specially drawn for this work.

The giant ran to the shore in rage, hurling great stones into the sea, hoping to strike the escaping ships.

waiting patiently for the day to come.

When the sun rose the giant took away the great stone from the entrance and let out his flock. But as the rams passed out, he ran his hands over the back of each one, to see that none of the men was escaping ; but he did not think of feeling underneath. All the men reached the open in safety, and, last of all, Odysseus.

He dropped from his ram and ran to the others. Very quickly he cut the ropes that tied them to their strange steeds. Then they all set off running to the sea-shore, where they had left their ships.

They hurriedly embarked, and soon they were sailing away in safety, rejoicing that they had escaped from the horrible land of giants. As for Polyphemus, he ran to the shore in rage, hurling great stones into the sea, hoping to strike the ships. But he could not see to aim aright, and soon the men were far away.

25—2

ODYSSEUS AND THE ENCHANTRESS CIRCE

Specially drawn for this work.

Circe, the enchantress of the palace, came to the door and smiled upon the sailors. She had long golden hair and bright eyes. She bade the sailors come in and said she would give them food and drink.

ODYSSEUS sailed on and on over the wide seas. One day he came to a fair island, and he and his men landed there. Odysseus climbed a hill, and from the summit saw a column of smoke rising up to the sky from a wood not far away.

He told his men of what he had seen. "We will draw lots," he said. "Half of you shall go to find what manner of men live here, and half of you shall stay by the ship."

So lots were drawn, and the company was divided into two. A man called Eurylochus was put in charge of the band that was to explore the island, while Odysseus himself remained with the rest of the men by the ship.

The company set out. It was not long before they came to the wood that Odysseus had seen from the hill. They entered it, and presently came to a wide clearing. In the centre stood a glittering palace, very fair to look upon. In front of it, pacing up and down, were mountain lions and shaggy wolves. The sailors gazed at them in terror, for they feared to be devoured.

But as soon as the beasts saw them, they ran up to them and fawned upon them, licking them with their rough tongues. They had once been men, but had been changed into beasts by the enchantress of the palace, Circe.

The witch was inside, singing a lovely song in a sweet and tempting voice. The sailors listened and were entranced. They called to her to come out.

Circe came to the door and smiled upon them. She had long golden hair and bright eyes. She bade the sailors come in, and said she would give them food and drink. They followed her, and sat down at the table.

Specially drawn for this work.

The enchantress brought the sailors a drink made of barley-meal, wine, honey and grated cheese, to which she added one drop of a magic drug. As she handed a goblet to each man, she touched him with her wand.

Specially drawn for this work.

"Listen to my words," said Hermes,
messenger of the gods. He stooped and
picked a plant from the ground.

Only Eurylochus stayed behind. He
did not like the look in Circe's bright
eyes, and was afraid. He peered into
the doorway and watched what happened.

The enchantress set food before the
men and brought them a drink made
of barley-meal, wine, honey and grated
cheese, to which she added one drop
of a magic drug. As she handed a
goblet to each man, she touched him
with her wand.

No sooner had the sailors drunk the
magic draught than each one changed
into a grunting pig. But, alas for
them! they still had the minds of men,
and could sorrow and grieve over their
changed state.

Eurylochus saw everything, and in
horror he ran back to Odysseus. He
was so terrified that he could tell his
chief nothing save that a dreadful
witch lived on the island. So Odysseus
took his great sword and set out to
find what had happened to his company
of men.

As he was walking through the wood,
he met a bright-faced youth, who was
Hermes, messenger of the gods. He
stopped Odysseus and bade him not
go lightly into terrible peril.

"Knowest thou that Circe the enchantress has turned thy comrades into
swine?" he said. "Wouldst thou suffer
the same enchantment? Listen to my
words, Odysseus, and thou shalt learn
how to defeat the witch."

Hermes stooped and picked a plant
from the ground. It had a milk-white
flower and a black root. Only the
gods could pick this plant, which was
called Moly, and held much magic.

"See," said Hermes, holding it out
to Odysseus. "Take this plant in thy
hand and go to the palace. None of
Circe's enchantments can harm thee
whilst thou hast this Moly-flower.
When she touches thee with her wand,
draw thy sword and rush upon her as
if thou wouldst slay her. Then she
will tremble before thee, and obey thy
lightest word."

Odysseus took the plant, and promised to do all that Hermes commanded. Then he went on his way once more. Soon he came to where the palace glittered in the sunlight. Circe saw him, and bade him enter.

The Greek followed her into the beautiful hall, and sat down at the long table. The enchantress brought him food to eat and set it before him. Then she mixed him a drink, and took it to him, striking him at the same time with her wand.

At once Odysseus leapt to his feet, drawing his sword. He sprang upon the witch, and made as if he would kill her instantly. She cried out for mercy.

"Thou must be that Odysseus of whom I have heard!" she said. "Pardon me, oh hero of Troy, and I will vow never to practise my magic arts on thee again."

Odysseus set her free. Tremblingly she commanded her servants to prepare a scented bath for the Greek, and to get ready a marvellous feast. But when Odysseus, bathed and clad in fine clothes, sat down once again at the table to feast on the wonderful dishes there, he could eat nothing. He sat mute, not saying a word to the enchantress.

"Art thou sad for thy friends?" she asked him at last. "Wouldst thou have them here with thee, oh Odysseus?"

She ran to the pig-sty, and anointed the inmates with a magic drug. In a trice their bristles fell away, they grew tall, and lo, they were men again! In joy they hastened to Odysseus and fell upon his neck, welcoming him gladly. Then one and all sat down to feast and make merry.

Circe made no more evil magic for them, but was kind and gentle. Odysseus stayed with her for a year, perfectly happy and content; and then, bidding her farewell, set sail once again for his own beloved kingdom of Ithaca.

Specially drawn for this work.

The witch cried out for mercy. "Pardon me, oh hero of Troy," she said, "and I will vow never to practise my arts on thee."

THE SIRENS AND SCYLLA AND CHARYBDIS

Specially drawn for this work.

The sailors rowed by Scylla's cave, trembling and fearful. Odysseus stood on the deck of his ship, ready to fight the monster if she appeared. He peered down into the dark depths of the cave.

AFTER Odysseus had sailed for some days in his ship, he spied a low-lying island on the horizon, and at the same time noticed that the wind had died down.

"We are near the island of the Sirens," he said. "You must take to your oars, men, but before you do so, I will mould wax to put into your ears. For you must know that these Sirens sing such sweet songs that all who hear them go to their island, and are devoured."

Odysseus took wax and melted it. Then he stopped up his men's ears with it, after giving them some commands.

"I wish to hear their songs," he said, "but I fear their power. So, for fear that I shall throw myself overboard to swim to the Sirens, I would have you tie me fast to the mast. If I sign to you to untie me, take no notice, but row steadily onwards all the time."

His men tied him to the mast as he commanded; and then, taking their oars, they rowed past the island. As soon as they came near it, they saw the beautiful Sirens, but they could not hear their enchanting voices. Odysseus gazed on the lovely maidens, and saw the garlands of flowers around them—but he did not see that the bright blossoms hid the white bones of sailors who had visited the island and had been destroyed by the cruel Sirens.

The men rowed on. They could not hear the songs, so the magic in the music had no power over them. But Odysseus, whose ears held no wax, could hear every word, and he longed to go to the maidens. He thought he had never heard such wonderful songs in his life, and the music melted his heart and turned it to water. He began to struggle, and cried out to his men to free him.

But they could not hear. So Odysseus signed to them with nods and frowns, bidding them release him; but they remembered his commands and would not. One of them rose and tightened the bonds, for he feared that Odysseus, in his anger, might tear them asunder.

So the ship passed by the island and the Sirens gazed in amaze to see it, for never before had a vessel resisted their enchanted voices. As soon as the wind sprang up again, and the ship was far away from the island, the men untied Odysseus. He marvelled at himself for wanting to go to the Sirens, and thanked the men for paying no heed to his signs.

Soon he gave his attention to two rocks not far ahead. One was tall and black, and towered to the sky. A dark cloud hovered over it, and never left it. Underneath was a fearful cave in which lived Scylla, a monster with six heads. Every ship that passed by was her prey, for she snapped six men out of it with her horrible heads, and devoured them. She had twelve legs, but no one could see farther down than her waist, for the rest of her body was hidden in the depths of the cave.

She yelped and howled loudly, and many a sailor loosed his oars in fright when he went by. Never a ship had passed without Scylla taking six men from it.

On the opposite side was a lower rock, on which grew a fig-tree, always in full leaf. Far below this rock, hidden in the restless, swirling water, was another monster called Charybdis. She sucked the waters down into her gigantic mouth, and

then spouted them forth again, making a fearful whirlpool in which many ships were lost. When she sucked the water down, such a vast hole was made that sailors could see the sand far, far below, and trembled with fear. When she spouted it forth the spray drenched the summits of both rocks.

"Steer close to the high rock," commanded Odysseus as they drew near. "We can lose only six men there, but we may lose the whole ship if Charybdis sucks us down into her mouth!"

So the sailors rowed by Scylla's cave, trembling and fearful. Odysseus stood on the deck of his ship, ready to fight the monster if she appeared. He was clad in bright armour, and held two

Specially drawn for this work.

His men tied Odysseus to the mast as he commanded; and then, taking their oars, they rowed past the island. Odysseus gazed on the lovely maidens and cried out to his men to free him.

strong spears. He peered down into the dark depths of the cave, ready to hurl his spears at Scylla, as soon as she showed her six dreadful heads.

Right through the strait the men rowed, shouting with fear when they saw Charybdis suck down the water into her mouth, leaving a monstrous hole in the sea. Then she spouted it up again, high as the rocks, and covered the men with spray.

Suddenly there sounded a yelping and howling from the cave on the other side of them. Scylla appeared, with all her six heads together, and before the horrified Odysseus could stop her, she had snatched six of his men, and darted back again into her dark cavern with them. His spears were of no use—the men were lost.

In terror the sailors ceased their rowing, but Odysseus shouted to them to continue, for he was fearful lest Scylla should once again appear and steal six more of his men. The sailors clutched at their oars, and rowed for dear life, hardly daring to glance round for fear the monster should spring upon them once more.

Then on went the ship again, but it was many days before the frightened sailors forgot the terrors of Scylla and Charybdis.

At last Odysseus arrived at Ithaca. Gladly he stepped ashore, and with joy he returned to his palace. Long years had passed since he had left Troy, and the hero was weary of voyaging, and longed for the joys of home.

His wife and son welcomed him with delight, and in peace and happiness Odysseus ruled once again over his rocky kingdom of Ithaca.

Specially drawn for this work.

Six of the men were snatched by Scylla and the ship went on again, the sailors frightened and distressed. It was many days before they forgot the terrors through which they had passed.

Fable,
Myth
and
Legend

Tales of
King Arthur
and the
Round Table

Specially drawn for this work.

As the knights were leaving the church they saw a strange thing. In the churchyard stood a large stone, which had not been there before. On it was a thick bar of steel and in this was driven a great sword.

THE SWORD IN THE STONE

LONG ago, when King Uther Pendragon died, every knight thought to seize the crown for himself, and for a while there was no king. Then Merlin the Magician came forth, and took counsel with the Archbishop of Canterbury.

"Let all lords and gentlemen of Britain ride to London, and meet on Christmas Day in the Great Church," commanded the Archbishop.

This was done ; and as the knights were leaving the church, they saw a strange thing. In the churchyard stood a large stone, which had not been there before. On it was a thick bar of steel, and in this was driven a great sword. About the stone was written in letters of gold these words:—

"Whoso pulleth out this sword is by right of birth King of England."

Then all the people marvelled, and each knight tried his strength on the sword. But none could move it even an inch, try as he would.

The Archbishop set two knights to guard the stone night and day until the rightful man was found, who should draw the sword forth with ease.

"On New Year's Day a tournament shall be held, and the strongest and most skilful knights may once more try their strength, and seek to draw out the sword," proclaimed the Archbishop.

When the day came all the knights went first to church, and then to the field to make ready for the tournament. Among them was a knight, Sir Ector, and with him was his son, Sir Kay, and his foster-son, Arthur.

Sir Kay, in his haste to ride to the tourney, had forgotten that he had unbuckled his sword the night before, and had left it behind him. He begged Arthur to go back to the house and fetch it for him.

Arthur at once rode back, but when he reached the house, he found it was locked, for all the servants had gone to see the tournament. In anger the youth rode away, despairing to think that his brother might not have a weapon with which to fight.

Then he suddenly remembered the sword he had seen in the churchyard, as he was coming out of church that morning.

"Kay shall borrow that!" he cried, and he rode forthwith to the church. The two knights who had been on guard were gone to prepare for the mock-fights, and no one was there. Arthur leapt off his horse, and ran to the stone. He took hold of the sword, and pulled. It came forth from the steel easily, and with joy in his heart the boy ran back to his horse.

He rode to his brother, and gave it to him. But Kay at once knew that it was not his sword, but the one from the enchanted stone. He went to his father and showed it to him.

"Am I then King of England?" he asked.

"Nay," said his father, "the one who pulled it forth is the rightful King. Who gave it to you?"

"Arthur," answered Kay. "But surely he could not pull it forth?"

The youth was called, and at once confessed that he had taken the sword from the stone. Sir Ector listened in astonishment. Then he bade the two follow him, and led the way to the churchyard once again. He bade Arthur place the sword in the stone, and the boy did so.

Then Sir Ector strove to pull it out, but could not, neither could Sir Kay; but Arthur drew it forth easily. When they saw that, they knew he was the rightful King of England, and both knelt to him in reverence.

"You are not my son," said Sir Ector, "but the son of Uther Pendragon, and were brought to me by Merlin when a babe. I did not know who you were, but now that you have drawn forth the sword, it is plain that you are no other than the prince."

The Archbishop was told that Arthur had drawn forth the sword, and came to see. But when the knights and barons saw that such a boy was to be

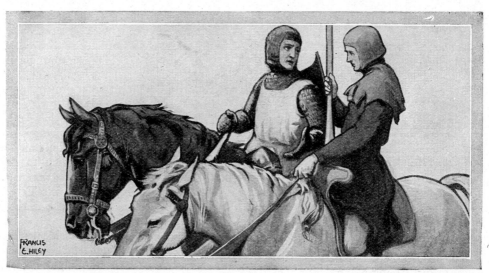

Specially drawn for this work.

Sir Kay, in his haste to ride to the tourney, had forgotten that he had unbuckled his sword the night before and left it behind him. He begged Arthur to go back to the house and fetch it for him.

THE SWORD THAT MADE A KING

Specially drawn for this work.

Arthur leapt off his horse and ran to the stone in the churchyard. He took hold of the sword and pulled. It came forth from the stone easily, and with joy in his heart the boy ran back to his steed.

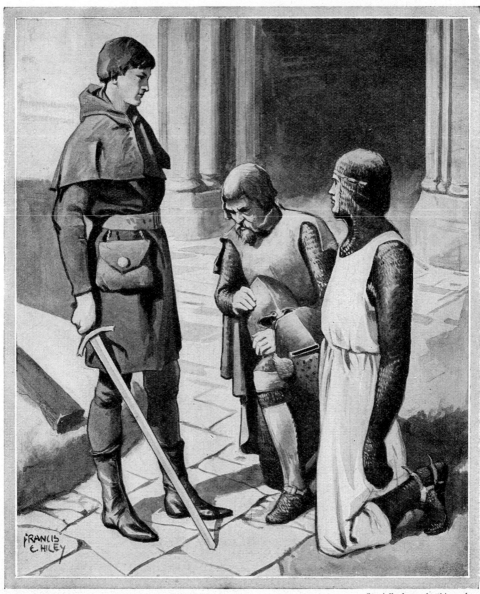

Specially drawn for this work.

When Sir Ector and Sir Kay saw Arthur draw forth the sword easily they knew he was the rightful King of England.   Then both knelt to him in reverence.

their king, they cried out in anger, and vowed that he should not rule them.

At Candlemas and at Easter many others tried to take the sword from the stone, but none could do so.   Only Arthur was able to, and at last the common people, who had watched him, cried out that they would have him for their King, and none other.

Then all fell upon their knees before Arthur, and the youth took the sword, and offered it upon the altar.   The crown was placed upon his head, and he was proclaimed King of England.   Humbly he vowed to be a true sovereign and to rule his people well as long as he lived.

GARETH AND LYNETTE

Specially drawn for this work.

" You may go to the King's court, Gareth," said the boy's mother, " if you promise that for a
year you will work in the kitchen and tell no one your name."

FAR away in the north there lived
a little prince called Gareth. His
big brothers had long since gone to
King Arthur's court, and were Knights
of the Round Table. They sat at the
great table with the King, and went on
his adventures, rescuing maidens in
distress and slaying evil-doers.

The little prince often thought of the
Round Table, and longed to join his
brothers. But his mother did not
wish him to go, for she feared she would
be lonely without him.

Gareth begged her so often to let him
be a knight when he was old enough
that at last she knew he would not
take no for an answer any longer. So
she made a condition, which, she
thought, would be too hard to make
his consent possible.

" You may go to the King's court if
you will promise that for a year you
will work in the kitchen and tell no
one your name," she said.

Gareth listened and rejoiced. He
would consent to anything, if he could
have permission to journey to King
Arthur. He knew he would not like
the year in the kitchen, for he was
a princely youth, unused to rough
work ; but that did not deter him.

He set off to go to the court, and at
last arrived. He came on a day when
King Arthur was holding a feast, and
all his knights were there. A splendid
assembly they seemed to the youth as
he entered the great hall, and gazed
around. He was dressed in rough
ploughman's clothes, and told no one
who he was.

" What is your wish ? " asked the
King.

" I ask three boons," said the youth.
" One I will ask now, and that is to
let me work for a year in your kitchen.
The other two I will ask when the year
is up."

In surprise the King granted the
youth's request, and Gareth was taken
to the kitchen. Here he was set to
work, and very rough and dirty were
his tasks. Sir Kay, who was steward,
disliked the handsome youth, and
jeered at him.

Specially drawn for this work.

" What is your wish ? " asked King Arthur.
" I ask three boons," said the youth. " One
of them is to let me work in your kitchen."

" Your hands are too white for a servant! " he said scornfully. " Since you will not tell me your name, I shall call you Fairhands! But I promise to roughen these lily hands of yours before the year is out! "

He kept his word, and gave Gareth all the roughest, hardest tasks to do. But the youth did not complain, and bore everything with a good grace.

When the year was up, the King held another feast and to it came a fair lady called Lynette. She was in great distress, and begged the King to give her a knight to rescue her sister the Lady Lyonors, who was besieged in her castle by a wicked knight.

Then Gareth, who was standing near by, waiting to ask the King for his two boons, saw here a great chance for himself, and he came forward.

" Sir ! " he cried, " let me ride with this lady to rescue her sister! My year is up, and I crave an adventure! "

King Arthur looked on the princely youth, and he was pleased to grant his wish, for he admired him. But the Lady Lynette was angry.

" What! " she cried. " Do you give me a youth from the kitchen? I declare, he smells of cooking! "

She ran straight out of the hall and mounted her horse to ride away. Gareth only stayed to don armour and mount a horse also, then he rode after her. Sir Lancelot knighted him, and proudly the young prince went out on his first adventure.

But his lady was scornful of him. She was angry to think she had a knight from the kitchen, and she jeered at him. He was gentle with her, and gave her good words for bad.

Soon they came upon a knight tied to a tree by six robbers. Gareth at once rode at the thieves, and slew one. Then he killed the second, and galloped after the third to slay him as he was running away. The other three vanished in terror. Gareth set free the knight, who was very grateful, and begged the youth and his lady to

stay the night with him at his castle
near by.

They did so, but Lynette was too
proud to sit at the same table with
the " Kitchen Boy," and bade the
knight of the castle set Gareth's plate
elsewhere. The knight forthwith took
not only Gareth's plate to another
table, but his own also, and the proud
maiden had to eat alone.

The next day they set forth again.
Soon they came to where two fierce
knights sat by a river, preventing all
who came that way from crossing.
Gareth rode fiercely at one, and sent
him headlong into the river, where the
current carried him away and drowned
him. Then he rode at the other, and
after a hard fight, slew him. But the
Lady Lynette gave him never a word
of praise.

They rode on once more and came to
a desolate-looking land, on the borders
of which sat a Black Knight. He was
by a black hawthorn tree, and his horse
and trappings were all black, as well
as his shield and banner.

For an hour and a half the two fought
fiercely, and then Gareth gave the
Black Knight such a blow that he fell
from his horse and died. The youth
took his armour and donned it, for it
was better than his own. Then on
he rode again, and presently came
to the Green Knight, who was
brother to the one Gareth had just
slain.

The knight rode at Gareth in anger,
when he saw him clad in his brother's
armour, and smote him fiercely. But
the youth struck him so strongly on
the helmet that he fell from his horse.
Gareth ran up to him, and was about
to slay him, when the knight called
to Lynette, asking her to beg for
mercy.

" Do you wish me to spare his life ? "
asked Gareth, turning to his scornful
lady. But Lynette at first would
answer nothing. Then, seeing that
Gareth was really going to slay the
knight, she thought better of her

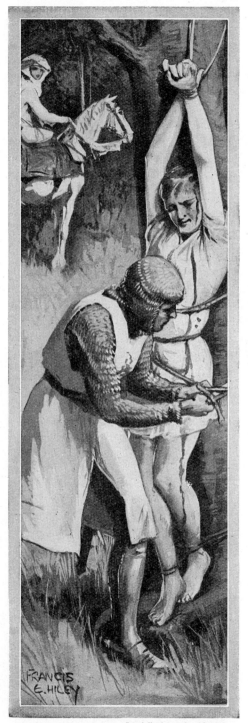

Specially drawn for this work.

Having killed or dispersed the six robbers,
Gareth set free the knight who had been tied
to a tree. The knight was very grateful.

muteness, and cried out to him to have mercy.

"I will grant anything you ask, lady," said Gareth, pleased that Lynette should beg him for anything.

Then the grateful Green Knight knelt before the youth, and begged him to come to his castle for the night. He and Lynette consented, and followed the knight. But when they reached the castle, Lynette again began to taunt Gareth.

"Do you not, a kitchen-boy, feel ashamed of your manners when you sit at table with those of noble birth?" she said.

Then for the first time Gareth reproached the lady Lynette and spoke to her sternly.

"Mock me no more," he commanded. "Have I not behaved to you as a true knight should?"

The Green Knight also reproached the scornful maiden, and she began to feel ashamed of her unkindness. She prayed Gareth to forgive her, which he did willingly.

Next morning they rode away together happily, and never again did Lynette utter a scornful word to Gareth.

Soon they came to where a great castle towered to the sky.

"That is Castle Dangerous, where my sister is besieged by the Red Knight," said Lynette.

Gareth rode up to it. He saw in the wood near by many knights who had been slain by the Red Knight and he felt afraid. Then, peering up to a window of the castle, he saw such a lovely lady looking down on him, that he felt courage spring up in him.

"There is the lady I would marry!" thought Gareth, gazing on the beautiful face of the Lady Lyonors. "I will slay this wicked knight, and take

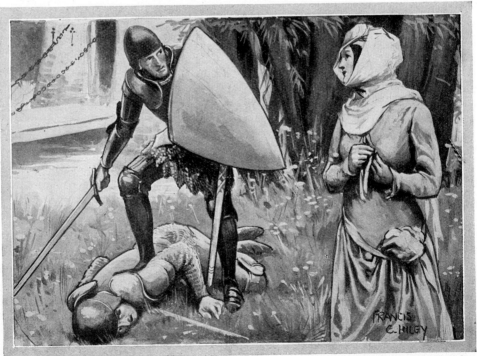

Specially drawn for this work.

Gareth ran up to the knight and was about to slay him, when he called to Lynette, asking her to beg for mercy. "Do you wish me to spare his life?" asked Gareth.

Specially drawn for this work.

"That is Castle Dangerous," said Lynette, so Gareth rode up to it and blew a great horn. At once the Red Knight armed himself and came riding forth.

the maiden to Arthur's court, where I will wed her!"

He blew a great horn, and at once the Red Knight armed himself and came riding forth to do battle with Gareth. Fiercely they rode at one another, and so hard did they smite that pieces of their armour were hacked out and each was sorely wounded. All day long the battle went on, till both were panting and weary.

At last Gareth struck his foe's sword from his grasp, and then flung himself heavily upon him, bearing him to the ground. He was about to give him the death-blow when the knight begged for mercy. Gareth granted him his life, and then went boldly inside the Castle to have his wounds tended.

For ten days the Lady Lyonors nursed him, and her sister Lynette helped her, sorrowing now for all the hard words she had given him. Soon he was well again, and proudly he asked Lyonors to go to Arthur's court with him and wed. She consented with joy, for she loved him with all her heart.

Back to the court they journeyed, and there at last Gareth told his true name, and made himself known. The King welcomed him with delight, for he found that Gareth was his own nephew.

Very soon he and the Lady Lyonors were married, and long and happily they lived at Arthur's court, Gareth ever making for himself a brave and honourable name among the Knights of the Round Table.

PRINCE GERAINT AND THE SPARROW=HAWK

Specially drawn for this work.

Geraint, with Enid at his side, rode back to King Arthur's court. Here Queen Guinevere
welcomed the maiden lovingly and remembered her promise to Geraint.

ONE morning, when the King had gone to hunt, Queen Guinevere arose too late to go with him. She went to a little hill to see the hunt in the distance, and whilst she was there a handsome prince rode up.

"It seems we are both late, Prince Geraint," said the Queen, smiling. "Come, stand by me, and we will watch the chase together."

As they stood there watching, a knight rode by with a lady, followed by a crooked dwarf.

"Who is that knight?" said the Queen, for she did not know his face. She sent one of her maidens to ask; but the dwarf answered the girl rudely, and struck her, so that she came tearfully back to the Queen. Geraint rode after the dwarf in anger, and demanded his master's name.

The dwarf would not tell it, and when Geraint would have ridden up to the knight himself, to demand his name, the dwarf raised his whip and struck Geraint on the cheek. The blood spurted out, and stained the prince's scarf.

Geraint rode back to the Queen.

"Madam," he said, "I will go after this knight who keeps such churlish servants and challenge him to fight."

"May good fortune go with you, Prince," said the Queen. "Mayhap you will bring back a bride with you, and if you do, I will dress her for your wedding with my own hands."

Geraint rode swiftly off. He soon saw the strange knight in the distance, and all day long he followed him. Over hills and along valleys they went, until at last, when evening came, Prince Geraint saw a town in the distance. The strange knight rode through it and entered the gates of a great castle that towered up to the sky.

"So that is where the knight dwells," thought Geraint. "Now I will buy me some armour, and then find shelter for the night. To-morrow I will challenge the haughty fellow, and revenge the insult paid the Queen."

The prince rode slowly through the town. All the people seemed to be busy, and none looked up to watch the knight riding by. Geraint wondered why the men were so hard at work. Some were sharpening swords, some were polishing shields and others were cleaning suits of armour.

"Where can I buy armour and weapons?" said Geraint to a busy workman. The man laughed scornfully, but did not look up, so busy was he.

"Armour!" he said. "That is foolish talk! Have you forgotten the Sparrow-Hawk?"

The Sparrow-Hawk? Now what did that mean, wondered Geraint. The man was too busy to talk further, so the prince rode on. Soon he came to another workman, a smith at his forge. "Where can I get armour?" shouted

Specially drawn for this work.

Guinevere sent one of her maidens to ask a question, but the dwarf answered the girl rudely and struck her, so that she came tearfully back to the Queen.

Geraint, making his voice heard above the sound of hammers. But the smith shook his head impatiently.

"You can get none," he said shortly, and went on with his work.

"Why not?" questioned Geraint.

"Because of the Sparrow-Hawk!" said the smith, and would say no more.

Geraint was puzzled. Who was this Sparrow-Hawk, and why was he keeping the town so busy? He could find no answer to the riddle.

He sought a lodging for the night,

but there was none to be had. Every house, every inn, was full, and would take no more guests. Geraint rode on until he came to a marble bridge crossing a deep river. On the other side stood a half-ruined castle.

An old man came to meet Geraint as he rode over the bridge. He had a courtly manner, though he was dressed in tattered clothes that had once been rich.

"Do you need shelter for the night?" he asked. "Come to my castle, and you shall have what hospitality we can give you."

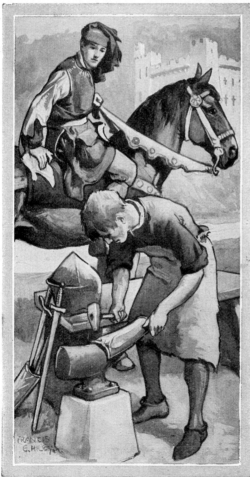

Specially drawn for this work.

"Where can I get armour?" shouted Geraint, making his voice heard above the sound of hammers. But the smith shook his head impatiently.

He led the way to his ruined castle. As they drew near, a shy and lovely maiden came out to take Geraint's horse from him.

"Here is my daughter, Enid," said the old man. "Go, my child, and buy cakes and meat in the town, so that we may feed our guest to-night."

Geraint did not want the maiden to go to the town, especially as he saw that she had to walk, but the old man would not let him say her nay. He led the prince indoors, and bade him seat himself.

Soon Enid came back, and cooked the food she had brought. Then she set it before her father and his guest, and waited on them. Geraint watched her, and thought that never had he seen such a sweet and modest maiden.

After the meal, the old man told Geraint his story.

"I am Earl Yniol," he said. "Three years ago my castle was untouched, and was splendid and strong. Then came my nephew, and bade me give to him Enid as his wife. I refused, and he marched against me, burning my castle and sacking it. He lives in the great castle yonder, and is known as the Sparrow-Hawk."

"So *he* is the Sparrow-Hawk!" cried Geraint. "It was he who insulted the Queen this morning. Now tell me, good Earl, why is the town so taken up with this Sparrow-Hawk to-day?"

"There is a tournament to-morrow," answered Yniol. "The Sparrow-Hawk holds one every year, and challenges all knights to do battle with him. The prize is a silver sparrow-hawk, which is set up on the battlefield. For two years my nephew has won it, and to-morrow if he should win it once more, it is his for always."

"Would I could fight with him!" muttered Geraint. "But I can get no armour."

Specially drawn for this work.

The Sparrow-Hawk rode straight at Prince Geraint and the two met with a crash. Their lances were shivered to pieces, but again and again they rode at one another. At last the Sparrow-Hawk was sent crashing to the ground.

" I have armour, but it is old and rusty," said the Earl. " Nevertheless, Prince Geraint, you cannot enter the tournament unless you have a lady to fight for."

" Grant that I may fight for Enid your daughter," begged Geraint. " She is the fairest and sweetest maid I have ever seen. Let me fight for her, and if I overthrow this bold Sparrow-Hawk, I will take her to Arthur's court and wed her! "

Enid blushed with delight when she knew that the famous prince wished to fight for her and wed her. Gladly she polished her father's old armour, and made it bright and shining for her knight.

In the morning Geraint rode to the tournament, with Enid by his side. He saw the silver sparrow-hawk set up on two forks at one end of the field, and heard the earl's nephew call loudly to his lady, who sat in a scarlet pavilion.

" The silver sparrow-hawk is yours! " he cried. " There is no knight here bold enough to fight me for it! "

Then Geraint rode eagerly on to the field.

" I claim it for a fairer and nobler maiden! " he cried.

The Sparrow-Hawk stared in anger, when he saw Geraint, and knew that his lady was Enid. He rode straight at him and the two met with a crash. Their lances were shivered to pieces, but again and again they rode at one another. At last the Sparrow-Hawk was sent crashing to the ground, and Geraint, drawing his sword, ran to him.

The Sparrow-Hawk sprang to his feet, and drew his sword also. Then fiercely the two fought, and their swords clashed together continually. Soon Geraint dealt his foe such a heavy blow on his helmet that it was cut right through and the Sparrow-Hawk fell to earth, groaning. The prince placed his foot on him, and touched him with the point of his sword.

" Now tell me your name, churlish knight, that I may pass it on to the Queen, whom your dwarf insulted yesterday! " he commanded.

" My name is Edyrn, son of Nudd," groaned the wounded man. " Have mercy on me! "

" Your life shall be spared if you will go to Arthur's court and beg the Queen's forgiveness," said Geraint, sternly. " Also you must restore to Earl Yniol all that you took from him two years ago."

" These things I will do," promised the Sparrow-Hawk, and he arose and left the field in shame.

Then Geraint took the silver sparrow-hawk and gave it to Enid. She gazed shyly on her knight, and thought him the noblest she had ever seen.

" To-morrow you shall ride with me to Arthur's court," said Geraint. " Wear the dress you have now, Enid, for the Queen has promised to array you like the sun, with her own fair hands."

The next day Geraint, with Enid at his side, rode back to King Arthur's court. He took his maiden to the Queen, who marvelled at her loveliness.

" Now am I pleased to see the one whom Prince Geraint has chosen for his bride," she said, and she welcomed the maiden lovingly. " I will deck you out in your wedding garments with my own hands," she told the blushing girl, " for so I promised Geraint before he set out upon his quest."

She took Enid to her own apartments, and laid out silks and satins, fair to look upon. Never had the maiden seen such lovely robes, and when she was arrayed in her wedding garments, all exclaimed in wonder at her beauty.

" You are the loveliest bride that has ever graced the court of Arthur! " cried the Queen, and she spoke truth.

The King himself gave Enid to Geraint, and proudly the prince took her for his wife. Many happy days they spent at the royal court, and then Geraint took his lovely wife to his own land.

Fable,
Myth
and
Legend

Tales
from the
Faerie
Queene

Specially drawn for this work.

Sir George, a young and lusty knight, vowed to kill the dragon. He set off with Una, he on his
great war-horse and she on her little white donkey, followed by her dwarf.

THE ADVENTURES OF THE RED CROSS KNIGHT

ONCE upon a time a lovely maiden called Una went to the court of the Queen of Fairy-land. She was in great distress, and begged for a knight to aid her.

"A fearful dragon has destroyed my father's kingdom," she said. "The King and Queen, my father and mother, are imprisoned in a brass tower. None dares to battle with the dragon, for it is a dreadful monster."

Then Sir George, a young and lusty knight, took the adventure upon him-self, and vowed to kill the dragon. He set off with Una, he on his great war-horse, and she on her little white donkey, followed by her dwarf.

Soon they were overtaken by a storm, and rode into a wood for shelter. They lost their way and came to a dark and gloomy cave, in which lay a horrid monster.

It had a great hideous head, and a long tail. It rushed at the knight in rage, for it could not bear the light that shone from his shield. Sir George smote at the monster's head with his sword, but it slipped, and struck its shoulder.

Then, with a horrible bellow, the creature leapt at him, wrapping him all round with its long tail. The knight began to struggle; and at last, when one of his hands was free, he struck the monster a fearful blow with his sword. He cut its head right off, and Una ran to him in delight.

Onwards they rode again, and travel-led many a mile. At last, when evening was near, they met an old

Specially drawn for this work.

A horrid monster with a great hideous head
rushed at the knight in rage, for it could not
bear the light that shone from his shield.

man. They thought he was a good
hermit, but he was Archimago, a
wicked magician. He greeted them,
and begged them to come and rest at
his cave for the night.

Gladly they accepted, for they were
weary. He showed them their rooms,
and left them to fall asleep. When he
saw that their eyes were fast shut, he
took his magic books, and began to
work spells. He bade a demon fetch a
false dream for the knight, and when
it was brought to him, he took it to
Sir George's room.

Then the knight began to dream
dreadful things. He dreamt that Una
was a false maiden, unworthy of his
help. He awoke, and laughed at his
dream. Then he slept once more, and
dreamed again. When he awoke, he
believed what he had dreamt, and
sadly he resolved to leave the maiden,
and go on his way alone ; for he was
sure she was not as sweet as she seemed,
but was false and wicked.

He called the dwarf, and bade him
saddle their horses. Then, as the
dawn was breaking, he galloped away,
leaving Una alone. The dwarf went
with him, and glad was the evil
magician to see them go, for he wished
to get Una into his power.

Sir George rode onwards, sad and
unhappy, for he hated to think bad
thoughts of Una. Soon he met a
stout knight on horseback, who was
with a lovely lady in scarlet. Her
face was fair, but her heart was false,
for she was a witch, called Fidessa.

Her knight, who was called Faithless,
rode fiercely at Sir George, eager for
battle. Their horses met with a crash,
and each knight's lance was broken.
Then they took their swords and
began to smite one another furiously.

Faithless hacked a great piece from
the knight's helmet, and Sir George, in
rage, struck him on the head. Faithless fell to the ground, and died.

The scarlet lady fled in terror, and
Sir George rode after her to comfort
her, leaving his dwarf to bring the

shield of the dead knight. He saw that the lady was fair, and promised to be her knight and protect her. He did not guess that she was a witch.

They rode on together, and presently came to a glittering palace, where they were made welcome. Sir George stayed there, enjoying the feasting and merry-making. Then, as he sat there with Fidessa the witch-lady, a knight came in. He was called Joyless, and was brother to Faithless, the knight Sir George had killed, and whose shield he had taken.

When Joyless caught sight of his brother's shield, he looked round in anger for the knight who had slain Faithless. Wrathfully he challenged Sir George to fight, and eagerly the knight accepted.

On the morrow the two knights fought. Joyless was a strong, powerful knight, but Sir George, believing that he would have Fidessa's love if he won, battled so fiercely that soon he dealt Joyless a death-blow. He ran to him to smite him for the last time, when lo! a great black cloud swept down, and covered the wounded knight. When it lifted, Joyless was gone!

Sir George had many deep wounds from the sword of the vanished knight, and for some days he lay recovering from them, tended by the false lady, Fidessa. Then one night his dwarf came to him in terror, and told him of dreadful sights he had seen in the dungeons of the beautiful palace.

"Master!" he whispered. "This place is evil. The lady Fidessa is false. The dungeons are full of weary, groaning folk. Let us haste away before we also are flung there!"

Hastily Sir George arose, and in the faint light of dawn, galloped away with his faithful dwarf. They travelled until noon; and then, hot and weary, the knight lay down by a fountain.

When Fidessa found he had fled, she hastened after him, resolved to win him back. So fair she seemed, and so

Specially drawn for this work.

Sir George saw that the lady was fair. He did not guess that she was a witch. They rode on and came to a glittering palace.

many tears did she shed when she found him, that Sir George listened to her, and promised to travel with her once more.

She bade him drink from the fountain and he did so. Little did he know that the waters were magic, and had the power of taking away the strength of all those who drank there. As soon as he had drunk, his limbs became feeble, and he could scarcely raise his sword.

Then, to the knight's horror, a great, hideous giant came stalking through the wood towards him. He rushed at the powerless knight and smote him. Sir George fell in a swoon to the ground. The giant picked him up and carried him off to his castle, where he flung him into a dungeon.

Fidessa followed, for she thought the giant was marvellous. She became his wife, and he gave her a terrible seven-headed beast on which to ride, and a crown of gold to wear on her head.

The faithful dwarf, who had watched all that happened, gathered up his master's armour, and ran off with it in sorrow, wondering whom he could get to rescue Sir George.

As for the wretched knight, he lay without food for many a day, and soon despaired of being rescued. For who could hear of his miserable fate?

Specially drawn for this work.

To the knight's horror a great hideous giant came stalking through the wood towards him. The giant rushed at the powerless knight and smote him. Sir George fell in a swoon to the ground.

UNA AND THE FAITHFUL LION

Specially drawn for this work.

Lawless seized the girl roughly and dragged her upon his horse. The lion heard Una's cry, and with a growl leapt at the rough knight. Lawless beat him off, but the lion once again sprang.

WHAT had happened to Una, when her knight had left her? She was full of sorrow when she found that he had gone away with her dwarf, and left her alone. She saddled her little white donkey, and rode off to find Sir George.

Day after day she travelled, looking for him. Then one morning, when the sun was hot, she alighted from her donkey, and laid herself down to rest.

Suddenly a great lion rushed out of the woods, and ran to Una as if it would devour her. But when it saw how fair the maiden was, and how frightened, the great beast's heart was touched. It fawned upon her, and licked her little feet.

When she mounted her donkey again, the lion went with her, marching by her side to protect her. She was glad to have him, for now that she had no knight, she was very lonely.

After some time Una saw a knight dressed in the armour of Sir George, and on his shield was a red cross, just as her knight had had on his. She thought it was Sir George, and gladly she rode to him.

But it was really the wicked enchanter Archimago, who had ridden after Una to see what further harm he could do her. In order to make her think that he was Sir George, he had disguised himself in armour like that of the knight; but when he saw the lion with Una he was afraid.

The maiden greeted him happily.

"At last I have found you, my own knight," she said. "Where have you been?"

Then Archimago, pretending to be Sir George, answered her falsely.

"When we were sleeping at the hermit's hut," he said, "the old man awoke me, and told me of a monster near by. I went to slay it, and when I returned, you were gone. But I am now happy again, since I have once more found you."

They rode on together. Soon they saw a fierce knight in the distance.

413

His name was Lawless, brother to Joyless and Faithless, and he had vowed to slay Sir George, who had killed both his brothers.

When he saw the enchanter, dressed in armour like Sir George's, he thought that the Red Cross Knight was before him. Furiously he rode at him, and the two began to fight.

The magician was struck from his horse, and lay wounded on the ground. Lawless leapt from his steed, and ran to give his foe the death-blow. But when he undid the man's helmet, he started back in amaze—for he saw the face of his friend, Archimago, the magician!

"Now truly did I think I was fighting Sir George!" said Lawless. Una came near to see, and when she found that it was Archimago on the ground, and not her own true knight, she was too astonished even to run away.

Then Lawless caught sight of her fair face, and resolved to make her his lady. He seized her roughly, and dragged her upon his horse.

Specially drawn for this work.

When the lion saw how fair the maiden was, and how frightened, the great beast's heart was touched. It fawned upon her and licked her little feet.

The lion heard Una's cry, and with a growl leapt at the rough knight. Lawless beat him off, but the lion once again sprang. Then alas for him! The knight was very strong, and drove his spear straight into the loyal beast's heart. The lion fell dead, and Una had now no protector.

Lawless rode off with her, and the little white donkey followed behind. Una was very much frightened, and screamed for help. The knight laughed at her, for he thought none could hear her, such a wild part of the forest were they in.

But some one did hear her cry! Not very far away were some wild woodfolk, dancing. They heard her call, and ran to see who was in distress. When the knight saw these queer folk, with horned heads, hoofed feet and long tails, he was frightened. He left Una among the trees, and rode off swiftly.

Specially drawn for this work.

No sooner did the knight see the queer woodfolk, with horned heads, hoofed feet and long tails than he was frightened. He left Una among the trees and rode off swiftly.

The woodfolk saw that she was frightened and tried to comfort her. They took her with them, and treated her kindly.

She stayed with them in the woods, teaching them many things, until her longing for her own knight overcame her, and she decided to leave the queer folk, and seek Sir George again.

A brave knight called Satyrane, whose father was one of the wild people of the woods, one day came to where she taught the strange folk, and saw her.

He soon made friends with her, and when he heard that she wished to seek Sir George, he helped her to run away.

He rode with her, and after a time they came to where a knight sat by a fountain. To Una's horror, it was Lawless, he who had tried to drag her away with him.

The knight Satyrane drew his sword and challenged him. They rushed at each other, and a fierce fight began. Una ran away in terror.

She stumbled on and on through the wood, and then suddenly saw a tiny figure coming towards her. Who should it be but the little dwarf! He bore Sir George's armour in his hands, and when Una saw it, she fainted, for she thought that her knight must be dead.

The dwarf ran to her in dismay. He fetched water from a nearby brook, and splashed it over the maiden's white face.

When she came to her senses the dwarf told her all his tale, and Una wept bitterly.

"Take me to the giant's castle, where my lord is imprisoned," she said.

The dwarf obediently led the way, and sadly Una followed him.

Specially drawn for this work.

Una suddenly saw a tiny figure coming towards her. Who should it be but the little dwarf?
He bore Sir George's armour in his hands.

THE FIGHT WITH THE DRAGON

Specially drawn for this work.

Soon the travellers came to the great castle, and the Prince blew the horn and awaited the giant.

BEFORE Una and the dwarf had gone very far, they met a shining knight called Prince Arthur. He begged Una to tell him why she wept so bitterly, and she told him how her knight lay deep in a foul dungeon, imprisoned in the giant's castle.

" I will rescue him," said the shining knight, and followed the dwarf, with Una at his side. Soon they came to the great castle, and the prince blew the horn, and awaited the giant.

The monster rushed out angrily, but Prince Arthur struck him so strongly on the knee, that he fell. Then the shining knight chopped off his head, and the giant lay dead. He killed the great seven-headed beast on which the false Fidessa rode, and captured the witch. She was stripped of all her fine clothes, and then, bald, ugly and old, she ran howling into the wilderness.

Prince Arthur broke down the door of Sir George's cell, and lifted him out. He was weak and ill, but as soon as he saw Una, he felt new strength flowing into him. Tenderly they kissed one another, and bitterly did the knight repent that he had believed his evil dream, and gone away from Una.

Una led him away to the House of Holiness where Faith, Hope and Charity lived. Here Sir George slowly recovered not only in body but in mind and spirit.

It was here, too, that he saw the vision of the Holy City which inspired him with new strength and greater courage for the tremendous task which still lay before him.

When at last he was fully recovered he set out once again with the maiden to fight the dreadful dragon that laid waste the kingdom belonging to her father. Long they travelled, and at last came to the land she loved so well. It was dreary now, and all blackened with the breath of the fierce dragon. Far away in the distance was the brass tower in which Una's parents watched and waited for her.

Suddenly the two travellers heard a fearful roaring, and saw the hideous dragon, stretched out on the side of a hill. When it saw Sir George, it arose,

Specially drawn for this work.

The knight smote the dragon heavily and the monster became suddenly angry and flew up into the air. Then **it** swooped down and picked up both horse and rider.

Sir George attacked the great beast fiercely, but his sword could not pierce the thick brass scales. The dragon lashed at him with its tail, and he and his horse were swept to the ground. They rose again at once, and the knight smote the dragon heavily but without really weakening the monster.

Then the dragon suddenly became angry, and flew up into the air. After that it swooped down and picked up both horse and rider, carrying them far over the plain. But when they struggled fiercely it was forced to drop them, and the knight, turning quickly, slashed the dragon under its outspread wing.

He made a great wound there, and the beast, furious with pain, belched forth fire and smoke at the knight. Sir George's armour became fiery hot, and burnt him. He longed to take it off, and feared that he would die. Then once again the dragon struck at him with its tail, and the knight fell to the ground. Night came down and Sir George was able to hide from the dragon.

He lay still through the hours of darkness, but his head was near a magic spring, whose waters healed all weariness and wounds. The spring flowed over him, and in the morning he was fresher than ever.

He rushed straight at the dragon, and dealt it such a blow on the head that the great beast howled like a hundred lions. It struck the knight with its tail, and fixed one of its stings in his shoulder. Sir George, in great pain, struck off the dragon's tail with his sword, which so maddened the monster that it caught hold of the

and came, half flying, half running, to kill him.

Its enormous body was covered with clanking brass scales, too thick for any sword to pierce. It had flapping wings, and a long tail armed with two poisonous stings. Two eyes blazed in its head, and from its mouth came fire and smoke.

knight's shield with one of its claws, and tried to wrench it away from him.

Sir George lopped off its claw, and then the dragon, in its rage, poured out so much smoke and fire that the knight, overcome with the terrible smell and heat, fell to earth. Once more night came down and saved him. The dragon, in fearful anger, waited near by to devour him as soon as day dawned.

Sir George fell at the foot of a magic tree from whose trunk there flowed a little rivulet of balm. This healed all wounds, and could even bring the dead to life again. All night long the stream flowed over the knight's limbs, and when morning came, he sprang up, strengthened and refreshed.

He drew his sword and shouted aloud. The dragon awoke from its sleep and gazed in amazement on the knight, for it had thought that by now he was surely dead. Sir George waited not, but ran at the great creature fiercely.

It opened its mouth, meaning to swallow the knight whole. Fiery smoke came out, almost blinding Sir George, but he was so full of fresh strength that he did not pause. He raised his sword and drove it down the monster's throat, up to the very hilt.

The dragon gave a dreadful groan, and then fell heavily to the ground, dead. The earth shook and trembled with its fall, and Sir George shouted in triumph.

Una saw that the dragon was dead and joyfully she ran to Sir George, filled with overwhelming gladness that he was unhurt. Together they looked at the dreadful beast which had wrought such terror to the countryside.

Specially drawn for this work.

When morning came the knight sprang up, strengthened and refreshed. The dragon was amazed, for it had thought him dead.

When the watchman in the brass tower saw that the dragon was indeed slain on this third day of the terrible conflict he ran to tell the King and Queen. Then glad of heart they told the news to their people. Soon the great gates were thrown open and hundreds of men and women came streaming across the plain to rejoice with Una and the knight. How glad they were to see the dragon lying dead ! How they welcomed the valiant Sir George whose courage had rid their land of this dreadful monster!

A great feasting and merry-making began, and the bells pealed out gaily for the marriage of Una and her brave knight, Sir George. Never was there such a lovely bride as the fair Una, nor so happy a man as the Red Cross Knight who had fulfilled his vow and gained this most precious reward.

Many more adventures befell the valiant Sir George, but, protected by the sign of the Cross, he came victorious through them all. Everywhere the fame of the Red Cross Knight was spread, and when he died he became a saint and his spirit still inspired men who fought against evil. Richard Cœur de Lion of England, when fighting in the Crusades, was emboldened and encouraged by the vision of St. George when the battle raged most fiercely. His shrine at Lydda was a place of pilgrimage to the Crusaders and his fame spread to many countries.

So it was that his name became a rallying cry for men sorely pressed in battle. " St. George for England ! " they cried, and it was in this way that St. George became the patron saint of England and his brave Red Cross was emblazoned on the country's flag. His feast day is April 23rd, and the highest British Order of Chivalry, the Order of the Garter, has St. George as its badge. To-day his cross has been joined with the cross of St. Andrew of Scotland and with that of St. Patrick of Ireland to form the Union Jack.

Specially drawn for this work.

THE WEDDING OF UNA
Never was there such a lovely bride as the fair Una, nor so happy a man as Sir George, the Red Cross Knight.

Fable,
Myth
and
Legend

The
Song
of
Roland

Specially drawn for this work.

Marsil sent messengers to the great King, begging for mercy, and promising many rich gifts if his desire was granted. "Do not trust him!" cried Roland.

THE TREACHERY OF COUNT GANELON

IN the days when the noble King Charlemagne held his court in France there were many bold and brave knights. Two of the noblest were Roland, the King's nephew, and Oliver, the friend of Roland. They did great deeds, and their fame was sung in many lands.

For seven years Charlemagne had fought the Saracens in Spain. Only one city now remained to be conquered, Saragossa, hidden in the hills. King Marsil, the Saracen leader, was full of fear, for he knew that Charlemagne would soon take his city.

So he sent messengers to the great King, begging for mercy, and promising many rich gifts if his desire was granted.

"Do not trust him!" cried Roland. "Never has Marsil proved himself worthy of mercy!"

Then Ganelon, who hated Roland, sprang up and spoke in his turn.

"Listen not to the counsel of fools," he said. "Take the gifts Marsil offers, and make peace with him."

Then the other nobles also advised Charlemagne to show mercy to the conquered king, and the Emperor consented.

"Who shall go to bear my message?" he said.

"I will!" cried Oliver, and many others cried the same, but the Emperor would have none of them.

"Send Ganelon!" said Roland. "He is a brave knight."

Then Ganelon was angry with Roland for he thought he had spoken thus in order to send him to his death; for it was well known that messengers to Marsil were like to have their heads cut off.

421

But Charlemagne beckoned Ganelon near, and bade him take the message to the Saracens. The knight was white with anger, and though he dared not refuse, he stood before the whole company and vowed to love Roland no more.

Then he went. But black anger was in his heart, and when the Saracens saw this, they began to try him, to see if he would play the traitor to his king. Soon they found out that he hated Roland, and was willing to do anything to have his revenge upon him.

After that it was easy to tempt the traitorous knight. King Marsil promised him much money if he would go back to the Emperor, and say that all was well.

"Bid him return to France," said Marsil, "but see that the rearguard is left in charge of this Roland, whom you hate so much. Then we will ambush him, and utterly destroy him and his men."

Ganelon rode back to the Emperor, who praised him for his success.

"Marsil will send you all he has promised and will himself come to you in France to be baptized a Christian," said the false Ganelon. "Therefore, my lord, command your men to return through the mountains to France, for each one of them is longing to rejoin his wife and children."

"Who shall keep the rearguard?" said King Charlemagne.

"Who better than Roland the Brave?" asked Ganelon. So the Emperor called his nephew before him.

"You and Oliver shall keep the rearguard," he said. "You shall have twenty thousand men; have a care that when our great army passes through the Valley of Roncesvalles, no enemy is nigh."

"Sire, you may go in safety," answered Roland proudly, "for while I live, you have naught to fear."

Then Ganelon laughed in his heart, for he knew Roland was lost.

Specially drawn for this work.

The Saracens began to try the knight, to see if he would play the traitor to his King. Soon they found out that he hated Roland and was willing to do anything to have his revenge upon him.

ROLAND SOUNDS HIS HORN

Specially drawn for this work.

Behind the great hosts of Charlemagne, keeping the rear safe from foes, were Roland and Oliver and their twenty thousand brave soldiers.

THE great hosts of Charlemagne passed safely through the mountains into the fair land of France. Behind them, keeping the rear safe from foes, were Roland and Oliver, and their brave twenty thousand.

As they marched, sounds of trumpets and shouting were borne to them, and they paused to listen.

"Methinks the enemy is near," said Roland.

Oliver ran to a tree on the summit of a hill, and climbed it. To his amazement he saw such a vast number of Saracens in front of him, marching down the next valley, that for a moment he doubted his eyes. Then swiftly he descended the tree, and went to Roland.

"The enemy is marching in such numbers that I doubt if we can defeat them," said Oliver. "Sound your horn, friend Roland, so that Charlemagne may hear and return to our aid."

"Not I!" said Roland, boldly. "We will fight these heathen ourselves, and send them scattering ere day is done!"

"I pray you sound your horn," begged Oliver. "Our few men can do little against such fearful odds."

But Roland would not. His horn was a magic one of carved ivory. When it was blown, the sound of it went for miles. Charlemagne would have heard it at once and returned, had Roland sounded it.

Soon the marching Saracens appeared, and the battle began. Fierce it was and very terrible. The Franks gave their battle-cry of "Montjoie! Montjoie!" as they rode to the conflict, and many a Saracen trembled to hear that sound.

Roland's lance was soon splintered and he threw it away. He drew forth his famous sword Durindal, and soon the bright blade shone and flashed

Specially drawn for this work.

Roland drew forth his famous sword Durindal,
and soon the bright blade shone and flashed
in the sun, as he laid about the Saracens.

in the sun, as he laid about the Saracens.

Oliver, too, did marvellous deeds, and so eager was he in battle that he did not notice that his spear was broken, and that he was fighting with the haft. Roland called to him to draw his sword, and he did so, dealing such blows with it that Roland marvelled to see them.

Wilder and fiercer grew the battle, and soon thousands of Saracens lay dead ; but many brave Franks were slain also. Then the enemy turned to fly, and the knights pursued them, cutting them down as they fled. Soon, of all that great Saracen host, but one man was left, and he, King Margaris, fled to where King Marsil waited for news.

"Master, Master!" he cried. "Your army is shattered! Gather a new one, and march on the Franks whilst they are weary!"

Then King Marsil, in terrible wrath, gathered together a fresh army. Next morning he marched once more on the weary Franks. When Roland heard their trumpets, and saw this new array, his heart sank.

But his men prepared themselves for battle, and dauntlessly they rode to meet the foe. King Marsil sent half his army to fight the Franks, and kept half by him, ready to send when his enemy was weary.

Then battle cries sounded once again, and soon a fierce encounter began. But so bold were the Franks that they broke the ranks of the heathen, and sent them flying in terror. The way was strewn with dead, but alas for the knights! small was the number left to them, for but three hundred swords now flashed, and but three hundred brave knights were left.

Then King Marsil mounted his horse, and led his last men against the enemy. The Franks fought them well and boldly, but they were weary, and feared the never-ending numbers of their foe. At last, when only sixty knights were left, Roland turned to Oliver.

"I will sound upon my horn!" he said. "Then Charlemagne will hear it, and return to help us."

"You should have sounded it before," said Oliver sadly. "It is thy fault, friend Roland, that so many Franks lie dead on the field of battle this day."

Then Roland raised his horn to his lips, and blew a long, long blast. Charlemagne heard it, leagues away, and drew rein to listen. Full and clear it sounded, and the Emperor turned pale.

"It is Roland's horn!" he cried. But Ganelon the traitor answered scornfully. "Not so," he said. "I hear nothing."

The Emperor rode on. Then, far away, Roland blew his horn a second time, but the sound came feeble and low, for the knight was weary and faint.

The Emperor Charlemagne stopped again, certain that it was his nephew's horn he heard.

"Ride on, Sire, ride on," said Ganelon. "None would dare to attack brave Roland. Your ears must surely deceive you."

So once more, though very unwillingly and sad at heart, Charlemagne rode forward.

Then, for the last time, Roland sounded his horn. He had so little strength left that the notes came pitiful and faint, and they wrung the heart of all who heard. The Emperor swung his horse round, and heedless of the traitor Ganelon, commanded the army to ride with all speed back to the mountains.

"Roland needs us!" he said. "Forward, forward, ere it is too late! As for that traitor Ganelon, take him, and keep him until I come again to give him meet punishment for his foul treachery."

Then back went the army, riding, riding all through the night. Strong knights galloped with fear in their hearts, and sobs in their throats, dreading to come too late to the help of Roland, brave Roland.

On they went, and on and on, never pausing, never resting, praying only that they might not be too late.

"Roland!" cried their hearts, "Roland! We come! We come to your aid!"

Specially drawn for this work.

Roland raised his horn to his lips and blew a long, long blast. Charlemagne heard it, leagues away, and drew rein to listen. Full and clear it sounded, and the Emperor turned pale.

THE DEATH OF ROLAND AND OLIVER

Specially drawn for this work.

With all their force the Saracens aimed lance, spear or arrow at Roland and the Archbishop,
and then turned to fly.

WHEN morning came King Marsil once more sent his Saracens against the few Frankish knights, and he himself came riding upon Roland, eager to slay him. But the knight, with one sweep of his sword, cut off Marsil's right hand, and then slew his son before him. In rage and terror the King fled away.

Then his uncle, the Caliph, rode upon Oliver, and with his spear struck him in the back. The lance pierced through the coat of steel, and wounded the brave knight sorely. He knew that he had received his death wound, and called to Roland:

"Come near, friend Roland!" he cried, and in fear and sorrow Roland rode up to him. Then Oliver dismounted from his horse, and knelt upon the ground. He said his last prayers, and so died.

In bitter grief Roland turned from his friend, and looked upon the battle-field. Only two knights were left beside himself. One was the brave Archbishop Turpin, and the other bold Count Gautier of Hum.

Back to them rode Roland, and the three noble Franks once more faced the Saracens. Soon Gautier fell, slain by an arrow, and then the Archbishop's horse was killed beneath him. Roland lifted his horn once again, and blew upon it, longing to know if the Emperor was near. Faint and feeble was the blast he blew, but it reached the ears of Charlemagne.

"Sound our trumpets!" he commanded. "Let every trumpet blow, so that Roland may hear and know we come speedily!"

Then arose the sound of sixty thousand trumpets, and the great clamour was borne on the wind to where the Saracens stood. When they heard it, they knew that Charlemagne was near, and were afraid.

"Let us fly!" they said. "But first let us each fling a spear, or shoot an arrow at Roland and his comrade, so that we may leave them dead."

ROLAND THE BRAVE

Specially drawn for this work.

Roland was left alone and he knew that death was near him. He sank upon the grass with his
horn in one hand and Durindal, his sword, in the other.

Then, with all their force, the Saracens each aimed lance, spear or arrow at the two brave knights, and then turned to fly. Roland and the Archbishop were struck, and Turpin fell heavily to the ground, wounded to death.

Soon he died, and Roland was left alone. He knew that death was near him, and he sank upon the grass with his horn in one hand, and Durindal, his sword, in the other. Behind him lay a Saracen, pretending to be dead. When he saw Roland lying there, he crept up to steal the wonderful sword from the dying knight.

But even as he grasped it, Roland opened his eyes and saw him. He raised his horn, and brought it crashing down on the robber's head. The man rolled over without a groan, and lay dead.

Then Roland rose to his feet, meaning to destroy his sword Durindal, for he feared that it might fall into the hands of the enemy.

He struck it heavily against a rock, but it would not break. Three times did the knight smite the rock with his sword, but not a scratch dimmed the shining blade. Then wearily Roland lay down again, with his face to the foe. Under him he put his horn and his sword.

He clasped his hands in prayer, and even as he prayed, his soul fled. Roland the brave was dead.

When Charlemagne rode into the Valley of Roncesvalles, and gazed around, what a dreadful sight met his eyes! Not a Frankish knight was alive to greet him, but all lay dead on that terrible field.

"Roland! Roland!" cried the Emperor, but Roland answered never a word.

"See!" cried a knight of Charlemagne's company, pointing to where a cloud of dust arose in the distance. "There fly the enemy! After them, Sire, and revenge the death of all these brave knights!"

Then grimly Charlemagne rode. Fierce were the battles fought, and dire the punishment of King Marsil and his men. Soon the victorious Emperor rode back to France, his foes vanquished. Then with great pomp and ceremony the bodies of Roland, Oliver and Turpin were buried.

Ganelon the traitor was punished by death. Never could he be forgiven for betraying Roland the Brave, Roland the Fearless.

Specially drawn for this work.

Soon the victorious Emperor Charlemagne rode back to France, his foes vanquished. Then with great pomp and ceremony, the bodies of Roland and his companions were buried.

Fable,
Myth
and
Legend

Tales about
Robin Hood
and his
Merry Men

Specially drawn for this work.

Robin Hood threw himself on the ground and wept bitterly.

ROBIN HOOD BECOMES AN OUTLAW

MANY years ago there lived a merry lad called Robin. He grew up in his father's great house, and played with his two friends, Maid Marian, and Will, his cousin, Often the three would play all day long in the Greenwood, and there were none so happy as they.

But all this came to an end one day when enemies marched against Robin's father. They surrounded his house and with their swords, bows and arrows killed and wounded the men that rushed to protect the house. Robin's father was slain and then the great building was set on fire. One by one all Robin's men fell, and when at last the house was destroyed, none of his trusty servants was left alive.

Robin had shot well all day with his bow, and none dared to challenge him, so sure was his aim. When evening came, and the youth saw his home in flames, and knew that his father and his men were all slain, he fell into despair. He ran to Sherwood Forest, his trusty bow with him, and when he came to the cool heart of the Greenwood, he threw himself on the ground and wept bitterly.

" What have I left ? " thought Robin. " My good father lies dead, my men are slain, my home is smoke and ashes, and my land is in the hands of my enemies. I will revenge myself! I will become an outlaw, and live here in the Greenwood. I will rob the greedy priest and take the gold from rich and haughty men, and I will give the money to the poor, who, like myself, have none to help them. The King's deer shall feed me, and I will take as followers men like myself. Ho, a merry life will we lead, caring for none! "

As soon as men heard what had befallen Robin, they were grieved for him, for he was a merry youth, and liked by all. Many came to serve him in the Greenwood, and rejoiced to become his Merry

Men. Suits of Lincoln green they wore, with hoods that they could pull over their heads, or fling back upon their shoulders.

It is said that Robin Hood gained his name from the hoods his men wore. He was first called Robin i' the Hood, which name soon became Robin Hood. A fine leader was he, and his men would have died for him, one and all.

Many a brave and goodly man did he have to serve him. Little John there was, Robin's right-hand man, a giant of a fellow, seven feet tall; Will Scarlett, Much the Miller's son, Allen-a-Dale who could sing so sweetly, and George-a-Green; Will Stutely, Gilbert of the White Hand, Arthur-a-Bland, the tanner of Nottingham, and fat and jolly Friar Tuck. Many others there were, and each loved Robin Hood and did his bidding in all things.

The common people, too, loved Robin and his Merry Men, for many a present did the bold outlaw send to them and much gold did he give them. Only rich priests and proud men did he rob, and none grieved for them.

"I will swear an oath," said Robin Hood, at the beginning of his adventures, "and this oath will I keep until I die!"

Then solemnly he made this vow:

I will honour God and the King,
I will help the weak and fight the
    strong,
Take from the rich and give to the poor,
So God will help me with His power."

This vow he kept faithfully throughout all his many adventures, of which you shall now hear.

ROBIN HOOD MEETS LITTLE JOHN

ONE fine morning Robin Hood set out walking through the forest. With him he took his bow and arrows, and gaily he bade farewell to his men.

"See that you keep within sound of my horn," he bade them. "I shall not be long gone."

Soon he reached the borders of the forest and walked out into the highway. He came to a brook over which lay a log bridge. He leapt on to it, and then saw that someone was crossing from the other side.

Robin ran to the middle, meaning to cross first, and the stranger did the same. He was a huge fellow seven feet high, and in his hand he carried a young tree for a staff.

The two met in the middle, and neither of them would go back.

"Let me cross!" commanded Robin. "Go back to the bank, fellow!"

Robin was used to giving commands to his men, and he was surprised to see the stranger laugh in his face.

"I give way only to one who is better than myself!" said the stranger, with a mocking laugh. "I shall not go back."

"Then I shall pitch you into the water!" shouted Robin, in a temper. "Go back, I say, or you will have a ducking!"

Still the big man did not stir from his place on the log.

"Push me in, my brave fellow!" he said. "If you are stronger than I, you will do it easily!"

"I will fight you then, if you are willing," said Robin. "Wait! I will go to the hedge and cut myself a stick like yours!"

He leapt off the bridge, and cut himself a strong oak staff from the hedge. Then back he went to the log and ran lightly to the middle.

"Come!" he cried to the big fellow. "We will soon see who is the better man! Are you ready?"

Robin flourished his staff and struck at the stranger, who parried the blow easily and smote hard at Robin. But Robin dodged aside, and got in a fine blow on the giant's head. Then the big stranger smote at Robin in his turn, and so hard was the blow that the outlaw nearly pitched into the river.

For a long time the two fought. Robin

was quick and deft with his stick, but the big fellow was as strong as an ox, and Robin could not make him take even one step backward from his place.

On arms, shoulders and heads fell the blows, and each man cried out in pain and anger, but neither would give in. The big fellow thought it a great joke at first, but when he had received a dozen smart blows from the nimble Robin, he became angry, and his face flushed red. He aimed a great blow at Robin, but he dodged it, and gave his foe such a resounding stroke that the stranger staggered and nearly fell into the brook.

Robin laughed joyfully, thinking to see the stranger pitch headlong into the water, but even as he laughed the big man lunged out at him, caught him smartly on the head, and sent him reeling back into the brook.

Then it was the giant's turn to laugh! How he roared to see Robin splash into the stream, splutter and gasp, and struggle for the bank. But soon he saw that Robin was half-dazed by the blow, and could not see where he was going. In a flash the big fellow ran across the bridge, caught hold of Robin's hand, and with one mighty pull, dragged him safely from the brook.

Robin rolled over on the grass, and then sat up, rubbing his head.

"What a blow you gave me!" he said, eyeing the stranger closely. Then he took his horn from his side, put it to his mouth and blew a long blast upon it. Hurrying to his call came a crowd of his Merry Men, who stopped in astonishment when they saw Robin on the ground, wet through and with a large bump on his head.

"What's come to you, master?" asked his men.

"This big fellow would not let me cross the brook," said Robin with a laugh. "I gave him a punch and he gave me a poke and over I went into the water!"

"Then we'll serve him the same!" cried Will Stutely. "Come on, boys, give me a hand!"

All the Merry Men seized hold of the surprised giant, swung him to and fro and then let him go. He flew over the water and splash! In he went and sank right beneath the surface.

Out he came in a fine temper, and began to lay about him with a right good will. Over rolled Will Stutely, and down went three others. The rest of the Merry Men leapt on the angry giant and tried their hardest to hold him

Specially drawn for this work.

The huge fellow lunged out at Robin, caught him smartly on the head, and sent him reeling back into the brook.

down, but they found it very difficult, for he heaved about like an earthquake!

"I'll fight three men at once!" he roared. "Wait till I get up, my mannikins, and I'll fight three of you at once."

"Let him free," commanded Robin, laughing to see such a struggle. "Such a goodly man as he have I never seen before. I would rather be his friend than his foe."

The men let go their hold of the big stranger, and he sat up and looked at Robin.

"Now, I like you well," he said, with a merry twinkle. "Who are you?"

"I am Robin Hood and these are my Merry Men," answered Robin.

"Now, by my life, here's a strange thing!" cried the big fellow in dismay. "I set out this morning to find you and your company, for I had resolved to ask if I might join it—but now I fear me you will turn me away, for I pitched you headlong into the brook!"

"And you got pitched in too!" said Robin, standing up. "You fought well and fairly, and glad am I to meet with you. What is your name?"

Specially drawn for this work.
The Merry Men leapt on the giant and tried to hold him down.

"John Little," answered the big man joyfully, clasping Robin's hand in his as a token of good fellowship.

"Welcome to our company," said Robin Hood. "Be true to us, mind, heart and body, till death!"

"That will I!" cried John heartily, his blue eyes dancing for joy.

"Now!" said Will Stutely, with a loud laugh, "we will christen you, little stranger!"

He splashed water over John from his horn, crying: "You shall be, not John Little, but Little John! That shall be your name!"

Then all the Merry Men laughed, for Little John was such a giant, being more than a head taller than any other man there. Robin laughed as well, for he was pleased to have such a fine new follower, and Little John clapped Will on the back, happy to be one of the Merry Men after all.

Then off they all went together, and very soon Little John became Robin's chief man, and was loyal and faithful to him till death, a true and loving friend through all the years.

THE WEDDING OF ALLEN-A-DALE

ONE morning, when Robin Hood was out in the Greenwood, he heard someone singing a merry song in such a sweet and tuneful voice that the outlaw hid behind a tree to listen. Soon he saw the singer. It was a young knight clad all in red, and very merry he seemed as he went on his way.

Robin told his men of this gay young knight and bade them capture him if they saw him, for he would speak with him.

Now the very next day, as Little John and Much the Miller's son were going through the wood, they saw the young knight, but how different he looked! His gay suit of scarlet was gone and in its stead he wore a tunic of dark grey. He sang no song, but sighed heavily as he walked slowly through the wood with bent head.

Specially drawn for this work.

Little John and Much the Miller's son marched the angry and struggling young knight up to Robin Hood.

Little John and Much the Miller's son came up behind him and seized the surprised knight's arms. They marched him off to Robin Hood, very angry and struggling hard, but he could not free himself from Little John's strong hands.

"Is this the knight you meant, Master?" asked Little John, when they came to Robin Hood.

"I misdoubt it!" said Robin in astonishment. "Are you the knight who yesterday was dressed in red and sang so merrily?"

"I am he," answered the young man, and he sighed dolefully.

"Now why are you so sad?" asked Robin. "Yesterday you sang as sweetly as a blackbird—to-day you have a long face, and do nothing but sigh. Let me hear your tale, and maybe I can help you."

"I am called Allen-a-Dale," said the young man. "I am but a poor knight, but gold mattered little to me, for the sweetest maid in the kingdom was pledged to marry me. Yesterday we were to have wed—but alas! there came a rich knight, old and ugly, who because of his gold is going to wed my maid to-day. I cannot fight him, for he is safe in his castle, and yesterday when I went to challenge him his servants flung me into the moat. Then no wonder I sigh so dolefully, for there is nothing I can do to save my own true love."

"I will help you to save her," said Robin. "It were shame that an old knight should wed your pretty young maid."

The young man was overjoyed; but soon his face fell again, and he sighed.

"I cannot reward you for your good will," he said, sadly. "I have no money."

"I want no gold from you," said Robin, clapping the knight on the back. "All I ask of you is that you become one of my Merry Men and make sweet music for us, for our company lacks a minstrel, and dearly would we love to hear your voice each evening when we sit around our fire."

"I could ask nothing better!" cried Allen-a-Dale, joyfully. "Gladly will I serve you, good Robin Hood."

"Tell me where this wedding is to be," said Robin.

"At Plympton Church, five miles distant," answered Allen. "Three o'clock is the time."

Then Robin laid his plans. He bade Friar Tuck to go to the church and sit down quietly at the back until he had

Specially drawn for this work.

Robin Hood strode up to the bridal couple. "Stop this wedding!" he commanded. "I like it not."

further orders. Allen-a-Dale he commanded to go to the church at three o'clock, with twenty-four of the Merry Men.

Then Robin disguised himself as a minstrel, took a harp with him, and set off to Plympton Church. Already many of the guests had arrived, and Robin spied Friar Tuck sitting solemnly at the back of the church. As he strode up to the door with his harp, he saw the fat Bishop of Hereford, who was come to marry the maid to the old knight.

"Ho, minstrel, who bade you come?" he asked Robin sharply.

"Sir, I am but come to play a tune to the sweet bride," said Robin meekly. "'Twill bring her good luck."

"Then you may stay," said the Bishop.

Robin smiled to himself, and set down his harp in the porch. Then arrived the bridal company. The old knight came foremost, tricked out in white satin. Old he was and ugly, and bad temper was in his wrinkled face.

Then followed the fair bride. Her hair hung over her shoulders in a sheet of gold, and very lovely and young was she. But her face was pale and her eyes were red with weeping for her own true love.

When the bride and bridegroom stood before the altar rails and the Bishop came forward to marry them, Robin deemed it time to interfere. He strode up to the bridal couple, and glared at the astonished Bishop.

"Stop this wedding!" he commanded. "I like it not!"

Everyone rose in their seats and gaped in surprise. The Bishop was so angry that he could hardly find words to speak.

"What mean you by this, minstrel?" he shouted at last. "You shall be thrown out of the church."

"Nay, hear my merry music first!" laughed Robin, and he put his horn to his mouth. Three long blasts he blew, and at that everyone cried, "Robin Hood! It is Robin Hood!"

The Bishop's servants rushed up to seize him, but Robin deftly drew his bow and none dared approach him.

"Keep your seats, wedding guests!" cried the outlaw to the excited people. "You shall see a wedding, but we will let the bride choose her own groom!"

In a trice the Merry Men came running into the church and the Bishop's servants were seized and held. The young maiden was afraid, and stood white and trembling by the altar rails, wondering what all the to-do was. Then to her side came running Allen-a-Dale, and smiled with joy on his love.

"Now, my fair maiden," said Robin, "you shall be wed—but you shall choose whom you will have. Look around and make your choice."

The maid threw her arms around Allen-a-Dale, and blushed a radiant red.

"The maid has chosen!" cried Robin merrily. "My Lord Bishop, I pray you go on with the wedding!"

"I will do no such thing!" shouted the angry Bishop. "You know that before a couple may be wedded the banns must be called three times in church! I will not marry these two! There shall be no wedding!"

"I say there shall!" said Robin, "and if you will not wed this man and maid, then I will find someone else. Ho, is Friar Tuck there? Come, call the banns, good Friar, and wed these two."

Forth came jolly Friar Tuck, chuckling to see the Bishop's anger. Robin stripped the Bishop of his splendid gown, and slipped it on Friar Tuck, who looked very comical, for he was twice as big as the fat little Bishop. Then the jolly Friar called the banns seven times instead of three, which made all the wedding guests laugh.

"Not so much merriment," said Friar Tuck, pretending to be angry, but all could see the twinkle in his eye. "Now say, who gives this maiden in marriage?"

"I do!" cried Robin, and he stepped forward.

Then Allen-a-Dale and his happy bride knelt down, and Friar Tuck married them, to their great joy. When the wedding was over, Robin led the way to the Greenwood.

"Come with me," he said to Allen and his bride. "I have a wedding feast for you!"

Then off they all trooped to the forest, the Merry Men laughing gaily as they thought of the angry Bishop and ugly old knight. And what a wedding feast

Specially drawn for this work.

Allen-a-Dale and his bride stayed in the forest with Robin, and every evening Allen's clear voice
was heard around the fire.

that was! Surely never was there such a merry wedding before!

Allen-a-Dale and his bride stayed in the Greenwood with Robin, and long and faithfully did they serve him. Every evening Allen's clear voice was heard around the fire, and so sweet and tuneful were his songs that all the Merry Men fell silent to listen.

ROBIN HOOD AND THE BISHOP

ONE day Robin Hood heard that the Bishop of Hereford, fat, rich and greedy, was going to pass by the Greenwood.

"We will have a fine joke with him!" cried Robin gleefully. "Where are our shepherd clothes, my Merry Men? Fetch them, and we will dress ourselves in them."

In a short time Robin Hood and six of his men had stripped off their Lincoln green and were dressed in smocks and wide-brimmed shepherd hats. They made their faces and hands dirty, and roared with laughter to see themselves look such scamps.

Specially drawn for this work.

A plate of meat was handed to the Bishop and he was commanded to eat.

"Now we will kill a deer, and cook it by the side of the highway as the Bishop rides past!" said Robin. "What a fury he will be in!"

The deer was killed with an arrow, and a fire was lighted by the highway. Then the meat was roasted over the flames, and a delicious smell rose up from it.

"Here comes the Bishop with ten armed men!" cried Will Scarlett, as he saw a cloud of dust in the distance. "Ho, now we shall see some fun!"

The fat little Bishop trotted up to where the shepherds were roasting their deer, his ten armed men close behind him. When he saw what the shepherds were doing, he reined in his horse, with horror in his face.

"How dare you eat the King's deer?" he roared. "What scamps are you?"

"No scamps, but only poor shepherds," answered Robin, with a deep bow.

"And who told you to eat the King's deer?" stormed the Bishop.

"None told us we might," said Robin. "But, Sir Bishop, we were so tired of eating mutton that we thought a meal of venison would be more than welcome. Will you not eat with us, your Honour?"

The Bishop spluttered in his rage. "You wicked fellows, to rob the King of his deer!" he shouted. "My armed men shall take you prisoners and you shall hang for this!"

Then Robin and his men pretended to be full of terror and fell on their knees.

"Mercy!" cried Robin. "We crave your pardon, good Bishop."

"I will grant you no pardon!" said the Bishop fiercely. "Men, seize these rogues!"

The armed men leapt down from their horses to seize the shepherds, but in a trice Robin and his men slipped away. The outlaw took his horn from beneath his smock and blew three loud blasts on it. At once his Merry Men came running to him from all sides, and dropped on their knees before Robin, awaiting his commands.

The Bishop's mouth fell open in horror. This was the outlaw Robin Hood, who had played him such a trick in Plympton Church, when Allen-a-Dale was married to his fair young bride. Oh, what a desperate plight he was now in!

"Take away the weapons of these armed men," commanded Robin, "and you, Little John, take the Bishop prisoner."

"Mercy!" cried the terrified Bishop. "I crave your pardon!"

"I will grant you no pardon!" said Robin in the same fierce tones as the Bishop had used to him, when he and his six men had craved pardon a short while before. "Did you not say you would have us all hanged? Well, tell me, why should I not hang *you*? Surely you do not expect an outlaw to be more merciful than a Bishop?"

The Bishop was so full of fear that he had to hang on to his horse's neck to prevent himself from falling off. His red cheeks were pale and he shook from head to foot.

Robin was delighted to think that he had so frightened the cruel Bishop, but he did not really mean to hurt him, for he had vowed never to slay any man.

"Do not tremble so," he said after a while. "I am not such a rogue as you, Sir Bishop. You would have hanged me—but I will take you to feast with us. Come, we will lead you to our haunts."

The half-cooked meat was bound on to the Bishop's horse, and the company moved off to the open space amid the great oak trees, where Robin Hood and his men met and made merry.

The Bishop sat down upon the grass, wondering fearfully what was going to happen. Soon a plate of hot roasted meat was set before him and he was commanded to eat.

And there he dined in the midst of all the Merry Men, who feasted and joked around him. But when he had finished his meal, the Bishop felt afraid. He

Specially drawn for this work.

Little John gave the beast a blow and it set off to Nottingham.

had four hundred gold pieces in his saddle-bags, which he had taken from a poor knight. Would Robin Hood make him pay for his dinner as he had made the Sheriff? Perhaps he would charge him no more than twenty gold pieces, but even that was a monstrous price to pay for a meal, thought the miserable Bishop.

At last he stood up on his trembling legs and spoke to the outlaw.

"I will pay for my dinner and go," he said, in as bold a voice as he could muster.

"Well, Sir Bishop, it has been such a pleasure to have you dine with us that I do not know how much to charge you," said Robin. "Give me your purse and I will see what money you have."

The Bishop began to shake, remembering all the gold in his money-bags.

"I have but little money of my own," he said. "You cannot take the gold in my saddle-bags, for that belongs to the church."

Little John laughed loudly at that, and at a nod from Robin went to the saddle-bags and took them. Then he counted out four hundred gold pieces into the Bishop's cloak, which he had spread on the grass.

" Ho, what a store of treasure! " said Robin, laughing. " You say this belongs to the church, good Bishop ? Nay, I know your cruel ways. You have taken this from someone who can ill afford it, so I, my lord Bishop, will in my turn take it from you, who can *well* afford it, and send it to many poor folk who will look on such riches with joy. Little John, take the gold away."

" Nay! " cried the Bishop, with tears in his eyes. " Leave me half, only half, I beg of you. I am a very poor man, Robin Hood."

" Do not tell such false tales! " said Robin in disgust. " You are one of the richest men in the kingdom, for everywhere I hear of the ways in which you extort money from others. You are a greedy rogue! "

The Bishop went red with fury and then white with fear, for never in his life had he been told such truths as this. Robin laughed.

" The Bishop looks gloomy! " he said. " Let us make him merry. Little John, take him to dance with you! "

Little John at once caught hold of the fat little Bishop and twisted and twirled him round and round in a merry, comical jig, whilst Allen-a-Dale played a gay tune on his harp. The Merry Men held their sides in laughter to see such a sight, and wept for joy.

At last the Bishop tumbled down, giddy and weary. Little John picked him up in his strong arms, set him on his horse with his face to the tail, and led him back to the highway. Then he gave the beast a blow on the back, and it set off to Nottingham, with the Bishop riding backwards.

" Ho, what sport we have had! " cried Robin in glee. " The Bishop will think twice ere he comes *this* way again! "

THE BISHOP HUNTS ROBIN HOOD

THE Bishop of Hereford was very angry because he had had all his gold taken by Robin Hood. He went to the Sheriff of Nottingham and told him what had happened.

" Give me a company of soldiers," he said, " and I will double the price you have set on the outlaw's head. I will hunt him till I get him him! "

" You shall have all the men you want! " said the Sheriff gladly. " The rogue took twenty pieces of gold from me! "

So off set the Bishop with a whole company of soldiers behind him, resolved to range the Greenwood through till he found Robin.

Now that very morning Robin Hood had wandered out in the Greenwood alone. He stood beneath a tree, listening to the birds singing—and suddenly the Bishop and his men came riding down the highway not far off. Robin ran out of the forest to see who was coming—and to his surprise it was the Bishop, with a great troop of armed men!

The Bishop gaped to see the outlaw alone.

" Here is a great chance! " he thought, and he shouted to his men. " See! This is Robin Hood! Ride at him, men, and take him! There is much gold for the man who captures him! "

Robin was taken aback. What could he do ? He could not fight the whole company of men, and his own followers were too far off to hear his horn. He must run!

He set off between the trees, running with all his might. The soldiers crashed after him on horseback, finding it difficult to ride through the trees, but even so they gained upon Robin.

The outlaw made his way to where the trees were thicker and many bushes and brambles grew beneath. He was at a loss to know what to do next, for he knew that soon he would come into a clearer part of the forest again and then the soldiers would find it easy to capture him. He glanced behind him—the horses were picking their way slowly between the bushes, and for the moment he was safe.

Suddenly Robin thought of an old woman's cottage not far from where he was. Perhaps he could find safety there. He made his way to it and rapped on the door.

" Who's there ? " cried an old woman's voice.

" It is Robin Hood, with the soldiers at his heels! " panted the outlaw.

The old woman flung open the door at once, and peered at Robin.

" Yes! " she said. " You are the good Robin Hood! Come in, come in! Now can I repay you for the many kindnesses you and your men have done me! Welcome, good Robin! "

Robin entered the cottage and the old woman at once bolted the door.

" Can you lend me an old dress, a cap and a cloak ? " asked Robin. " If I disguise myself as an old dame I can go through the Greenwood in safety."

" You shall change clothes with me! " cried the sturdy old dame in excitement. " Give me your Lincoln green, and you shall have my dress and cloak! I will remain here in my cottage, and then when the Sheriff's men come, they will think I am you, and will delay following you! "

" Old Dame, you shall be well rewarded for this! " said Robin, swiftly taking off his Lincoln green and putting on the old woman's garments. " Have no fear when I am gone. Bolt your door and wait for me and my Merry Men, for we will soon return to your help."

When Robin was ready, the old dame let him out by the back door, giving him her stick to hobble along with. Then she bolted her door, and dressed herself in Robin's green suit. Round her shoulders she flung his cloak, and over her face she pulled his feathered hat. Then she waited for the soldiers to come, laughing to think of Robin hobbling through the wood in her old clothes.

Robin went through the trees with bent back and slow steps. As he went he mumbled to himself, and wagged his head to and fro. Soon the Sheriff's men saw him, but Robin dared not hasten, for he knew that if they saw him running they would guess he was not an old woman.

Then a soldier rode up to him and caught him roughly by the arm.

" Old woman, have you seen Robin Hood ? " he asked.

Specially drawn for this work.

" Yes," said the old woman, peering at Robin, " you are the good Robin Hood. Come in, come in, and welcome! "

Specially drawn for this work.

" See ! " cried the old woman, pointing to the outlaw with her skinny finger. " There is Robin Hood."
The Bishop stared at her in horror.

" Let go my arm ! " whined Robin in a quavering voice. " Do you want me to lay a curse upon you ? "

The soldier feared that the old dame was a witch and quickly dropped her arm. The Bishop rode up and spoke fiercely to Robin, thinking he was in truth but a poor old woman.

" I'll have you burnt for a witch ! " he said angrily. " Tell us quickly, have you seen Robin Hood ? "

Then Robin pretended to be afraid and fell on his knees.

" Yes, your Honour," he quavered; " he is even now in my cottage, but I pray you let him go, for he has done me no harm."

" Ho, ho ! " shouted the Bishop in glee. " Now we have him ! Surround the cottage, men, and break down the door ! A purse of gold to the one who takes the outlaw alive ! "

The soldiers at once rode off, forgetting all about the old woman. Robin rose from his knees, glad to escape so easily, and hobbled off. As soon as he was out of sight he ran with all his might to where he knew his men waited for him.

It was a long way off, but at last he came in sight of Little John and the others. The Merry Men were amazed to see an old woman running so quickly and thought her to be a witch. Little John fitted an arrow to his bow and shot at her. Robin felt the arrow touch his hat, and he cast it off in a hurry, showing who he was.

" Stay your hand ! " he panted. " I am no witch, but your leader, Robin Hood ! "

" Why are you dressed like this ? " cried Little John, turning pale to think how nearly he had killed his master.

" There is no time to tell now," panted Robin. " Fetch me a suit of Lincoln green, and then summon all my men, every one. Let them follow me quickly."

What had happened to the brave old woman ? She was having the adventure of her life ! The soldiers had surrounded her cottage, and finding the doors bolted, had tried to break them down.

Crash ! the front door fell in, but no one dared to enter, fearing that Robin stood there, an arrow in his bow, ready to aim at the first man who stepped across the doorway. Then at last a daring soldier peered in, and saw a green-coated figure standing silently in the shadows of the little kitchen.

" There he is ! " he cried. " Come on ! We'll have him ! "

All the soldiers rushed into the cottage and seized the green-coated figure, thinking it to be Robin Hood ! The old woman smote left and right with her stick, and many a good blow she gave ! But at last the soldiers pinned down her arms, and dragged her out to the Bishop.

The old dame stood with downcast

head, for she did not wish the Bishop to see that she was not Robin.

" Ha! " cried the fat Bishop in joy, " so you are in my hands at last! Now will you be hanged, my fine fellow, and bitterly will you repent taking from me my four hundred pieces of gold! "

The old woman said never a word. Two soldiers lifted her on to a horse and tied her there firmly. One of them looked into her face and was astonished to see it old and wrinkled, for he had thought the outlaw to be young and handsome.

" How ugly Robin Hood is ! " said the soldier in surprise.

" Ha, that is because of the wicked life he has led! " said the Bishop.

The old dame longed to cuff the Bishop, but she still said nothing and rode with her head bent. She wondered when Robin would come to rescue her, but she was not frightened, for she knew that he would be sure to keep his word to her.

Suddenly, as the company rode along the highway, headed by the Bishop and the old dame, they saw a strange sight. Under the trees stood a hundred men or more, all dressed in Lincoln green, their bows in their hands.

The Bishop began to tremble—but then he took heart.

" If these men try to rescue their master, I will have him straightway slain," he thought.

The old dame saw the men and knew that the one who led them was Robin.

" See! " she cried, " there is Robin Hood! " and she pointed with her skinny finger to the outlaw.

The Bishop stared at her in horror.

" Who are you, then ? " he cried.

" I am but an old dame," she answered, and looked him straight in the face. When he saw her grey hair and her wrinkles he knew that she spoke truth, and his heart sank within him.

He wheeled his horse about, shouting to his soldiers to gallop away, but Robin ran up and caught his bridle.

" Stay, my lord Bishop! " he said,

with a laugh. " Methinks you have money with you—the purse of gold you promised to the first man who captured me! Give that purse to this old dame, I pray you, for you have battered down the door of her cottage and she cannot afford to pay for a new one."

The Bishop went red with fury. He saw that his soldiers had been surrounded by Robin's men, and had laid down their weapons. There was no way out—he must do as the outlaw commanded. He took his purse of gold and threw it fiercely on the ground. Then, almost weeping with rage, he galloped off down the road to Nottingham, leaving behind him a band of laughing men. His soldiers followed him, angry and ashamed at having been taken in by an old woman.

As for the old dame, great honour was shown her by Robin and his men! She was taken to feast in the Greenwood, and there she sat, cracking jokes in her suit of Lincoln green, as gay as any of the Merry Men. When she went home at last, she carried with her the Bishop's purse of gold, and her heart was lighter than it had been for years.

As for the Bishop, he never again went to the Greenwood, for he deemed Robin Hood to be more than a match for him or any man!

THE GOLDEN ARROW

THE Sheriff of Nottingham longed to catch Robin Hood, and punish him for all the tricks he had played on him and on other rich men and greedy priests. But no matter how he tried, he could not capture the bold outlaw.

" If I cannot take him by force, mayhap I can catch him by trickery," thought the Sheriff at last. " Now I will bethink me of a plan whereby the outlaw and his men may fall into my power."

He thought deeply for many days, and at last hit on a clever trick.

" I will proclaim a great shooting match! " he thought gleefully. " It shall be to prove who is the best archer in the shire of Nottingham. I know that Robin and his men think themselves to be the finest archers in the countryside, and they are sure to come to the match. I will post my soldiers at the gates of the city, and as soon as they see the men in Lincoln green, they will surround them and capture them, one and all!"

The Sheriff rubbed his hands in delight.

"Now this is a fine plan!" he said. "I will offer a golden arrow as the prize for the best archer, and I am certain that nothing will stop Robin Hood and his men from trying to win it!"

Then he sent out his proclamation, so that soon in every village of the shire the great news was known. It was not long coming to Robin's ears, and he rejoiced.

"We will all go to the match!" he said to his men in glee. "We will win the Sheriff's golden arrow and fill him with rage!"

But David of Doncaster caught Robin by the arm, and spoke gravely to him.

"Master, it were folly to go to the shooting match," he said. "I have heard that it is all a trap of the Sheriff's to get us there and capture us."

"Now that is sad news," said Robin in disappointment. "Dearly would I have loved to go, but our Lincoln green would give us all away. The soldiers would have an easy task to see us and capture us."

"Master, we can dress ourselves in different colours!" cried Little John. "We can each get a suit of red, blue, brown or yellow, and none will know us then! We can mix with the other townsfolk when they enter the gates, and shoot in the match unknown by any!"

"That we will!" cried Robin, and he laughed for joy. "Now, my Merry Men, take your bows and practise well until the great day comes—for one of us must surely win the golden arrow!"

Day after day the Merry Men twanged their bows and sent their arrows flying. David of Doncaster went to Nottingham and brought back with him cloth of many colours, which Allen-a-Dale's pretty wife soon made up into gay suits.

Robin's suit was bright red, David's was yellow, and Little John's was blue. Each man made his choice, and all longed for the great day to come.

At last it dawned. All the Merry Men donned their new suits, and then set off with their bows and arrows to take the road to Nottingham. Down the highway were walking many villagers, and in twos and threes the Merry Men slipped among them, talking and laugh-

Specially drawn for this work.

The news of the Bishop's prize was not long in coming to Robin's ears, and he rejoiced. "We will all go to the match," he told his men.

Specially drawn for this work.

The Merry Men donned their new suits and set off with their bows and arrows along the road to Nottingham.

ing as if they were villagers themselves.

The Sheriff was up early too, and saw that his soldiers were posted at the gates, in readiness to capture any man in Lincoln green. The Sheriff sat on a high seat with his wife beside him, and anxiously he looked for Robin and his men. But never a man in Lincoln green did he see.

"Husband, it grows late, and the people are anxious for the match to begin," said his wife at last.

"Be silent," growled the Sheriff. "Robin and his men are not here yet. I will not begin until they come."

But not a sign of the outlaw and his band was to be seen, and at last the Sheriff knew that he could not postpone the match any longer.

"I had not thought Robin Hood to be such a coward as not to come," he said angrily. "My golden arrow will be wasted on some village archer, and my money spent in vain!"

At last a trumpet was blown to say that the match was to begin. All the archers went to the targets, and the Sheriff looked at them closely. They were dressed in red, yellow, blue and brown, but not a man was in Lincoln green. All talked merrily to one another,

and the Sheriff groaned, thinking that they were but villagers or townsfolk. Little did he know that quite half of them were Robin's band, laughing to think that they were so near the Sheriff and he did not know them.

Then the match began. He who struck the centre of the target oftenest was to have the golden arrow. Each man shot in his turn, and if he missed the target altogether he had to withdraw from the match.

Not one of Robin's men missed, and all got nearer to the centre than any other archer. Some hit the target full in the middle, and were loudly cheered.

"There are some fine archers here this day!" said the Sheriff. "Methinks that if Robin Hood had come with his band, he would have been well beaten by these men shooting now!"

One by one the men fell out, and soon there were none but Robin's followers left, shooting against each other. The people cheered excitedly. What marvellous archery this was!

"Go on, Browncoat!" called one. "You will win the golden arrow!"

"Nay, I back Bluejacket!" cried another. "See how deftly he strikes the target every time!"

Specially drawn for this work.

At last the match began.   Each man shot in his turn, and not one of Robin's men missed the target.

"Yellowcoat, Yellowcoat, that's the one for me!" cried a third. "He will win!"

"But see yon man in red!" cried another. "Each of his arrows has flown to the centre of the target. Not once has he missed! He will win the prize!"

Robin Hood was the man dressed in red, and by him stood David of Doncaster in yellow. Little John was in blue and Much the Miller's son was in brown. Bravely each shot at the target, but soon Little John and Much missed, and only Robin and David were left.

Trembling with excitement, David sent his arrow singing through the air. It struck the target almost in the centre and everyone cheered. Then Robin Hood shot—and his arrow flew swiftly right to the very middle of the target. He had won the match!

Everyone shouted madly, and the Merry Men threw their caps into the air and cheered too. Then Robin marched boldly up to the Sheriff to receive the prize. He took the golden arrow from the Sheriff's wife, and bowed before her and the Sheriff, hiding his smiles. Then off went he and his men to enjoy the sights of the fair nearby.

Later on they slipped out of the city gates as they had come, in twos and threes, mixing with the villagers. And how they laughed and joked when they got back to the Greenwood and talked over the great day! The golden arrow was passed round for everyone to see, and all were proud to think that their leader had won it.

"If only the Sheriff might know that it was I, Robin Hood, who bore away his arrow!" sighed Robin. "Then should I indeed be happy!"

"Well, write him a letter to tell him it was you who won the prize," said Little John. "Tell him that we were all there, laughing to see him lying in wait for us!"

"But how shall I get my letter delivered?" said Robin. "Whoever takes it to the Sheriff will be clapped into prison."

"Write it, Master, and *I* will show you how to deliver it!" said Little John.

So Robin wrote the letter and gave it to Little John; and early the next morning, before anyone was astir in the city, Little John stuck the letter on an arrow and shot it into Nottingham. It fell into the street near the Sheriff's house, and a soldier found it and took it to the Sheriff.

How furious he was when he read it!

"To think that I laid my trap for Robin Hood and he walked into it and I never knew!" he wailed. "Oh, my lovely golden arrow! Little did I think that it was to Robin Hood I gave it!"

KING RICHARD COMES TO THE GREENWOOD

MANY were the tales that had come to King Richard of the brave outlaw, Robin Hood, and at last the King made up his mind that he would go to seek this outlaw and see what sort of fellow he was.

So he set forth to Nottingham, taking a strong bodyguard with him. He went to the castle in the city, and feasted royally there, hearing many more tales of Robin. Some of the stories made him laugh, and he longed to see the bold outlaw face to face.

"I will ride each day in the Greenwood, and I shall soon see Robin Hood," said the King.

So on his horse he rode each morning in the forest, and he and his men scoured the Greenwood through, yet never once did they see any sign of Robin or his men.

"Now this is strange," said the King at last. "Methinks the outlaw must have withdrawn from the forest."

"Not so," said a lord. "It was but yesterday that a rich abbot rode into Nottingham and complained to the Sheriff that he had been robbed by the outlaw."

"Well, why can I see no sign of the robber when I ride through the Greenwood?" wondered the King.

Robin Hood could have told him why. He knew well that Richard Lionheart was in the forest every day, but he loved the King and was loyal to him, as were all his men. Robin gave orders to them to hide away when they saw the King, and to follow him when he went into dangerous parts of the forest, in case he was attacked by wicked men.

One night the King sat next to the fat Bishop of Hereford, and complained that although he had been in the forest every day, never once had he set eyes on Robin.

"If you really wish to meet this robber," said the Bishop, "I can tell you how to do so. Dress yourself in the guise of a rich abbot, and take with you six men dressed as monks. Drive six asses before you, laden with bags which look as if they contained gold. Then without a doubt will you meet Robin Hood and his men, for they will fall upon you and rob you!"

Now the Bishop did not really mean the King to do this, and he was filled

Specially drawn for this work.

King Richard and his men scoured the Greenwood through, yet never once did they see any sign of Robin or his men.

with horror when Richard clapped him on the back and cried out that it was a good plan.

"But, my Lord," he stammered, "you must understand that this outlaw is a fierce and cruel man, and will show you no courtesy and no mercy."

But the King had made up his mind to try the Bishop's plan, and next day he disguised himself as a rich abbot in a fine cloak, with a tall hood that almost hid his face. He made six of his nobles dress in grey cloaks and hoods so that they looked like monks, and then, with a train of laden asses, he set out for Sherwood Forest.

Into the Greenwood they went, looking to right and left for Robin—and when they came near the heart of the wood, out stepped the bold outlaw, with his men behind him!

"Hold, Lord Abbot!" said Robin, catching hold of the King's bridle. "I would speak with you."

"Who are you?" asked Richard.

"I am Robin Hood," said the outlaw. "And it is plain to see who *you* are! You are a rich abbot taking gold to your monastery! Some of it you shall leave with me."

"Now why should I do that?" asked the King, pretending to be angry.

"Because such gold as you have comes from the poor who can ill afford to give it!" said Robin. "I take from rich men such as you and give to the poor who need what gold I can send them."

Then Robin blew on his horn and to him ran his Merry Men. They surrounded the King's men, and with bent bows prevented them from riding away.

"You are a bold fellow, methinks," said the King to Robin. "Do you dare to stop one who is on the King's own business? See, I bear Richard Lionheart's ring on my finger. Look on it, and stop me if you dare!"

Robin looked at the ring, and in a trice he knew it to belong to the King. At once he dropped the bridle he was holding and bowed low.

"No harm will I do to one who is the King's messenger," he said. "I love Richard Lionheart, and I and my men are loyal to him. Woe to all traitors, say I!"

"But you and your men are traitors," said the King.

"Now would I slay you for those false words, if you were any other than the King's messenger!" cried Robin fiercely. "I am loyal to Richard, and would let no harm come to him. All these days that he has wandered in the forest I and my men have followed him and kept him safe."

Then Richard knew why he had not seen the outlaw before, and he rejoiced to meet such a loyal man.

"You steal from the King," said Richard. "You eat his deer."

"'Tis only to feed my men," said Robin angrily. "Must they starve, with plenty round them? Oh, my Lord, if Richard could see what fine men I have he would not begrudge the deer they kill."

"That may be so," said Richard with a smile. "But now, let me go, I pray you."

"Will you not come and dine with us this day?" asked Robin. "You shall see our haunts, and we will feast you right well."

Richard thought of the fine meal awaiting him in the castle, and had half a mind to refuse and go back—but he liked Robin, and thought that for the sake of seeing more of the brave outlaw he would put up with the poor fare he would doubtless be offered.

But what a surprise lay in wait for the King! Under the great oak trees were spread cloths of snowy white, and on them were laid fine dishes, plates and mugs. And what an array of food was there! Freshly caught fish, finely cooked fowl, venison from the King's own deer and new-baked bread. Wine and ale were set in tankards, and the hungry King looked with delight on the feast before him.

Some of Robin's men came up and

Specially drawn for this work.

The Merry Men wrestled with one another, and the King watched in amazement, for never had he seen such sturdy, skilful wrestlers.

took the King's horse and those of his men. Then up ran page-boys in Lincoln green, and kneeling down before the King and his nobles, presented before them basins of cool water in which the guests washed their hands.

When the meal was all ready Robin blew a short blast on his horn. A hundred and ten men in Lincoln green marched up in a row. When they came before Robin each man bent his knee, and then took his place at the feast. The King watched in amazement.

"Now would that my men gave me as much honour as these outlaws give to their master!" he thought. "Never in my life have I seen so gallant a sight as these fine men marching up to their feast, their good yew bows in their hands."

Friar Tuck said grace, and the men began their meal. The King fell to with a hearty appetite, and never had he enjoyed a dinner more. The sun shone down through the trees, the wind blew fresh and sweet, and the birds sang merrily around. Jokes were cracked and loud laughter rang out. The King found it in his heart to envy Robin his fine free life, and wished that he too might have a band of such strong, loyal men.

"What think you of the King's meat?" asked Robin slyly. "Do you not think he would forgive my taking his deer if he could see the fine men that eat it?"

"Mayhap he would," said the King, smiling to himself.

When the feast was finished, Robin sprang to his feet, holding a mug of brown ale in his right hand.

"Rise to your feet, my Merry Men!" he cried. "Drink a toast to our good King, Richard Lionheart!"

Up leapt every man and drank heartily, crying, "God save the King," at the tops of their voices. The King had to rise too and drink his own health, for if he had not done so, Robin might have guessed his secret.

Then Robin commanded his men to set up the wands and the garlands of roses, so that their guests might see their skill at shooting.

Little John set out slender willow wands, and over one he hung a garland of roses, through which the archers had to send their arrows, without touching a single rose.

The willow wands were a great distance away, and the King thought that surely no archer could hit them. But man after man shot so truly that each of the slender wands was split in half and every man shot an arrow through the rose garland.

Then when the shooting was finished the Merry Men wrestled with one another, and the King watched in amazement, for never in his life had he seen such sturdy, skilful wrestlers.

When all the games were finished, Robin went up to the King and bowed.

"My lord Abbot," he said, "when you next see the King, I pray you tell him of my fine men. Tell him that we are one and all loyal to him, and ask that he will grant his pardon to us for killing his deer."

"I will tell the King this," said Richard. "But suppose that he wanted you to leave your wild life in the Greenwood and go to serve him—would you be willing to do this?"

Robin turned to his men and shouted loudly to them.

"Would you be willing to leave the Greenwood and go to serve the King?"

"Ay, ay!" shouted back every man, and many cried out, "God save the King!"

Richard Lionheart flung back his dark hood and let every man see his face.

"I am your King, your sovereign King!" he cried.

All the Merry Men stared in silence. Then with one accord they fell upon their knees, Robin too.

"Rise up, Robin Hood," said the King. "I grant my pardon to you and to each of your Merry Men."

Then every man leapt to his feet, flung his bow into the air and shouted joyfully, crying out that he would serve Richard to the end of his life.

"Then come with me to Nottingham!" said the King. "You are outlaws no longer."

Off they all went to Nottingham, cheering loudly, the King riding at the head. All the townsfolk came running out to see what was happening.

"The King has pardoned Robin Hood!" cried the people, and they surrounded the Merry Men and cheered them wildly. The Sheriff came forth from his house to see what was happening, and how dismayed he was to see the King riding side-by-side with the bold outlaw!

Then all the people made a great holiday, and the King sent a proclamation throughout the city to say that Robin and his men were now his own followers, and were outlaws no longer.

Then off to London Town went the King, and with him he took Robin Hood and his Merry Men. Robin was made Earl of Huntingdon, and faithfully and well he served Richard, who vowed that no king in the world had so fine a bodyguard as he!